# The
# U-Boat
# War

# The U-Boat War

The German Submarine Service and
the Battle of the Atlantic, 1935–1945

DAVID WESTWOOD

CONWAY MARITIME PRESS

Copyright © David Westwood, 2005

All rights reserved. No part of this publication may be
reproduced, stored in a retrieval system or transmitted in any
form or by any means; electronic, electrostatic, magnetic tape,
mechanical, photocopying, recording or otherwise,
without permission in writing from the publishers.

First published in 2005 by Conway Maritime Press

An imprint of **Chrysalis** Books Group plc
The Chrysalis Building, Bramley Road,
London W10 6SP

Published in North America by:
Casemate Publishers, 2114 Darby Road, Havertown,
PA 19083, USA

David Westwood has asserted his moral right
to be identified as the author of this work.

British Library Cataloguing in Publication Data
A catalogue record for this book is available
from the British Library

Library of Congress Cataloging in Publication Data available

ISBN 1 84486 001 9

Edited and designed by DAG Publications Ltd
Designed by David Gibbons; edited by Michael Boxall
Printed in Great Britain.

# CONTENTS

# INTRODUCTION

The Second World War was marked by a series of campaigns, mostly on land, which were of long duration. Among these were the campaign in North Africa (1940–3), the German invasion of Russia (1941–5) and the air war against Germany (1939–45). However, none of these campaigns stands against the Battle of the Atlantic, which had a similar duration to the air war (1939–45) but also carried with it the weight of grand strategy.

The other campaigns were all of significance, and for Germany a successful conclusion would have been of immense importance. However, the campaign in the Atlantic was one in which the victor could hope to create or eliminate the threat of a cross-Channel invasion that would then threaten Germany with war on two fronts. If Germany had managed to close the Atlantic to merchant shipping there would have been the extra benefit of Great Britain strangling in the grip of starvation, deprived of the food brought across the ocean from the United States. Furthermore, military aid would also have failed, and US troops would not have been able to assemble in Britain prior to D-Day.

Winston Churchill referred to the Atlantic as a 'lifeline', and it was just that. Britain was greatly dependent upon supplies (military and civilian) from the United States, and the threat of the U-boats was that they might, even in 1943, stop the convoys to the United Kingdom, thereby reducing the war effort here to a minimum, and even bringing the fear of capitulation or withdrawal from active prosecution of the war into reality.

Luckily for Great Britain and the western Allies, Germany had no great strategist in its senior ranks, not even in the German Navy. Hitler himself was no sailor, while Raeder and Dönitz were more than able seamen but failed to impress upon Hitler the real significance of the Atlantic as a supply route: eliminating that supply route could have forced Great Britain out of the war, or at least reduced the potential of these islands as a base for the masses of US troops and airmen who would pose the final threat to Germany.

Dönitz commanded the U-boat fleet throughout the war (even after his promotion to Head of the Navy in 1943), but he himself failed to grasp fully what his force was capable of, had he concentrated all his efforts on the Atlantic. Further, if he had had the courage to gainsay Hitler's strange ideas about Norway, the Indian Ocean and other faraway places, he would not have been constantly bemoaning the fact that he was short of U-boats. Mistakes were undoubtedly made by both sides, but the biggest mistakes were made by the Germans. It was for this reason more than any other that they lost the war.

This book attempts to describe the character of the war in the Atlantic and the measures implemented by each side in fighting that long campaign. Many factors came into play; perhaps one of the most obvious is the reluctance by the air supremos on both sides to see how important the convoy battles were. In England the RAF leadership continually blocked the provision of suitable long-range aircraft to Coastal Command, and in Germany Göring failed to provide the U-boat arm with the long-range reconnaissance force that might have swung the battle the other way.

The book looks at the strategic, operational and tactical aspects of the battle. It examines the technology that was developed to combat the U-boats as well as German counter-technology. Radar, Sonar (Asdic), acoustic torpedoes, aerial searchlights, codebreaking, deciphering operations, decoys, radar detectors, escort carriers and forward-throwing anti-submarine mortars all played a part in this conflict, as well as many other technologies and techniques. It is hoped that the narrative answers some of the reader's questions, and clarifies what was often a confused field of battle.

If the Allies had lost control of the Atlantic sea lanes, it is quite possible that D-Day would never have occurred, and that the Russians might then have gained control of Europe to the Atlantic coast of France and down to the Mediterranean. That scenario would have augured badly for the post-war situation.

# 1 'NOT A SINGLE SUBMARINE'

## Article 188

On 7 February 1919, the State Secretary of the *Reichsmarineamt* wrote: 'For the foreseeable future Germany is not to have a single submarine.' This succinct statement reflected the terms of Article 188 of the Treaty of Versailles, which condemned Germany for her actions in causing and perpetuating the First World War. European life had been in turmoil for more than four years and relief at the cessation of hostilities soon turned to plans for vengeance. The reparations in monetary terms were enormous, and Germany, as the main country of the vanquished, was saddled with an externally-imposed debt worthy of the Middle Ages. Among the terms restricting her capacity to maintain armed forces was the absolute limitation in respect of submarines, with which the German Navy had been so close to forcing a result at sea to the body-consuming stalemate on land and indeed in the air.

The Secretary felt that this ruling was too extreme, for even the smallest of nations had coastal submarines for defensive purposes. He was concerned about territorial aggression by other nations, to such things as important islands, fishing areas and harbours. This fear of German seas lying unprotected by German submarines (some elements of a surface fleet had been allowed) led him to suggest that some small part of the machinery relating to U-boats should be preserved. However, his protests to the Allied Commission had no hearing, and the full Treaty, promulgated on 28 June 1919, reiterated the conditions as to submarines just as he had feared. Article 188 stated that within one month of the signing of the Treaty all U-boats, bases and yards must be handed over to the Allies. U-boats were to proceed wherever possible under their own power to a port designated by the Allies, and that any unable to do so were to be destroyed unconditionally *in situ*. The latter condition had to be fulfilled within three months of the date of the Treaty.

The Article further specified that all ship-building machinery and equipment was to be handed over to industry or to farming if it could be useful in those areas. Finally, Article 191 ruled that the building and acquisition of submarines, even for commercial trading purposes, was absolutely forbidden.

A total of 176 U-boats was brought to the United Kingdom where some remained, the rest being dispersed to America, France, Italy and Japan. This was the last act of the U-boat Inspection Office and Submarine Bureau of the Imperial German Navy, already de-imperialised upon the abdication of Kaiser Wilhelm II in favour of Chancellor Ebert. In 1920 a new Torpedo and Mine Inspectorate was formed, but its job was simply to assemble the requisite documents for compiling a history of the U-boat campaign during the war; in 1922 the Inspectorate was wound up, and the papers were transferred to the *Reichsarchiv*.

The yards, which had been so busy during the war, lay empty. Interest still remained however, and this was supported clandestinely by the newly-appointed leadership of the German Navy. The experience and ability gained during the war was of interest also to various foreign and friendly nations. Germany could still provide plans, advisers and constructors. In 1920 Germaniawerft (GW) and Vulkan (two of the yards) were selling their plans for the U-cruiser *U142* and the large minelaying design *U117* to the Japanese. Construction in Japan (one of the victors of the recent war) was supervised by German engineers, occasionally even by Dr. Techel, who had joined GW in 1907 after the innovative designer d'Equivelley had left.

In 1921 Argentina was planning to build her own submarine fleet, and set about this by obtaining the services of three highly experienced U-boat engineers, Karl Bartenbach, Friedrich Schürer and William Krankenhagen. This trio went to South America to supervise the building of a planned ten submarines. German Naval Command in Hamburg was informed, and they in turn contacted the Vulkan yard and two of the Krupp yards (Germaniawerft and A-G Weser). The Navy suggested that the yards form a consortium to deal with the project. At the same time German technical ability was being hired in Italy (from Vulkan) and Sweden (from GW). The conditions of the Treaty however forbade any U-boat activity on German soil, and so the yards had to find a friendly neighbour where work could go on.

Doctor Hans Techel, earlier chief designer and engineer for GW, now moved to the Hague where the company *Ingenieurskantor voor Scheepsbouw* (telegraphic abbreviation 'Inkavos') was formed, with Captain Ulrich Blum as purchasing director. This was not a purely private company, for the board came from the three main U-boat yards of the war years, and profits and losses were to be split three ways. Initially little capital was available, and the Dutch government refused to register the company, relegating it to an office in a shed within the GW yard at Kiel. There work continued on plans for Argentina and Italy, but the Argentinians decided to go elsewhere and the Italians dropped the idea.

This set-back was followed by a Spanish decision not to proceed with a six-boat order (Electric Boat got the design order, Vickers-Armstrong and the Spanish national yard to do the building). Ties with Spain were much sought after by the German Naval Command at the time, and the Spanish-speaking Captain Canaris (later head of German Intelligence, *Abwehr*) had been sent to Spain to act as liaison officer for this contract. In 1924 Spain decided to build 40 boats in all: 28 were on option to Vickers-Armstrong, twelve were left on tender. The tender boats were subject to a specification demanding long range, a high surface speed of 20 knots and about 1,000 tons displacement. Inkavos tendered their own design, in competition with Blohm & Voss (with new MAN diesels) and French and Italian designs. German influence through the Spanish industrialist Don Horacio Echevarrieta helped the B&V design to win the competition, but the boat was to be built by a Spanish yard. Krupp had no control of that yard, and so Inkavos was successful in its bid for the building contract.

Once more Inkavos's hopes were dashed, for the Moroccan crisis intervened and the Spanish decided to shelve the U-boat fleet plan. After three years Inkavos had nothing to show for its efforts. Suddenly however the Dutch government dropped its objections to the registration of the firm, and in the summer of 1925 the company moved into new offices in the Hague, which it occupied up to the end of the Second World War (it was run by Techel and Blum up to 1938.) In 1925 there was still insufficient capital invested in the company, and the three parent yards were unable to cover the financial risks involved in tenders that Blum was presenting, especially for two 500-ton boats for Turkey.

Naval Command now backed its initial support for the firm by deciding to inject financial support. Because the Navy could not be seen to be directly (or even clandestinely) involved, a dummy firm 'Mentor Bilanz' was formed on 1 July 1925, with funding from one of the Navy's secret appropriations, and an ex-U-boat commander, Korvettenkapitän Robert Moraht, as managing director. With naval financial backing Mentor Bilanz soon became the major shareholder in Inkavos, and the driving force behind it.

The main naval interest stemmed from the fact that German submarine design and construction had formed a major portion of the war effort, and naval support would ensure that the experience gained would not be lost. In addition, new design developments would be available to the Navy, as well as a possible wealth of information about the state of the art in countries with which Inkavos had dealings or knowledge. For a few million Marks there would be the return of experience, development knowledge and pure intelligence. It was not a high price to pay. Naval command also set up a second dummy company, 'Tebeg GmbH', whose task was to examine equipment and supply with a mind to remobilisation. 'Tebeg' and 'Mentor Bilanz' were housed in the same building as the German Naval Office in Berlin, and both had retired naval officers as their managing directors.

Canaris now advised Naval Command that if they wished they could easily set up a U-boat department if they camouflaged its activities under the title of Anti-Submarine Warfare School (Unterseebootsabwehrschule). On 1 September 1925 Captain Arno Spindler took command of this unit. In 1927 another covert department was established under Friedrich Schürer, with the job of supervising future German U-boat construction. This organisation was eventually forced to be incorporated within naval command, after the Lohmann scandal. The paymaster to the naval staff, Lohmann, was revealed in the Press as having involved German money in the proscribed activities of Inkavos. The Reichstag investigated, and the firm folded. Moraht had foreseen such an eventuality and had recommended one of his men for promotion – a serving naval lieutenant, Schottky. The end result was that all naval interests were concentrated in the firm *Ingenieurbüro für Wirtschaft und Technik GmbH*, another name for the Navy's own design and construction department (Igewit). Spindler retired in 1929 (to write the history of the German U-boats in the First World War), and Schottky succeeded him as overall director.

In 1926, however, before the Lohmann scandal had come to light, Turkey placed an order for two boats. German engineers had already been evaluating the earlier designs to establish those which would bear redesign work, and how easily they could be modified to update them. The Turkish order meant that they could find out whether their conjectures were valid. The boats for Turkey were based on the Type UBIII boat, having a project designation Pu46. Displacement was to be 505 tons surfaced, 620 tons submerged. Two diesels (combined rating 1100hp) and two electric motors (combined rating 780hp) would give speeds of 14.5 knots surfaced/9.5 knots submerged; 59 metres long, range 7,500 nautical miles at 6 knots surfaced/80 at 4 knots submerged. They were fitted with six torpedo tubes (including 2 external stern tubes above the water line): ten 45cm reserve torpedoes.

During the negotiations Inkavos had insisted that one condition of the contract be that the firm was to take part in testing the boat, and would have the final say as to the personnel involved. This reflected the hopes of the Lützowüfer (where the *Marineamt* was based). It was hoped that the Navy would get a detailed report on the boats, together with details of problems arising and means of solution. As a sop to Dutch opinion the Navy ruled that only retired officers could be eligible as members of the testing programme, and then promptly retired Korvettenkapitän (Eng) Walter Hülsmann. Spindler and 'Mentor Bilanz' worked together to assemble the team.

The two boats were launched on 1 February (*Birindçi Inönü*) and 12 March (*Ikindçi Inönü*) 1927. Testing began at the end of April, the second boat starting her tests from July. Schottky had been able to get only two suitable men for the job, and so the boats had to be tested consecutively. The benefit to the Navy was that they had two modern U-boats to examine for four months at least, instead of just half that time. In the event the Turkish Navy was not ready to accept the boats until early in 1928. To get them to their destination two crews of (supposedly) retired naval personnel were arranged. They sailed from Rotterdam on 22 May 1928, arriving safely after an 18-day passage which served as a valuable sea time evaluation for the Germans. Two of the crew remained in Turkey to set up a U-boat training school.

A second opportunity of this nature resulted from a Finnish request to Inkavos to prepare designs for a medium, combined torpedo/minelaying, submarine. Bartenbach, who had been a member of the abortive mission to

Argentina, had been in Finland since 1924. On his own initiative he negotiated an order in 1926. Three boats were to be built at the Chrichton–Vulcan yard at Abo (now Turku) in Finland. Design Pu89 modified the original UC-type U-boat to carry mines in external shafts, allowing torpedoes to be fired forward and aft from within the boat. Displacement was 493/715 tons; two 580hp Atlas diesels and two 600hp electric motors gave combined speeds of 14/8 knots maximum, with ranges of 4,000 nautical miles at 10/75 at 3 knots. There were two forward and two stern tubes within the pressure-hull with six torpedoes, and twenty 200kg mines fitted in five shafts outside the pressure-hull. The design was complementary to the larger UBIII type for the Turks, but was more powerful than the original UCIII, although there was no surface displacement increase.

The keel of the first boat, *Vetehinen*, was laid down in September 1926, and German supervisors from Inkavos started work early in 1927. The other two boats, *Vesihiisi* and *Iku-Turso*, were laid down at the same time. Total building time was over three years, because of the yard's ignorance of submarine building techniques and the tolerances required, and the long lead-time for materials. Further interruptions were caused by the weather; winter work was impossible because of the extremely low temperatures. But on 1 June 1930 the first launch took place, and the second on 2 August. Schottky himself super-vised testing, in view of the importance of the results to future German plans, and he was accompanied by many active service officers, many of whom were to become instrumental in the future U-boat programme.

Testing ended on 6 September and Schottky reported that 'diving, seawor-thiness and battleworthiness, having regard to their displacement, are far superior to any foreign boats'. From the Navy's point of view the exercise had been a complete success, and the Finnish Navy was happy. Various other contracts were also considered by Inkavos, but the majority of their work, including foreign excursions, was rationalised into an evaluation of future work should the Treaty conditions be removed. The efforts of Inkavos and its successors in this field led directly to the designs and building methods for the Types II and VII U-boats of the Second World War.

As can be seen, Inkavos was working with some success on foreign orders, and using the experience gained to further their knowledge in preparation for the U-boat Arm they were sure to be asked to design and build once the restrictions of Versailles were removed. Elsewhere, in 1924, plans had been drawn of a small boat design, which became Project 'Lilliput' (the CV707), and in 1926 plans for another design were drawn, based upon the UBIII Project 51a (the Type G). Plans for the first production boat (soon designated *E1*) were sent to Inkavos.

Once the Moroccan crisis had subsided, Spain renewed her interest in a submarine fleet, assisted by the pro-German attitude of Echevarrieta. In August 1926 Canaris and Lohmann went to Spain with the plans of a modified UBIII, hoping to get approval to build a test version of this boat. The Spaniards were interested in boats of 1,000 tons surface displacement (and were perhaps influenced by American Fleet Submarine thinking) and would not therefore issue an order for a boat of only 745 tons surface displacement. Negotiations of a sort continued, however, and Echevarrieta visited Berlin in July 1927, the Spanish Defence Ministry having asked him to discuss further details with Canaris.

One objection to co-operation with the Germans was the financial interest Inkavos had with the Spanish shipbuilder ENL; Krupp immediately severed the link, and the German Navy agreed to underwrite the costs of building the boat, which was now designated Project Pu111. Financial aspects of the contract were settled on 23 August 1927, when it was decided that construction would be backed by a sum of 4 million Reichsmarks, from the secret supplies fund. A total outlay of RM 4.6 million was expected. In a memorandum of 17 October the contract was detailed in full and referred to the benefits expected to accrue to the German Navy:

> To avoid the conditions of the Versailles Treaty in the area of U-boat building, and to make small increases in present and future personnel, IvS (Inkavos), which has little chance of survival otherwise in the present climate, is to be given every support ... the friendly relationship with Spain will now allow this, and by expending RM 1.5 million immediately, and a total of RM 3-4 million (spread over three years), its use by IvS will bring our target nearer – namely to design the most modern and the very best U-boats possible, to acquaint our shipbuilders and yard personnel with this, and to train seamen and technical branch members of the Armed Forces in their use?

This was a clear statement of two intentions – to circumvent the provisions of the Treaty, and to build a new U-boat Arm.

Negotiations between Canaris, Echevarrieta and the Spanish Government came to a satisfactory conclusion at the end of 1927; furthermore, Echevarrieta had ordered (privately) a Type G from Inkavos. The hull of the latter was to be built in sections at Fijenoord in Holland (the yard that had built the two Turkish boats for Inkavos) and then be shipped to Echevarrieta's own yard at Cadiz for assembly and fitting out. This boat, Pu111, also interested the Spanish Navy; they did however specify that 1,400hp diesels were to be fitted so as to increase surface displacement. They also specified a good surface range and transition from 50cm torpedoes to the international standard of 53.3cm. The boats as laid down had displacements of 745/965 tons, with two 1,400hp MAN diesels and two 500hp electric motors. Speeds were 17/8.5 knots, range 7,000 at 10/ 160 at 4 knots. She had four forward and two stern torpedo tubes in 53.3cm calibre, and carried ten torpedoes. Overall length

13

was 72.38 metres, beam 6.2 metres, draught 4 metres. Her crew was 32, including officers.

She was laid down (under yard title Ech21 or E1) in February 1929. Given the preparatory work which had been done in Holland and the experience of Schottky and his team, gained from building the Turkish and Finnish boats, she was finished in eight months, but during that time Echevarrieta became bankrupt. Unwilling to see it fail for lack of money, the German Navy financed the entire project, and Spain merely had the right to buy her. She was launched on 22 October 1930, only to run aground. Further difficulties followed the fitting-out, and she was not ready for sea trials until the summer of 1931.

Earlier in the year a crew was chosen for her sea trials, consisting once more of German naval officers, some still on the active list. From May to 4 July 1931 she underwent trials, including those of the new Kunze anti-surge torpedo-firing equipment. Schürer joined the testing crew on 24 July to write his report for Naval Command. He praised the boat, but unrest in Spain and in particular the precarious situation of the monarchy delayed the sale of the boat to the Spanish Navy.

As mentioned above, there had been an earlier project, the CV707 or Project 'Lilliput'. This had its genesis in a request from Finland in 1924 for a small mine-laying boat. Bartenbach laid this out as Pu23, of 99 tons surface displacement. Following the incorporation of modifications from Inkavos designs, the final designation was Pu110. She was built by the Hietalahden Laivatelakka Yard at Helsinki, and launched on 2 July 1930. Schottky's team tested her, the team being already in Finland to test CV702 and CV703 (*Vetehinen* and *Vesihiisi*). On commissioning in the Finnish Navy CV707 became *Saukko*, at that time the smallest submarine in service in the world. Length overall was only 32.95 metres, with beam and width both of about 3.2 metres. Propulsion comprised one 200hp diesel and one 120hp electric motor. Her range was limited to 500 nautical miles at 8 knots/50 at 4 knots, but these were practical in the limited spaces of the Gulf of Finland.

The design excited great interest at Tebeg in 1926, and they proposed its adoption as the basis for small German boats, especially as each boat would be quick to build. At a naval conference in April 1926 the plan was not adopted, the committee preferring 250 tons surface displacement for the smallest class of future U-boats. They classed *Saukko* with the much earlier *Forelle*, and added that experiences during the late war of UBI-type boats (reported in the War Diary of the Flanders Flotilla, and in Captain Bartenbach's own report) demonstrated that such a small boat had little or no tactical value.

The committee was also informed that diesel engines were now being developed with a weight/power ratio of 5kg/hp compared to the earlier 22kg/hp, and that this development, and the parallel development of a much more compact gearbox, would reduce engine weight and space requirements. The committee then decided in favour of development of the earlier Type UBII, with a planned displacement of 250 tons. The idea was not immediately accepted, because of continued support in the Navy for the UF type (from the first war Scheer programme) which seemed to have some very good naval and military advantages. By the end of 1929, however, the general feeling in the *Marineamt* was that there would have to be some type of small U-boat of 200–250 tons displacement to allow rapid construction if re-armament came. Then Schottky was installed as Chief of Department A II u, the U-boat Office of the Marineamt, and he wrote a paper in which he examined the whole range of U-boat designs then available.

His first point was that the most important consideration should be given to designs for a 200-ton boat that was easily and quickly built. He favoured a single-hulled design with a surface speed of 12 knots, armed with three 53.3cm tubes. His second point was that one such boat should, if possible, be built abroad, if the money were available. If not, then as soon as spare materials from the already building *E1* in Spain became available, they should be moved to a yard where building could start. He hoped that either the cost of building (RM 1.5 million) or the provision of the spare material could be made in 1931. Such action, he wrote, would, allow German shipbuilders to gain valuable planning experience and practical training in U-boat building methods, together with the means of coping with the problems and day-to-day administrative and managerial tasks involved.

Schottky did not leave the matter at planning in the abstract however, for he went on to design a quick-assembly programme for the Type I. All equipment, he wrote, such as torpedo tubes, electric motors, auxiliary machinery, batteries, periscopes, gyro-compasses, castings, pressure-hull plating and armatures, as well as the many other items peculiar to the submarine, should be prepared in advance to allow a build of six boats from scratch in the shortest possible time. Given experienced personnel, he expected the boats to be completed in about eight weeks. These six boats would constitute only one-third of the Type total requirement. As to crews, he commented that the U-boat course at the camouflaged Torpedo School would adequately provide the boats with trained officers and men.

Support for the new design was rapidly forthcoming from the newly appointed Chief of the Navy, Admiral Raeder. His interest had been quickened by the short build time, and he ordered that although the U-boat allotment (of money) had all but been exhausted by the unexpected cost of *E1* (caused by Echevarrieta's bankruptcy), RM 1 million was to be made immediately available for this project, code-named 'Lilliput'. The full cost (RM 1.5 million) would be paid out of the 1931 Naval Estimates. So, until the Finns actually paid for *Saukko* she was the property of the German Navy, which underwrote all costs for 'Igewit' (the new name for covert companies owned and run by the Navy).

Once the three Vetehinen-class boats and the Saukko had been completed there was little difficulty in persuading the Finns that the 250-ton design was of value to them in addition.

Small submarines with both torpedo and minelaying capacity were utterly suitable for the Finnish Navy, in view of her geographical situation. Her main seaways lay through the Gulfs of Finland and Bothnia, with Russia, Estonia, Latvia, Lithuania and Poland all having adjacent coastlines. To control access to the sea lanes and thence to the North Sea and the oceans, she had to deny access to aggressors, and ensure her own freedom of movement to the south and west. She looked to Germany for help; Captain Bartenbach was obviously a good salesman, who additionally had a good product. The competition was quite limited!

The result was the design for Project 179 (CV707). Externally, she was attractive, as had been the Vetehinen boats. When she was first laid down under the control of Inkavos' naval architects and engineers at Abo, she was built without her saddle tanks. The appearance of the single-hull form gave rise to the conviction that she would be well able to withstand attack by depth-charge, and have a fast diving time. Her lines plan at this stage shows that she was as nearly circular in cross-section as internal equipment arrangements would allow. The main bow feature was the 'eyes and nose' arrangement of the three torpedo tubes. This design was very close to that of the later Type II of the Kriegsmarine. There are three internal compartments, the forward torpedo room/crew's quarters, the control room and superimposed attack tower, and the after engine/motor room.

It can be seen from the Plans that although only a development of the 1917 UF Type, planned for North Sea use, she was a boat with which the German Navy could start its new crew training programmes. The build was hampered by dreadful weather, and she was not launched until 10 May 1933, but this was not allowed to delay the embryo training programme. In the autumn of 1932, on the date of promulgation of promotions and duty changes, a number of engineering officers had been ordered to U-boat theory training, with prac-tical work to follow when a boat became available. This was planned to take place during the sea- and acceptance-trials of the boat.

Ten officers were therefore assigned to a course beginning on 3 January 1933: three months on the technical aspects (theory) of the U-boat, and tactical methods resulting from experiences during the First World War. Then they progressed to the acceptance trials of CV707 when they were joined by two further (so-called 'retired') officers; all had sea time on board. This led to an illegal situation whereby German naval officers were training in the proscribed art of submarining in a Finnish U-boat in Finland's national waters. However this did not affect the performance of the boat, which lived up to all expectations.

She dived easily at any speed, no matter what rudder angle was set, and her depth-keeping was such that she ran for five minutes at 4.7 knots without requiring any hydroplane angle adjustment. Remarkably, when a salvo of torpedoes from all three tubes was fired, although she lost 2m in depth, she maintained longitudinal stability, and showed no tendency whatever to break the surface. On the surface she exhibited acceptable sea-going qualities, and her time trial realised a maximum surface speed of 13 knots. Criticisms levelled against her were that she needed 45 seconds to dive to thirty feet, her range was limited to 2,000 nautical miles (compared to 3,700, also at 8 knots, of the UBII type), and her unsilenced exhausts were very noisy at maximum speed (for a coastal boat this is of importance as sound travels well at sea disclosing the presence of a boat to listeners within range ashore or at sea).

Although CV707 was ready for acceptance by the Finnish Navy by the end of 1933, Bartenbach exercised his persuasive talents again, getting approval from the Finns for more sea-trials by the Germans in 1934, so the boat was not handed over to the Finns until 1936, when Germany already had some of its new U-boat fleet at sea. This extended period allowed the so-called 'Anti-submarine School' (*Unterseebootsabwehrschule – UAW*) to give many officers and crew sea time and handling experience, being in actuality the Navy's new Submarine Training School, and was to be responsible, from this time until the end of the Second World War, for all training of officers, petty officers and ratings of the submarine fleet.

The Treaty of Versailles was still in force, but the Navy had been making plans for many years for the action to be taken once the restrictions were lifted. The actions described above were not legally in contravention of the provisions of the Treaty, but its intent had been circumvented to such an extent that the only thing the German U-boat Arm did not have was a submarine fleet based in German waters. By 1935 even the letter of the law was cast aside by the London Naval Agreement which gave official approval to Hitler's new Navy and its U-boats, and the boats themselves were actually building while that conference was taking place.

The redevelopment of the U-boat Arm was always part of German naval strategy, and even as far back as 1926 Arno Spindler had begun identifying enemies. He saw Poland and France as being the main antagonists. U-boat building during the First World War had reached prodigious proportions, but Spindler and some of the younger ex-U-boat commanders from that war wanted faster building times. They borrowed the idea of production line construction, reasoning that with sufficient pre-planning the submarine would be as easy to build as the motor car. Spindler looked at the various types that had been available during the First World War, and put proposals to a conference which approved his ideas. He claimed that, if the Vulkan, Germaniawerft and Blohm & Voss yards were used to maximum capacity, 86 boats of three types could quickly be built. His plan allocated a specific boat type to each yard, simplifying both construction and raw and finished material supply. He also argued for a preponderance of medium-sized boats, despite the successes of the shorter-range boats at the end of the war. He also proposed the construction of some longer-range minelaying boats for deployment in the Mediterranean.

The plan was amended slightly in 1928 to an all medium-sized boat programme, and Schürer was appointed to command the technical section at 'Mentor Bilanz'. His job there was to plan material requirements and equipment supplies. The Navy took over control of the allotment and planning of the future use of the shipyards. The main point of note is that all this was done in 1928, when the northern hemisphere was drifting into fiscal disaster and no country was contemplating war.

Experience with the *E1* design and its minelaying capability convinced the planners that a boat of some 500 tons surface displacement might well serve as the intermediate category, but the boat that resulted was extremely unsatisfactory from the Navy's point of view. It was the Type IA of which only two examples (*U25* and *U26*) were built. This intermediate category boat did not have the capacity to carry an effective number of torpedoes and TMB or TMC torpedo-mines, the invention of which had simplified boat design. Prior to this, U-boat minelayers required mine shafts built into them as part of their construction, or mine tubes of a special calibre. This was *in addition to* the torpedo tubes (with few reloads capable of being fitted into an already stretched hull) and was necessary because torpedo U-boats could not carry and lay mines. The unitary calibre of torpedo and mine meant that all U-boats could carry either mines or torpedoes, or more frequently a mix of the two. A U-boat so equipped was able to lay a minefield as the first part of an operation, and then go on to operate offensively with its torpedoes, rather than having to return to base to re-arm.

From 1932 to 1937 seven main U-boat designs were submitted, of which three were built (one was the Type II as noted above). Types I to VII were examined in detail, their main function being to sink merchant shipping. Types I and II were built in small numbers; Types III to VI stayed on the drawing-board. The Type VII became the mainstay of the U-boat Arm, more of them being built than all other boats built during the Second World War.

Hitler's accession to power on 30 January 1933 brought a quickening pace in military activity, which was felt as much in the Navy as in the other armed forces. The pre-planning carried out for the U-boat Arm was paralleled elsewhere, but U-boats took less time to build than virtually any other warship, and they had a significance remembered from the First World War. But even before Hitler and the National Socialist party came to power, the naval staff had plans extending as far forward as 1938. By that year the Navy wanted a battleworthy and modern fleet at sea. This aim was published in a paper of 15 November 1932 by the office of the Reichsminister with responsibility for the Navy. The planning report detailed the fleet, including its submarine component. This was to include eight each of the 500-ton *Vetehinen*-type boats and the 800-ton *E1* class, the boats to be ready by 1938. They were to be organised into three half-flotillas, each of four boats, two for training and two for experimental purposes.

The boats were designated by a code-word *Motorenversuchsboot* (experimental motorboat). Of the boats already built and building, the Navy hoped to obtain both the *E1* and CV707 to serve as the basic boats around which the rest of the fleet could be designed. The main intention was, if boats were to be built in German yards, to build boats to the CV707 design. The result would be a U-boat fleet in being in a very short time. It was planned to build at Deutsche Werke in Kiel-Wik, which had docking facilities for six boats. The final decision as to the yard to use went however to DWK in Wilhelmshaven, for geographic and economic reasons. The construction plan was then extended by Admiral Groos, who confirmed the plans for the CV707 and added the *E1* to the future building plan. However, he changed the numbers to three of each type, postponing the development of the 500-ton class to a later date.

The plans for Kiel-Wik as the founding base for the U-boat Arm were approved, and 100 officers and men were posted there to staff the unit. Their job was to lay the foundations of the U-boat Arm organisation as far as recruitment, training and postings was concerned, as well as establish procedures governing boats – supply, armament, fuel, equipment, repair and modification, acceptance trials and all engineering matters.

The Navy now examined the plans of *E1* and CV707 in detail, and some non-fundamental alterations were requested. One request common to both boats was that the tower be reduced to the lowest silhouette possible, commensurate with safety. This points to the fact that tactical use of the boats was to make attacks on the surface. Even before Dönitz produced his various papers on U-boat use and tactics, the U-boat men were thinking in terms of surface approach and attack. This was partly imposed upon them by the low submerged speed and duration of the boats, and the possibility of being unable to execute an attack or escape an escort because of flat batteries. Another engineering and weapons requirement was that torpedo tubes be modified to take G7a and G7e torpedoes, as well as Torpedo Mines Types A and B. One benefit was that the reduced weight and space requirements of the new MAN diesels and the much shortened gearbox meant that the shortfall in weight could be made up by increasing hull strength without exceeding the original specification; this meant in turn that the boat's performance would be as planned.

On Monday 30 January 1933 Hitler took power, and immediately appointed his cabinet. His defence minister was General von Blomberg, who authorised the formal establishment of the U-boat School at Kiel-Wik on 2 February. In deference to the Treaty it was named the *Ubootabwehrschule*. This was originally part of the Torpedo Inspection Department. By the end of

March the first order went to Igewit for a U-boat, and this was followed by further orders within a month, raising the total to three 250-ton boats. By May it had been decided to build them at the DWK yard at Wilhelmshaven, starting in October 1933. In addition, three of the larger *E1* boats were to be built by GW, to be laid down on 1 April 1934. These boats were built under the cover name noted above, as MVB9 (*Motorenversuchsboot*) IA, and two of them were completed to become the only two Type IA boats to see (limited) service during the Second World War. The third was never built.

Plans for various building programmes were examined at the Lützowüfer and much of 1933 was spent in working out how many boats, of which type, would be ready and when. The plan arrived at by the end of the year was for a total of 24 boats by the beginning of 1938 (five MVB IA and nineteen MVB IIA). It is clear that Raeder had no inkling of Hitler's opportunistic method, and that in this and the Z-Plan, he relied on Hitler's assertion that war would not occur before 1944. He planned a main fleet and reserves including a limited submarine force. There was no thought then of long-range incursions into the Atlantic, and attacks against the east coast of the USA, operations against Brazil and South Africa, or of patrols into the Indian Ocean.

Raeder was a professional naval officer, born in Wandsbek near Hamburg in April 1876. He had been appointed Chief of Naval Command at the age of 52 in 1928, and continued to command the Navy until January 1943. He was an advocate of steady progress towards a goal, rather than the inspirational approach favoured by Hitler, who in any case had little appreciation or knowledge of the problems facing Raeder and his staff in re-equipping the Navy almost completely. To design and build warships, even as small as the Type IIA U-boat, involved a long lead-time when all the imponderables were included. There was also the not insubstantial problem of finance, although this gradually became less problematic as the Nazi Party gained control and industrial backing increased.

In December 1933 there was a meeting between the Navy and the managerial staff of Deutsche Werke, Kiel. DWK had to build an erection shed for the boats, partly to alleviate weather conditions, but more importantly to camouflage the operation from the inspectors of the Treaty. The laying down of keel number 1 could, said DWK, be done in May 1934, although the shed would not be finished by then. But time was becoming a factor for the Navy which wanted to take advantage of a change of government and the pro-armed services atmosphere that was prevalent. It would also mean that the Navy was once more to build the weapon most proscribed by the Treaty. At a subsequent meeting in January between Igewit and DWK verbal contracts were agreed.

Ruhr steel production had continued after the First World War. To play safe, now that U-boats were to be built again, to avoid the eyes of the Allied Control Commission (what was left of it) as well as those of the German left-wing movement and French agents, the steel for U-boat production was first exported, and then re-imported to Kiel. Holland was the natural choice with Inkavos the client to carry out this covert plan. The plan did run into one problem however, which was that customs duty had to be paid on the steel when it was moved around.

The urgency of the project began to permeate everything that happened at the DWK yard. The erection of a second shed was begun in May 1934, in which the six smaller boats were to be built. Already the tower of *U25* (first of the Type IA boats) had been completed, but then had to be modified to accept the larger of the two periscopes. By the end of June the first two boats (*U25* and *U26*) were fitting-out, and on the 27th Raeder, who may have been a little affected by the euphoria, ordered the next six boats, this time of Type IIA, which became *U1—U6*. Further discussions resulted in work on Type IIA boats being transferred to Germaniawerft. The final result, after much discussion and many changes of mind, was that the two Type IXA boats were to be completed and launched by Deschimag, Bremen. Deutsche Werke, Kiel, built the majority of the Type IIAs, fourteen were built by Germaniawerft. (Two later IIAs, *U120* and *U121* were built by Flender-Werke, Lübeck.)

The speed with which the Navy had proceeded with its plans led, almost inevitably, to confusion, which in turn led to exasperation in the yards, but the whole matter was shrouded in such secrecy that all mention of U-boats was specifically forbidden. In June 1934 Raeder had a long discussion with Hitler as to how new shipbuilding was to be handled in talks outside the closed circle of the High Command. Raeder noted that 'Hitler demands complete secrecy on the construction of the U-boats.' Secrecy was such that the German Army List had not been published since 1932, and the Navy was even more vulnerable to the Commission, for it was also building two 26,000-ton battle-cruisers (*Scharnhorst* and *Gneisenau*), both 10,000 tons over the Treaty limit.

So far as the Type II boats were concerned, the many problems arising out of the shroud of secrecy as well as practical difficulties made it quite clear that the first boat could not be completed until at least February 1935. This was then extended for practical and political purposes so that the first Type IIA was not launched until 15 June 1935, and the first IA went into the River Weser on 14 February 1936.

# 2 CREATING THE NEW U-BOAT FLEET

Political reactions during 1934 had suggested to Hitler that not all the signatories of the Treaty of Versailles would be implacably imposed to German re-armament under this new National Socialist government. In May 1934 Sir John Simon, British Foreign Secretary, had actually proposed equality of armaments to Germany, but the French rebuffed the idea. By 1935, however, it was clear that either the Powers would have to enforce the terms of the Treaty or cancel it, and start negotiations with Germany about her re-armament. The Admiralty was aware of German plans to re-arm, and a White Paper of 4 March made this abundantly clear at the Wilhelmstrasse, where it caused concern; furthermore, Sir John was due in Berlin for talks on the whole question, with the prior knowledge that Germany already had an embryo military air force, and that naval construction was in progress.

If Hitler were to take unilateral action and tear up the Treaty, he still had to be able to justify it. He found his excuse in a French bill extending national service from eighteen months to two years (which had been necessitated by the shortage of men in the call-up class caused by the losses of the First World War). Hitler decided to test the water before taking this decision. He had Göring inform the military correspondent of *The Daily Mail* what was already common knowledge – that Germany had the *Luftwaffe*. Sir John and Anthony Eden were due to visit Berlin on 6 March, but the White Paper had brought on one of Hitler's colds; then Germany informed the world that she was re-arming, and still Sir John confirmed his willingness to come to Berlin.

The next step was inevitable. Knowing that British opinion would at least be divided, and mainly in his favour, and that Great Britain had the major say in European diplomatic matters, Hitler took the major step of declaring (on Saturday, 16 March) the introduction of national military service and that Germany was to have a peace-time army of 36 divisions. At half a million men, this was a flagrant breach of the Treaty. Shirer commented that when he went at noon to the ceremony at the State Opera House on Sunday, 17 March (*Heldengedenktag* or Heroes' Memorial Day), he '... witnessed a scene which Germany had not seen since 1914. The entire lower floor was a sea of military uniforms ... It turned out to be a jubilant celebration of the death of Versailles and the rebirth of the German conscript Army.'

In fact the new German Army had been beaten to the off by both the *Luftwaffe* and the *Kriegsmarine*. Planning had started in 1919 (when Noske lamented that Germany did not possess a single submarine) and was now given some freedom of action. The surface fleet was to take precedence, but the U-boat building could be brought into the open. Reaction took a month, and was utterly devoid of the sanctions which were contained in the Treaty. When representatives from France, Italy and Great Britain met at Stresa on 11 April, there were ineffective mutterings about support for the Austrians and the Locarno Treaty, and an almost incidental condemnation of German actions. The League of Nations appointed a committee to suggest steps that might be taken *the next time*. The full strength of the Utopian ideals which were the product of the First World War were seen to be utterly ineffective against Hitler, as they were in the face of Mussolini's aggression in Ethiopia.

The German High Command remained nervous for some time at this apparent closing of ranks, especially when France signed a mutual assistance pact with Russia. Hitler now relieved the situation with a master stroke, removing European fears of German re-armament. In keeping (apparently) with the spirit of the time, and, more to the point, in keeping with his own methodology and character, he made a public and widely reported speech. On 21 May 1935 he stood before the Reichstag and 'exuded a spirit not only of confidence but ... of tolerance and conciliation.' Shirer wrote that the speech was 'perhaps the most eloquent and certainly one of the cleverest and misleading of his Reichstag orations ...' Hitler spoke out against war, saying that '... dynastic egotism, political passion and patriotic blindness ... by shedding rivers of blood has ... not substantially altered their (the combative nations of the First World War) fundamental characters. If these states [and he slyly included Germany – the old Germany] had applied the merest fraction of their sacrifices to wiser purposes the success would certainly have been greater and more permanent.'

He went on to declare that 'National Socialist Germany wants peace because of its fundamental convictions ... The principal effect of every war is to destroy the flower of the nation ... Germany needs peace and desires peace.' The statement was what Europe needed to hear, and in any case there was no resistance to the dictators in Europe who were speaking softly and rarely, as yet, using big sticks. In the UK Churchill was disregarded as an anti-Hitler scaremonger; in France there was sabre-rattling and the building of the Maginot Line, but here the full circle of reaction to Germany had been reached, with a pure defensive policy adopted once again. Had the élan of 1914 been present in 1935 or 1936, or indeed at any moment prior to 1939, the world might have been spared the most disastrous war ever fought. But the Maginot mentality suited a France sickened and decimated by the First World War, and where the resultant manpower and other shortages were still being felt. This inactive malaise was an ideal scenario in which Hitler's plans for the future of Germany would flourish.

Nevertheless, Hitler was careful in what he said in his speech of 21 May. He reinforced the effect of his platitudes by saying that 'Germany declares herself willing to agree to any limitation whatsoever of the calibre of artillery, battleships, cruisers and torpedo-boats. In like manner the German Government is ready to agree to the limitation of tonnage for submarines, or their complete abolition.' Throughout the period since Hitler had taken power, the British had pursued their policy of appeasement, and had not even had the courage of the French sabre-rattlers to say what they were really afraid of. Instead of admitting fears of German re-armament, they 'trusted' the Germans to behave like gentlemen. Hitler's speech seemed to justify that trust. In fact it was justification for their complacency, not only with benefit of hindsight.

The main British interest in Hitler's offer to restrict re-armament was in relation to the naval proposals. Hitler had publicly offered 35 per cent of the strength of the Royal Navy as his upper limit, and the Government and the Admiralty accepted this without question and with relief. Hitler had stated in *Mein Kampf* that friendship between Great Britain and Germany was fundamental to German interests, and he amplified this in his speech saying: 'The German Government recognises the overpowering vital importance, and therewith the justification, of a dominating protection for the British Empire on the sea ...' and here and elsewhere in the speech he effectively castigated the 'old Germany' for its naval aspirations before and during the First World War. What he did not say was that he would eventually attempt to gain control of an Empire as vast as that of the British, but linked to Germany by land, not sea.

Hitler's opportunism has been mentioned before; he was learning quickly just how far he could push the rest of Europe politically, and even militarily, and he reaped great benefits until September 1939. In all of his dealings up to that time he was proved right in his assertion that he knew how much the Powers were prepared to give away of others' rights to prevent war. After September 1939 he proved himself initially an intuitive military leader, but neither he nor Germany was prepared for, or even aware of, the problems that a long-term war would pose. Before the speech had been made, the (postponed) visit of Sir John Simon and Anthony Eden to Berlin took place. At the meeting, Hitler had proposed a British–German naval accord, and the proposal was met with a response that *The Times* accorded his May speech: 'It is to be hoped that the speech will be taken everywhere as a sincere and well-considered utterance meaning precisely what it says.'

On 12 April the British Naval Attaché at the British Embassy had a conversation with Leopold Bürkner of the German Naval Staff. Knowing of this impending meeting, Raeder had the previous day given Bürkner permission to inform the Attaché that Germany was now building five destroyers in addition to the already published total. Bürkner added that work on seven more destroyers and two cruisers was shortly to commence. The report of the conversation notes that the British Attaché 'was not shocked, but asked why no figures for submarines had been given to him.' The reply was 'we haven't got that far.' Obviously the injunction of secrecy still applied to U-boats, Bürkner being barred from saying that the first U-boat would go for fitting-out in just two months, or that sixteen more would be launched by the end of the year.

Bürkner added that he 'had the impression that we could have given the British Naval Attaché simultaneous information about submarine construction without arousing more unfavourable reactions; he is certainly thoroughly prepared to hear such news, and so, I suppose, is the Admiralty'. The main concern of the Admiralty thus seemed to have been tonnage totals and not types. They also seemed little concerned about the quality of the vessels Germany was building, as Bürkner said 'he knew that we did not want to say anything about displacement, but he supposed that the two cruisers were not of the *Deutschland* type'. (*Deutschland*, later the *Lützow*, displaced 15,000 tons, *Scharnhorst* 38,900 tons and *Gneisenau* 31,800 tons. No comparison can be drawn between *Deutschland* and the others, they being in the true battle-cruiser class.) This tolerant sympathy no doubt reflected that of the Admiralty at the time.

The conversation then turned to the real matter of the day: the Anglo-German Naval Accord. The first meeting to discuss this was due to take place at the end of April or the beginning of May, and Bürkner told the Attaché that the German team had already been chosen. The Attaché ended the conversation with the sympathetic comment that the Admiralty attitude to such talks was that the consent of the other four Powers would be necessary to invite Germany, but that Great Britain would not take part unless Germany were present. No longer were France, Italy, Japan and the United States (with Great Britain) to dictate naval programmes and policy to Germany. Then came the formal invitation to Germany from the British Foreign Office to send a delegation to the UK for discussions, to which Berlin replied that Germany was convinced of the usefulness of the talks, but that as the Chancellor, Hitler, intended to make a statement on foreign policy in reply to the League of Nations resolution of April 17, a postponement would be appreciated. This was agreed, and in due course Hitler made the 21 May speech, effectively drawing the fire of both the League of Nations and individual countries with respect to his re-establishment of conscription and the attendant military programmes.

Two days after the speech a 'Top Secret Military' policy directive was issued to the participants in the forthcoming conference, with a copy for information to German Naval Command. Certain matters were *not* for discussion, these being:

1. Qualitative German equality of rights as regards all types of vessels, fortifications, weapons, etc., and consequently the abolition of Part V of the Treaty of Versailles relating to the Navy ...
2. The fixing of the German fleet establishment at 35 per cent of the displacement of the British fleet, taking the British Treaty displacements (of 1930) as the basis.

3. Germany's readiness for such *limitations of naval armament* as all Naval Powers may, on the basis of the negotiations conducted during the 1935 Naval Conference, undertake to carry out at the same time ... (Author's emphasis)

This was to include even the abolition of submarines, and had the concomitant effect, later noted, that 'If an increased submarine establishment should be allotted to all the larger naval powers generally, as was provided for in the London Treaty (and also in the Hoover Plan) then Germany would also share in this settlement.'

The document later states: 'The size of the Budget estimates and financial questions are internal German affairs, discussion of which shall be refused.' This seemingly harmless proviso camouflaged the relationship of the Defence Budget to the total German budget of the time, and could have indicated not only the magnitude of the re-armament programme, but by careful analysis, the individual size of large ships then building. As to dates of completion, should the British have asked, the dates planned were between 1942 and 1946, which was probably the true consensus of naval opinion at the time, and the information given to Hitler.

The document finally turns to the matter of U-boats. It states that:

Since the war Great Britain has been constantly striving for the limitation of or outlawry of submarine war on commerce, as well as the abolition of submarines. At the conversations she will probably ask us, too, what are our views on this problem. In this case our reply should be: Germany would welcome a general humanisation of war on commerce such as is attempted in the 1922 Washington draft and is to some extent achieved in Part IV of the London Agreement. Germany subscribes to the general principle that all provisions in the sphere of armaments *should be general and applicable to all*. In order to further British efforts for a more humane code of war and as further proof of her peaceful intentions, *Germany declares herself willing to accede at once to Part IV of the London Agreement*, even if it should not prove possible to achieve general agreement on the part of the other Powers concerned. [Author's emphasis]

*U1* was three weeks from launching when the document was issued, and although other U-boats were building, had the London meeting decided upon no submarines, Germany would have lost little. The offer to scrap them cost nothing to make however, and in the event had no effect. The Admiralty was probably not going to scrap its own 31 submarines then in commission, as well as cancelling those in build. The Royal Navy submarine strength in September 1939 had risen, as had Germany's, to 57 boats, but the role of the submarine in the Royal Navy was somewhat different from that of the German U-boat.

The effect of Hitler's speech in May was obviously to ameliorate, and it drew from the British Ambassador a letter to the German Foreign Minister, Baron von Neurath, expressing 'the hope that the German Government would send their experts to London for naval conversations as soon as possible ... my Government [is] most anxious to lose no time in beginning these conversations.' The talks were planned to begin on 4 June 1935, the day chosen that year for the ceremony of Trooping the Colour in honour of the official birthday of King George V. The conference was to last until 22 June.

As in Berlin, Sir John Simon was in charge of the British negotiations, accompanied by four Royal Naval officers and a Mr. Craigie. The German delegation was led by Joachim von Ribbentrop, specially appointed for the occasion, and he was accompanied by three naval officers and two diplomats. Sir John began by thanking the Germans for attending and then said:

The British Government and the British public had noted with satisfaction that, in his speech on 21 May, the Reichs Chancellor had stated, with reference to British defensive naval requirements, that he had no wish to enter into competition with Great Britain in the naval field, any more than she intended to compete with Germany in the field of land forces.

He went on to state that agreement would probably never result if limits were laid down that were quantitative, which was entirely counter to the instructions the German delegation had received.

Von Ribbentrop then launched into a monologue paying tribute to a number of the shibboleths of the time – the arms race, Great Britain's 'historic claim to supremacy at sea', and then suddenly injected the demand that unless the British accept immediately the 35 per cent ratio, the talks could not proceed. The meeting had started at 10 a.m., but when this proposal, or rather demand, was made, Simon found that he had to go to a meeting with the Prime Minister. Mr. Craigie took the chair, and commented that the German proposal was rather like arriving at an answer before the question had been put. Von Ribbentrop replied that the 35 per cent matter was a 'final decision by the German Chancellor', and that the situation was 'take it or leave it'.

If von Ribbentrop had waited, he would have been informed by Mr. Craigie that he was prepared to leave the matter to further discussion, which might have resulted in a higher ratio for Germany, but von Ribbentrop then 'drew attention to the great restraint which the Reichs Chancellor had imposed upon himself in making his historic offer'. Acceptance of this hallowed writ by the British Government was the *sine qua non* for further talks. Craigie replied 'if the German Delegation represented the claim for 35 per cent as a final and unalterable decision of the Reichs Chancellor's, the formal consent of the British Government was really superfluous ...' This discussion, if it can be called that, went on until 1.45 p.m., with Craigie trying to establish some mutual agreement, and von Ribbentrop repeating the same demand at regular intervals. One agreement was reached however, that there should be secrecy regarding the subjects under discussion, and any proposals made and conclusions reached.

The meeting resumed at four that afternoon and von Ribbentrop proposed that there should be only one meeting per day, between 11 a.m. and 1 p.m. There was no dissension to the proposal. Discussion then took place as to whether Great Britain and Germany could ever come to a workable agreement on ratios, Mr. Craigie arguing that the other Powers should be consulted. Von Ribbentrop suggested a joint statement without further consultation, but Craigie was not to be bulldozed into a quick decision. He felt that the British reply to the initial proposal should first be heard.

In the days that followed the meeting continued in the conference room, at von Ribbentrop's hotel, and on the telephone (particularly between the two senior naval officers, Admiral Little and Admiral Schuster.) The Admiralty was trying to tie the Germans down to a more definitive phrase than the 'global tonnage' insisted upon by Hitler. Submarines were discussed as well, with Schuster tossing in the bait of German agreement of tonnage by categories, if Germany had submarine parity. Luckily the naval members of both delegations were capable of reasoned argument, despite von Ribbentrop's pompous party attitude. The first result of these talks was that Great Britain agreed if there were to be no *international* accord on Germany's allowed tonnage, then Britain and Germany were free to arrive at some agreement themselves. This had taken only two days, and on the evening of the 6 June 'Sir John Simon ... expressed his satisfaction that agreement had been reached and that the way was open for the task ahead'. Despite von Ribbentrop, Hitler had succeeded, and Great Britain would now inform the other nations concerned of the results of the Anglo-German agreement, rather than consult them before making decisions.

The delegations then departed for the Whitsun weekend, but Berlin was still working on the declaration by Raeder on the method of classification to be used in relation to the German fleet to be, including the tonnage available in submarines. The reply from Naval Command recommended that as far as submarines were concerned:

When announcing our claim for parity of submarine tonnage in principle ... it seems better to limit ourselves for the near future (perhaps for the period of expansion) to a smaller tonnage, in order not to give the British unnecessary cause for suspicion, *particularly since on personnel grounds we cannot go substantially beyond our present programme.* [Author's emphasis]

This referred to the 35 per cent in submarine tonnage in comparison with the Royal Navy. The brief added that while claiming parity throughout with the British, the delegation should represent German capacity at, say, 45 per cent, reserving the right to increase U-boat tonnage to 100 per cent, should the need arise. The French were always uppermost in German strategic thinking, posing the most immediate potential threat to Germany on land and at sea. The final point made was that if any higher percentage were proposed, although it would lead to a larger building programme, it might harden the British attitude to total opposition to Germany having any submarines at all.

French reaction to the 35 per cent proposal was swift and angry, and the British modified their tacit agreement. This angered the Germans, but they were mollified by a statement from Mr. Craigie to the effect that the British Government was still on all fours with Germany over the 35 per cent, but that a suitable clause would be inserted into the final agreement to allay French fears. This drew the reaction from von Ribbentrop that he was pleased to note the British attitude, but that he could not understand how the French could possibly imagine, because Germany was rebuilding her fleet, that escalation was involved! Such is the language of diplomacy that German re-armament and new naval construction became the first step 'towards a real limitation of armaments'.

By 18 June the matter had been decided. Sir Samuel Hoare (Secretary of State for Foreign Affairs) chaired the meeting that day, to which came the First Lord of the Admiralty as well as the regular British delegation. The First Lord remarked how good it was to conclude the mutually beneficial agreement, and said that the British delegation was handing the German delegation the Note defining the Agreement 'although it is an unusual procedure to sign a Naval Agreement until the details have been examined'. The Note was then signed and the German Navy had the right as far as the British were concerned to a Navy of 35 per cent of the British Fleet in being. *The Times* had put the matter into context in its leader on 4 June, when it said that 'thirty five per cent would mean parity in European waters' in that the Royal Navy was, by necessity of its role, 'scattered over the seven seas'. Hitler of course had claimed that the German fleet was merely 'to secure our existence and freedom on the Continent'.

The Note had agreed the 35 per cent, but went on to add (ominously) in section (f) that:

In the matter of submarines, however, Germany, while not exceeding the ratio of 35:100 in respect of the total tonnage, shall have the right to possess a submarine tonnage equal to the whole submarine tonnage of the British Commonwealth of Nations. The German Government, however, undertake that, except in the circumstances indicated in the immediately following sentence, Germany's submarine tonnage shall not exceed 45 per cent of the total possessed by the Members of the British Commonwealth of Nations. The German Government reserves the right, in the event of a situation arising which *in her opinion* makes it necessary for Germany to avail herself of her right to a possession of a submarine tonnage exceeding the 45 per cent above mentioned, to give notice to this effect to His Majesty's Government in the United Kingdom and agree that the matter shall be the subject of friendly discussion before the German Government exercise that right.

On 20 June, the German Naval Attaché in London, Wassner, had lunch with Captain Dankwerts, one of the naval members. Dankwerts told Wassner that the Admiralty had been the driving force behind British acceptance of the 35 per cent agreement, despite general governmental dislike. Then Germany officially informed Great Britain that she intended to lay down a battleship a year for three years, which meant that Admiralty *bonhomie* towards the German Navy disappeared beyond the horizon. French opinion became once more 'extremely agitated' about this timetable, but Dankwerts suggested that if the time-scale were doubled, further agreement might be possible.

Now that there had been quantitative agreement, it was thought that there would have to be a qualitative distribution of the tonnage, to include the total number of submarines. Germany proposed to build forty submarines in 1935 and 1936, and take up the slack of the remaining tonnage in the years up to 1942, but in the light of French reaction was prepared to reduce the numbers to an extent. French opinion was affecting British attitudes, including that of the Admiralty. This rapidly produced statement was telephoned to Wassner at 5.30 p.m. on 25 June, and as soon as it became known it had a remarkably favourable effect upon Parliament, the Press, the Admiralty and the British people. Then the matter was obfuscated by the French proposal to lay down a 35,000-ton battleship, and submarines disappeared from general concern.

In the *Marineamt* there was relief; the French statement had removed the focus from the U-boats, and planning could continue, this time with the certainty that the plans would mature into reality. The first two Types (I and II) had been designed, laid down and from that moment, launched (of the Type IIA boats *U1* had launched on 15 June, *U2* then launched on 1 July; *U25* – the first Type IA – launched on 25 July 1936, but by then a number of Type II and VII boats had been launched). Furthermore, the Type IX boats were due to launch in 1936 (although, because of technical problems, *U37* – the first – was not launched until May 1938). The first of the Type VII boats, *U33*, was launched on 11 June 1936, to be followed by more than 700 of the Type.

The two Type IA boats were, as has been noted, the offspring of the Spanish *E1* boat, built in Spain with German Navy money, and later sold to Turkey as the *Gür*. Although superseded as early as 1936 by the Type VII, the IAs gave some value in the early part of the war before being lost in 1940.

They had, however, been valuable test pieces. They were in the class of 'High Seas boats', differentiated from coastal boats, and although their official displacement for the Treaty was 712 tons, their true operational displacement was 862 tons surfaced. Designed within the specification for an 800-ton torpedo and mine boat, they had severe technical limitations in diving, and frequently 'porpoised'. No more were built, other than *U25* and *U26*, for the reason that the Type VII boats had the same performance (except range), and yet were of some 240 tons less displacement. Four Type VIIs could be built from the same materials as three Type IAs, thus allowing more U-boats to the tonnage of the Agreement.

The matter of the extra range (which the Type IA did have) had to be solved, but with a better design. The freedoms of the Agreement meant that Germany could now build experimental boats at home and thus get results faster, especially in view of the invaluable experience already gained abroad. The concept of a primarily minelaying U-boat, which could then go on torpedo patrol, could now be addressed. The torpedo-mines developed, TMA and TMB, had a common calibre of 53.3cm, and were respectively a moored mine 3.64 metres in length, and a ground mine of 2.3 metres. They were ideally suited to laying by U-boat, but there was no suitable boat, not even the Type IA, that could carry enough of them to be effective.

In 1934, one solution had been to lengthen the Type IA by 7.5 metres, to increase carrying capacity. The original design carried 30 TMA or 45 TMB, increasing to 54/75 if no torpedoes were carried. The lengthening proposed would increase displacement to 970 tons (fully laden), with a surface speed of 18.5 knots and a range of 12,000 nautical miles at 10 knots. But the internal re-arrangement would have meant the tower being in a very forward position, and while this would have improved stability, the overall displacement was considered to be too high in relation to the Type VII of which more could be built.

Various designs were considered, including some which were of amusing rather than practical value (see Chapter 3 and Appendices). What concerned the submariners most was the crucial factor of diving time, coupled with the need to be able to dive to considerable depth to avoid surface ship attacks. The consensus seemed to be that what was needed was a general-purpose boat of about 500 tons with the fighting potential, although not the range, of the Type IA, and which could dive in 30 seconds, and reach a depth of 100 metres.

The original form of the Type IIA boats without their saddle-tanks has been mentioned above; this hull form was considered to offer possibilities in increasing diving depth, in that it rendered the hull, with a near circular cross-section, less liable to crush either during a depth-charge attack or at increased depth. The Type IIA hull design was therefore re-evaluated, and it was decided to take this hull form and increase the size. The aim was to produce the larger boat of 500 tons, with the desired diving time and depth. Saddle-tanks and an outer casing could be grafted on to improve range and seaworthiness. Further diving tanks were to be added forward and aft between the pressure-hull and the outer casing, but most importantly the main diving tank was to be placed within the pressure hull, below the control room. Situated around the centre of gravity of the boat, this would shorten diving time dramatically. It was also decided to put the main fuel tanks within the pressure-hull; this would further augment the dive rate and reduce the possibility of oil-traces which could lead a hunter straight to the U-boat.

The design was discussed in January 1935 and the MVB VII eventually became the Type VII. The designed displacement was 550 tons, with speeds of 17/9 knots. Ranges were 6,000nm at 8 knots/75 at 4. Engine power-weight ratio was 15/16kg/hp, and weight 38 tons. The electric motors and their batteries weighed far more however, and were unchangeable to any great extent, at 138 tons. Just over 32 per cent of the boat's capacity was occupied by power units and batteries. Tests with models showed that drag on the saddle-tank version only increased at speeds between 11 and 13 knots. The design, produced by Schürer and Bröking, was accepted.

As soon as the design had been approved, production orders were issued on 25 March to Germaniawerft (*U33–U36*) and on 1 April 1935 to Deschimag (*U27–U32*). *U33* was launched on 11 June, *U36* on 4 November 1936. *U27* was launched on 24 June 1936, *U32* on 25 February 1937. The first boat to commission into the German Navy was *U33* on 25 July 1935, having taken fifteen months to build, and a further six weeks to fit-out, trial, undergo acceptance tests and commission. No doubt the boat was rushed into service for political reasons, and needed some time on its shake-down cruise. The planned schedule proved remarkably accurate, with *U33* only eleven days late, and *U34* only two days adrift.

Deschimag had been included because Deutsche Werke, Kiel, had no slip available until, at the earliest, 1937, being committed to other contracts (*U1–U6*, Type IIA), and Germaniawerft was building *U7–U12*. The London Agreement was taken as fact, even before the British Government had been told of the proposals; the German Navy had in fact originated the idea for it in 1934, and it had then been passed to the Reich Chancellery for diplomatic action.

Orders were issued in February for a further eight Type IIAs at GW, and four at DW. Small modifications were included from *U7* onwards which were included in all new builds (including a lower silhouette and an extra steering position on the open bridge in the tower). The final total was therefore 24 Type II boats, due for completion by 15 May 1936. Only the last four were late, and *U24* was launched on 24 September 1936 at GW; the delay was due to political considerations, not to the yards or the building plan.

The plan projected to the end of 1938 included these 24 Type II boats, plus the two Type IA and ten of the basic Type VII 500-ton design. The London Agreement left Germany with another 6,000 tons. Initially, more

Type I boats were planned, but this was changed to twelve more Type VIIs (*U37–U48*) spread over three years. Although the Navy had jumped the gun over the Agreement, it had adhered to the tonnage provisions, due to the build capacity of the yards then used for naval construction. At this point, French counter-reaction to the Agreement began to have an effect, and the building of *U37–U48* was put back to a start date of 1 October 1938, with the last launch planned for 1 January 1940. Furthermore, delays were applied to the building of *U21–U24* (as noted above) and four of the Type VIIs previously ordered.

In June 1935 Admiral Raeder appointed captain Karl Dönitz to the post of Commander U-boats, responsible for the training and leadership of the burgeoning U-boat fleet. Interestingly, Max Horton had been appointed to command the British First Cruiser Squadron on 7 June, during the conference in London. Appointed to command of the Western Approaches after the war started, he would become Dönitz's major opponent. At this time Dönitz's influence was limited, but he was a convinced U-boat officer, having served in U-boats during the First World War. He was very much in favour of the medium-sized boat, but he seems to have had no influence on the planning decisions at the time. However the importance of the appointment was to be felt later, during the first half of the war in the Atlantic.

General opinion in the Navy saw the U-boat as a part of the main fleet (as did all other major navies at the time), and not as a weapon in itself, to be used against merchant fleets. This stemmed in part from German fears of the French Fleet, and the feeling that sinking merchantmen was incidental to the U-boat commander's real task of laying waste to the iron colossi on the surface. Furthermore, the efficacy of the submarine was under question, given the development of Asdic and pre-set fuses for depth-charges by the British. These and other problems faced Dönitz upon taking up his command in Kiel-Wik.

Then, on 28 September 1935, Dönitz was also appointed Commanding Officer of the first operational U-boat unit – the Weddigen Flotilla. His command consisted solely of *U9*, the Type IIB boat commissioned on 21 August 1935. He knew that his job would become more substantial, and he was an energetic man, and so he threw himself into the job wholeheartedly, despite, as he said himself, having been appointed with 'neither orders, instructions nor guidance'. His command was one which was ideal to a reasonably senior officer; he had almost total freedom of choice in what he did, and how he did it. Raeder's evaluation of the man was right. Dönitz was not entirely alone, however, for a number of officers and men had already received training, and there was a corpus of experience available in the veterans of the previous war.

Training programmes under Admiral Spindler had begun in 1927, although these had naturally been theoretical. Later some sea training had been provided, thanks to Inkavos' activities, and quite a number of officers and men had also benefited from Schottky's specialised U-boat course. This course, which also ran from 1927 onwards, was divided into three sections:

A. i. The origins of various submarine types, and talks on the meaning of the submarine within the field of naval warfare.

ii. Lectures on foreign submarines and their weapons, with a constant feedback of Intelligence from abroad, and particularly from Inkavos and the various officers who had sailed in the boats designed by them.

iii. Talks on the basic means of maintaining depth, submerged manoeuvring and submarine steering equipment.

iv. The weaponry, periscopes and the organisation of protective measures to counter anti-submarine attack.

v. Lectures on attack tactics, backed up by experience from the previous war.

(The whole of Part A of the instruction programme was given to every young ensign of the U-boat Arm.)

B. Staff courses in submarine subjects (down to the rank of lieutenant). These were given from 1930 by Schottky, from 1932 by Schürer and Fürbringer.

C. The training of small groups of serving seamen and engineering branch officers on the various Inkavos boats. Until 1932 Fürbringer, who had crewed one of the Turkish boats, was running a submarine training school for the Turkish Navy, and three young serving officers had been attached to his staff in Turkey for some time.

In addition to these special-to-arm courses, Schottky asked for, and got, lectures on U-boat matters given at the Naval School at Kiel-Mürwik, and the Naval Academy at Kiel.

Until 1932 none of the training had any practical purpose, but then the first definite plans were laid for future U-boat building. Hitler supported the armed forces' expansion programmes, and the U-boat training became more formalised within the general training structure; Fürbringer was put in charge because he was the most experienced of the training officers. In May 1932 he gave his first six-day course to 49 naval ensigns. Further training plans for 1932 included starting intensive yearly courses for seamen's branch and engineering branch officers. This training was to be far more extensive, lasting twelve weeks. There were to be 207 hours' teaching, and one or two hours daily on the simulator. Sea time was spent in CV707, and an increasing number of officers experienced the benefits of both theoretical and practical training. Regular courses became standard, and von Blomberg (Minister of Defence from 1933) put the matter into the normal training programme by establishing Kiel-Wik as the new submarine school from 1 October 1933.

The Commanding Officer was Korvettenkapitån Karl Slevogt; the senior lecturers were Fürbringer, and Hülsmann who was to become one of the most senior U-boat engineering officers, and eventually Chief of the U-boat acceptance board. Lecturers were Rösing (who had tested a Swedish submarine in 1932) and Freiwald (later aide-de-camp to Raeder). The first course assembled at Kiel in the summer of 1933.

It comprised eight officers and more than 70 petty officers and ratings. Still operating as the 'anti-submarine training school', this was actually the only class of this nature at the school until submarine production prospects improved in 1934. The second entry reported on 30 September 1934. In both cases the course consisted of theoretical instruction in U-boat construction (from the point of view of both seamen and engineering branch), together with lectures on stability maintenance (including load planning and trim correction, surfaced and submerged). Seamen got basic torpedo handling training and firing, and senior rates and officers were practised in periscope use. Engineering officers went through a much more detailed description of the power units, and all other machinery for which they would be responsible. Practical models of steering equipment, periscopes and gyro-compasses were used, to increase the value of the training.

Further practical training was carried out on the simulator fitted in a minesweeper. A periscope stub was fitted in an enclosed deck compartment, and an engine replica gave half the power of a Type II; control was through another replica, of the submarine's steering equipment. A number of officers were trained in this way, and as many as possible sent to Finland to experience the real thing in CV707. During her extremely lengthy trials period, thanks to Fürbringer, many officers benefited from training in her, including Braütigem, Papenberg and Freiwald.

Thus, when Dönitz took command of Uflotilla Weddigen and his one U-boat, he was not short of trained crews. These now had to undergo further training, and much of that, which took place at Kiel and Mürwik (for ensigns and lieutenants), was concerned with Asdic, and the counter-measures to it. Dönitz was responsible for all of this. He had, as noted above, been promoted Commander U-boats on 6 June 1935, his command of Uflotilla Weddigen dating from September that year, and training was part of his job. At the time 28 seamen's branch and nine engineering branch officers had been posted to UAS, among them Lieutenants Prien, Schepke, Schütze, Godt (later Admiral and Commander U-boats) and Frauenheim. All were to become 'aces' in their time.

Uflotilla Weddigen was officially established at Kiel on 27 September, and Dönitz arrived to take command two days later. The Flotilla was planned to be equipped with U7–U12 (all Type IIB), but eventually received U9, U13, U15, U17, U19, U21 and U23. The last boat arrived on 10 October 1936. The training Flotilla (US Flotilla) received U1–U8, U10 and U11, which arrived during the period 29 June 1935 to 16 December 1936. All boats had completed acceptance trials before being taken on the Flotilla strengths.

Although Dönitz was essentially on his own as far as training and organisation was concerned, he was looking forward to the task. He wrote that he had his 'own ideas about the training of the Flotilla and had set myself certain, clearly defined fundamental objectives'. He went on to give details of these:

1. I wanted to imbue my crews with enthusiasm and a complete faith in their arm, and to instil in them a spirit of selfless readiness to serve in it. Only those possessed of such a spirit could hope to succeed in the grim realities of submarine warfare. One of the first things that I had to do was rid my crews of the ever recurring complex that the U-boat, thanks to recent developments in British anti-submarine defence, was a weapon that had been mastered ...

2. The U-boat crews had to be trained as far as possible for war conditions. I wanted to confront them in peacetime with every situation with which they might be confronted in war, and to do it so thoroughly that when these situations arose in war my crews would be able to cope with them.

3. As to the range at which a U-boat should fire, both in surface and in submerged attack, I laid down the short range of 600 yards ... During the summer of 1935 the UAS had been teaching the young crews that when a U-boat discharged its torpedoes submerged, it must do so at a range of over 3,000 yards from the target, in order to avoid detection by the British Asdic apparatus ... I strenuously opposed this conception ...

4. I considered that the U-boat was ideal as a torpedo carrier, *even at night and in a surface attack*. (Author's emphasis)

5. The primary emphasis of my appreciations, objectives and consequent training methods had, however, to be laid on the tactical considerations. And here new problems presented themselves for solution.

   a. It is essential, in an attack on any given objective, to be able to deliver the attack in as great strength as possible ... to bring a number of U-boats to attack the given objective simultaneously ... A massed target then, should be attacked by massed U-boats.

   b. The U-boat has a very restricted radius of vision and is slow, even on the surface ... Tactically then it must act in co-operation with a branch of the armed forces more suited to reconnaissance duties. And for these the best is the aeroplane.

This summary gives an outline of Dönitz's method, and how he trained his crews during peacetime, and what he put into effect as soon as war broke out. He had not however the size of force he required, nor the air reconnaissance facilities that he implies were needed to put the plan into immediate, and devastating, effect. First results were therefore not too encouraging, but the situation improved as numbers grew and pack tactics became more effective, until there was a danger to the Allies that the Atlantic supply routes would be cut permanently.

To ensure that all crews received a very firm grounding in general boat handling, they had to make 66 surfaced and 66 submerged practice attacks before being allowed to fire their first live (practice) torpedo. Crews also trained in handling their craft in enemy waters, surfaced and submerged, inshore and off-shore. Then they were taught when to submerge when enemy aircraft or surface vessels were sighted, and when to remain on the surface; there was however one main rule, which was 'dive if in doubt'. During the interminable 132 training attacks and during later training torpedo attacks, they had to trim the boat to minimise periscope exposure, and this was done at night as well. They were taught to use background light behind the target at night, to illuminate it, and to minimise their own silhouette at all times. Combined with this was training to improve seamanship in the attack, thereby using the effects of wind and sea to lessen chances of being seen. In essence they were being taught stalking tactics.

During training a number of tactical points were dealt with that had arisen from the First World War. Other matters were the product of Dönitz's close analysis of what the enemy might do, as well as what the U-boats could do. Crews were taught how to maintain contact with a target while, when possible, getting ahead of it. This was particularly important in convoy attacks, for only one attack might be possible, and therefore it must be effective. Crews also received instruction in 'housekeeping' – watch routines by day and by night, and how to change over routines. This was particularly important at night, when bridge watches had to be kept in a darkened space for their night vision to develop, without which they were ineffective for up to half an hour.

Further tactical training was devoted to actions to be taken by commanders when faced with enemy defensive action. Captains had to know when it was possible, and necessary, to withdraw at high speed on the surface, and when to creep away submerged. In the latter case there was an inherent danger of losing contact with the target, and so this method was reserved for situations in which the boat would otherwise have been in danger. When withdrawing they also practised zig-zag, and when escaping submerged, they learned to operate silent routines. They had repeated practice in technical control of the boat, and in diving and surfacing techniques. Above all, the crew had to learn to operate as a coherent team, at all depths and all the time. Finally they were trained in surface gunnery, and in anti-aircraft defence. The course in all lasted for a year.

One U-boat commander wrote the following about the course:

The knowledge acquired during this single year of intensive training, in which the crews were tested to the limits of human endeavour, was the foundation in so far as the choice of types, armament and training were concerned, upon which the future structure of the U-boat Arm was built.

In the years that followed, tactics underwent refinement and modification. When it became evident that Great Britain might take the field against us, these tactics had to be modified to meet the conditions imposed by warfare on the High Seas and the introduction of the convoy system. But the principles remained unchanged.

The salient feature of this training year, 1935-36, was in fact that it eradicated from the mind of all commanders and their crews the inferiority complex, which had undoubtedly been prevalent among them, and the idea that the U-boat had been mastered and rendered impotent as an instrument of war by recently developed anti-submarine devices.

This course was standard to all crews who served in the U-boat Arm until strategic requirements forced truncation. The detail in it, and its scope, explain how Dönitz and his training staff were able to inculcate such an exceptional *esprit de corps* in the U-boat Arm, which considered itself an élite within the élite of the Navy. National Socialism did not pervade the Navy, and long periods away from base, or in such training courses, encouraged professionalism rather than any need of political justification. The greatest achievement was undoubtedly that crews were rid of the feeling of despair when confronted by Asdic, and that they were welded into a first class naval force.

While Dönitz was training his officers and men, the military power of Germany was increasing, mainly at a far faster rate than that of his U-boat Arm. But the situation improved slowly. Flotilla Weddigen had been established in September 1935, and Flotilla Saltzwedel followed in April 1936 (with two Type IA boats *U25–U36*, and the first of the Type VII boats). UFlotilla Lohs was set up at the same time as Weddigen, the first boat arriving on 30 September 1935. The full complement was to be *U12, U14, U16, U18, U20, U22* and *U24*. The three Flotillas and the training Flotilla were the sum total of Dönitz's command until 1938, when three further Flotillas were set up, Uflotillas Emsmann, Hundius and Wegener.

When Dönitz first assumed command he had the following units:

US Flotilla ten boats, Types IIA and IIB
Uflotilla Weddigen eight Type IIB
Uflotilla Saltzwedel two Type IA, nine Type VII
Uflotilla Lohs seven Type II

Bases for the Flotillas were Kiel (UFlotillas Lohs and Weddigen), and Wilhelmshaven (Hundius). Kiel was chosen for the smaller boats, having immediate access to the Baltic (and the coast of Poland), whereas

Wilhelmshaven had access to the Atlantic (and the French coast and lines of communication).

The new U-boat fleet was thus established, it had a commander, a training establishment, enough boats for three Flotillas and sufficient men trained in the basics to begin further, advanced, training in preparation for war. The commander was sufficiently experienced to do his job, and to enthuse his men. He was able to use experience in planning actively for his role in any future war. The period from the beginning of 1936 to 1 September 1939 saw the U-boat fleet double in size, and the development of new Types, some of which saw extended service during the war, others spawned new ideas, and some disappeared from sight. Throughout the period, however, the theme that war would come was ever present, although Raeder certainly prayed that it would not come before his balanced fleet was ready.

# 3  PREPARING FOR WAR

On 5 April, Dönitz had 36 U-boats in service, but he continued to plan and to train personnel as if ever increasing numbers would become available to implement his strategy of mass attack upon merchant fleets. His plan was quite simple: a maximum concentration of all available boats on each available target. This demanded some form of tactical as well as strategic control – strategic control to get the boats to the most valuable targets, and tactical to get the boats into position to attack in the most effective manner.

The first priority, however, was to locate the enemy, report his position to Headquarters, and attack with maximum available force. To locate the enemy Dönitz adopted a tactic already used with success by the earlier torpedo boats. A reconnaissance patrol formation was organised; once any boat of this force had located the enemy, the position and course was signalled. The finding boat would attack immediately, and all other boats were moved to an interception position calculated from the first signal, where they too would attack. The tactic would only be effective against ships steaming at a relatively slow speed.

To cope with higher target speeds the patrol line was to be backed up by the presence of one or more extra U-boat groups whose task was to operate against targets located by the patrol line. Various tactical formations were tested during this period, from which it emerged that if a ship cut a curved patrol line the U-boats would have the best chance of success. In an ideal situation the U-boat that made the first contact would maintain it, while the 'horns' of the curve, in the manner of the Zulu impi, would move in from either side of the target (a convoy), attacking as two separate groups as soon as they came into contact.

All the lessons that were being learned in the almost continuous exercises which Dönitz insisted take place were incorporated into technical instruction handbooks, which were continually updated with new information and results. The training had a background in the then political situation, in which was growing the conditions which would lead to practical application of these theories. German naval thinking foresaw France as the main enemy, and once the London Naval Agreement had been signed the German High Command published its report on the politico-military and -naval position. One section of the report dealt with the submarine weapon, and gave reasons for the design and construction of a third type of U-boat.

The report began by saying that there was only a limited amount of tonnage remaining within the terms of the Agreement which Germany could legitimately construct, even though Germany had reduced the pace of submarine building, even if not the final total of boats. After a restatement of the planning undertaken during, and often in spite of, the currency of the Treaty of Versailles, the report concentrated upon the Mediterranean theatre from the naval point of view. Germany had to ensure that supplies could not reach metropolitan France via the sea routes to Marseilles. The weapons of paramount importance in denying access to both French and neutral shipping were the torpedo and mine, both capable of delivery by the U-boat. The use of the U-boat and these weapons would disrupt, if not halt, shipping movement, and would also be valuable for reconnaissance.

The problem in executing this strategy lay in the U-boat designs available at this time:

(a) the Type II boats would never be able to function effectively in waters other than those within easy reach of German bases, such as the Baltic Sea, the Gulf of Finland, the North Sea and the English Channel.
(b) the Type VII boats were equally limited because their range, although greater than that of the Type II, was still too small to be effective in the Mediterranean without bases in that area. It was stated that a new type of U-boat with a much greater range was required.

The specification sought a boat with sufficient range to reach and enter the Mediterranean from bases in Germany, and to be able to operate there for some time. This meant a larger boat than the Type VII, in order to accommodate the requisite amount of fuel. The second requirement was that the boat have an increased surface speed (in comparison with other designs) thus cutting transit time to the operational area, but without demanding too high a rate of fuel consumption. The report recognised that there was a natural competition between the advocates of numbers and those who were in favour of boats being of sufficient size to be able to perform useful military functions. The main aim was a boat with longer range, higher surface speed and space for sufficient torpedoes and/or mines to make patrols viable, and preferably fruitful. The report proposed that the E1/MVB III design be used as the basis for such a boat.

The specification that MVB III be used as a design basis allowed the designers to complete initial plans in a short time, and the new design was suitably enhanced to come up to the revised requirements. Surface speed was projected as 20 knots by using 9-cylinder diesels (instead of the 8-cylinder engines fitted in the Type I A), and the range was increased to 20,000 nautical miles at a cruising speed of 10 knots. She could carry twelve torpedoes internally for the four forward and six aft tubes, all of which were internal to the pressure-hull. Further reserve torpedoes could be carried externally below the casing deck. As an alternative, a total of 44 TMA, 60 TMB or 22 of the latest

TMC torpedo-mines could be carried, or a combination of torpedoes and torpedo-mines.

Displacement was 730 tons, and speed had been enhanced, partly by increasing the engine rating, partly by redesigning the outer casing to reduce friction and drag, and finally by increasing the length-to-width ratio to impart an increase in its speed coefficient. Internal alterations included a new air circulation system to ensure adequate air supply to the diesels. Externally the casing deck was widened to accommodate the reserve torpedoes, and increased Flak weapons were installed (a 3.7cm immediately aft of the tower, and a 2cm weapon on the tower afterpart).

The decision to build this design was made quickly, and a total of thirteen boats would take up the last of the tonnage allowed to Germany under the London Naval Agreement. Admiral Raeder showed great interest in the new type, but there still existed a core of opinion that wanted numbers rather than size, arguing that two Type IX boats took the tonnage and the resources of three Type VII boats. Dönitz could have been one of the backers of this argument; he wanted the maximum number of boats at sea within the terms of the Agreement, with an ultimate aim of a large number of submarines available for economic warfare. If the larger, longer-range boats were built they would almost certainly be used as individual units, operating beyond the main Atlantic and Mediterranean convoy routes. It was on those convoy routes that Dönitz saw the decisive field of action. His opinion as to the planned use of the Type IX boats was confirmed in a letter of 8 June 1936 in which the role of this large boat was seen as operating in areas where the Type VII could not, because of its smaller range of action. This role was important, especially in view of the experiences gained in the First World War, and the new boat had the advantage that its superior surface cruising speed would allow it to reach its far-flung operational area in a relatively short time. It was also seen as a future transporter and as a substitute for the U-boat cruiser that was frequently proposed, and was to appear again in the form of the Type XI boat.

The decision whether to go ahead, and in what numbers, was twice postponed by Raeder, who finally came to a compromise decision: U37–U44 would be built (Type IX), and the remaining tonnage could be devoted to Type VII boats if reports on them, when they had finished their trials, were favourable. It seemed the best solution to the problem, affording the Navy a number of long-range boats and simultaneously leaving tonnage available for more boats of either type. On 9 June 1936 he ordered that trials with the Types IA and VII be completed as soon as possible, so that he could come to a decision as to whether to build another six Type VII boats by the autumn of the year. At the same time he asked whether the present Type VII could be modified to include external storage for torpedoes and mines (perhaps by removing the external stern torpedo tube), and whether the speed and range of the boat could be improved. This latter improvement might be brought about by the installation of superchargers fitted to the engine air intakes. His final decision on the Type IX was to issue an initial order for four boats (*U37–U40*) to Deschimag on 29 July 1936.

This order was for a boat already modified to increase its range to 11,000 nautical miles at 10 knots, and 15,000 at 8 knots. Surface maximum speed was 20 knots, submerged she was designed to make 8.5 knots. Her displacement was 740 tons, and she carried twelve internal and ten external torpedoes for her six tubes. This design (of 28 September 1936) was formidable, and she was similar in range and offensive potential to any fleet submarine of a foreign navy, despite her low surface displacement in comparison with larger foreign boats.

Dönitz now committed his thoughts to the question of which of the two designs was going to be of the most value. He argued, basing his contentions on his experiences in U-boats in the First World War, and on common sense applied to his knowledge of warships, that the U-boat would always be slower than surface vessels, even if it could make 17–20 knots. Whereas surface ships had increased their speeds dramatically since that time, submarines still had virtually the same submerged speed, and a surfaced speed that could not compete with that of surface vessels.

He wrote that 'the chances for a U-boat to come upon the enemy in the open sea are very limited unless the boat is able to get itself into a position ahead of the enemy and on the course he is sailing.' To have the greatest chance of making successful attacks, U-boats must remain stationary at convergence points of enemy convoy routes, and in close proximity to enemy strong points. During daylight the U-boat would maintain a silent, submerged position.

Given the speed problem, he saw only two possible situations where an enemy could be successfully attacked:

1. On convoy routes, especially at points of assembly, in areas where there was limited sea room in which the convoy could manoeuvre, and at rendezvous points, and
2. When military targets were considered, the U-boat had to be within short range of prospective targets.

His aim was to cover all the known and possible enemy convoy concentration points, and to do this he needed the maximum number of U-boats. His conclusion was that as Germany was limited as to tonnage, the boats must remain small, so that 'the more boats there are, the more points can be covered by U-boats, increasing the chances that the enemy will pass through one of these points.' He went on to define the requirements of the U-boat:

As a torpedo carrier it must have good attack performance, as a submarine of the first line it must have good underwater performance. Among these characteristics are: fast diving time, equipment simplicity (which reduces to a minimum the dangers of diving accidents in an alarm dive), good underwater steering, must create the least possible noise, have a limited turning circle, a low silhouette and a fast dive time. The small boat (the Type VII) has all these characteristics in its design.

He went on to compare the two types, concluding that the turning circle of the Type VII would be better than that of the Type IX if double rudders were fitted just behind the twin screws. As far as diving time was concerned, the Type VII was ten seconds faster to fifteen metres, and another five seconds reduction would result when better inlet valves were fitted for Diving Tank 3 (the main, midships, diving tank). He then went on to criticise the underwater steering of the Type IA (originally MVB III), the basis for the design of the Type IX. Due to longitudinal stability problems the metacentric height of the boat was located six metres in front of the control room, making the boat dive prone. He even cited the example of a Type IA hitting the bottom and burying itself as far aft as the forward gun platform because of this tendency, and further, the inability of the underwater steering apparatus to control the tendency, and power failure in one of the forward hydroplanes completed the disaster potential.

Dönitz was supported in his opinion of the Type IX by Korvettenkapitän Scheer, CO of the (then) Saltzwedel Flotilla, who said that the Type VII had such positive rudder and hydroplane controls that as far as he was concerned it could not be bettered, and that the handling was far better than the Type IA. On the surface both boats had good seagoing qualities, although the IA was down by the head at higher speeds. In bad weather trials the Type VII proved its superiority once more, and could remain stationary long enough for rust to appear on the diesels!

In terms of range the Type IX was far superior, but the naval architects looked at the idea of fitting the Type VII with larger saddle tanks. The extension of these towards the keel would be beneficial, bringing the metacentric height of the boat nearer to the longitudinal centre of gravity. There would also be increased stability when the saddle-tanks were blown, but the main advantage would be a 50 per cent increase in fuel capacity. Surface and submerged speeds would however be reduced by 0.5 knots, and reserve buoyancy reduced by some 10 per cent. Dönitz was generally in favour of this proposal, despite the fact that one of the Type VII design characteristics would now be lost – fuel would be outside the pressure-hull, and if the saddle tanks were damaged a slick could indicate the boat's position.

However, he was willing to accept this as a small risk when compared with the increased fuel capacity, especially when a further proposal suggested a slight increase in the boat's length. Overall, the proposals increased the Type VII fuel load by some 40 tons (the original design was for 67m$^3$ fuel oil, whereas the Type VII B had a total capacity of 108.3m$^3$). The range increase was some 2,500 nautical miles greater than the original 6,200 of the Type VII. Discussion continued as to the total number to be built, and final agreement was not reached until mid-December 1937.

The decision led to eight more Type VII boats being built up to the end of 1939 (of the VIIC version), and eleven Type VIIB, together with ten Type IX (eight Type IX, two Type IXB). So, including the earlier boats (Types IA and the Type II range), a total of 65 boats was built by the end of 1939, with 57 of them being available to Dönitz on 3 September 1939, when England and France declared war on Germany.

It was mentioned above that the 1935 Anglo-German Naval Agreement had caused the estrangement of France within Europe from Great Britain and Germany. In December 1935 the signatories to the 1930 Washington Naval Agreement met to discuss extensions to the Treaty, in accordance with the provisions of the original document. Japan soon left the conference, having her own ideas on the subject of territorial expansion, leaving the United States, Great Britain, France and Italy around the table. Some qualitative limitations were agreed, with size restrictions imposed on certain types of warship and on main armament, but the whole conference was overshadowed by the individual naval (and other) plans of the participants and of other allied or influential nations, all of whom intended to increase ship sizes and naval numbers. The British decided upon re-armament a year later, as did the United States, in response to Japanese plans, and Italian plans caused some concern in London and Paris.

In 1936 the London Submarine Agreement was discussed in detail, and this led to the ruling that all attacks by submarine were to be preceded by a warning to the ship about to be attacked, and that the safety of the crew of that ship had to be assured before the vessel could be sunk. This concept was diametrically opposed to Dönitz's tactical plans and, as will be seen later, he cajoled Hitler incessantly for freedom to attack without warning, particularly as soon as war began. Germany became a signatory after the event of this Agreement (the London Protocol), but, as Roskill comments: 'The sincerity of this declaration by Hitler did not exceed any of his other avowals, and the entire Anglo-German Agreement was abrogated by him on 26th April 1939.'

Throughout the period from Hitler's accession to power in 1933 to the outbreak of war in 1939, German naval planning was based upon the assurance given by Hitler that war would not occur before 1944 or 1945. But, aware of the inevitability of this war, and armed with the tonnage allowances of the 1935 Agreement, Germany planned (through Raeder) a main fleet which would complete building by that time. In addition, and before this plan was put into effect, an isolated war with France was seen as requiring a contingency plan, and so a number of fast, well-armed surface vessels (the 'pocket battleships') as well as the planned submarines (up to the tonnage allowed) were to be built as soon as possible, and certainly by the end of 1939.

The arguments over the total numbers of each U-boat type to be built had one objective in common: a fleet capable of defending the German coast against the French northern fleet, and to be able to carry out limited offensive operations both on the surface and submerged. Full-scale construction of a fleet that could compete with the Royal Navy only began in 1939 after Hitler unilaterally abrogated the 1935 and 1936 accords in that year.

With new U-boats (in addition to the Types IA and II already commissioned) now being laid down and building, Dönitz had to reorganise his command. Up to 1938 he had a training flotilla (*Ubootschulflotilla*) and three operational flotillas under his command (Weddigen, Saltzwedel and Lohs – named after First World War U-boat aces). In October 1937, when all were nearly up to complement, he appointed three flotilla commanders for the three operational flotillas, and a month later a commander for the training flotilla. All were directly responsible to him. To accommodate the influx of a further 29 boats, of which sixteen were to go to operational units (and the remainder to the USFlotilla), he created three new flotillas. By 1 October 1939 he had under his command:

**UFlotilla**
Weddigen eight Type IIB
Saltzwedel ten Type VII, two Type IA
Lohs nine Type IIB plus, created in 1937
Emsmann eight Type IIC
Hundius eight Type IXA, one Type IXB
Wegener seven Type VIIB
UA (eventually)
Unnamed (7 Fl) three Type VIIB, four Type VIIC
Unnamed (8Fl) four Type IXB

In fact only the named flotillas with their complement of 57 boats were available to Dönitz on the eve of war in 1939, the two unnamed flotillas being added by the end of December 1939. Of the total, 43 boats were ready for operations, the remaining twelve being under repair or in the USFlotilla. U-boat bases were in existence at Kiel and Wilhelmshaven, and plans were drawn-up for a further base at Emden.

These organisational arrangements allowed Dönitz to double his U-boat availability, and to increase the training function. He had four types of U-boat available (IA, II, VII and IX), and eight flotillas were planned for 1 October 1939. There was still a further need – for a minelayer – if tonnage were available. Political considerations soon outweighed compliance with the letter, and soon even the spirit of the London Agreement, and naval architects were charged with designing an ocean-going minelaying U-boat. Torpedo mines made this a profitable area of study. The TMB (length 2.306m, weight 740 kg, explosive charge 580kg) and TMC (length 3.385m, weight 1,115kg, charge 1,000kg) were both of torpedo calibre (53.3cm) so they could be laid by ejection from torpedo-tubes, making every U-boat a minelayer as well. The mines were ground-lying or ground-anchored, however, and were only effective in depths up to 20 metres (60 feet). Most had a magnetic firing pistol, although some were acoustically fired.

Development of the TMA (a moored mine, designed to operate in up to 270 metres (900 feet) of water) proceeded slowly. It had the same length as the TMC, but with the inclusion of the sinker and cable, the explosive charge was reduced to a mere 215kg. To increase the size of the mine would involve an increase in the size of the vessel chosen to lay it, and the mine under development was the SMA. This was 2.15m long, 1.331m. in diameter, and weighed 1,600kg. Even at this weight the charge was only 350kg, such was the weight component of the mooring tackle. Like the others, it had a magnetic pistol. The U-boats designed to carry these mines was designated Type XB, and was a development of *U117–U126* of the First World War.

The redesign involved fitting six internal mine-shafts in one longitudinal row, and two external rows of twelve shafts fitted on each beam. It was planned that the first of build should be laid down on 1 October 1938, with an expected launch date of 1 October 1940. In the event, the first (of only eight built) came off the slip at Germaniawerft, Kiel, on 3 May 1941. The last of the boats, all built at GW Kiel, was launched on 23 April 1943.

U-boat cruisers have already been mentioned, and had been a concept in their own right since the First World War, exemplified by *U151–U157*. Post-war, further developments were crystallised in Projects 47 and 50. The boats were to displace some 3,140 tons surfaced, and carry medium naval guns in two enclosed turrets, forward and aft of the control tower. Naval Command specified:

1. The boat should have the fighting ability of an auxiliary or light cruiser, and be able to engage in anti-merchant shipping warfare. It had to be able to dive to escape superior forces, return to the surface role without delay, and have enough speed to evade enemy reconnaissance. The boat to be of such size and offensive potential that the enemy would be forced to deploy his forces in small groups to search for it, its presence being very dangerous to merchant shipping.

2. Its operational area would avoid naval establishments and be located of the east coast of the United States or the west coast of Africa (Casablanca and Dakar for example), as well as the Arctic as far as the White Sea, and the Mediterranean (subject to political considerations – especially in view of British interests in the Suez area).

3. From (1) and (2) came the general requirement that the boat be fitted with powerful enough guns to take on a light cruiser, and have the requisite high rate of fire and effective fire control mechanism. Guns were to be four 15cm or five 12.7cm, with additional Flak to counter low-level attack.

Furthermore, the boat was required to have four torpedo tubes and room for reserve torpedoes and/or torpedo-mines. Speed was to be 20 knots, maintainable for long periods and the boat was to have good seagoing qualities. The radius of action was to be 25,000 nautical miles at 10 knots.

This design was given the Type Number of XI on 24 July 1937, but Article 7 of the London Agreement stated that no submarine was to displace more than 2,000 tons or be fitted with a deck gun of a greater calibre than 13cm. This led to a redesign with four, and even six, 12.7cm weapons (the latter housed in two triple turrets!).

When the designers had had their day, they had a boat capable of cruising at 20 knots (maximum surface speed 23–25 knots) maintainable for some hours. Range was 20,000–25,000 nautical miles at ten knots. Diving time was a remarkably short one minute, but this required the guns to be housed in water-tight and pressure-resistant turrets. A further refinement was that an Arado Ar 231 light aircraft for reconnaissance purposes and with a range of 500 miles could be carried (manually folded into a container mounted vertically just forward of the tower). The problem with the aircraft was that it could only be launched in a zero sea state. The first of these ocean-going U-boats was to start building on 1 October 1938, as was the Type XB, with launch some two years later. The boat was considered to be of great significance within the Z-Plan.

Another large boat design was planned for a proposed U-boat-merchant raider co-operation role. The Type IX was a little too slow at 18.2 knots, the magic figure of 20 knots surfaced speed being the target. The design designated XII displaced about 2,000 tons. Externally very similar to the Type IX, it had a designed surface speed of 22 knots/10 knots submerged. Power was from two 10-cylinder GW diesels and two electric motors. Power ratings were 7,000hp (each diesel) and 1,720hp (each motor). The design was still under consideration when the war began, and was then dropped.

By 1938 it was becoming clear that Great Britain would be on the enemy side in any future war. In April Raeder took part in a naval *Kriegsspiel* with the scenario of war against both France and Great Britain. How would naval planning cope with this? Raeder devoted time to the problem together with the probable situation should war break out before Hitler's promised 1944. One factor above all others limited German warship building – the physical capacity of her yards. The allotment of 35 per cent of Royal Naval strength simply could not be built until the mid-1940s; added to this was the re-armament building in progress for the Royal Navy, which began on 31 December 1936. This caused Hitler to step-up production, especially of U-boats, but meant that the achievement of the 35 per cent would be even further delayed.

Hitler was in a quandary when deciding which type of naval warfare would best be pursued. Göring trusted his *Luftwaffe*, boasting that it was more than a match for any ship; Hitler was partly convinced by this. In general the High Command was (as Hitler) land-oriented, but Hitler gave a degree of support to Raeder. The latter, however, continued to trust Hitler's assertion that war would not be a factor until at least 1944, and this led him to plan and start to build the balanced surface fleet which, although not on a par with the British fleet, would be more than adequate in waging economic war against the British extended lines of communication. The plan was carefully balanced against the building capacity of Germany's yards, and modified as circumstances dictated.

In parallel with the Z-Plan, detailed appreciations were made of naval strategy and tactics. The results of these deliberations were published in the *Battle Instructions for the Kriegsmarine* in May 1939, but this was after the Munich crisis of 1938. This had ushered in a supposed era of peaceful co-existence and so the battle plans were regarded as extreme contingency plans, rather than matters of urgency. In fact, in 1939 only the *Luftwaffe* had any hope of waging war in the west, the Army and Navy being ill-equipped and unpractised in their art. Events in Poland did little to enhance the Navy's potential for operations against the western allies, and any threat posed by the Navy was minimal for many months.

In 1938, with war inevitable and only the date to be decided, Raeder was faced with the bottleneck of German shipbuilding capacity. He nevertheless drew up his plans based on the facts, hoping that Hitler would note that in any future war the Navy could be of little significance until the plans were carried to fruition. Only in one area could he act quickly, and to effect. He aimed at increasing the U-boat Arm to the parity allowed by the 1935 Agreement, and in accordance with the term that Great Britain be so informed, arranged discussions with the British at the end of the year. This would result in reduced capital ship construction for the time being, but some of the punch could be put back into the programme by building some of the Type XII boats as well as laying down a large number of Type VIIs as a stop-gap in the event of war. Had there been no war, the Type VII boats would have been good training vessels for their larger sisters.

All of this was decided at a conference on 25 May, when it was hoped that by increasing the number of yards involved in warship building the yearly production of U-boats, then 24, could be stepped up to 36. By 1942/43 a total of 129 would have been built, the 100 per cent under the 1935 Agreement. The planning department reported, however, that plans to build the heavier Type

XI (two were to be built by GW) and Type XII (two at Deschimag) would detract from builds of in-service types. The two yards were scheduled to produce four Type II, four Type VIIB and two Type IX boats monthly under the mobilisation plan, which would be impossible if they were to build the four larger boats.

The outcome of the conference was a flurry of orders for further builds:

8 Type IXB (*U103–U110*) Deschimag
8 Type VIIC (*U93–U100*) Germaniawerft
4 Type VIIB (*U73–U76*) at the new Bremer-Vulkan yard at Vegesack
4 Type VIIB (*U84–U87*) Flender-Werke, Lübeck
The end result of the plan was to be a total of 98 boats in service at the end of 1941:
32 Type II
2 Type IA
10 Type VII
31 Type VII B/C
21 Type IX
1 Type X
1 Type XI.

To complete the orders necessary to fulfil this target, Deschimag got an order for one further Type IX (*U111*), and a boat being built for export at Flender-Werke was commandeered as *U83*.

The Type VIIC boat (which now appears for the first time) was a further modified version of the Type VII general design range. Active sound location equipment was installed, causing an overall length increase of the pressure-hull of 60cm, and it was decided to make improvements on earlier designs at the same time. The small tower was enlarged slightly, but more importantly two new pressure-tight diving tanks were added. These were forward of the port and starboard regulating tanks, and improved diving ability. The internal fuel tank was increased by $4.8m^3$ to $62.1m^3$. Oil cleaners were fitted to the lubricating oil outlets, allowing engine oil to be cleaned before re-entering the engines, and a Junkers air compressor was added to reduce power consumption. Finally the electrical controls were re-arranged. Unknown to the General Staff at that time, and to the naval architects and engineers and the yards themselves, these were to be the last peace-time modifications.

What the British and French were unaware of was that building capacity in Germany was severely limited, despite the plethora of plans. Furthermore, although there were a number of yards, merchant demands had to be satisfied as well, which left only five yards with warship capacity. The demands of war changed this, and many yards which had never built a warship before became involved, especially when almost all naval building was of U-boats – which situation arose after 1943.

The Skl (*Seekriegsleitung* – Naval High Command) required a balanced fleet to conduct *any* form of warfare against the British. It knew from the outset that the only effective strategy would be to attack British economic supply lines, and to do this the aim was to engage in cruiser warfare. All contact with the enemy fleet was to be avoided; all German units would attack commercial targets of opportunity. This was a repetition of the strategy that nearly succeeded in the First World War – cutting the convoy routes to the UK and thus denying re-supply of foodstuffs and other supplies without which the British could not continue to wage war against Germany. Skl concluded its statement of intention with the comment that 'wide-ranging effects cannot be expected from a campaign conducted only by U-boats'. At the time this probably reflected Dönitz's conclusions exactly, but Skl had based its conclusions on an exaggerated opinion of the value of Asdic equipment as it then was, coupled with the expectation that U-boat warfare would be waged under the Prize Regulations.

Raeder had a meeting with Hitler on 1 November 1938 and presented three building plans which extended as far forward as 1947. Hitler approved the plan that gave equal weight to battleship and U-boat construction. This plan envisaged 174 U-boats completed by the end of 1943, and a 1947 final figure of 249. This included 60 Type II, 90 Type VII and 60 Type IX boats, and was published on 24 November.

On 10 December 1938 German naval representatives met members of the British Board of Admiralty and presented their 100 per cent plan. By the end of the month the Admiralty had concurred, but asked that the plan be completed in stages. Yet another round of new building orders were issued in January 1939:

13 Type VIIC (*U77–U82*) Bremer-Vulkan, (*U88–U92*)
Flender-Werke, (*U101,U102*) GW
3 Type XB (*U116–U118*) GW
4 Type XI (*U112–U115*) Deschimag

Up to then total building and orders for building totalled 64,573 tons of U-boats, against a ceiling of 70,000 tons. This detail, and the Z-Plan (as the modified plan of November 1938 was now called) were presented to Hitler for his assent on 17 January 1939. Fascinated by big ships, the prospect of having six battleships of the H-Class commissioned by 1944 must have been a heady tonic. Hitler gave the Navy the highest priority to get these ships built; even so, Raeder and his Staff were not overly optimistic.

With the final details of the Z-Plan decided, Dönitz cannot have been utterly displeased with the U-boat programme, especially as neither he nor

Raeder had any reason to suspect that war with Great Britain would begin in eight months' time! The completions planned for U-boats were:

| Type/Year | 1939 | 1940 | 1941 | 1942 | 1943 | 1944 | 1945 | 1946 | 1947 |
|---|---|---|---|---|---|---|---|---|---|
| II | 32 | 32 | 32 | 32 | 33 | 39 | 45 | 52 | 60 |
| IA/VII/IX | 34 | 52 | 73 | 88 | 112 | 133 | 157 | 161 | 162 |
| XB/XI/XII | – | – | 6 | 10 | 16 | 22 | 27 | 27 | 27 |
| Totals | 66 | 84 | 111 | 130 | 161 | 194 | 229 | 240 | 249 |

The boats were to be organised into 22 flotillas (19 of nine operational boats with two reserve boats, and three flotillas of seven operational boats with two reserves, and a training flotilla of fifteen boats) which were to be based along the German North Sea and Baltic coasts. The first six flotillas had already been established, and either were, or in the process of being, equipped with their boats. The situation on 1 September 1939 was:

| Flotilla | Total boats commissioned | Flotilla | Total boats commissioned |
|---|---|---|---|
| Weddigen | 8 | Hundius | 7 |
| Salzwedel | 11 | Wegener | 9 |
| Lohs | 7 | USFlotilla | 10 |
| Emsmann | 6 | **Total** | 58 |

A further reorganisation took place at the end of the year which will be dealt with at the appropriate point in the narrative.

This organisation was intended to fit into both the U-boat plan mentioned above as well as the entire Z-Plan which foresaw the building of:

| | | | |
|---|---|---|---|
| Six battleships by the end of 1944 | | Four aircraft carriers | 1947 |
| Eight heavy cruisers | 1945 | 221 U-boats | 1947 |
| Seventeen light cruisers | 1948 | | |

As noted, the planned submarine total had been increased to 249 by the end of 1947, and to this would have been added the fleet in being of February 1939 (seven battleships and pocket-battleships built or completing), eight cruisers and 46 U-boats – in all a total of:

| | |
|---|---|
| Thirteen battleships | 267 U-boats (295 under the amended |
| Thirty-three cruisers | plan) |
| Four aircraft carriers | |

together with a large number of destroyers and lesser craft as well as the auxiliaries required for such a fleet. This would have been a formidable fleet, which

Roskill says would have caused a threat to Great Britain which 'is not pleasant to contemplate, particularly when the age of the majority of our own warships is remembered'. He continues:

> Hitler's erroneus estimate of when war would break out may therefore be considered one of his most important mistakes, since it forced Admiral Raeder to abandon the long-term programme of building a balanced fleet and obliged him to build what he could use quickly to strike against our shipping. This mistake can be compared in its magnitude with his declaration of war on the United States on 11 December 1941, Hitler's sole firm compliance with a treaty with another Axis power, and which led to the ultimate destruction of (inter alia) the U-boat Arm.

The decision to invade Poland was made very soon after this however, on 3 April 1939, when he ordered the Wehrmacht to prepare for the campaign, and in so doing set in train the disastrous series of events leading ultimately to 1945 and total defeat. On 10 May he further ordered the Luftwaffe and the Kriegsmarine to prepare for an immediate start of war against merchant shipping. Hitler's main fear at the time seems to have been the growing level and scope of re-armament in the nations which would eventually oppose his schemes; if he opened his bid for pre-eminence in mainland Europe any later, he would be confronted with greater military power than his forces could hope to defeat.

On 26 April 1939 Hitler unilaterally abrogated the Anglo-German Naval Agreement and the London Submarine Protocol. In May German Battle Instructions for the Navy were issued; the war would, they stated, be fought against Poland or Russia in the east (Russia was eliminated for the time being by the Russo-German non-aggression pact of 1939), and against France and Great Britain in the west. The Navy's tasks, including the U-boats, were:

> to protect the German North Sea and Baltic coasts
> to defend German, and attack enemy, sea communications
> to give support to land operations along the coast
> to serve as a 'politico-strategic instrument of war to ensure, for example, the neutrality of the Scandinavian countries'.

These instructions were utterly practical in the light of the mix of warships in the Kriegsmarine at the time. Germany could not aspire to a maritime strategy, because the Navy was too weak, and even the tasks set for it within the limited war plan meant that 'the Navy is faced with a task for which its present development does not correspond'.

Much was said at the time and subsequently about German U-boat building. The actual monthly building figures are shown below:

| Year | Jan | Feb | Mar | Apr | May | Jun | Jul | Aug | Sep | Oct | Nov | Dec | Total |
|------|-----|-----|-----|-----|-----|-----|-----|-----|-----|-----|-----|-----|-------|
| 1935 |     |     |     |     |     | 1   | 2   | 5   | 4   |     | 1   | 1   | 14    |
| 1936 | 3   | 1   | 1   | 1   | 2   |     | 1   | 3   | 3   | 2   | 2   | 2   | 21    |
| 1937 |     |     |     | 1   |     |     |     |     |     |     |     |     | 1     |
| 1938 |     |     |     |     |     | 1   |     | 2   |     | 1   | 2   | 3   | 9     |
| 1939 | 1   | 2   | 1   | 2   | 1   | 2   | 3   | 1   |     | 2   | 3   |     | 18    |

Total 63

The effect of fears of French military reaction and the subsequent reduction in production during 1937 shows up clearly, for all the boats shown in the Table were built in pursuit of the London Naval Agreement. New production, which led to increasing U-boat numbers in the third quarter of 1940, does not show among completions. Immediate plans to increase production were:

| Planned production after | 10 | 11 | 12 | 13 | 14 | 15 | 16 | 17 | 18 months |
|--------------------------|----|----|----|----|----|----|----|----|-----------|
| Type IX                  |    |    |    |    |    |    | 1  | 2  | 2         |
| Type VII C               |    |    |    |    | 1  | 1  | 2  | 3  | 4         |
| Type II C                | 1  | 3  | 3  | 3  | 3  | 3  | 3  | 3  | 3         |

The plan was subject to the proviso that there was no alteration in yard priorities; but if production were turned over to naval construction, instead of mixed merchant and naval building, these figures would naturally increase.

It is obvious that the Navy in general (and the U-boat Arm was no exception) was in no position to fight a war on any large scale. The Navy was fully aware of this, but Dönitz (and Fürbringer) wanted to use the U-boat Arm to its best advantage, and they did not consider the reconnaissance role to be particularly productive. Dönitz had long thought about the problem, and his great fear was that despite all his training to the contrary, British Asdic developments would deny the U-boat any hope of success in anti-merchant shipping warfare. In 1937 the Staff of the Royal Navy had reported to the Shipping Defence Advisory Committee that, because of Asdic, 'The submarine should never again be able to present us with the problem we were faced with in 1917.'

This comment had the double-edged quality of a Delphic oracle. It had by its inherent, albeit basic, truth forced Dönitz to research counter-measures, and the results were to be felt in increasing losses to Allied and Neutral shipping as the war progressed. Dönitz was in fact convinced that Asdic could and would nullify any attempts by his men to attack convoys, whether off-shore or on the high seas. The reason for this was that convoys, by their nature, are escorted and the warships escorting would be equipped with Asdic. The problem was in fact due for solution by the most simple expedient, but he was as yet unaware of the limitations of Asdic, or of the calm courage of his boat commanders and their crews.

Fürbringer wanted to 'immunise' the U-boats against the Asdic sonic transmissions; his ideas seemed unreal at the time, but his concept was valid, although this was not realised until later in the war. Modern submariners will echo his fervent desire to camouflage and conceal the submarine from surface warships equipped not only with detection equipment which locates the underwater enemy, but also with dire means of removing the submarine from the field. Fürbringer, like Dönitz, recognised that the one way to bring the British to their knees was by cutting what Churchill later called the 'diver's lifeline' – the supplies from overseas which enabled the British first to survive, and later to fight back.

Fürbringer not only wanted immunity from location however; he also wanted the U-boats to have the means of retaliating against the attacking warship. He proposed that all U-boats should carry small bombs which could be released into the water, which would arm themselves on rising to the surface and strike and damage or even sink the pursuer. This idea led the Naval Staff unknowingly to the main weakness of Asdic. Their point was that the U-boat commander had no means of knowing the relative positions of his boat and the attacker. In fact Asdic could only establish range and bearing, but could give no indication whatsoever of the depth of the target, and it would become 'deaf' the moment the attacker's depth-charges exploded. It was also rendered ineffective within the range of the attacker's own engine noise.

This was not the end of Fürbringer's proposals however. He explained to the German Naval Staff (in March 1938) that he had also hit on the idea of defensive torpedoes. These would be steered to their target by radio, or by cable, and might even be rocket-propelled, or simply dropped in the track of the oncoming escort vessel. The rocket-propelled concept was in fact passed on to Helmut Walter's scientific team for evaluation; Siemens-Schuckert had in fact been developing radio-control systems for torpedoes since 1906.

Fürbringer had also turned his mind to radio traffic, and later in the same year published his recommendations. He commented, quite rightly, that radio transmissions would lead to radio-location fixes on the U-boats. (This was *one* of the methods used.) He also pressed upon the Naval Staff the concept of the cable-guided anti-escort torpedo, which he said could be steered by using sound-location equipment fitted to the U-boat. Sound-location equipment was standard on the Type VIIC boats. Further ideas were proposed, but they demanded a technology beyond the reach of military science at the time.

Despite all this, there still remained the present and insistent problem of Asdic. The answer was provided by the U-boats themselves. Their lack of underwater speed, even in comparison with First World War types, meant that to have any hope of success the U-boats would have to operate on the surface. In daylight this would be suicidal, but night attacks were feasible. This had been tried towards the end of the First World War: Kapitänleutnant Wassner wrote in 1922:

> In my experience the greatest results in 1918 were achieved on the
> surface ... in two nights in September 1918 I got into a firing position
> nine times, including one period of twenty minutes when I was in a posi-
> tion to attack three separate targets.

He added that much of the time spent by escorts trying to find U-boats was
wasted when the convoy was on the high seas, and concluded with the recommendation that the use of a number of U-boats to attack a convoy could
reduce the efforts of the escort to nothing, as far as preventing attacks on
merchantmen was concerned.

It only remained for Kretschmer to add his own refinements to the general
technique to prove Wassner's argument, and show that early in the Second
World War night surface attacks were almost always undetected and even
undetectable. Asdic was no answer, with the U-boat on the surface. The
chances of success were to be heightened further if a group of U-boats was
assembled in the track of the convoy, controlled from a land-based Headquarters, and observing radio silence itself.

As frequently noted, the forces available to Dönitz on the eve of the Second
World War totalled 57 U-boats, of which two were Type IA, thirty Type II A-
C, eighteen were Type VII including Type VIIC and seven Type IX. Ranges
varied from the 3,800 nautical miles of the Type IIC (of which he had six) to
the 12,000 of the Type IX (seven boats). The small Types IIA and IIB had a
range of only 1,600 to 3,000 nautical miles, and these were in the majority. It
was clear to him that he would have only a very limited number of boats available for a *guerre de course* in the Atlantic.

Dönitz summarised his position in a note to Raeder on 1 September 1939:

> 57 U-boats were commissioned, with eighteen in the Atlantic
> 21 in the North Sea or intended to be
> ten in the Baltic
> three not ready for active duties
> four undergoing trials
> one set aside for anti-submarine experiments

Of the 26 suitable for Atlantic operations (Types IA, VII and IX), eighteen were
on station, with three in the Baltic, three unready and two undergoing trials.
There were no reserves, and he had included the boats of the US (training)
Flotilla in these figures. His true strength on 1 September 1939 was 48 U-
boats, of which 31 were the small, limited range Type II boats, each carrying
merely five torpedoes. His offensive capability in terms of the number of
torpedoes his U-boats could fire was severely limited.

Germany had developed her torpedoes in the Baltic before the war, and
had settled on the G7e design, which was electrically driven, leaving no

bubble trace as had earlier compressed air designs. The original contact pistol had been improved by fitting a magnetic proximity fuse, which was to prove a problem. The torpedo so fitted was designed to explode not against the side of the hull of the target but beneath its keel where water pressure would increase the explosive effect. A torpedo hit on the side of a target, not too far from the water line might sink the target, but if it did not the large hole resulting could be overcome by a resourceful master who, by careful shiphandling and patching could bring his ship and its cargo to port. The detonation of the warhead beneath the keel would cause irreparable damage, and could even break the ship in two. A weapon with great potential, the G7e suffered from design faults which caused erratic depth keeping and frequent premature detonations, problems not solved as early as Dönitz and his U-boat captains would have liked.

In September 1939 Dönitz was unaware that the torpedoes would prove a mixed blessing, but he knew that he had too few U-boats. The Z-Plan (see above) was, with this precipitate outbreak of hostilities, not likely to be fulfilled within the terms of its original aim of a balanced fleet. He was also unaware, as was the rest of the world, that Poland and then western Europe would fall so quickly to German force. He told Raeder that the Navy in general, and the U-boat Arm, were in no position 'to play anything like an important part in the war against British commerce'. But he did see that the U-boats could become 'the backbone of warfare against England, and of the political pressure on her'. His argument was that to enable the U-boat Arm to take advantage of the speed of building available to it, production figures had to be stepped up, and he proposed a total U-boat force of 300 boats, allowing him 90 active boats in the Atlantic. The higher total was required to allow for boats in transit, re-supplying in harbour, and for mechanical repairs that the campaign would necessitate.

As things stood, construction figures were too low, and he recommended that Hitler set up a central office with the sole task of increasing U-boat production, and which would be responsible only to Raeder, so that he would get his required number of U-boats as soon as possible. Raeder agreed with Dönitz and replied on 3 September that he considered 190 to be the minimum required and further that 'the pocket battleships ... cannot be decisive for the outcome of the war'. As is noted above, the rapid fall of Poland, and the more important fall of France had great effect upon Dönitz's ability to wage war in the Atlantic; the latter event gave him Atlantic bases and cut a considerable distance from the transit mileages required to get the U-boats to their theatre of war.

Four days earlier Hitler had issued Directive Number 1 for the conduct of the war. Among the matters contained in it were strictures binding upon the Navy's conduct of the war at sea. Germany had been portrayed throughout the document as the aggrieved party in the Danzig Corridor affair and he cited this and other grievances to justify his present stance. However land and air action against Poland were one side of the coin; the other was the possibility of Great Britain and France entering the conflict on Poland's side. In the hope of mollifying them, he gave specific orders to the Navy:

> In the west it is important that the responsibility for the opening of hostilities should rest unequivocally with England and France ... The neutrality assured us by Holland, Belgium, Luxembourg and Switzerland should be scrupulously observed. The German land frontier in the west is not to be crossed at any point without my express consent. The same applies to warlike actions at sea or any which may be so interpreted. (Paragraph 3)

On copy number 2 of this document is a pencil note (by Raeder?) that reads 'According to this Atlantic U-boats must remain in their waiting positions for the time being.' The Directive continues:

> If England and France open hostilities against Germany, the task of those sections of the Armed Forces which are operating in the west is to uphold, while conserving their strength as far as possible, those conditions necessary for the successful conclusion of the operations against Poland. Within the scope of this duty, damage should be done to enemy forces *and their economic sources of supply* [Author's italics] as far as resources allow. (Paragraph 4)

The paper continues, on the subject of economic warfare:

> In its warfare on merchant shipping the Navy is to concentrate on England. To intensify the effect of this, a declaration of danger zones is to be expected. The Supreme Command of the Navy is to announce in which sea areas and within what limits danger zones are considered expedient.

Further matters relevant to the Navy included permission to all branches of the forces to make effective attacks on 'massed English naval units, especially on battleships and aircraft carriers'. These instructions would naturally only come into force when the invasion of Poland had started, and only if France and/or Great Britain took steps to place themselves within the scope of the Directive.

Dönitz's communication to Raeder of 1 September fell upon receptive ears, but Raeder, like Dönitz, was extremely pessimistic about the prospect of war with England and France at such an early stage, even if Poland could be defeated in the short time the Army and the Luftwaffe claimed. As soon as Prime Minister Chamberlain had completed his fateful declaration that 'a state

of war' existed between Great Britain and Germany, Raeder dictated his reflec-
tions to his aide (Assmann):

> Today the war against France and England broke out, the war which,
> according to the Führer's previous assertions, we had no need to expect
> before about 1944 ... At the turn of the year 1944/1945, by when,
> according to the Führer's instructions, the Navy's Z-Plan would have
> been completed, Germany could have begun a war against Great Britain
> with the Navy at the following strength:
> For merchant warfare on the High Seas
> 3 fast battleships
> 3 converted pocket-battleships
> 5 heavy cruisers
> several mine-laying and reconnaissance cruisers
> 2 aircraft carriers
> about 190 U-boats, including six gun U-boats, six fleet U-boats, and six
> mine-laying U-boats (Types XI, X and XII respectively).

He added that Great Britain, contrary to Hitler's hopes, had gone to war over
Poland, and he confirms that Hitler had chosen 1939 as the year in which to
begin the fight. His conclusions were:

> 1. The Navy was in no way 'very adequately equipped for the great
> struggle with Great Britain', and
> 2. although much had been done to build up the submarine arm in the
> short time available, and despite many delays and side-tracks, it was 'still
> much too weak to have any decisive effect on the war'.
> 3. The surface forces were such that all they could show the British was
> that they knew 'how to die gallantly', and
> 4. The pocket-battleships would, when trained, be able to contribute
> something to economic warfare, if skilfully used. They would be a factor
> for some time to come, until the British tracked them down, but 'they
> cannot be decisive for the outcome of the war'.

The whole paper is despondent in tone, possibly reflecting Raeder's unspoken
reaction to Hitler's declaration of war five years too early.

Then, at twenty-one minutes to eight in the evening of 3 September 1939,
at 56°44' North, 14°05' West, *U30* torpedoed the SS *Athenia*, on passage for
the USA from England. She sank at 10.40 a.m. next day, and for the German
U-boat Arm the die was cast.

# 4  THE OPENING PHASE

In view of the worsening political situation, Raeder had ordered a number of German naval units to sea in August 1939. Among these were sixteen U-boats which sailed 19–23 August from Kiel and Wilhelmshaven to selected positions in the Atlantic. *U30* (Kapitänleutnant Julius Lemp) had sailed on the 22nd to a position west of Ireland, in square AM on the German coded chart of the Atlantic, and had been at sea for thirteen days when she torpedoed SS *Athenia*. Like the *Lusitania* twenty-five years earlier, *Athenia* was a passenger liner, and was carrying a number of US citizens. Of the 1,200 passengers, 112 died, 28 of them Americans. British reaction was one of outraged shock; Goebbels counter-claimed with his conspiracy theory directed against Churchill. The general conclusion was that a German submarine had fired the torpedoes, but in the air of unreality surrounding the first few days of the war, little was heard except rattling sabres from the Press. In fact there had been no detailed clarification of German declared danger zones around the United Kingdom, and advertisements warning of the dangers at sea in specified areas around the UK were only, belatedly, published in US newspapers.

The immediate reaction of the British naval staff was that unrestricted U-boat warfare had started. In fact, to prevent any similar action, Hitler signalled all U-boats that 'on no account are operations to be carried out against passenger steamers, even when under escort.' This went beyond the requirements of mercantile law, for any escorted vessel was a legitimate war target, as were all armed merchant vessels. But *Athenia* was sailing alone, and unarmed, and was registered in the UK. What measures had the Admiralty instituted to combat the apparent menace of unrestricted U-boat warfare?

The First World War had proved the efficacy of the convoy. Although not brought into general use until 1917, against the objections of the Admiralty, but on the insistence of Prime Minister Lloyd George, it had reduced merchant shipping losses to tolerable limits. Plans for convoying had existed well before September 1939, and some vessels had sailed in convoy as early as August. Admiralty books of the time defined a convoy as 'one or more merchant ships sailing under the protection of one or more warships.'

This was developed in 1939 and later into regular convoy runs sailing at mainly fixed intervals. The system became immense in the amount of traffic it involved, but at all times during the Second World War there were obstinate merchant captains who would not comply, and who too frequently fell foul of a U-boat. However, almost all merchant shipping as well as military transport became part of a massive, interlinked system of routes and schedules, with escort groups and air patrols closely co-ordinated for protection. Support Groups of naval vessels and air support were also made available until the convoy system, with the aid of certain assets denied to the U-boats, succeeded in beating off attacks. But more than three years were to pass before this could come about, and in the meantime a small but increasing number of U-boats positioned around the British Isles managed to threaten the continued resistance to Hitler's territorial ambitions.

In September 1939, however, Dönitz had neither sufficient U-boats nor freedom of action to make any serious inroads into the defensive screen around the British Isles, nor did his men yet have the experience to exploit the many weaknesses of the system. This was despite the fact that the convoy and escort system only operated as far as 12° West; thereafter the ships dispersed to sail independently to their destinations. At the time Dönitz was also hamstrung by the restrictions Hitler placed on all forms of aggression towards merchant shipping; only British and Allied vessels were to be attacked, the neutrals remaining safe from disturbance.

On 7 September Hitler and the Naval Staff held the first wartime Führer Conference on Naval Affairs (FCNA). By then the Polish Air Force had been annihilated, and the Polish Navy sunk (a total of four destroyers, one minesweeper and some submarines, all lost in the Gulf of Danzig). Raeder's main concern was the political situation, and Hitler seemed to want some form of peace, once the land campaign in Poland was over. At the conference the discussion included the 'political and military restraint' showed by France, and noted the 'still hesitant conduct of British warfare'. To avoid exacerbating the situation, the German surface raiders, which had been on station since before September 1939, were ordered to their waiting positions. In general, attitudes in favour of neutrality were hardening, 'and the fact that the USA, at least outwardly, claims strictest neutrality' led both men to order a restriction in submarine activity. There were to be no offensive acts against the French, passenger ships were to be spared, even in convoy (a direct outcome of the *Athenia* incident), and some U-boats were even to be withdrawn from operations to act as replacements for boats already at sea. Raeder saw the situation as follows:

1. Great Britain is unable to draw France into the war unconditionally.
2. France fails to see any war aim and is therefore trying to stay out of the war.
3. After the collapse of Poland, which can be expected soon, it is possible that France, and perhaps afterwards Great Britain, might be ready to accept to a certain extent the situation which has been created in the east.
4. Therefore an attack should not be forced and our strength should be saved for the time being.

Hitler was in full agreement, and it was decided that, as a general policy in the west, restraint was to be exercised until the situation became clearer. The *Athenia* matter was to await the return of the boats at sea, U-boats in the Atlantic were to spare passenger ships and French ships altogether, and *Graf Spee* and *Deutschland* were confirmed in their orders to remain at their waiting positions.

The next FCNA took place on 23 September. By then 35 ships had been sunk in the North Sea and the Atlantic (including three by U-boat-laid mines). Of these, one had been Belgian and two Finnish. Only one vessel had been in convoy, and the system appeared to be working, despite efforts of some masters to cram on speed and the effects of lack of maintenance by some owners, causing ships to run ahead or straggle. By the end of the month the figures had risen to 48 ships of 178,621 tons, but no further vessel had been sunk in convoy.

The conference also noted that British counter-measures were beginning to take effect. Convoys were proving an effective defensive system, and further measures were also proving valuable. The Northern Patrol and submarine mine barrages were causing the *Kriegsmarine* difficulties in operating. The Northern Patrol was a surface warship patrol which forced outward bound U-boats to dive to avoid its attentions, and the Dover mine barrage was an effective barrier, causing U-boats the necessity of sailing around northern Scotland, wasting time and fuel. Raeder now reported to Hitler:

> The first phase of the submarine war in the Atlantic and the Channel is now over. When the war broke out, numerous U-boats were at sea; a great stream of ships was returning home to England and France; [the British merchant fleet at the time was approximately 3,000 ships of 21,000,000 GRT. On average, some 2,500 of these were at sea on any one day] as yet there were no armed merchantmen; defences were not yet fully organised. It is true the U-boats sank 232,000 tons so far [actual sunken tonnage was, as noted, 178,621 GRT. Faulty G7e pistols were encouraging inaccurate claims by U-boat commanders – a failing that persisted throughout the war, and was to lead to a formula for disaster in the first half of 1943] but they are hampered by political restrictions ... it hampers our operations [wherever there was a possibility of French involvement]. The Navy considers the disruption of British transport traffic a special duty.

Raeder went on to give examples of his being frustrated in the main aim of interfering with British merchant shipping. Hitler then promptly lifted previous restrictions relating to French vessels and ports, no doubt in view partly of Raeder's request that he be allowed to attack transports carrying the BEF to France and supplying it there.

In further response to Raeder's pressure he gave the Navy permission to attack any armed merchantmen without warning, although retaining the embargo on attacks on passenger liners. U-boats could in effect now assume that all enemy merchant ships were armed. To mollify international reaction he then added that the occasional neutral vessel should get special treatment. The semantics of what was being planned were also considered, and Hitler ruled that 'submarine warfare' was in future to be referred to as the 'war against merchant shipping', and the 'notorious expression "unlimited submarine warfare" is to be avoided', to be replaced perhaps by the expression '*die Belagerung Englands*' (the siege of England).

The Führer and the Commander-in-Chief of the Navy then discussed submarine production. Raeder made it clear that losses would soon outstrip production, and reminded Hitler of the 1918 Scheer programme, under which was planned a monthly launch of 30 U-boats. The same political decision was being debated now as was then decided: unlimited submarine warfare, no matter what Hitler preferred as a euphemism. To be able to sustain any offensive at sea, Raeder and Dönitz had to have more U-boats. Hitler once more gave his consent (in the euphoria of the moment probably), and gave Raeder priority over Junkers Ju88 building, the bomber upon which the *Luftwaffe* based its campaign against England. He also ordered Raeder to look at the Navy programme to see if any construction could be shelved to provide even more U-boat building facilities. Raeder was to inform Hitler of what he needed in the way of labour and material to produce between 20 and 30 submarines per month. Unfortunately for the Navy, although approval to increase production had been given, no date was set for the programme to start.

The first four weeks of the war had produced little other than U-boat activity at sea. *Athenia* had been a temporary embarrassment, but this was solved by altering the log of *U30* (the only occasion upon which a German naval vessel was subject to such censorship), and by placing Lemp under 'cabin-arrest' for a short period. Thereafter the matter was forgotten until the time of retribution. From Dönitz's point of view decisions of fundamental importance were made, albeit undated, which would eventually enable him to carry out economic warfare against Great Britain, and the means to sustain it.

One target which had been available to the U-boats from 3 September had been British warships (the French were denied to them for some time). An action took place on 17 September reminiscent of the dummy attack on the *Empress of India* by a Royal Navy Holland Class submarine in 1904. Three days previously *U39* had narrowly missed hitting *Ark Royal* operating west of the Hebrides; *U39* was then sunk by the carrier's escorts, HM ships *Faulknor*, *Foxhound* and *Firedrake*, and her crew captured; she was the first Type IX boat to be lost. *U29* unexpectedly sighted HMS *Courageous*: the meeting took place in the Western Approaches, and the Type VII boat saw that she was escorted by two destroyers, and had just turned into the wind to launch aircraft; her other two escorts had been detached to search for a reported U-boat. This was just before 2000 hours, some two hours after the reported sighting. Schuhart in *U29* found himself favourably placed for an attack, and he fired three torpedoes at under 3,000 yards, two of which hit *Courageous*. She sank at 2020 hours, taking her captain and 518 of the crew. The two remaining destroyers depth-charged *U29* until midnight, but she survived to return to base. Surprisingly this was not empha- sised to Hitler at the next FCNA, a week later; it would have strengthened his case even further. Then, at 1023 hours on 14 October, the last pages of the log of HMS *Royal Oak* recorded her being hit by torpedoes while at anchor in Scapa Flow. The Official Historian describes Prien's entry into the Flow:

> At about midnight on a clear, moonless night, while the Northern Lights flickered overhead, Lieutenant Prien, who remained throughout on the surface and had chosen a time near the top of high water, passed between the blockships and the northern shore. Though she touched bottom and also fouled a blockship's cable with her stem, the U-boat got clear without damage, and at twenty-seven minutes past midnight, entered the Flow.

Prien fired four torpedoes in his first attack, of which only one hit, causing the Captain and the other officers who 'went forward to investigate' to believe 'the explosion to have been internal'. He then fired his stern tube without effect, and finally, having reloaded his forward tubes on the surface within the Royal Navy's own redoubt, he fired three more times. All torpedoes hit. Twenty-four officers and 809 crew died. The passage in Prien's log recounting his escape from Scapa reads like a novel:

> At high speed both engines we withdraw. Everything is simple until we reach Skildaenoy Point. Then we have more trouble. It is now low tide, the current is against us. Engines at slow and dead slow, I attempt to get away. I must leave by the south through the narrows, because of the depth of the water. Things are again difficult ... I pass the blockship with nothing to spare. The helmsman does magnificently ... we are once more outside ... A pity that only one was destroyed. The torpedo misses I explain as due to faults of course, speed and drift. In tube 4 a misfire. The crew behaved splendidly throughout the operation ...

Dönitz himself had ordered Prien to enter the Flow and attack any warships found there. That he did so with skill and daring is beyond dispute, and he earned the respect of the Royal Navy for that, and of all by his acceptance of faults in bad shooting and his compliments to his crew.

Prien's chivalry was exemplified both during this attack, and in his subse- quent meeting with the Norwegian steamer *Meteor*, on the return passage to

Wilhelmshaven. *U47*'s radio operator mistakenly told Prien that *Meteor* was signalling and Prien, in full accordance with Maritime Law, fired a shot across her bows. Once he had established that she was in fact carrying 238 passengers bound for Newcastle-upon-Tyne, he 'immediately allowed her to proceed'. Naturally, upon arrival home, crew and Captain were fêted and rushed before Hitler, Prien being awarded the Knight's Cross to his Iron Cross on 18 October.

The main task facing the U-boat Arm was not the sinking of battleships in one-to-one combat, but the drudgery of denying essential supplies to Germany's main enemy by blockade. But it had been a stunning propaganda coup for Germany, ably exploited by Goebbels. The Royal Navy had, in the two actions, lost an aircraft carrier and a battleship. As later events were to show, the aircraft carrier became the supreme capital ship of the Second World War and later, but even old battleships had a significant part to play, escorting troop convoys and shore bombardment (a role which was still relevant in the 1990–1 conflict in the Gulf). The reaction from the Royal Navy was simple – aircraft carriers were withdrawn from a task for which they were eminently unsuitable, anti-submarine sweeps – and Coastal Command was charged with mounting anti-submarine patrols, an order which proved highly unpopular with Bomber Command.

Four days before the attack on Scapa another FCNA took place, and Raeder emphasised once more the need of increased U-boat production. He argued that 'the U-boat construction programme ... is indispensable and of decisive importance, for the war against Great Britain can be carried out with certainty only by giving it priorities over all other programmes'. He submitted a draft of his revised programme, knowing that he needed active support from Hitler, not just assent. Other factions were competing with the Navy for labour and material, and the Navy had little in the way of success to claim apart from U-boat successes. He knew too that U-boats needed an enormous financial, material and manpower budget to enable the required expansion to become a reality. His trump card was that with an expanded U-boat Arm, Great Britain *could* be removed from the Order of Battle, and the later news of Prien's operation doubtlessly helped his case.

Prien's success at Scapa meant that the *Kriegsmarine* had audaciously bearded Churchill's Fleet in its lair; a cause for rejoicing, although it begged the question noted above – what was the real role of the U-boat Arm in the war? The day before Prien docked, Raeder saw Hitler again, and Dönitz was promoted to Flag Rank. In the euphoria Raeder, hard-headed as always, presented Hitler with a demand for the intensification of U-boat warfare. Hitler agreed, giving the following permission:

(a) All merchant ships definitely recognised as enemy (British or French) can be torpedoed without warning.

(b) Passenger ships in convoy can be torpedoed a short while after notice
has been given of the intention to do so.

Raeder then pointed out that the U-boats were already torpedoing passenger
ships proceeding without lights, for he had extended all the loopholes in
previous orders as far as possible. He, Raeder, was more aware than anyone
of the strength of the Royal Navy, and the importance to Great Britain of her
merchant fleet. If he were to do anything significant at this stage of the war
he had to have total freedom to operate, with no political or legal restraints.
His strategic analysis was correct. He had to inflict as much damage as
possible on the merchant fleet and the Royal Navy before the latter in conjunction with Coastal Command found the means to destroy his one true strategic
weapon. His larger surface units could be extremely troublesome to the Allies,
but because of their paucity in numbers they would never have any real
strategic influence. As was shown by later operations, both Raeder and Dönitz
were forced to use the threat of operations by large surface vessels as a
bargaining counter, and the few piecemeal attacks they made (*Graf Spee*,
*Bismarck*, for example) resulted in the destruction of those units. Raeder thus
forced upon Hitler his view that the U-boats would make the one significant
contribution of the German Navy to the conduct of the war.

All the ideas that had been put to Hitler at various times were stated in a
paper which Raeder read to Hitler at their next meeting on 23 October. He
stated that, above all:

> To exert political pressure Germany should weaken the enemy economy,
> promote her own economy, create a united front of neutrals against the
> enemy, cause the financial isolation and cultural boycott of the enemy
> and cripple enemy production ... *Purely economic measures should be
> taken to prevent entirely all commercial traffic of neutrals and allies with Great
> Britain and France*, and to reorganise German trade relations in Europe
> in order to establish a German war economy which would be capable of
> supporting the war indefinitely. Military measures should consist of the
> proper coordination of all three branches of the *Wehrmacht*, particularly
> the *Luftwaffe* and the Navy – for the destruction of enemy industries,
> commercial centres, bases, and trade communications by land and sea.

Had Hitler assumed all the wisdom in the above statement, he might yet have
won the war.

Raeder's main request was all-out war at sea, and proper *Luftwaffe*–Navy
co-operation. As a necessary part of U-boat operations, long-range reconnaissance was needed, and only Göring could supply the men and the aircraft for
this. The task of the U-boats would be rendered far simpler by the provision
of a number of Focke-Wulf Fw 200 aircraft; the reconnaissance value of the

U-boats was low, because of the boats' low (economic) surface speed and the physical restrictions imposed on watchkeepers by the tactical requirement of low tower silhouette. Until good radar was available (and few real efforts were made in this direction until it was too late) the only aid to the U-boat crews was the S-Gerät, a sound direction set being then fitted in the Type VII and IX boats.

The surrender of Warsaw on 27 September had meant the end of land warfare on the Continent for the present, and indeed little of moment occurred on land until the spring of 1940. The situation was similar in the air, with small-scale raids on England and France, and coupled with the phony war and the Maginot mentality on land, only at sea was Germany on the offensive. On 23 October Hitler, having accepted Raeder's argument, ordered that:

> The war against merchant shipping and all other measures for attacking the economic installations, resources, and trade connections of the enemy are to be directed uniformly by the OKW according to my orders. The Chief of Staff, OKW, will appoint a staff for the comprehensive treatment of the problems arising therefrom and for preparation of my decisions ...

A handwritten note added that Admiral Schuster was appointed Chief of the *Sonderstab für Handelskrieg und wirtschaftliche Kampfmassnahmen* (Special trade and economic warfare staff). This was the same officer who had been head of the German naval element of the staff at the London Naval Conference in 1935.

During the first months of the campaign British reaction was generally optimistic as far as U-boat warfare was concerned. With the Prime Minister's permission, Churchill addressed the House of Commons as First Lord of the Admiralty on 16 September:

> ... The whole vast business of our world-wide trade continues without interruption or appreciable diminution. Great convoys of troops are escorted to their various destinations. The enemy's ships and commerce have been swept from the seas.

This was essentially true, despite the journalistic bombast, as the efforts of the Northern Patrol were being amply rewarded, with only a few blockade-runners making the attempt to get vital *matériel* to Germany by sea. He continued:

> ... Again, I reiterate my caution against over-sanguine conclusions. We have in fact however got more supplies in this country this afternoon than if no war had been declared and no U-boat come into action. It is

not going beyond the limits of prudent statement if I say that at that rate it will take a long time to starve us out.

This was direct evidence, however, that such a thing was a possibility, but in September 1939 the war was a novelty, and most of the guns being fired in the west were by propaganda companies. He continued:

From time to time the German U-boat commanders have tried their best to behave with humanity. We have seen them give good warning and also endeavour to help the crews to find their way to port. One German captain signalled me personally the position of a British ship which he had just sunk, and urged that rescue should be sent. He signed his message 'German submarine'. I was in some doubt at the time to what address I should direct a reply. However, he is now in our hands, and is treated with all due consideration.

The boat in question was probably U27, which had been sunk and her crew captured on 20 September, the first Asdic sinking of the war. Whether she also sent the message (which may have been apocryphal) is another matter.

Great Britain was now standing in near splendid isolation in Europe, however, with only a defeated Poland and the reluctant French at her side. The USA, although ostensibly neutral, had just elected Franklin Delano Roosevelt to his second term as President, when the title had greater meaning in diplomacy and statesmanship than now. His foresighted attitude in forging a friendship and later a full-blooded partnership with Churchill was fundamental in ensuring that Europe would eventually see the end of Hitler, especially when coupled with the later military might of the Soviet Union. The remarkable number of communications that were to pass between the two men (some 2,000 letters and communiqués) became enormously more significant once Churchill became Prime Minister on 10 May 1940, the same day that Germany opened the campaign in the west against France and Belgium.

American friendship towards Great Britain took a turn for the worse after the First World War, but rallied during the thirties as an amicable, albeit strongly contested, rivalry in all matters, including military affairs. The dangers Hitler posed to Europe's stability and peace did not go unnoticed, and despite the pro-German lobby and the isolationist attitude of many of its citizens, the USA enabled a Royal Naval staff officer and staff officers of the US Navy to confer in secret in May 1939. The fear of German naval activity was so great that the British representative was forced to concede that the Royal Navy would be so occupied in fighting the Kriegsmarine that the western and southern Atlantic, and the whole of the Pacific, would have to be secured by the US Fleet. The American naval attitude was in favour of the Pacific being their concern, leaving the Atlantic to the British. Once the USA entered the war this attitude caused some minor problems, but they were soon solved by the 'Germany first' policy.

When war broke out in Europe with the invasion of Poland in September 1939, Roosevelt was facing serious opposition internally, as well as being bound by neutrality laws. He could not even give aid to both sides in order to succour the British. King George VI had visited the USA in June 1939, and Roosevelt had made it quite clear that he wanted to set up a western Atlantic patrol, relieving the Royal Navy of an enormous patrol responsibility. The King had been glad to get this information, but wondered whether Roosevelt could manage it without declaring war. By October the problem had been solved, and Roosevelt declared a 'neutrality zone' some 300 to 1,000 miles to the east of the east coast of the Americas. In definition it did not include Canada, but in real terms it did. The British reaction was approving, Churchill writing to say that unqualified government approval was subject only to the proviso that 'it is effectively maintained. We should have great difficulty in accepting a zone which was policed by a weak neutral. But of course if the American Navy takes care of it, that is all right.' Churchill's aim, to be achieved *at any cost*, was to get the USA into the war.

The Neutrality Zone was established by Presidential Order on 5 September. German war aims did not include giving cause to the USA to enter the war on Great Britain's side, even biased neutrality being the preferred status. Keeping his eyes firmly fixed on Europe, Hitler hoped that Japan would involve the Americans' attention to such an extent that if Japan pursued her expansionist programme in the east by military means, subsequent American involvement would preclude any aid to the British from that source. Roosevelt was equally determined that Great Britain should not be defeated for want of equipment and armaments, even if he had no reason or opportunity to send men. There is no doubt that without this friendship, and its subsequent material expression, Great Britain would not have survived the war.

If Churchill had not returned to the Admiralty only recently before Prien's attack at Scapa, the opprobrium it caused might have resulted in his being asked to resign as First Lord. As it was, however, he used the situation to some advantage, in writing to Roosevelt that the sinking of the *Royal Oak* was 'a heavy blow to Anglo-American sea power'. It was nothing of the sort, being a defeat for the Royal Navy and the Admiralty, which reflected heavily upon both. If the fleet base could be penetrated by a U-boat, where could the fleet be safe? In a more optimistic vein Churchill continued that successes with Asdic 'have been hitting the enemy hard'. This was also untrue, although Churchill didn't know that. In the speech to the Commons already mentioned, he had claimed that:

Even taking six or seven U-boats sunk as a safe figure [implying that more had been sunk] ... it is probably one-quarter, or perhaps even one-third, of all the U-boats which are being employed actively. But the British attack on the U-boats is only just the beginning. Our hunting force is getting stronger every day. By the end of October we hope to have three times the hunting force that was operating at the beginning of the war.'

In fact two U-boats, *U27* and *U39*, were lost in September, both prior to Churchill's speech. They represented nearly 5 per cent of the available operational U-boats (a total of 48, as noted above). There were others building, however, and even more were planned. Furthermore, the hunting groups to which Churchill referred were almost totally ineffective once they got to sea. Churchill's optimism at this time was to suffer a reverse in 1940, until he was left apparently without any practical help after the withdrawal from Dunkirk.

Neither Raeder nor Dönitz was in such an optimistic frame of mind. They still had to persuade Hitler to give them the practical means to enlarge the U-boat Arm. The Economic Warfare Committee had been set up under Schuster, but Germany was still no nearer to unlimited U-boat warfare or to getting the requisite priority for U-boat construction. Again, on November 10, Raeder tried to get this priority allotted to U-boat building, and he also tried to get extensions to his target list. Neutrals were still, declared Hitler, to be left alone, but armed passenger ships known to be carrying troops could now be attacked, as long as 'the names of the large ships concerned are known previously.' Hitler was still hopeful of some form of armistice, if not peace, with France and Great Britain, and he was wary of upsetting neutral opinions, especially if the neutrals had some influence with the British.

While these political matters were being discussed, the U-boat Arm continued to operate against their targets, the merchantmen. The campaign had begun with ships under the British flag, and had been extended, on Raeder's insistence, to French ships. Then it extended as far as the European neutrals, especially the Norwegians, Dutch, Swedes and Danes. This had been a gradual process, effected by Raeder without Hitler's official sanction. From the tactical point of view there had been a number of individual operations, although none which could compete with Prien's adventure in Scapa. Among his earlier tactical plans Dönitz had, it will be remembered, counted the group attack (later named the *Rudeltaktik* or 'wolf-pack' method). The first attempt to put such a group together and into operations got off to a bad start. On 10 October nine U-boats were ordered to the area west of the Bay of Biscay, on the route of the UK–Gibraltar convoys.

Of the original nine, only six sailed. The group consisted of *U37* (with the tactical commander, Hartmann, aboard), *U40, U42, U45, U46* and *U48. U40* ran into the Dover mine barrage and was sunk. *U42* attacked a straggler from Convoy OB.17 en route and was sunk by the escort vessels of the convoy, and the same fate befell *U43* at the hands of the escorts of Convoy KJF.3. By 14

October Hartmann's group had been reduced to three, *U37*, *U46* and *U48*. They contacted Convoy HG.3, homeward-bound from Gibraltar on 17 October, and attacked between 0835 and 2035 hours. Each boat succeeded in torpedoing one merchant vessel. HG.3 was not a convoy by definition, because it had no escort, and had it been, in the light of what befell *U42* and *U43*, there seems some doubt as to the outcome. The operation was almost a total failure apart from the attacks on the 17th, but another opportunity to test the theory soon occurred.

On 15 November *U53* was on patrol to the west of Gibraltar when she sighted KS.27. She was in turn sighted by the escorts of this French convoy, and the destroyers *Frondeur* and *Sirocco*, the sloop *Chevreuil* and the heavy destroyer *Chevalier-Paul*, together with a seaplane, contrived to drive the U-boat off repeatedly. But *U53* doggedly maintained contact until the 20th. This was in compliance with Dönitz's order that the first boat to sight a convoy should shadow it, reporting position, course, speed and composition (number of merchant ships and number and type of escort) to Dönitz's headquarters. These radio messages had *U41*, *U43* and *U49* sent to assist in the operation, but their arrival was constantly delayed by encounters with independents and the nearby OG.7 Convoy. Finally *U53* withdrew without attacking, and the other three boats never came into contact. This seems at most a non-event, but combined with the operation lead by *U37*, the following conclusions could be drawn:

1. The U-boat locating a convoy could shadow it, if the escorts did not make every effort to drive it off, having the destruction of the U-boat their aim. Half-hearted efforts by the escort would not be enough to force the U-boats away. So the 'shadower' U-boat concept was valid, as evidenced by *U53* spending six days in contact with the convoy, and logging its every movement.

2. Once a convoy had been sighted, directing other U-boats into contact would result in a higher total sinking rate. Although untested in battle, it was clear that the more U-boats attacking, the more distracted would be the escort, and the more thinly spread.

What Dönitz needed was more opportunities to put his theories into practice. It would be too late when he had large numbers of boats; lessons learned at this early stage in the war, when circumstances were still relatively forgiving, could save many boats and lives later on. It was not, however, until August 1940 that he was able to take the opportunity again, for losses were fast over-taking production. In August 1940 he had once again 57 boats in commission, and many of them were battle ready to a much greater extent than in 1939.

As the technical descriptions of the U-boats makes clear, they were capable of operations other than single or group torpedo/artillery attacks on independents and convoyed ships. There had been a minelaying campaign in which a number of boats (mainly Type II but some Type VII) laid small fields at various points around the British coast. Most of the mines laid (including those laid by aircraft) had been contact rather than influence detonated. Germany had very small reserves of magnetic mines at the beginning of the war and this, combined with some very courageous work by British naval mine-disposal and mine-sweeping teams, had combined to limit what had been a serious threat to British freedom of navigation. The submarine campaign as a whole, in the period to the end of 1939, had resulted in the sinking or loss of 147 ships of 509,321 GRT. Mines were responsible for 25 of those losses, of 72,111 GRT. Mines had also damaged HMS *Nelson* (a 33,950-ton battleship) and HMS *Belfast* (a cruiser of 11,500 tons), off the west and east coasts of Scotland respectively.

Another type of operation which had a short heyday was the fleet operation. An example of this took place in November 1939. The fleet submarine proper had been adopted as a concept by the Americans, and demanded a submarine of sufficient surface speed and displacement to be capable of co-operation with surface ships of the line. If this were feasible, it would add a further dimension to combined fleet operations. The Germans had designs for such boats (particularly the Types XI and XII), but they had fallen foul of Germany's lack of time to develop the Z-Plan fleet. The Americans found also that the plan could not be realised, partly because of the maintenance problem. The first trial undertaken by Raeder was in conjunction with the sortie by *Gneisenau* and *Scharnhorst* under Admiral Marschall, with the task of gaining access to the Atlantic despite the presence of the Northern Patrol.

At that time *Admiral Graf Spee* was under close scrutiny by the Admiralty, for she was at large in the Atlantic and Indian Oceans, sinking a number of merchantmen without interference. *Gneisenau* and *Scharnhorst* by their sortie were to relieve the impending pressure on her. Following the gallant suicide of HMS *Rawalpindi* (a British armed merchant cruiser which, in protecting her convoy, engaged the German ships and was sunk by 11in gunfire), British cruisers and destroyers formed patrol lines to avenge her loss, and to stop this excursion. In support of Admiral Marschall's sortie, *U31*, *U33*, *U35*, *U47* and *U48* were positioned in the area of the Orkneys (in advance of the surface ships' arrival). Only *U47* (Prien was at sea once more) made any contribution, an attack on the cruiser HMS *Norfolk* which failed because of the persistent problem of torpedo pistol failure. Prien claimed *Norfolk* as damaged, but her log shows that his torpedo exploded prematurely, quite near to the cruiser's side, but without causing damage. The rest of the patrol group saw nothing of the considerable large ship activity, apart from *U35* which was attacked and sunk without ceremony by the destoyers HM ships *Kingston*, *Kashmir* and *Icarus*.

Without exception during this period, operations were concentrated around the British Isles and in the Atlantic as far south as Gibraltar. This was due to the restrictions in range imposed upon the U-boats by the Dover mine barrage. Three U-boats were lost there to mines in October 1939, and no other boat ever sailed through these waters to reach the Atlantic. The long outward and inward passage around the north of Scotland was further complicated by air patrols in the North Sea and around Scotland, as well as the Northern Patrol. This meant that the fuel they carried had far less value, and the Type II boats were effectively limited to coastal work and the Baltic. Only the Type IX boats had any real endurance beyond the Bay of Biscay (*U53* which shadowed convoy KS.27 was a Type IX).

At the FCNA on 10 November, Raeder told Hitler that six U-boats had been lost since the war began (in fact there had been seven losses, for *U40* – a Type IX – had also been lost, but this was as yet unknown to the BdU). He also told Hitler that all replacements due for delivery in 1939 had now been taken up, although he hoped that Dönitz's training would result in fewer losses. Raeder and Dönitz both knew that they could not carry out an offensive U-boat policy without losses, and Raeder may have hoped to further sway Hitler with this information. He did not, although Hitler asked Raeder if he had any use for the Dutch and Belgian naval bases. In view of the mine barrage Raeder replied in the negative.

This constant demand for more U-boats must have seemed monotonous, but it was the only way to get the message through to Hitler, who had no real sea sense at all. Losses at least had to be replaced, and for the Navy to compete with the other armed forces, it needed U-boats. When war broke out, Raeder's greatest fear was realised – he was to take on the largest fleet in the world. Naval building had been increased, with orders for 24 new destroyers, 48 torpedo-boats, 132 minesweepers and 108 U-boats (24 Type IXC, 48 VIIC and 36 IID). Completion was speeded up as well on *Bismarck*, *Tirpitz*, *Graf Zeppelin* (aircraft carrier), *Prinz Eugen* and *Seydlitz*. The plan was modified in the light of events, and the U-boat programme planners seem to have been taking serious thought to the future, as was presented to Hitler on 22 November.

At this FCNA the new U-boat building plan showed an increase in total U-boats available for operations from 45 in November 1939 to 116 in November 1941, within which the total of training boats increased from twelve in 1939 to 75 in 1941. The figures had been further extended to 1943, when the available total overall was to be 320, with a fixed number of 75 boats attached to the training flotillas. Of the remainder, 95 were intended to be operational at any one time. The rest would be in harbour replenishing and resting, training and acting as reserves. This would result in Dönitz's original target of 90 boats at sea. (The actual figures for 1943 were 368 U-boats in all, 193 operational and 175 in training and working-up.)

The requirements of the programme in terms of materials and labour were enormous. Other naval construction, particularly destroyers, torpedo-boats, fast patrol craft, minesweepers and inshore mine clearance vessels, would have to be curtailed, if not abandoned. Raeder was quite prepared to forgo these ships if he could have the U-boats. German naval opinion had been firmly in favour of the U-boat since the First World War, and isolated exploits by the great ships did little to dampen enthusiasm for the type. One of the main reasons (learned during the First World War) was that U-boats took individually less time and material to build than any comparable craft of similar battleworthiness; they could escape patrols and operate with considerable freedom compared to surface craft, and they could lay mines and fire torpedoes during the same patrol if required. Raeder resented Hitler's decision to go to war in 1939, because it had precluded any hopes he had for the Z-Plan (balanced) fleet. But he was determined that the Navy should nevertheless play its part, and an increasingly important part if possible, in the war against Great Britain. He had to get Hitler to agree to increased building. Raeder prepared a survey, which he delivered to his Heads of Department in the Skl. At this secret briefing he began with a resumé of the current political situation. Great Britain, he said:

> is determined on a war of extermination against Germany. At present she is not sufficiently armed. The Army is not yet appreciable in numbers, is insufficiently trained, and has no modern equipment. The Navy is only capable to a limited extent of maintaining supply routes from overseas, since it was disarmed considerably after the last war. Expansion of the fleet is not practically possible until after 1941. The Air Force (including the French Air Force) is at present inferior to the German Air Force offensively as well as defensively.

This was essentially an accurate assessment. He said that in view of increases that would accrue to the British and French fleets 'In one or two years they will be equal to Germany in armament' and he concluded that 'victory can be achieved by offensive action alone'. He noted, in passing, that military equipment would be forthcoming from overseas; (he meant the USA). He had decided, he said, that by taking the offensive in the west, and by advancing along the French Channel coast, the Navy should 'seek to obtain favourable strategic bases for an offensive war against Great Britain by U-boats, mines and aircraft'. He was aware of the threat the British Isles posed to Germany, which had to be neutralised or even removed entirely. To achieve his aim he was prepared to do anything, and 'Neutrality questions are irrelevant in the cause of victory'. But he had to convince Hitler that this was the way to victory. In this he was as yet unaware of plans for the invasion of France and Belgium, and that in less than a year Dönitz would be operating his increasing U-boat fleet out of French Atlantic harbours. The Army would solve some of the problems for the Navy.

The next meeting between Hitler and Raeder was on 8 December, when they discussed both strategic matters and matters of specific note for the Navy. The strategic discussion covered U-boat activities in the North Sea and future attacks on convoys from and to Halifax (Nova Scotia) and Freetown (Sierra Leone). These attacks would demand deeper penetration of the Atlantic than hitherto. Economic warfare was discussed with specific reference to Scandinavia, and Hitler said that if the British controlled Norway, Swedish iron-ore supplies to Germany would be endangered. Furthermore, the naval war would be extended into the Baltic – an intolerable state of affairs. They discussed the forthcoming invasion of Holland and Belgium, which indicates that the matter was in detailed planning. The conference then turned to internal naval matters, and it was reported that U-boat production would be delayed because of steel and other metal shortages.

The economic importance of Sweden to the German military economy could not be underestimated. Germany had to import iron ore for military (and civilian) purposes, and some 70 per cent came from Sweden. Without these imports Germany was finished. The invasion of Norway by Germany would ensure continued supplies of ore which came via the Norwegian ports, and as a corollary Germany would have some extra naval bases. The Navy was closely concerned with the operational plan for this invasion, because the ground troops had to be transported by them at least across the Belts, and they also had to ensure that the British could not establish a permanent presence to the north. The strategic port in the north was Narvik, linked by rail with the iron ore mines at Kirunavaara and Gellivaare. The use of surface vessels (including possibly merchant ships) meant that there had to be suppression of Norwegian resistance to the invading troops. Hagelin and Quisling were brought into the discussion in December. Rosenberg reported that Quisling had solid support in the Army (he was a Norwegian staff officer), and that about 10 per cent of the nation was behind him. Raeder met both men during the month.

The Norwegian Parliament, the Storthing, was generally pro-British, and Quisling said that secret arrangements had been made between Norway and Great Britain for the landing of British troops in Norway if there were any hint of German interest in invasion. He then said: 'the National Party' [which Quisling led] desires to anticipate any possible British step in this direction by placing the necessary bases at the disposal of the German armed forces.' He added that the key men in the coastal communications network had been 'bought' (his word) to facilitate this. Public opinion remained anti-German however, and this needed to be altered. He hinted that when the Storthing was dissolved constitutionally on 10 January 1940 there might be civil unrest, which could be used by the National Party to put itself into power.

Raeder reported the substance of this discussion to Hitler two days later, adding a caution about self-interest, and at the same time hinting that German control of Norway would solve the iron-ore and Baltic problems simultaneously. He also pointed out the dangers of trying to protect the Norwegian coast with surface vessels. This was part of Raeder's overall strategic thinking, and could in no way foresee the results of the lightning campaigns of 1940, and the strategic results that followed, results which altered the global view of Europe. Hitler agreed to meet the two Norwegians, and was convinced. The General Staff was ordered to prepare plans that would either support a pro-German Quisling led government or, if that failed to materialise, would ensure a rapid capture of all stategic points by the German military, even against Norwegian and British resistance. This was eventually to be Operation 'Weserübung' and the Navy's part would involve all available vessels. It was in fact the only example of a strategic operation carried out by all three of the German armed forces together.

The last naval conference of 1939 was on 30 December, when Hitler and Raeder could take stock of four months of war. *Graf Spee* had been lost, scuttled on 17 December off the River Plate. This blow to German naval pride had been in part salvaged by the Royal Navy's loss of HM ships *Royal Oak* and *Courageous*, and the strategic balance had been altered. It was hoped that Italy was nearly ready to come into the war, for the addition of her fleet and her control of the Mediterranean should affect the strategic balance once more in Germany's favour. Submarine warfare was still subject to some restrictions, although these restrictions were becoming less onerous. The declarations of mined areas helped here, for U-boats could operate in the declared areas (often unsown) and sinkings could then be attributed to mines. This was particularly important in respect of neutral sinkings. Raeder reported also that:

> In January a large number of U-boats will be ready for torpedo attack [42 U-boats were operational at the beginning of the month] and for co-operation with the surface forces.

The surface forces were also being prepared for action, in Norway, and then the Low Countries. Raeder then turned to the intensification of submarine warfare:

> Previous experience has shown that gradual intensification without special proclamation is the best method. If a proclamation is planned in conjunction with general intensification of warfare, as advocated by the Führer, only a general statement concerning intensified naval warfare should be made, without specific details; moreover it is requested that the Naval Staff be authorised to introduce intensification according to the general situation and the state of preparedness of the forces, subject always to fundamental agreement previously obtained

from the Führer. The same procedure is recommended in case no proclamation is made.

Hitler was still not ready to free the Navy; he allowed ships of neutral nations to be sunk if that nation had sold ships to Great Britain. In the US Neutrality Zone ships could be fired upon if the attacks could be blamed on mines, and he also specifically mentioned the English Channel. As far as a reply to the British decision to seize all German exports as contraband (Order in Council 27 November, French Decree 28 November), that matter could wait until there was a general intensification in warfare, and especially the U-boat offensive.

One piece of news was given to Raeder at the meeting for which he had waited a considerable time. The minutes of the meeting record that:

Negotiations are in progress with the Chief of Staff, OKW, about a U-boat construction programme which by January 1942 would provide us with 316 more submarines than we have at present. This would be done by drawing on metal, particularly tin, reserved for the Navy for later years. The Chief of Staff, OKW, confirms this and intends to investigate the industry thoroughly to see if any more tin can be obtained.

This meant that Raeder could go into future stocks, rather than restrict the U-boat programme because of material shortages. Earlier he had told Hitler he was short of 30,000 tons of steel, and this announcement eased the situation. This incidentally shows how unprepared Germany was for anything more than a campaigning war, with even the minimal losses suffered up to the end of 1939 illuminating the weakness of the forward planning under Hitler's régime, and the inherent catastrophe ever present during the war.

During these first four months of war, almost all the U-boats and their officers and crews had seen some action. Some were already accumulating sinking totals that would increase dramatically in the next stages of the war at sea. Dönitz had, as is noted above, started the war with six operational flotillas and a training unit, but losses and, more importantly, operational requirements brought about a reorganisation. The new flotillas were to be numbered, and the old names of the First War heroes had disappeared by February 1940, as if the U-boat Arm was becoming a more compact and role-dedicated entity. The Weddigen, Lohs and Emsmann flotillas were amalgamated to form the 1st Uflotilla, Saltzwedel and Hundius formed the 2nd, and Wegener alone formed the 7th. Losses to the end of December totalled nine U-boats, three to mines, five to escort vessels and one to an enemy submarine patrol. Production in the same period (or rather release of boats then in training to the operational flotillas) had replaced six of them, and the strength at midnight 31 December 1939/1 January 1940 was 51 U-boats. The allotment of the boats under the new organisation was:

1st Uflotilla sixteen Type II
2nd Uflotilla fifteen Types IA, VII and IX
7th Uflotilla eight Types VIIB and UA
USFlotilla (training) nine
Training three
Total 51

The 1st and 7th were based at Kiel, the 2nd at Wilhelmshaven. The Type II boats were to be phased out because of their limited range, although some surviving boats were transferred at a later stage of the war to the Black Sea where they operated with some success against Russian sea traffic. The organisation of 1939 stayed in force until the further expansion some months later when additional flotillas were raised according to availability of U-boats and naval requirements.

This period of the war may be summarised, from the point of view of the U-boats, as merely training, from which a number of lessons learned would be incorporated into training and tactics. The U-boats had proved, even in this short period, that they alone would be the main contribution to the Navy's effort in the war ahead. In the next period they were to increase dramatically in numbers, and their effect upon Great Britain and later upon the USA was to be remarkable. The problem facing the British during this period, and indeed until 1943, was how to defend ships against the U-boats; not until a later stage would it be possible to take the offensive against them in a way which would have strategic effect.

# ELECTRONIC ANTI-SUBMARINE WARFARE

The question of locating a submarine had arisen during the First World War. Although only crudely addressed then, submarines could obviously be detected by sight from warships and aircraft when they were on the surface, and then attacked. The more significant problem arose when they were submerged, which was their real operational advantage. The surface of the sea would, except when an injudicious periscope broke the plane, give no indication of position. Furthermore, there was need of strategic information about the whereabouts of each U-boat, in harbour or at sea, the name of its Captain, whether the boat had reported sinkings or more importantly its position and intentions, damage to itself, and the myriad questions that appeal to the intelligence officer.

The function of intelligence is to procure, by any means, information about the enemy. But mere information alone is of little value to commanders actually engaged in battle. The mass (when there is a mass) has to be sifted, sorted and then published in such a way that the importance or otherwise of the information is stated, but the source remains a secret. Numerous sources were used by the intelligence staffs of both sides in both wars, but the really fundamental information in the Second World War came from radio and electronic devices. It came from radio signals transmitted by the enemy, as will be discussed later, and it came from electrons. Electronic equipment became practicable during the war, and only refinements to it have appeared since then.

The study of sound and electricity since the end of the First World War had advanced knowledge considerably, and research teams were still engrossed in the practical military applications during the thirties. The characteristic of the submarine, its ability to submerge, gave it a method of escaping enemy attack, and initially there was no remedy, and there was no way of establishing the position, course and speed of the submerged boat. In 1937, Asdic was thought to be the ultimate answer to this problem. Dönitz, with the ability of hindsight, said of it that:

> Thanks to the possession of these anti-submarine devices which worked under water, the British Navy between the wars really had lost sight of the U-boat menace and had underestimated its importance.

However, Asdic (later Sonar) was a step in the right direction, and it had taken long years of training to remove the fear of it from U-boat crews. From the

Royal Navy standpoint it meant that they could establish a bearing to the underwater target at least, but unfortunately they would not be able to read range and depth for some years.

There were few signs of the presence of a submerged U-boat to help the surface ship observers: perhaps a trail of bubbles, an untimely periscope exposure, or occasionally an oil trail which might lead to the boat. But all of these were only visible at a relatively short range, and gave no detailed information. During the First World War a number of experimental defensive devices were tried, with limited success. Nets were laid as a counter to submarine movement, whose use was partially circumvented by bow netcutters fitted to U-boats. A more successful device was the minefield, used by both sides, and explosive devices were sometimes trailed (as were minesweeping paravanes). At least one U-boat was sunk by this method during the First World War. Another method of locating submarines received only passing interest, involving the training of seagulls to perch on exposed periscopes.

Then came the genesis of sound location. It had been noticed that a ship's screws could be heard by a microphone trailed from a surface vessel and switched on below the surface of the sea. This method had superseded attempts to locate submarines by magnetic field readings (the idea is perfectly valid, but the instruments were too crude at that time). In January 1915 experiments tested the hypothesis in the Firth of Forth, and six months later an experimental station was set up at Hawkscraig. This produced, at the end of the year, a non-directional hydrophone which could hear a U-boat's screws at three miles, if the listening ship were stopped and the weather calm. Two hundred such hydrophones were ordered, on the basis that something was better than nothing, and if a U-boat was heard, a lot of noise could be made in the hope of scaring it off. Unfortunately for the listener, he was extremely prone to attack by his very target, which had a sitting duck to shoot at. Further testing showed that the microphone was actually more effective when fitted to a submarine, and if two were fitted, one to port, the other to starboard, target direction could be calculated with an accuracy within plus or minus 2 per cent. However the boat itself had to swing to get this directional indication, and measuring the variance between the two receivers required a finely tuned ear.

When twin hydrophones were fitted in a trawler, however, the experiment failed, and it was established that the hydrophones were too close to the water surface, thus receiving interference from the surface effect of the water against the ship's side. Then, on 6 July 1916 the motor-boat *Salmon* reported a U-boat off Lowestoft detected by hydrophone. The report was erroneous, but use of hydrophones was given a boost and the Admiralty ordered 800 portable units. At that time there were 2,500 non-directional sets in use, fitted mainly in small patrol vessels. The technique had developed of using two vessels to triangulate bearing and range of the target, a method used by escort commanders during the later conflict. During the Second World War the technique was refined, and once a range and bearing was established, one escort guided one or more others on to the target.

The entry of the USA into the war in 1917 led to a pooling of effort by Great Britain, France and their new fighting allies. The following problems were common:

1. All vessels in the area of a hydroplane search had to stop and maintain a silent routine.
2. The system would only operate in calm weather and water, for surface water movement caused sounds which disturbed operations.
3. The technique had to be practised frequently, and with submarines, otherwise operators lost their 'ear'.
4. Communication between the searching ships had to be very good.
5. The submarine still had the upper hand, because it could choose to go to the bottom and adopt its own silent routine, defeating the purpose of the exercise. Furthermore, during an attack, the accuracy of the echo for ranging purposes was only plus or minus 400 yards.

Results in general were disappointing, although it was clear that continued research could yield a better outcome. But in 1917 even the adoption of the 'fish' hydrophone equipment did not allow accurate attacks to be made. This was a 12-foot long, torpedo-shaped device, some 18 inches in diameter. It was towed aft and fitted with a horizontal directional microphone. Accuracy was in the region of 90 to 95 per cent, but this was not enough to enable the towing vessel to attack accurately, although she could move, even if only slowly, in search of the enemy.

The Allied Submarine Detection Investigation Committee (from which came the acronym ASDIC as an abbreviation, later SONAR after the American acronym) was set up in 1917 to work in the field, and it was established that if alternating current were applied to a quartz crystal, the vibrations of the crystal caused a short burst of sound waves to be transmitted through the water in the direction chosen by the operator. This significant breakthrough meant that if there were an obstacle in the line of these constantly repeated tranmissions, a return (the echo, or 'ping') was made to the emitting crystal. By halving the total time elapsing between emission and receipt of the echo, the range to target could be calculated. But as late as 1921, however, only the 'ping' was available, heard by the operator by means of a valve heterodyne receiver. This established the presence of a reflective object and its bearing, but range-calculation was yet to come.

The equipment was designed by a M. Langevin, and sea trials took place aboard HMS *Antrim* in 1921. Results were encouraging for, contrary to received wisdom, the crystal sound-ranging equipment could operate independently of

hydrophones, for which the crystal equipment had been designed as a complement. It further showed a capability up to 2,000 yards, and allowed the transmitting ship to proceed (albeit at, as yet, only two knots). Moreover it over-
came the stumbling-block of the hydrophone – it could detect a stopped U-
boat under silent routine. The device was made of quartz crystals sandwiched
between steel plates. The protective housing for it projected below the transmitting ship's hull; the keel was found to be best, allowing the apparatus to
operate as far below the surface as possible. It rotated, but could not be
angled vertically.

The operator could therefore control the attitude of the Asdic head in relation to, but independent of, the ship's heading, and, by means of a key similar
to a Morse key, could transmit the sound wave from the crystal at will. There
were still natural complications such as bottom echoes, shoals of fish, large
mass water movement such as tide rips and the wakes of other ships, all of
which could confuse the operator. Unknown at that time, and to be of help
initially to the U-boats, was the layering characteristics of ocean water, where
temperature stratification can occur. A layer of cold water can cause a bottom
echo, and U-boats could lie concealed below such a layer. This problem as yet
appears unresolved in its entirety. Rough weather could also 'quench' the
sound wave, which produced yet another problem for the operator.

By 1924 the shroud or dome of the oscillator cover had been refined into a
very thin steel casing, allowing operation at up to 12 knots, and in 1925 a
wide-beam transmitter was tried out. The idea behind this development was
that wide beam could be used until target location, then switch to narrow
beam for precise location. This idea was dropped because results did not
encourage further experiment at the time. By 1926 submarines could be fitted
with Asdic, which could by then also be used in the passive mode. This meant
that sets could be set to receive, without transmissions betraying the presence
of the listener. The crystal receivers were very sensitive, and supplanted
hydrophones in accuracy. But Asdic on its own was insufficient, for means had
to be found whereby the listener could become an effective attacker.

The answer to that problem was the depth-charge, which is merely a
container of fused high-explosive, detonated below the surface in sufficient
proximity to the target to allow the laws of physics to cause a rupture in the
pressure-hull of the submarine. Once this had been done, the U-boat had little
chance of survival. Although unsophisticated, it would do its job if it exploded
close enough to the boat's hull to cause the rupture. Used in conjuncture with
Asdic to locate the submarine, it was thought that the evil days of 1914–18 had
been banished, and the U-boat as an offensive weapon was negated. The
evolution of depth-charge patterns, necessary because of the infelicities of
Asdic, would, the statisticians thought, remove the significance of operational
errors attendant upon the use of Asdic. This was coupled with the 'pounce'
attack, whereby the attacker made a slow approach to within 400 yards of the

target, aided by Asdic, followed by a full-speed dash and the release of a five-charge pattern which would, it was hoped, despatch the submarine. Such were the results of experiments carried out with this technique that all experiments with hydrophones were abandoned by the Royal Navy, leaving Asdic alone to be the anti-submarine detection equipment on issue to the Navy.

Although not members of Asdic, the Americans were conducting similar experiments at the same time Their apparatus was called Sonar (from Sound Navigation and Ranging), and experimental sets were available for sea trials by 1927. They were limited in range (very short in fact at the time) and could not operate at speeds in excess of 3½ knots. Further development led the Americans to passive Sonar in 1929, and to submarine echo-ranging equipment.

In Germany the development of sound-ranging equipment as originally known was begun after the loss of the *Titanic* in 1912. Her loss after hitting the submerged part of an iceberg led the German engineer Behm to try to solve the problem of whether sound waves could be reflected in water, under control, so that ships could be alerted to similar danger of collision. His experiments proved the Behm Echo rule. His apparatus was used in the First World War, although not in anti-submarine work. He also realised that by using ultra-sonic waves enemy sound interference could be countered. If the waves were put into 'bundles' and transmitted at 1,435 metres per second, the apparatus had a practical application; it was installed in U-boats a few months before the end of 1918, and was used for navigational (obstacle avoidance) purposes.

Further experiments refined the process, without Allied knowledge of course, and in 1935 the first *Gruppen-Horch-Gerät* was completed. First installations proved their worth and by the time they were fitted into the Type IX boats there were eleven receiving heads fitted on the bows, later rising to two sets of 23 receivers. The range of this equipment, and its directional accuracy, proved to be of great help to the U-boat commanders when searching for convoys. The KTB records Prien in U47 hearing a German bombing attack on British surface units some 100 miles away. This apparatus was passive, as was another piece of equipment, the *Navigations-Horch-Gerät* (NHG), developed to receive signals from light vessels for navigational purposes. A further development was rotational sound location; although not used by surface craft because of speed limitations, it was found to be suitable for submarine use and was installed as the *Kristalldrehbasisgerät* (rotating crystal set). In this six quartz crystals, suitably housed, were fitted to the decks of U-boats, abaft the forward bollards. Development included the active mode and by 1938 German scientists had developed the *S-Gerät* which caused a small length increase in the Type VII boats when it was installed (for the operator's cabin and equipment).

This *Sonderanlage* (or the *S-Gerät*) operated in exactly the same way as Asdic, transmitting a horizontal pulse which echoed to the receiver part of the combined sender-receiver crystal head, and gave the direction *and the range* of submarine obstacles/targets. Performance was affected by the speed of the boat, however. Later developments of this original equipment saw service in the more sophisticated submarine designs of the latter war years, being installed as a matter of course in the Types XVII, XXI and XXIII U-boats.

As noted above, and held as sacrosanct by the Royal Navy, the greatest single enemy of the U-boat was Asdic. What it could do was shown on 19 September 1939. The Admiralty had been notified that a U-boat, in fact U27, had been stopping and sinking fishing vessels in the area of Tory Island, off Donegal, and further to the south-west the following day. On about the 17th she turned northwards and was operating in the area of the Butt of Lewis, off the west coast of Scotland. There she was located by Asdic by the ten destroyers sent to deal with her, and she was sunk and her crew captured. But this was a single success, aided by accurate intelligence about the whereabouts of the U-boat and her intentions (and see later about Enigma/Ultra matters). Furthermore, it should be remembered that Asdic was limited in range to a few thousand yards of the searching vessel, and became utterly ineffective when Dönitz's U-boats began their convoy attacks at night and on the surface. Then only radar could combat the attack.

Other methods of approximating U-boat positions were available at the start of the Second World War. Direction-finding techniques had been highly developed during the previous conflict, so that whenever a U-boat signalled to base its signal was recognised by Allied listening-stations. By rotating two or more aerials to register the strongest signal bearing, the U-boat position could be 'cocked-hat' plotted. This allowed for estimates to be made not only of locations, but of the number of boats at sea, and even their movements in relation to Allied shipping movements. Orders to change course could then be sent to enable convoys and individual ships to avoid the waiting U-boats. The next step, taken at the beginning of the Second World War, was to develop these D/F sets for ship use. On land a number of listening-stations were set up, which had great success in locating the general position of a transmitter, but that transmitter had to be more precisely located for the information to have tactical value. The general strategic value, however, was significant.

Direction-finding and the development of radio-location was one form of electronic warfare, albeit passive. An active form was involved in the development of radar. Just as sound can be returned to the sender, so can electronic waves. By 1945 radar was almost universal at sea and in the air, but in 1934 it was in its infancy. When Hitler was elected with the NSDAP into power in Germany in 1933, realists in the UK saw the probable course of events. The then Secretary of State for Air, Lord Londonderry, set up a committee under Sir Henry Tizard to investigate means of countering the envisaged heavy enemy air attacks. The first task was locating the enemy when he was beyond normal vision, or at night, or in fog. This was to become radar, and at the time it was thought that radar would not only be able to locate the enemy in the dark and in fog, but, as a Death Ray, destroy him as well. The memorandum which lead to the development of radar was in fact on the more science-fictional properties of electro-magnetic energy in radio waves.

Mr (later Sir Robert) Watson-Watt, who was working at the National Physical Laboratory at the time, wrote a paper on this subject, and although the committee was apparently unimpressed by his treatment of the destructive ability of this energy, the paper was farsighted enough in, and technically capable of, asking for further thoughts upon the subject. This was the subject of Watson-Watt's second paper, on 'Definition and Location of aircraft by radio methods.' Earlier work in examining the ionosphere had established that its height could be calculated by bouncing short pulses of radio frequency energy off it, and timing the results. Theory said that the same principle should be true with aircraft caught by such a beam.

German development in this field was in parallel with the work in the UK, although there the main interest lay in developing a radar gunnery ranging set for the Navy. Using a short-wave transceiver the Navy had a 50cm set working in 1934, capable of detecting a 500-ton ship at a range of seven miles. By 1936 a 70cm set was fitted in *Graf Spee, Königsberg* and *G10* (a minesweeper). The claimed range was 17km against a large ship, and 8km against a cruiser. The accuracy of the set was acceptable, at plus or minus 0.2% in azimuth. When fitted in a battleship it would have an effective range of gun-ranging at eleven nautical miles, eight miles in a destroyer and three in an MTB. It could not however locate fall of shot, this technique eluding the scientists. By 1939 twelve sets were available to the *Kriegsmarine*, but no more had been installed for use at sea. Radars, however, they were not. They were merely ranging radio sets. But the Germans had not stopped at that point.

German radar development had begun with the work of the GEMA Company in 1934. By 1938 this firm had designed and built the 2.4m *Freya* radar, capable of locating aircraft at fifty miles' range. Naturally this set was allotted to the *Luftwaffe* for air defence. In the UK emphasis in radar development had always been on aircraft detection, and so when the Royal Navy was invited to participate, thay saw the equipment as giving surface vessels air activity intelligence. The invitation to the Admiralty to participate was issued on 11 March 1935, only two weeks after the first, and successful, demonstration of radar had taken place at Daventry. An aircraft flying in the 50m beam of the BBC transmitter at Daventry had returned an echo which could be, and was, ranged. It was eight miles away. Facilities were immediately made available for further development work at Orfordness. The aims were to provide aircraft detection at the maximum range possible, and to so present the result that air and ground defence systems would have current information on which to base their use of available counter-measures.

Convinced of the practicality of radar, the Admiralty decided that naval and air radar development should separate, their needs being different. This reaction contrasts sharply with the attitudes of 1928 and 1931 when the Admiralty was offerred two projects for the use of electro-magnetic waves for ship detection. They were dismissed as peremptorily as the death ray idea. In 1937, while the Air Force and the Navy were settling down to deal with their specific requirements, the first Chain Home stations were being built. These had a range of 100 miles, but could not be modified to naval use because of aerial size; initially 50 metres high, they were reduced to 26 metres, but still on top of a 250-foot ground mast.

Development at the Naval Signal School resulted in the first naval radar, on a wavelength of 1.5 metres. Unfortunately the power requirement was too great for any ship then in service, and the wavelength had to be increased. (The power requirement for radar is inversely proportional to the wavelength of the signal, a 7m wavelength requiring less power for projection than a wavelength of 1.5 metres.) The prototype set of the second design was available in March 1937 and, as a bonus, it picked up aircraft as well. The set was a pulse transmitter with a narrow beam, having separate transmitting and receiving aerials attached to the fore and mainmast tops. They were rotated by means of a Bowden cable linked to the operator's station, and the returns were displayed on an 'A' scope. This was a cathode ray tube calibrated to show the returns from left (the source) to right (extreme range) with intermediate returns shown at an approximate range. Returns were shown as a vertical deflection of the horizontal signal trace on the tube. Ranging was quite accurate. This was the Type 79 radar, installed in HMS *Rodney* (August 1938) and *Sheffield* (November). The power output was 20kw, and the anti-aircraft range was 50 miles, the upper limit being 10,000 feet. The next version, 79Z, had a range of 90 miles and a ceiling of 20,000 feet, and was fitted in HMS *Curlew* in August 1939, at the same time as a further 40 sets were ordered.

By this time the Royal Air Force had developed its radar to the stage that it was air-portable, and had been fitted experimentally in Anson aircraft in 1936. It was 1.5m wavelength, with a power output of 50 watts. It was limited in power, and only capable of locating *Courageous* at five miles. Although this was within visual range, it should be remembered that radar worked at night, and in adverse weather conditions. This was the ASV (Anti-Surface-Vessel) Mark I set, with its beam set at 25° each side of the aircraft's nose. Ranges were improved until large ships could be detected at up to fifteen miles from the aircraft, and such sets were fitted in Coastal Command aircraft by September 1939. Unfortunately they were not yet operational, being fitted for familiarisation only.

As in Germany, gunnery ranging was an application which received attention; in this country it was developed by the Army. The set (the CD) had a range of 17,000 yards, and was capable of picking up a 2,000-ton ship at that range. It was so finely tuned that it could also locate shell splashes, but instead of going to the Navy, development was turned over to the Air Force, from which evolved the Chain Home, Low radar, for low-flying aircraft detection. The Navy had been looking at a gunnery ranging set, with 50cm wavelength, and this had undergone sea-trials in HMS *Sardonyx*. At the time fears began to arise in the Navy that the sets might be detectable by virtue of their own emissions (which is possible), thus supplying the enemy with the information that a radar set was transmitting, and that logically there had to be a ship carrying the transmitter.

During the war the Germans failed to take full advantage of this weakness, although they did use (initially French) equipment to detect radar transmissions. The device (later the Metox, Naxos, etc., types) was fitted in U-boats when radar became a significant factor, giving warning of aircraft approach, if the aircraft had its radar on, and if the wavelength were detectable. Naturally the British made every effort to reduce wavelengths, and once they had, emissions once more were undetectable. A further tactic was to reduce the power of the signal as the aircraft approached the U-boat, thus deceiving the target as to the aircraft's range.

Ultimately, seaborne radar was effective against the U-boats at up to 8,000 yards' range; at the same time the Admiralty Tracking Room was using high-frequency Direction-Finding sets to locate the U-boats in mid-Atlantic. Furthermore, there was the insidious feeding of information via Ultra. All these means and a number of others were to end the U-boat threat. By the end of 1941 there were sixteen listening-stations in the UK, Iceland and Newfoundland, covering the North Atlantic alone, and a further five in the Mediterranean, and three each in the West Indies and the South Atlantic. They were also listening in on medium-wave frequencies for homing signals from U-boats grouping other boats prior to an attack.

Further British development in radar led to the arrival of a more 'user-friendly' display system, the Plan Position Indicator (PPI). This meant that any member of the crew of a radar-equipped craft could understand the general trend of the information displayed, with the home craft being in the centre of the screen, and echoes displayed in a 360° layout around it. Needless to say, the trained operator was still needed, to distinguish between an upturned ship's boat, a whale or a submarine's tower.

Asdic too had its use expanded for although well developed in 1929, only 25 out of a total of 250 ships in commission were so equipped. The Admiralty was fully aware of the value of the equipment, and authorised Asdic compartments in all destroyers, even though many were still without the set itself. By the early thirties the Type 119 set was in use, which could be controlled remotely from the bridge, bringing the Asdic operator and the captain together. When the new D-class destroyers were built (HMS *Daring* was launched by Thornycroft on 7 January 1932, and seven others joined her in class) they were fitted with retractable dome sets, solving the problem of transceiver damage in shallow waters. By 1932 the Admiralty was so enthralled by the Asdic phenomenon that it changed to an offensive policy; the role of the Navy in anti-submarine warfare would henceforth be to seek out the submarine, rather than defend against its attack.

As has been mentioned, and will be seen later in detail, anti-submarine patrols in themselves were of no value; the escorts and destroyers were better equipped to deal with the U-boat danger at its inevitable point of concentration – at the target, the convoy. But the policy did have the advantage that even more ships were retro-fitted with Asdic, and all new ships were equipped at build. Older craft were prepared for subsequent installation in the event of war. Furthermore, the Admiralty built up a reserve of sets to be installed in trawlers, and two ship designs were even aimed at improving Asdic performance by building them round the sets. (These were the ships of the *Bittern* convoy sloop and the *Kingfisher* coastal sloop classes.) Thus, by 1939, the Royal Navy had more than 100 destroyers, 45 sloops and a number of older destroyers fitted with Asdic, and had made provision for extension throughout the anti-submarine fleet.

In the USA, surprisingly, anti-submarine techniques had lagged behind those of Europe. One factor in this may have been the range requirement for a European or Japanese submarine to reach the Atlantic or Pacific coasts of the continental United States, but in view of the technical state of submarine development in America such laxity seems strange. Sonar could now be operated at up to 10 knots, and this was installed in the ships of Destroyer Division 20, but as the manufacturers were only producing 20 sets a year, the expansion programme was slow. By 1939 some 60 destroyers were Sonar equipped, but operator training lagged considerably behind that in the Royal Navy. The centre for sound training for the US Navy was not commissioned until 1936, at San Diego, California, and it had a lot of ground yet to cover.

This short evaluation of Asdic, Radar and Direction-Finding is intended to set the scene for the operations of the U-boats during the first phase of the war. A later chapter will describe the developments and their effect on the campaign. However, another matter needs to be considered at this stage, for it was a matter that had created a field of intelligence all of its own – the Enigma machine. The equipment mentioned above has an immediate value only in intelligence, for it tells what is happening. Only signals and similar intelligence sources can get at the mother lode of information to reveal enemy plans and intentions, and what the enemy knows about the other side.

German naval codes were read with great frequency during the First World War, and post-war officers in signals branches were fully aware of this. They determined to eliminate this source of intelligence in the future. To understand what they were attempting to reverse is shown in the affair of the *Magdeburg*, which went aground early in the First World War. On 26 August 1914, while at sea near Odensholm, this German cruiser went aground in fog, fifteen of her crew losing their lives. Scuttling charges were set and she was abandoned.

The Russians searched the wreck and found (astonishingly) her code book. This was sent to the Admiralty in London where it was passed to Commander (later Admiral Sir William) James in Room 40. This so-called 'room' was the Admiralty centre for the cryptanalysis of German naval signals. The code book gave a start in an important task and Room 40 was able to keep abreast of German naval codes for the rest of the war, especially when aided by further code books from sunken U-boats (retrieved by intrepid divers) and from Zeppelins later in the war (the latter being under command of the German Navy). It should be added that it took some time, as in the later war, for the relevant information to be passed down to those on the spot who needed it, but after the Battle of Jutland this downward transmission became more frequent and valuable.

Indeed, in 1917 Room 40 became the operational intelligence centre for the Royal Navy, as well as the intelligence-gathering and evaluation centre. Commanders at sea now had all relevant information, but it was left to them to decide how to use it. But the system still had failings, such as no central filing system, no central study of the German Navy, and still a restricted flow of intelligence. Naturally it is easy to sympathise with the intelligence officer who does not wish to reveal his sources; from the other point of view the commander at sea does need all available information to be able to formulate his own plans, and he is unconcerned with the future of the source, only in the actuality of the moment. Such problems were never fully resolved, and Room 40 was disbanded soon after the end of the war.

Until 1937 naval intelligence played no further real part in the activities of the Royal Navy. Code-breaking, which had always provided a multitude of high-grade naval intelligence, was then concentrated at the Government Code and Cipher School (GCCS), near Cheltenham. In June 1937, Paymaster Lieutenant-Commander Denning (brother of the famous High Court Judge and later Master of the Rolls) was appointed to the Naval Intelligence Division (NID), with orders to reorganise the entire establishment. He realised that there had to be a close liaison between GCCS and NID (as there had to be later between NID and Bletchley Park, when Enigma decodes became available). By 1938 Denning had altered NID structure and had Admiralty consent to direct communication with ships at sea. He was passing raw, unedited intelligence at the time. He also increased GCCS' role to include radio-location of ships at sea, both merchant and naval.

In 1938 he also managed to get a staff increase from the original one clerk and himself, and other officers took over the supervision of intelligence relating to the Japanese, Italian and Spanish navies. This left Denning free to concentrate on the *Kriegsmarine*. He then began to look for staff to join him in the event of war, and one officer interviewed at the time was Lieutenant-Commander Peter Kemp, who later took over the submarine tracking room and ran it with phenomenal success throughout the war. Denning established that the existing five direction-finding stations would be too few and forced an increase to fifteen, including six high-frequency (locating) stations and four medium-wave (locating) stations in the United Kingdom, staffed by civilians.

NID went onto a war footing as early as the Czech crisis in 1938, and never relaxed thereafter until 1945 (as far as the Axis powers were concerned). Sources available to NID included the Secret Service, reports from warships and merchantmen at sea, naval attachés, RAF and other aircraft, and data from the direction-finding stations and Bletchley Park among many. The last source was geared up in 1939. Bletchley Park (BP) had one task: to 'translate' signals sent by German stations via the Enigma encoding machine. The sources of the signals ranged from domestic police reports, the SS, the Army, Navy and *Luftwaffe*, and indeed anyone who had the use of such a machine. The Navy from the outset was a hard nut to crack, and eventually used thirteen different codes, not all of which were solved. The U-boat codes were the most sought after, and the codes 'Hydra', 'Triton', 'Thetis', 'Medusa' and 'Shark' were all decoded at various times, with varying degrees of success.

Gaps in the decoding of U-boat material had to be filled wherever possible from other sources, and NID had the benefit of almost always being first to see operational information about the enemy, but there followed the problem of how to interpret that information. It also had to keep its 'friendly forces' information up-to-date, to be able to answer all the questions inevitably put to it as the fount of knowledge. This meant a constant liaison with the other two services, as well as the Foreign Office, and the various Ministries of the Crown, especially those of Shipping and Economic Warfare. This led to rapid inter-departmental specialisation for NID. Under the new DNI of January 1939 it was sub-divided into:

a. Trade – dealing with all movements of enemy shipping.

b. Operations – enemy and own forces.

c. Anti-U-boat – under Paymaster Captain Thring and the section's future chief, Commander Rodger Winn.

d. Operational Intelligence – under Captain Jock Clayton, also the Deputy DNI.

Even more specialised was to be the man who interpreted direction-finding information. For this job Denning called in Kemp, who, although his section was never large, managed to maintain a standard of evaluation (often intuitive, sometimes inspired guesswork) which served the country well throughout the entire war. He was often the only source of intelligence available to the Operational Intelligence Centre. Their job was to offer solutions to problems posed by the commanders at sea. By the early months of 1939, GCCS had moved to

Bletchley Park, and Hut 8 there was being staffed with mathematicians and similar thinkers for the stupendous task of breaking the German naval codes. NID was organised as follows:

OIC Rear-Admiral Clayton
Deputy Commander Colpoys
Japanese and Italian Sections Barrow-Green
D/F Plotters Kemp
U-boats Thring
German surface ships Denning

Communication from all sections was direct to the Admiralty, the Commanders-in-Chief of the Fleets, and to independent warships. There was to be no repetition of Jutland. In various appreciations prepared by OIC, the following list contains some of their conclusions; recommendations were more difficult to make, as everything seemed unavailable or in very short supply:

1. Trade protection was a severe problem. The Royal Navy relied too much on Asdic. Furthermore, there were too few destroyers and other escort vessels available to give adequate protection to convoys.
2. The controversy between the Royal Navy and the Royal Air Force over command of the Fleet Air Arm had gone on too long, and to little effect, except to hold back the development of the FAA.
3. Escorts had a continental attitude; they were limited in range and in strength, sometimes consisting of just one armed merchant cruiser.
4. U-boat signals until later in 1940 were so short in duration (Dönitz had had the signal book coded in itself so that a single letter or number could relay a much longer message) that Direction-Finding were having great difficulties in getting a fix on the U-boats.
5. Air reconnaissance was either non-existent or so limited as to be valueless. This did improve later as aircraft types improved and photographic reconnaissance units increased their skills.

As the war progressed the Submarine Tracking Room became more and more important, for it was quite clear that the German leadership was convinced that the main role of the German Navy would be an all-out assault on merchant shipping, conducted chiefly by U-boats. The location of every U-boat was at all times of paramount importance. Ultra material had tremendous value, most of which was actual U-boat traffic. The establishment of *Rudeltaktik* increased German radio traffic enormously, as did the growing number of boats at sea. The increasing amount of material available for decoding, plus the benefits gained from errors by German signallers all helped in the decoding effort.

In the course of tracking the U-boats in the First World War the staff of Room 40 had noticed that occasionally patterns would emerge. Intelligent and informed interpretation led them to make certain predictions of next moves, which were sometimes proved correct. Captain Winn, in the STR, also came to these conclusions, but his rate of achievement was much higher than that of his predecessors. The radio information he received was routine traffic (short signals, sightings, sinkings and weather reports, long signals of damage or refuelling and end of patrol calls). The turning-point came when Winn was put in command of the STR, for his intuition, added to his knowledge of the enemy, combined to provide some very accurate assessments which were always reliable and very often acted upon. The other result of Winn's promotion was an improvement in the relationship between OIC and NID, which had formerly not always been amicable. Relations between GCCS and OIC also improved, so that only the Trade section was removed from the centre of the operation. But what they did not have on a regular basis initially were 'translations' of German naval signals, which were increasing in volume daily.

The settings used by the U-boats for their Enigma machines were changed frequently, and their codes on a monthly basis. When a U-boat sailed it would carry with it the settings and codes, together with the planned changes for perhaps the next three months. The German naval staff was mainly confident in the security of their communications, although on a number of occasions the KTB records concern about this security. In fact 'plants' by British Intelligence (an RAF prisoner of war on one occasion, constant references to 'radio location' on others) fooled the Germans into thinking that radio location equalled precision position-finding, and radar did the rest of the job, despite the fact that they were reading the U-boat Situation Report almost currently in 1943, which was a transcript of Enigma material. In fact GCCS had begun to make inroads into the codes before May 1941. In February of that year had occurred the first of a number of important material captures which ended in the decipherment of the U-boat settings and the codes. On 23 February the Royal Navy attacked and captured the German armed trawler *Krebs*.

The capture of *Krebs* was part of a campaign to get Enigma equipment, and was followed by the capture of the weather vessel *München*, which provided documents relating to machine settings, followed by the capture of another weather ship, the *Lauenberg*, and the acquisition of more documents and cipher considered to be of 'inestimable value'. Last of all, but of supreme importance, *U110* was captured on 9 May 1941, still commanded by the man who had sunk *Athenia* on the first day of the war, Kapitänleutnant Lemp. With other boats, she had been attacking convoy HX.122 west of the Faroes, but after sinking two merchantmen she was attacked by HMS *Aubretia*, whose depth-charges forced her to surface and surrender. Lemp was killed during the action. The U-boat was then systematically raided by a Royal Naval boarding party who garnered a good crop of Enigma and other documents. This capture, combined with the intelligence captured from the other ships, meant the penetration of Hydra, the current U-boat code.

Dönitz was of course aware of the problems arising from U-boat radio traffic, but to have control he had to receive information from all boats (local tactical control was tried early in the war, but discarded as ineffective, which it was). He needed to know not only about his U-boats, but about enemy traffic (air, naval and merchant), weather, and inshore, details of lights, shoals, sandbanks and harbour defences. All this and more was needed to keep BdU in the picture. To cut transmission time to a minimum, the system of short signals had been developed, but non-standard information needed non-standard signals. He hoped to balance the value of the information he received against the risk to the U-boats. To try to reduce the risk he ordered that:

a. U-boats in operational areas should only transmit important tactical data (especially relating to convoys and their escorts).

b. En route to or from operational areas U-boats could transmit situation reports and sightings, taking care not to compromise other U-boats whose operational area it was, or which were soon to be in it.

c. Technically, there were to be frequent frequency changes, and German signals experts added extra wavelengths and enforced wireless discipline. This last measure was aimed at making direction-finding more difficult.

For the British direction-finding teams the situation was that they could establish where a signal came from, but they could not establish the status of the transmitter. The transmitting unit could be an operational U-boat (that is, in its designated operational area), or in transit, or might not be a U-boat at all, such as an aircraft, surface vessel or a neutral. The answer lay with GCCS, who had to establish the status. Fortunately, GCCS was frequently helped by errors in transmission, but German naval radio operators were in general less prone to error than their counterparts in the *Luftwaffe* or the SS.

The U-boats' operators were well aware that their own lives were dependent upon their radio security, as well as the lives of their crew-mates. But the U-boats were ordered to make certain fixed reports and to report when off their home port on their return. If sailing from Germany, and later from Norway, all boats had to report a successful transit of the Iceland–Faroes gap; if sailing from France they had to report when passing 15° W. In the latter case the signal would also include whether the boat was proceeding north to the North-West Approaches, west to the mid-Atlantic or south towards the Canaries and the South Atlantic. D/F fixes would give Winn in the STR a reasonable idea of the number of boats at sea, and GCCS translations could give details of their intentions. Adding all the current information into one main Atlantic Plot then showed Winn and his staff where the U-boats could be aiming for, and whether they were on individual patrol or joining a wolf-pack via a rendezvous point.

A transmission from U-boat headquarters was of greater importance, containing almost certainly orders, or perhaps an intelligence update on convoys at sea and escorts. Until 1943 the *Funkbeobachtungsdienst* (abbreviated to *B-Dienst*) was able to read the British and Allied Merchant Ship code (BAMS) and much of Dönitz's intelligence came from this source. (In passing, it seems strange that when the British were cracking the Enigma codes nothing was done to make this code less accessible to *B-Dienst*). The efforts of Hut 8 at Bletchley Park in reading some of the German radio traffic did not affect the signals to the merchant convoys to such an extent, and so the intelligence Dönitz received was of some value. Dönitz was also provided with Allied intelligence summaries transmitted to the escorts and convoy commodores, so he frequently knew what was known about his own dispositions, certainly until mid-1943. But Winn held the upper hand for he was frequently aware of what Dönitz knew, and could turn this into convoy routings that avoided U-boat concentrations, thus saving many merchant ships from attack.

Air co-operation with naval forces was frequently a matter of intense argument on both sides during the war, but whereas the solution was to mutual benefit in the Allies' case, the German resolution never came, and often left Dönitz and his crews in the dark. The problem of Coastal Command was forever bedevilled by the Royal Air Force, particularly by Air Marshal Harris. The Air Force saw every 4-engined aircraft as a bomber, the sole role of which was to 'export' bombs to Germany and the occupied countries. Personal feelings are aroused by this controversy, but studies carried out after the war certainly suggest that a proportion of the four-engined long-range aircraft produced during the earlier part of the war would have been far better employed in patrol and convoy support than in dropping loads of frequently defective bombs on German fields. But Coastal Command eventually became an enormous force in its own right, and was extended at sea by carrier-borne aircraft, so that the gaps over the Atlantic were eventually closed. The German picture was far less satisfactory from Dönitz's point of view.

Aerial reconnaissance did not figure highly in Göring's view of the war, for he, like Hitler, was continental in train of thought. His *Luftwaffe* had never really had a strategic role, having been subordinated to the Army initially as extra artillery. The twin-engined bomber was too short in range to be of any effect after the first months of the war, apart from lightning raids in the North Sea, the Channel and off the North Cape of Norway. However, I/KG.40 was equipped with the longer range Focke-Wulf Fw 200 (nicknamed 'Kondor'). After the fall of France these aircraft were posted to Bordeaux (Mérignac) airfield. The trouble was there were far too few of them and they were rarely able to do their job, being 'maintenance-intensive'. As the narrative will show, these aircraft were able to gather significant intelligence, as well as attack merchant shipping, but they did not get the priority of production that would have made them an effective strategical element.

The *B-Dienst* has been mentioned above; such was the importance accorded to this aspect of intelligence-gathering that the Germans had more than 5,000 personnel in the service during the war. Operational intelligence, a more practical branch, also grew, and was responsible for monitoring such things as conditions at sea. It was this branch that plotted swept passages in minefields in the coastal waters off the Norwegian coast, in the Baltic, the Kattegat and the Skaggerak, in the area of the Heligoland Bight, the English Channel and the Bay of Biscay. Allied minelaying in these areas meant that swept passages had to be maintained. An advantage accrued from this via Enigma to the Allies, for the minesweepers reported on the same machines but in different code from that used to inform U-boats of minefields. The repetition of one message in two codes helped Bletchley Park arrive at an often quicker solution of settings and often the messages themselves. From 1941 onwards British intelligence relating to the minefields and the state of their clearance was equal to, if not better than, German intelligence.

In all, by the end of 1941 Allied Intelligence and the operations function were benefitting greatly from the GCCS translations and from air and surface reconnaissance and reports. It was beginning to function expertly, but the process had taken two years to develop. If any of the major intelligence sources had been compromised, and especially Ultra, the ensuing result could have been disastrous. During 1941 the Atlantic Plot display grew to show the locations of all Allied convoys and warships, most neutrals and many enemy positions, particularly the main enemy, the U-boats. The next step was not merely to know where the U-boats were, but to go out and defeat them conclusively, and to drive them away from the rich pickings to which they were accustomed.

The style of warfare engaged in by the U-boats during the period to the end of 1941 is reflected by the *Kriegstagebuch* (War Diary) kept by Dönitz's staff. Until 1 November 1941 it has an erratic style, seemingly written initially as an afterthought, mentioning matters of importance and trivia with no emphasis whatsoever. The reader gets the feeling that it is not a serious military document initially, but which slowly comes to demonstrate the growing importance of the role of the German Navy in the mammoth conflict developing in the Atlantic. Events during 1939, 1940 and 1941 fall into the following summary:

Phase I. The war expands into pan-European dimensions.
Phase II. U-boat building begins to expand the U-boat Fleet (after August 1940) rather than merely keeping pace with losses, and includes the first serious attempts to stop trans-Atlantic traffic to the British Isles.
Phase III. Attempted air–sea co-operation by the Germans,
Phase IV. Concerted attacks on the Atlantic convoys and the entry of the USA into the war.

During the first four months of the war very few ships had been sunk in convoy in comparison with the number of ships sunk. Trade Division of the Admiralty had put convoy into effect before the commencement of hostilities and they seemed in January 1940 to be effective. The definition of a convoy has already been mentioned, and so ships sailing together for convenience but without a naval escort do not fall within the definition. Coastal convoys ran around the coast of the British Isles, and were subject to frequent air attacks, and were in danger from minefields at nodal points, such as the Thames Estuary and the Liverpool roads. North Sea convoys sailed to and from Bergen, often passing convoys and ships bound for Germany, Norway trading with both sides at the time. The Atlantic convoys, upon which so much depended, were of course the most important. Although convoys had been instituted, it was another matter to convince merchant skippers of their necessity, and many ships sailed alone, at great cost to themselves and Great Britain. Neutral shipping, of which there was still a great amount at this time, sailed as and when it would, and all ships that could cruise at a minimum of 15 knots, and the unfortunates which could not maintain 9 knots, were specifically excluded from the convoy system. It was the independent sailings that formed the bulk of the U-boat's targets at this stage.

The main concentration area for the U-boats against the convoys was in the South West Approaches, and it was there that the longer range boats (Types IA, VII and IX) gathered. The defences against this small number of U-boats were provided by the Royal Air Force and the Royal Navy. The Air Force was bomber–oriented even in 1939, whereas the role of Coastal Command was trade protection, and reconnaissance for, and co-operation with, the Royal Navy. The Command was formed in 1936, just before command of the Fleet Air Arm passed finally to the Royal Navy. Staff officers of both forces realised that when convoy was introduced there would be a concentration of targets for the enemy. The Navy assumed Asdic would cope, and both services then agreed that the main danger to the convoys would be armed raiders at large in the Atlantic. The threat of the U-boats seemed to have been minimised, and when war looked inevitable in 1939, Coastal Command had three main tasks:

a. To patrol the exits northwards from the North Sea.
b. To co-operate with the naval forces in anti-submarine operations.
c. To co-operate with the Northern Patrol.

The first task was impossible to perform, because the Avro Anson aircraft allotted had insufficient range to cross the North Sea and return to base. This had been realised and some Lockheed Hudsons had been ordered from the USA; when they arrived they in turn released the Ansons and those Royal Navy submarines drafted in to supplement the weak air effort.

Coastal Command was all but denied any hope of performing its role because of the pro-bomber attitude which pervaded all levels of the Royal Air Force. But despite resistance, Coastal Command managed to increase its strength, and the figures below show to what extent expansion was achieved.

| Type    Date | 9.39 | 1.40 | 7.40 | 1.41 | 7.41 | 1.42 |
|---|---|---|---|---|---|---|
| VLRange | | | | | 1(9) | 1(9) |
| L Range | | | | | | |
| Med Range | 1(9) | 3(72) | 5(105) | 9(174) | 13(242) | 15(300) |
| Short Ra | 9(200) | 8½(182) | 8(162) | 7(138) | 4(82) | 1(18) |
| F/Bs | 5(40) | 6(48) | 7(46) | 7½(60) | 10(81) | 9(76) |
| Total | 15(249) | 17½(302) | 20(313) | 23½(372) | 28(414) | 26(405) |

Note: 1. The squadron establishment was not necessarily the actual total of aircraft on strength.
2. The first figure in each column denotes the number of squadrons, the second the number of aircraft.

Coastal Command organised its three Groups so that their boundaries coincided with Naval Command boundaries. This was to reduce confusion, and ensure that the two command staffs would work in parallel. The remainder of the Royal Air Force was left to pursue its own, increasingly unproductive, bombing offensive against Germany. The main task of the Coastal Command aircraft was, initially, to keep watch on sea lanes within range, and to report U-boat presence to surface vessels. The Command was virtually weaponless at that time, because the anti-submarine bomb was totally ineffective. It was an aerial bomb fitted with an acoustic fuse, but the aircraft had no low-level bombsight. Also, the bomb proved to be fickle in the extreme, sometimes exploding on contact with the water, sometimes not exploding at all. This was later resolved with the issue of small quantities of aerial depth-charges from the middle of 1940 onwards. Royal Navy demands for an effective anti-submarine weapon were finally met by the Royal Air Force, and, as noted above, the strength of the Command began to increase; it did not exert any real influence over the conduct of the war in the Atlantic until a much later stage, when the Command will be referred to again.

Naval escorts for the convoys were also in short supply in 1939 and 1940. There were some purpose-built escorts (escort destroyers, sloops and corvettes), and main fleet ships could be pressed into this service when circumstances dictated. This meant however that any extra demands made upon the fleet would result in the convoys having their escorts weakened, or even withdrawn. This latter case was not an exception during the early part of the war. In 1939 the Royal Navy had 73 escort vessels, and it knew that this was inadequate for the task. It was further recognised that losses from enemy action and other exigencies would quickly erode this figure. The plans for future construction included:

| 1939 programme | War Emergency | 1940 programme |
| --- | --- | --- |
| 20 fast destroyers | 36 fast destroyers | 30 fast destroyers |
| 58 escort vessels | 60 escort vessels | 70 escort vessels |

This would increase the escort force, by the end of 1941 at the latest, from the original 73 to a total of 347 escorts (minus losses). The race was on, with Dönitz's U-boat programme competing with the British escort building programme. At stake was the future of North Atlantic trade and the viability or otherwise of the convoy system.

In early 1940 the escort system included some air cover and sea patrols as far as 15° West and no farther. For convoys sailing southwards, escorts accompanied them as far as 47° North (the approximate latitude of St.-Nazaire on the French Atlantic coast). In both cases the convoys were then left to their own devices. The shortage of escorts meant that there would be no continuous naval presence throughout the voyage. The escorts saw the ships both ways through the Approaches, and whenever possible released one outgoing convoy to join an incomer. Air cover was even more limited.

While all these constraints were coming to light, Hitler and the German

Navy were debating further plans. Above all Hitler needed a fast decision about a land campaign in the west. If he waited too long, the Allied war programmes would build up defences that would stop him, even if not defeat him. There was too the growing inertia in the west, partly for fear of the dreaded static trench stalemate of the First World War. Hitler had plans drawn up to invade Norway (to secure the Northern flank and ensure continued iron-ore supplies), followed by an attack into the Low Countries and France. While the discussions and planning went on, Dönitz's boats were once more plying their trade in the North Sea and the Atlantic.

During the first part of 1940 they benefited from the Admiralty policy, to hunt for the U-boats rather than concentrate naval strength at the point of attack – the convoys. The independents were not only ships captained by the impatient and the ill-equipped, but also those released from convoy as the escorts turned about at 47° N or 15° W. During January 1940 the U-boats attacked three convoys, but in each case only one U-boat made an attack. This was due to the shortage of U-boats, and their being spread over a very wide area. There were 54 commissioned boats at the beginning of the year, of which 42 were operational. The total sinkings in convoy during the month amounted to five ships.

This is a typical picture of the early months of 1940; the U-boats were stretched to the limit and reconnaissance merely made their task even harder. When they came upon a target, whether or not it was a convoy, they attacked. The escorts seemed to be getting the upper hand too: U55 was lost to the two naval escorts to OA.80G (HMS *Whitshed* and a French destroyer, *Valmy*); the single escort to OA.84 had similar success against U41, sinking her for the cost of one merchantman. Again, U63 was sunk by HM ships *Narwhal*, *Imogen* and *Inglefield*, escorting HN.14 in the North Sea. The only comfort Dönitz got from these three losses was that the escort was unaware of the presence of a U-boat until it had attacked. The picture did seem to bear out the Navy's trust in Asdic, and fully justified the escort-with-convoy policy of the Admiralty.

In February, a further attempt was made to operate against a convoy with a group attack, Hartmann in U37 being local commander. U37 was to attack a French convoy, 10.RS, in the Bay of Biscay, with U53, U54, U26 and U50 in the tactical group. U54 was lost to a mine en route and U26 and U50 never made the rendezvous. Finally U37, moving in with only U53 for support, attacked and sank one ship. Attacks throughout February were made in the Bay of Biscay and the North Sea against convoys, but the end result was generally disappointing. The U-boats attacked seven convoys, sank six ships, and lost two of their number.

However, independent ships made up in tonnage for the comparative failures with regard to the convoys. Forty-eight independents were sunk in January and 45 in February. But the U-boats were still not ranging far afield, for ample targets were available to them in the North Sea, Western

Approaches and off the Spanish and French Atlantic coasts. The restrictions on the U-boats were still having a serious effect; their range was limited by the long transit from Germany to their patrol areas, and this in turn emphasised that they carried too few torpedoes. From March to May, however, these factors were unimportant, for the U-boats were engaged much nearer to home, operating as part of the combined operation against Norway, in the North Sea and the inhospitable fjords. During this operation a total of only 47 independents was sunk, and no convoys were attacked; the effort did not resume until June 1940, by which time the strategic situation of the U-boat Arm had changed for the better.

The overall strategic position of Germany was threatened in the north by her necessary supplies of iron ore from Sweden, which arrived via Norwegian ports and the coastal sea routes off Norway. The total tonnage of iron due (and very much needed) in 1940 was 11,550,000 tons, of which one-third came by this route. In November 1939 Churchill had tried to bar this vital supply route to the Germans by proposing a North Sea mine barrage, extending into Norwegian coastal waters. The War Cabinet did not accept the proposal, but Germany was fully aware of what the effect would be of any British intervention. Scandinavian iron ore represented no less than 77 per cent of Germany's requirement, and the importance of Norwegian neutrality at least was fundamental to Hitler's plans for the continuation of the war. Naturally, if Norway were to fall into the German sphere of influence, this would be an even better state of affairs. Quisling and Hagelin were encouraging Hitler towards this latter case, and Raeder was able to tell Hitler that there was a good chance of landing adequate German forces in Norway to remove the British threat.

At the FCNA on 23 February 1940, Hitler and Raeder discussed the Norwegian problem, and Raeder came down in favour of Operation 'Weserübung' as long as all forces involved synchronised their operations; this included a series of defensive patrols by the U-boats. Further discussion included the idea of buying two Estonian submarines to add to the boats expected from Italy. This shows once more how desperate was the need of U-boats at the time, especially in view of the shortage of surface craft. Hitler agreed to this, but was diametrically opposed to Raeder's plan that his Type IX U-boats should operate off Halifax after mine-laying, concealing torpedo attacks under the camouflage of a declared minefield. Hitler's fear of the entry into the war of the United States had been aroused by the *Athenia* sinking, and would not go away until the Japanese attack on Pearl Harbor.

In March Raeder presented his appreciation of the prospects for the invasion of Norway, and now included Denmark, to gain complete control of the Baltic entrance once and for all. He said that the plan was

> contrary to all principles in the theory of naval warfare. According to this theory, it could be carried out by us only if we had naval supremacy.

'We do *not* [emphasis in the original] have this ...' In spite of this the C-in-C Navy believes that, provided surprise is complete, our troops can and will successfully be transported to Norway.

This meant that Raeder was prepared to risk much of his Navy in the attack, basing his decision on the element of surprise. As it turned out the destroyer action in Narvik roads proved that the Royal Navy was more than a match for German surface forces, and nine German destroyers were lost. But Raeder was obviously aware of the risk, commenting that 'the fate of the German Fleet is hanging in the balance'. The point was, however, that without action, if the Swedish iron ore supply contracted, or worse, dried up, the German fleet was relegated to insignificance anyway. Ships lost in a successful action could be replaced, however, providing a powerful incentive for action.

Dönitz was naturally involved in the planning and he considered that one factor fundamental to success was air cover, and the air preparations to back this up. He asked for a minelaying sortie by the *Luftwaffe* including laying mines in Scapa Flow. His overall aim was to deny freedom of action to the Home Fleet. The minelaying operation against Scapa was in fact called off at short notice, on 27 March, by Göring himself. This was an act of childish venom on Göring's part, seemingly brought on, as was disclosed the next day in front of Hitler, by Raeder's refusing Göring free access to naval aviation fuel. These squabbles were put aside however. On 6 April the British Operation 'Wilfred', the mining of Norwegian coastal waters, began, but the Germans had already completed their preparations, and their invasion of Norway began next day. Eleven groups of troops with attendant transport and naval support attacked fifteen major ports in Norway and Denmark. Denmark was totally unprepared for war, and capitulated on 9 April, the same day that German troops landed in Norway. They were supported by most of the German Navy, and by no fewer than eight U-boat groups, patrolling as follows:

Group 1: *U25, U46, U51, U64, U65* off Vestfjord
Group 2: *U30, U31* off Trondheim
Group 3: *U9, U14, U56, U60, U62* off Bergen
Group 4: *U1, U4* off Stavanger
Group 5: *U47, U48, U49, U50, U52* (later *U37*) off Shetlands
Group 6: *U2, U3, U5, U6* off Pentland Firth
Group 8: *U7, U10* off Shetland–Orkneys

These 31 boats were from a total strength that had dropped by April to 37; there was also a massive surface presence, Raeder being forced to take the risk for the sake of the iron ore. He also had to risk his fleet to impede the Royal Navy and prevent it from making an attack on the invading land forces and their transports. This one operation was make-or-break for Raeder; if he failed there would be little of the Navy left, and no prospects of building replace-ments. If he succeeded, the Navy would benefit enormously, especially in view of the needs of the U-boat Arm for replacements and eventually new building.

There were many opportunities for the U-boats to attack during the naval battle and the targets had little room to manoeuvre in the confined waters of the Norwegian fjords; but the U-boats only managed to sink the British submarine HMS *Thistle* on 10 April off Skudesnes (*U4*) and the Norwegian minelayer *Fröya* in Trondheim Fjord on 13 April (*U34*). There was a series of unexplained torpedo failures, among which were the following documented attacks in which the magnetic pistols fitted to G7e torpedoes failed to cause detonation:

1. At 2107 hours, 11 April, *U25* fired torpedoes at two British destroyers of the Task Force in Ofotfjord: no detonations.
2. At 1234 hours, 13 April, *U37* attacked a light cruiser north of the Shet-lands with no result.
3. At night, 15/16 April, *U47* fired on troop transports and cruisers lying at anchor. Eight torpedoes fired, no results.
4. At 1519 hours, 16 April, *U13* attempted to torpedo a destroyer north-east of the Shetlands: no detonations.
5. At 1248 hours, 20 April, *U9* attacked the Polish destroyer *Blyskawica* in the Shetlands area: premature torpedo explosion, and no damage as a result.

The high incidence of torpedo pistol failures was disastrous. The failure was in part due to magnetic anomalies which were even more pronounced in the Norwegian area than in the Atlantic, where some similar effects were felt. The G7e was hastily withdrawn from service in its entirety, for there was a depth-keeping problem as well. This left the U-boats with the older, standard contact pistol and the G7a torpedo, which meant that more torpedoes would be consumed in attacks, because the G7a only detonated if it struck and holed a target's hull. The G7e was planned, with the aid of its magnetic pistol, to deto-nate under the target, which frequently resulted in the target sinking, its back broken by the severity of the pressure caused by an exploding torpedo beneath its keel. The problem was not remedied until 1942, when the G7e came back into service.

The Operation as a whole was a success, however, and an example of tri-Service co-operation never again tried, let alone equalled by the *Wehrmacht*. For Dönitz it was a total failure. In addition to the torpedo failures, he had lost four U-boats during the campaign. Luckily for him three new boats had been commissioned by the end of April, but he still had a net loss of one boat. Sink-ings in April not connected to 'Weserübung' totalled just six merchant ships, and there were no U-boat operations at all beyond the confines of the North Sea.

In May the invasion season continued, but the next operation was far more important than the preventive effort of '*Weserübung*'. On 10 May 1940 German forces invaded Holland and then Belgium in the north, and broke through once more via Sedan into France. The rapid collapse of France meant far more than any of the other, almost peripheral, campaigns carried out up to that time. For the Army it was a victorious campaign against their supposed superiors, the French and the British, whom they eliminated from the continent in weeks. For the Air Force it was more practice in *Blitzkrieg* and their extraordinary role as airborne artillery, but it had the by-product of bases nearer to England from which to carry on their bombing campaign; for the Navy it meant just one thing – bases on the Atlantic coast.

The Norwegian campaign had brought the Navy near to breaking point, and had even demanded the use of U-boats as transports, to get aviation fuel to Trondheim because of the denial to the Germans of the use of surface vessels by the Royal Navy (*U101*, *U122* and *UA* were used). Furthermore, the U-boat Arm had been reduced not only by sinkings but by the withdrawal from operations of the Type II boats, which were too small to have any significant effect. The Type II U-boats were to form the backbone of the new training organisation that Dönitz was setting up, in anticipation of the arrival of the new boats which could be built thanks to the Norwegian conquest. The albeit limited new building begun in 1939 was now beginning to come off the slips, and the programme as a whole began to show a profit later in the year. The actual figures for 1940 were as follows:

| 1940 | Jan | Feb | Mar | Apr | May | Jun | July | Aug | Sept | Oct | Nov | Dec |
|---|---|---|---|---|---|---|---|---|---|---|---|---|
| Commissioned | 1 | 1 | 2 | 3 | 3 | 3 | 3 | 5 | 7 | 7 | 6 | 9 |
| Lost | | 2 | 5 | 4 | 4 | 1 | 2 | 1 | 2 | 1 | 1 | 2 | 0 |
| Total U-boats | 53 | 49 | 47 | 46 | 48 | 49 | 51 | 54 | 60 | 66 | 70 | 79 |

Not until September 1940, a year after the war began, did Dönitz see the total number of U-boats begin to rise above the number he had when the war started. But the die was now cast, and the increase in totals went on for three years before he suffered any real setback in strength. His task now was to make good strategic use of these slowly increasing numbers, otherwise he might lose the advantage to greater numbers of escort and other vessels ranged against him, and to the development of sophisticated methods of locating and destroying the U-boats. His main aim, of which he could not lose sight if he were to achieve it, was to deny Great Britain the supplies and reinforcements she needed to oppose Hitler's advances.

As mentioned '*Fall Gelb*', the invasion plan for the west, resulted in the French Atlantic bases falling into German hands. These were at Brest, St.-Nazaire, Lorient and Bordeaux, with La Pallice coming into use a little later. The bases were of strategic and tactical value in that the U-boats no longer had to contend with the long and dangerous passage around the north of Scotland; the transit time to the Atlantic would be cut by at least seven days. The bases of course had facilities for surface ships, but these did not concern the U-boat Arm except in connection with the *Bismarck* operation in May 1941.

In May some U-boats had operated in support of the land operations, and were in action in an old stamping-ground off the Belgian coast and the north-eastern coast of France. *U9* sank the French submarine *Doris*, and *U62* the British destroyer *Grafton*, together with fourteen independents. In June, however, the operational area once more included the Atlantic. Raeder had correctly judged that British fears of invasion across the Channel (after Dunkirk) would cause the Royal Navy to restrict convoy duties to the bare essentials, assembling as much of the fleet as it could in anti-invasion concentrations within easy reach of the English Channel. Dönitz now sent his boats to sea with the same orders as before: attack convoys, sink ships, but with the advantage of heightened morale (how much easier to return to France rather than Kiel or Wilhelmshaven), and use of highly acceptable tactical and strategic bases on the eastern edge of his battle area.

Despite previous disappointments, Dönitz persevered in his attempts to make *Rudeltaktik* work. Groups Prien and Rösing sailed in June 1940, tasked with attacks on Convoys HX.48 and US.3 respectively. Group Prien consisted of seven boats, and was to operate west of the English Channel and in the Bay of Biscay; Group Rösing, five boats, west of Cape Finisterre (the first operation in that area). At the same time he ordered that the armed merchant cruisers of the British Northern Patrol be attacked if possible, and two were sunk by boats from the two groups. A third was lost to Convoy UA. The final results of the operations carried out by the two groups were not excessive in comparison with the total sinkings for the month (four ships from HX.48 were sunk, none from US.3; 58 independents were sunk), but they showed that the tactic was beginning to work. The Rösing group also operated against the French convoy 65.X, off the Spanish coast, but only one sinking resulted. Prien's group had managed to attack with *U47* and *U38* together, and although the rest of the U-boats did not get up, the result was pleasing. (Three ships including one straggler were sunk in this attack. The fourth ship was sunk later.) This was only the second occasion since the First World War when two U-boats together had approached a convoy. The difference this time was that this war had only just begun.

From the morning of the 6 July 1940 Lorient became available and *U30* (Lemp) docked there two days later. The weather at sea was not kind, and gales during the month limited U-boat successes. With other causes taken into account as well, only 38 ships were sunk, but eleven of these were from convoys. The German presence on the west coast of France meant that all traffic that had previously left the United Kingdom via the South-West Approaches now had to pass round the north of Ireland, which made targeting much easier for Dönitz and his staff. Searches could concentrate off the Rockall Bank, and with the increased traffic in this area, sinkings should automatically increase. *U61* located and attacked two convoys in the area of Rockall Bank in July, and Rollmann and Kretschmer enjoyed significant individual success at the end of the month. Oesten had sunk two ships on 10 and 16 July, while Rollmann and Kretschmer were in the Bay of Biscay, but when they moved north they found targets in the approaches to Liverpool. Operating separately, they sank six and damaged three others (in early August), all from convoys to the north of Ireland. This gave Dönitz a foretaste of the future, especially now that the U-boats' range had effectively been doubled; patrols were also lengthened by the same token, the U-boats being able to refuel and re-arm (even in mid-patrol at this time) in western France.

The U-boat Arm was reorganised at this time, reflecting its burgeoning fortunes. U-boat commissionings were increasing, as noted, and new bases were available. Although only 2nd Uflotilla moved to Lorient at first, it was followed by the 7th in October 1940, and the 1st (when it was up to strength) in June 1941. The organisation now was:

| | |
|---|---|
| Skl | **Operational Training** |
| BdU | 1st Uflotilla 1UAA |
| Torpedo Inspection: UAK | 2nd Uflotilla 1ULD |
| | 7th Uflotilla 2ULD |

Notes:
1. The UAK or *Ubootsabnahmekommando* (U-boat Acceptance Command) had been responsible for all U-boat acceptances from the constructors since 1937, and it continued in that role as part of the Torpedo Inspection Department until the end of the war.
2. The UAA or *Ubootsausbildungsabteilung* (Submarine Training Department) was set up in 1940 at Plön, and trained raw recruits in submarine techniques.
3. The ULD or *Ubootslehrdivision* (U-boat Training School) was based at Neustadt, and carried out practical U-boat training with the boats of 21st Uflotilla. 2 ULD was established in June 1940, and started crew training in November of that year, using the U-boats of its attached 22nd Uflotilla.
4. Officers were usually trained at the U-boat training flotilla, which became 1st U-boat Training Flotilla in April 1940, only to be renamed 24th Flotilla three months later. The 25th Flotilla took over the role of 2nd U-boat Training Flotilla in July, dealing with gunnery and torpedo training for ratings and petty officers, and 27th Flotilla began officers' tactical training at Gotenhafen in the same month.
5. The Uflotillas at the front were simply administrative units, charged with providing bases for the boats, rest and recreation facilities, and re-supply and repair facilities. They were not tactical formations as were flotillas in the Royal and other navies.

By July, extensions to the original organisation meant that the training function was taking a more important part in the overall U-boat Command structure. So when more new Flotillas were established a year later (4th Uflotilla in May, 5th in June 1941) there were enough crews trained and ready to operate their boats, new from commissioning. By 1941 the effects of increased U-boat building were beginning to appear, and the operational total was much nearer to Dönitz's original demand of 1939. The figures for 1941 were:

| 1941 | Jan | Feb | Mar | Apr | May | June | July | Aug | Sept | Oct | Nov | Dec |
|---|---|---|---|---|---|---|---|---|---|---|---|---|
| Commissioned | 10 | 9 | 11 | 14 | 24 | 14 | 19 | 19 | 15 | 24 | 23 | 22 |
| Lost | 0 | 0 | 5 | 2 | 1 | 4 | 0 | 4 | 2 | 2 | 6 | 10 |
| Total | 89 | 98 | 104 | 116 | 139 | 149 | 168 | 183 | 196 | 218 | 235 | 247 |

Only a proportion of these boats were operational (see Appendix: Operational Strength), many being held in training or working-up. The training function was increased, apparently at the expense of the operational flotillas, but with the aim of ensuring an enlarged and trained operational force as the process worked itself out. Increases in the number of operational U-boats from 1942 were most marked. So, until the end of July, the U-boat Arm had done little of great import operationally, but it had started learning how to operate *Rudeltaktik*, was increasing in strength, and had new bases close to the theatre of operations.

The period to the end of 1940 saw an initial improvement in the weather from the earlier Atlantic midsummer storms, only to see it degenerate into midwinter storms later in the year. But now the U-boats were able to sail farther and longer in their main operational area. Operations against convoys could now extend much further into the Atlantic, although this summer was typified by a majority of independent ships attacked and sunk, but the in-convoy sinking figure rose to 25 per cent. In August the first three-boat group attack took place, by *U38*, *U52* and *U58* on HX.60 in the North-West Approaches as the convoy neared landfall in the UK. The three U-boats were near the convoy early on 4 August, and during the day sank five ships. *U58* continued the pursuit alone and sank a further vessel on 7 August. Six merchant vessels were sunk, and no U-boat was lost. This operation laid a standard for later convoy attacks. There was a number of other, individual attacks, during the month, but in the last week of August there came a series of attacks that set the tone for some months to come.

It has already been mentioned that *B-Dienst* could translate the BAMS cipher, and intelligence from this source, and the base at Lorient, allowed Dönitz to assemble a tactical group of U-boats (varying in strength between eight and ten boats) off the North Channel throughout the month. *B-Dienst* located an HX convoy in the middle of the month and *U36*, *U46* and *U48* were sent to locate and attack it, but the attack had limited success. By 23 August there were still nine U-boats off the North Channel, and they attacked no fewer than five convoys, with considerable success.

The first attack was a solo effort by *U57* against OB.202, ending with two ships sunk and one damaged; then *U37* and *U48* contacted SC.1 and HX.65A respectively. From these a further six ships were sunk and one damaged, and *U37* added the scalp of HMS *Penzance* to her tally for the operation. Then came attacks by *U100* and *U32* on HX.66 and OA.204, these two boats sinking seven merchantmen and damaging one, and the same day *U38*, *U59* and *U60* grouped for their attack on OB.205. That day and the next the three boats sank one, damaged one beyond repair, and damaged two other ships of the convoy. In eight days, fifteen ships had been sunk, and a number damaged, by a relatively small number of U-boats. During the whole month 53 ships were lost of which 20 had been in convoy. The U-boat Arm had only 44 U-boats operational at the time, and in the months they had been operating as a strategic arm (discounting the period of the invasions of Norway and France) they had sunk a total of 257 merchant ships; *Rudeltaktik* was proving to be a very viable tactical concept, which could well lead to strategic results.

This of course was the gospel Dönitz had preached before the war: a sufficient number of U-boats concentrated against a convoy could make easy pickings. Further, the grouping of boats meant that when one of their number located a target convoy, the others were easily brought into the action and, as had been proved, the increase in sinkings assumed a geometric ratio. Dönitz had advantages of course, such as the nearness of his bases to the operational area, and the necessary concentration of targets into the narrow seaway of the North Channel. British air patrols were still limited by shortage of aircraft, although the new aerial depth-charge was now in service. Bomber Command was still engaged, and perhaps for once correctly, at the Channel ports, where the German invasion fleet of barges was assembling. Not until September did submarines appear among the targets in Air Council Directives to Bomber Command.

With his operational fleet now increasing in size, Dönitz could send greater numbers into battle, and at the same time he had enough boats to operate in other, as yet unexplored, areas. His aim was partly to dissipate the effort of the escorts, which would otherwise be able to concentrate all their forces in one small area, but also to give new crews sea time before committing them to the serious battle. The opportunity was also there of reconnoitring new areas, and sinking targets of opportunity. It should be noted that although these patrols were sent far afield, they were always ordered into known shipping lanes, and never to empty tracts of the ocean where only warships were to be found.

The anniversary of the start of the war came round, and during September there was a number of single U-boat attacks on convoys with the by-now expert commanders sinking seventeen vessels and damaging one up to 22 September. HMS *Dundee* had also been lost, sailing as an escort to SC.3, on 15 September. But the major operation took place against HX.72, and was the first of a number of highly successful U-boat operations that would threaten the 'lifeline' across the Atlantic during the next eighteen months. Convoy HX.72 comprised 41 merchantmen, and had been escorted across the Atlantic by the armed merchant cruiser *Jervis Bay*, but she turned away from the convoy on the 20th, just before the convoy was sighted by *U47* (Prien again). *U47* had already used most of her torpedoes in an attack on SC.2 earlier in the month, and she was now stationed to the west of the main group of U-boats as a weather boat. When Prien sighted HX.72, he shadowed it in accordance with tactical orders, signalling its presence and details to U-boat Command. The convoy made a number of unsuccessful efforts to escape. In the meantime Dönitz, commanding the operation from ashore, ordered in *U29*, *U43*, *U46*, *U48* and *U65*, but before they could arrive Kretschmer in *U99* made contact and attacked. The convoy was, at this time, due to be escorted into harbour, but the escort did not arrive until after *U99* had torpedoed three ships, all of which were eventually lost.

The escort had arrived late, on the morning of 21 September, and the U-boats were already grouping for attack; *U47* and *U48* had already attacked. *U47*'s last torpedo missed, but *U48* sank one ship. Nine U-boats were now concentrating on the convoy and *U100* and *U32* went in for the kill. The commanders of the boats involved were the best U-boat commanders Germany had at the time: Kretschmer, Prien, Schepke, Bleichrodt and Jenisch being among them. (Lüth, another ace, was absent; he was attacking OB.216 at the time). The escort consisted of five warships, HM ships *Shikari*, *Lowestoft*, *Calendula*, *Heartsease* and the French *La Malouine*. The escort commander sent *Shikari* off to aid the ships damaged by Kretschmer, and his four remaining escorts were overpowered by the U-boats, especially by Schepke's attack during the night. From just after 2300 until 0210 hours, *U100* made eight attacks and sank seven merchantmen. Bleichrodt and Jenisch also attacked, damaging one each; at 0646 hours *U32* was driven off after an attack, the escort having been reinforced by HM ships *Scimitar* and *Skate*, which helped *Lowestoft* to drive Jenisch away. By now the convoy had been reduced to 30 ships and two of those were damaged. Relief was at hand, however, in the shape of air and sea support from Northern Ireland and the British mainland. The U-boats were called off.

Analysis shows that the operation had involved nine U-boats. Eleven ships had been sunk and two damaged by the five U-boats that made contact (*U29*, *U43*, *U46* and *U65* failed to reach the convoy). The entire attack took place within twenty-seven hours of *U100* firing her first torpedo until *U32* was driven off at first light on 22 September. The operation was near to a total success for the U-boat Arm, and proved conclusively that Dönitz's tactics had been correct. Four escorts (one sloop, *Lowestoft*, and three corvettes) had been totally outmanoeuvred and outfought by five U-boats; Asdic had helped locate *U32* but had not been enough to sink her.

This action had taken place after an instruction had been sent from the Deputy Chief of the Air Staff to Air Marshal Sir Charles Portal:

> I am to inform you that the enemy submarine campaign in the north-west approaches has now assumed such serious proportions that, in addition to strengthening our attack on the operational submarines [by bombing the U-boats bases, which was ineffective] it has become neces-

sary to adopt a longer term policy against this menace. By agreement with the Admiralty it has been decided ... to divert the effort of the three squadrons engaged to the enemy submarine organisation ashore ... [to] submarine building yards ... [to] additional yards ... [to] the only known factory employed on producing batteries for submarines ... [and to] the principal establishment for training crews.

The Air Staff was aware of the problem posed by the U-boats, but failed to realise that Bomber Command at that time was utterly incapable of hitting such targets. They were incapable of even getting the majority of their aircraft on a mission to the target, and bombing the actual site of the target was a matter of supreme chance, as far as the crews were concerned.

In September, as in August, the U-boats had been operating almost exclusively in the area of the highest concentration of ship targets, off the North Channel. Air cover was inadequate there, and escorts so far ineffective at warding off attacks. The same pattern was repeated in October, during which there were two major convoy battles, even more effective for the U-boats than the previous occasions. Until the middle of the month only Bleichrodt, in *U48*, had contacted and attacked a convoy – HX.75 – of which he sank three ships during the night of 11/12 October. Then Korth in *U93* and Lüth in *U138* attacked OB.228 and sank two and damaged one of its ships. But during this attack, *U93* had located SC.7, on passage for Liverpool.

On 9 October *U47* and *U124* were positioned well to the west of the North Channel as weather and outpost boats, and *U48*, *U101*, *U93*, *U100*, *U46*, *U99*, *U28*, *U123* and *U38* were concentrated around the Rockall Bank. There were 30 ships in the convoy including four stragglers; before the attack started the inward escort had joined, being the sloops *Scarborough* and *Fowey* and the corvette *Bluebell*. *U48* went in immediately and sank two ships in three attacks; Sunderlands of Coastal Command then appeared and drove Bleichrodt off. The time was 0553 hours on the 17th. Before committing his U-boats to the attack, Dönitz had been informed by radio of the convoy position and course, and he now ordered supporting U-boats to join the attack. A patrol line of five boats was formed ahead of the convoy and on its expected route. *U38* gained contact at 0204 hours (having already sunk a straggler the previous morning). The corvette *Heartsease* and the sloop *Leith* had joined and they drove *U38* off, but only after the latter had made a successful attack on a steamer, leaving it damaged.

The daylight hours of the 18th were uneventful, but at 2100 hours *U123*, *U46*, *U101*, *U99* and *U100* were in position to intercept. In 27 attacks they sank fifteen ships and damaged four; by morning only seven ships remained undamaged. In less than 48 hours more than 1,700 tons of merchant shipping was sunk in each hour. This was not, however, to be the end, for *U47* had already located Convoy HX.79 nearby. Liebe, in *U38*, who had been driven off by the escorts of SC.7, was the first to attack this new target, and he was followed by *U46*, *U47*, *U48*, *U100* and *U124*. In the space of fourteen hours and sixteen minutes, twelve ships were sunk, and one damaged. The escorts had been unable to shake off *U47*, and were swamped by the combination of night, surface attacks, and the weight of numbers. The rate of sinking was nearly 19,000 tons per hour.

Of the U-boats ordered to these two convoys, only *U28* had failed to achieve any success. The other seven had sunk 33 ships totalling 158,273 tons, and damaged six totalling 31,891 tons. These totals amounted to 54 per cent of all sinkings in that month, and were the ultimate proof of Dönitz's tactic. And yet more firepower was arriving. In October a second flotilla, the 7th, had begun operating from St.-Nazaire. Dönitz was concentrating all his efforts on the North Atlantic convoys for the simple reason that there were no other targets. The lack of German air reconnaissance was the only leavening of the situation from the British point of view.

British reaction to these successes was concentrated on determining how they were possible. The answer was readily available: there had been too great a reliance placed on Asdic. In the minds of the Naval Staff the submarine threat of the First World War had been negated by the mere presence of Asdic, and the majority of training of both the Royal Navy and Coastal Command had been devoted to anti-surface raider tactics. Submariners in the Royal Navy were of the same persuasion: anti-merchant shipping attacks would be from below the surface, and Asdic would stop that. Dönitz had, as has been said, countered this with his training, insisting upon surfaced attacks at night, thus robbing the Navy of the advantage it thought it had in its anti-submarine equipment. The escorts and other defending craft had to return to visual observation, and at night the U-boat's profile was easily missed; in even a slight swell they were almost impossible to see. Another factor was that many of the escorts were no faster on the surface than the aggressors, and often less manoeuvrable.

Prien even went one step further, entering the body of the convoy itself and attacking from there, where the convoys were utterly defenceless. Added to all these factors against the defenders was the constant and chronic shortage of escort vessels, lack of experienced officers and crews, and lamentably bad communications between ships at sea. From Dönitz's point of view nothing could have been better; his tactic worked, he was sending more U-boats to sea every month, and losses were negligible. Up to the end of October only two U-boats had been lost since June, and *U32* was only lost after she had sunk her target, the 42,348-ton *Empress of Britain*, on 28 October 1940.

Dönitz's tactics were both a strength and, surprisingly, a weakness. The two salient factors were the shadowing U-boat and radio communications. The shadower acted as a mobile information centre, relaying course, speed and details of a convoy to U-boat Command, and from there the information was transformed into orders for other boats. The weakness came if the shadower were sunk, or effectively removed from contact, for then the link would be broken and the mass of U-boats rendered ineffective. On the other hand, if German radio signals could be read, convoys could be re-routed to avoid concentrations. Unfortunately for the British, the U-boat cipher 'Dolphin' was not being read at this time, so there was little more than direction-finding to go on, and guesswork as a substitute for hard intelligence.

Whereas October ended with 42 convoyed ships having been sunk of a total of 69 ships sunk in all, November was much less successful for the U-boats. Attacks on OB.244 and SC.11 garnered seven sinkings from each, but only three boats, U100, U103 and U123 managed to contact these two convoys. In fact only six boats made attacks at all that month, proving that luck had been on their side in October, especially in view of the still small number of U-boats available to patrol an increasingly large operational area. Indeed Dönitz's methods did not meet universal success. In September the operation against SC.2 should have involved a total of six boats, but only two arrived. Even the attack on HX.72 was short by four boats. In October a patrol line of five boats established north of the Rockall Bank made no contact whatsoever with the enemy, and a similar instance occurred during November, when nine U-boats and four Italian submarines were operating together west of the North Channel. Only one of the Italian boats made contact with HX.84, and this despite its being attacked by an Fw 200 of Kampfgeschwader 40.

But perhaps the most important single occurrence of the month from the point of view of both sides, although known at the time only to the British, was the sighting of either U47 or U100 when approaching HX.84. This sighting was on the A-scope of an ASV-I radar set, newly fitted into a Sunderland of Coastal Command. Although the flying-boat could do nothing, this first radar location of a U-boat meant a great deal to the Royal Navy, which could now begin to fill the gap created by their inability to locate surfaced U-boats except by eye. The weather and night were no longer an enemy, so long as the set was working.

November, as noted above, was relatively quiet; 36 ships were sunk, of which sixteen were in convoy. Two convoy attacks were pressed home during the month, with seven ships from each being sunk. OB.244 was sighted by U103 on the 20th when the U-boat was part of a patrol line to the west of the North Channel. The line consisted of nine U-boats and three Italian submarines. Following normal tactics, U103 signalled details to U-boat Command, and then attacked. She sank two ships with one salvo from her forward tubes, but was then driven off in a depth-charge attack by HMS Rhododendron. Contact was lost for two days until U123 regained it, just as the convoy was dispersing, and Moehle proceeded to sink five ships. But his attack had been luck, for the mass of U-boats had been unable to approach and finish off U103's initial assault.

SC.11 was contacted at almost the same time by *U100*, and Schepke sank seven ships from that convoy in seven attacks between 0018 and 2105 hours on 23 November. Schepke had been on his own, and he pressed home an attack because the enemy coastline of Donegal was in sight. Schepke was truly one of the 'aces' under Dönitz's command, and while he was alive contributed a great deal to the history of the U-boats. Many other U-boat commanders were still untried, and had one of them had the same opportunity, the result might not have been the same.

The following week saw no contact with convoys, and it was not until 1 December that the Italian submarine *Argo* attacked HG.47 in the Rockall Bank area. She was on patrol with two other Italian submarines and nine U-boats, when she made her approach and sank the Canadian destroyer *Saguenay*. But the U-boats were more interested in a convoy sighted further west by *U101*. This was HX.90 with a sole escort, the AMC *Laconia*. The Ocean Escort had departed, and during the night of 1/2 December, before the local escort arrived, *U101*, *U52* and *U47* torpedoed nine ships, of which six sank that night. Further north another auxiliary cruiser, HMS *Forfar*, was lost to *U99* when her escort was diverted to HX.90. When that ship, the destroyer HMS *St Laurent*, came into contact with the convoy she was joined by the sloop *Folkestone*, the corvette *Gentian* and another destroyer, HMS *Viscount*. An Italian submarine was swiftly driven off, and contact with the convoy was lost, despite attempts by aircraft of I/KG40 to re-establish it. Then, in the afternoon *U94* found the convoy again and *U95* and *U99* joined in. Three ships were sunk, including the already-damaged *Conch*. The final score in favour of the U-boats was nine ships sunk and three damaged for no loss to themselves.

There were other convoy attacks during the month, but none on the scale of that on HX.90; individual boats were involved in most cases, and Lehmann-Willenbrock in *U94* sank four ships from HX.92. In fact by the end of the month the Italians were more active against the convoys than the Germans. So ended 1940, and Dönitz could take stock, consider the results of his tactics, and whether changes were necessary. His U-boats had sunk 658 ships totalling 2,948,448 tons, of which 158 (839,469 tons) had been in convoy. This latter figure represented 28.5 per cent of total sinkings, but was only a very small proportion of the total sailings in convoy during the first sixteen months of the war. He had for much of the period been short of operational U-boats, and only three true group operations had taken place: a group of four U-boats in January, and two groups of seven and five boats in June. Other convoy contacts had been accidental, and, as noted, mainly by individual boats. In 1941, with increasing strength, he would be able to mount 22 group operations against convoys. As early as 26 April Dönitz had reported to Hitler his decision to plan for the future, and withdraw some U-boats from operations to form a training establishment, to prepare for the increase in U-boats soon to come.

The year 1940 had seen another strategic advantage for Dönitz; not only was he to have a strong U-boat Arm, but also Atlantic bases from which they could operate. He also had a base being prepared at Trondheim in Norway. He had a further slight advantage in the presence of Italian submarines in the Atlantic, often co-operating with the U-boats. Although they were obviously not too happy about the Atlantic weather, they were additional sources of intelligence to the BdU. They did not press home their attacks with the same zeal as the German U-boat commanders, but they can perhaps be forgiven for taking the attitude that this particular war was very much of German choosing.

It has been mentioned frequently that Raeder and Dönitz had been pressing Hitler for more U-boats since the beginning of the war. Until July 1940 the land battles had occupied his mind to the exclusion of the Atlantic, no doubt regarded as essentially a side-show to the events in the main arena. Then, on 31 July, Hitler gave the Navy what it wanted. He gave them the steel and other materials required, and more importantly he made the manpower available to build the new U-boats. Many shipyard workers had been hurriedly called up into the Army in 1939, to swell its numbers in view of impending war. These men could now be released to the yards again, where there contribution would be far greater than in the front line. On 13 August Raeder made a further point to Hitler, after discussing the time-scales of Operation 'Seelöwe'. He pointed out that torpedoes and torpedo tubes also needed priority, because of increased torpedo consumption and the needs of the new boats respectively. Torpedo expenditure had increased because the use of Lorient as a base speeded up the pace of the U-boat offensive, with U-boats spending a much higher proportion of their time at sea actually in their operational areas. Göring was also pressing for new equipment as the *Luftwaffe* was now seriously engaged against the Royal Air Force over England.

The matter was left to the Chief of Staff, OKW, General Halder. He was of the pre-Nazi old school, and he gave Raeder his priority, balancing this with some concessions to Göring. The German attitude to its Air Force was less committed than the British, and it never managed to become a 'strategic' element in German planning. Despite some efforts (failure of which led to at least two suicides by very senior officers) Germany never had an effective long-range, four-engined, high-load bomber, already developed in the United States and Great Britain. The *Luftwaffe* had condemned itself by virtue of its efficiency to the roles it had so effectively performed in Poland and the west – as aerial artillery preparing the ground for advancing troops, and as immediate cover for those troops at the front. But it had another role which was highly important to the U-boat Arm, and which it had yet to fulfil. The problem was common to both sides; charismatic air force leaders unwilling to release aircraft for truly strategic tasks, which had the disadvantage of not covering those commanders with the glory emanating from the heat of battle.

The strategic situation at sea had been presented to Hitler by Raeder on 14 November 1940, when he described the Atlantic (i.e., the North Channel) operations area:

> The great successes of our submarines at the end of October are now decreasing. This is unavoidable in view of the necessary overhauling and relief. It will be offset somewhat by operations of Italian submarines in the North Atlantic ... Recently there have been appreciable losses in supplies for Great Britain resulting from the successful warfare waged against merchant shipping by submarines and the Air Force. Reports from Great Britain confirm the seriousness of the situation and the anxiety felt there regarding the supply situation. In his last speech Churchill said that the submarine danger is more serious than the continual air attacks, and that large-scale preparations will be necessary in order to meet the very serious dangers from submarines in the coming year.

He went on to say that the main aim of Germany's war against Great Britain had to be the interruption of supply shipments. He also warned that American aid was becoming very significant in this field, for the weakness of the escorts was slowly being eliminated by the provision of more ships from the United States. He added that 'an increase in anti-submarine activity is already perceptible'. To combat this he argued that submarine building had to have superior priorities in materials and manpower. It was typical of German resource allocation throughout the war that too many projects, often duplicated, were pursued, all of which called for resources that would have been better used by allocation to war-winning projects, such as the submarine building programme, and a co-ordinated aircraft and tank programme. Luckily for the Allies, at this time there was no one man who had the power to co-ordinate all these efforts, and when one (Speer) was appointed, it was too late for him to do more than increase production for defence.

By 3 December the respective roles of the *Luftwaffe* and the Navy were clearly delineated: the Navy was to attack communications at sea, while the *Luftwaffe* was to attack British industry and harbour installations. It would be of advantage if the *Luftwaffe* were to sink escorts, for Dönitz saw torpedoes fired at escorts as wasted. In fact, had he at this time embarked upon a secondary anti-escort campaign he could have benefited greatly later in the war. Christmas saw a gathering on 27 December at tea-time, when Raeder reviewed the whole naval situation. He stressed the United States' assistance again, pointing out the value of it, and said, 'Great Britain's ability to maintain her supply lines is definitely the decisive factor for the outcome of the war.' He added that the naval staff was utterly convinced that 'German submarines ... are the decisive weapons against Great Britain.' He was right. The relationship with the United States was fundamental to Great Britain's survival and eventual resurgence, and is of primary importance to an understanding of the Second World War.

Hitler now began to think again in terms of the requirements of the Navy, and declared that production of U-boats at the figure of 12 to 18 per month was too low. He accepted Raeder's advice on this, and agreed with the proposition that 20, and preferably thirty, U-boats per month was the correct figure. Unfortunately Hitler was already engrossed in plans for the east, and the U-boats were peripheral to the mainstream of his thought. He said, 'It is necessary at all costs to eliminate the last enemy on the continent before he can collaborate with Great Britain. For this purpose the Army must be made sufficiently strong.' Only after the defeat of Russia would Hitler release to the Navy and the Air Force the resources they desperately needed. The Navy never actually achieved its target, and the highest wartime production of U-boats came too late. Maximum production up to the winter of 1942/3 was 24 U-boats in one month, with an monthly average of below 20.

Hitler's reluctance to commit resources to the Navy was the product of his inability to understand and sympathise with naval strategy. Fighting as an infantryman in the First World War, and constant exposure to the German Army in the thirties does not make a staff officer, and certainly not a consummate Grand Strategist. He had proved himself an adept opportunist, but this very ability left him bereft of the mind spread to plan on a world scale. Large troop movements are relatively simple to conceive, global strategy and forward planning are something else, and he had no imagination beyond the land battle. The German fighting man was on average superior to his opponents, and had there been sufficient equipment available to the Navy at this stage, the Battle of the Atlantic might still have been won. The lightning successes of the Army in the west led everyone to believe that the same was possible in the vastness of Russia.

What the Germans failed to realise was that if there were any setbacks to a speedy conclusion in the east, the German economy would be hard-pressed to cope with them. Men alone were not enough, despite all their bravery, loyalty and undoubted skill. The technical demands of warfare were becoming so great in terms of *matériel* and equipment that only a fully-geared war economy could cope with them, and even the United States was nowhere near being on such a footing: Germany was still economically at peace. Great Britain had to rely upon the US warehouse for the very basics of existence. Germany had almost gone too far, even in 1940, into the area where productive capacity was the winner of wars, not merely skill. In planning to invade Russia Hitler was committing cardinal errors of judgement: he would involve Germany in the long-dreaded two-front war, and he was sending a largely horse-drawn Army into a land where only efficiently mechanised, massive armies could hope to prevail.

The Navy could however look back on 1940 as being a relatively successful year, bearing in mind the size of the U-boat Arm (in particular). For the loss of 22 U-boats the operational Flotillas had sunk 510 ships, 139 of them in convoy. Operations had not been solely confined to the North Channel, where the British still had no remedy against the U-boats. Limited range aircraft, and no ocean escorts of value left ships very much at the mercy of the U-boats, which could virtually queue up to torpedo targets. UA (the ex-Turkish submarine *Batiray*) had been sent south down the African coast in July and August, and had had some limited success. In December *U37* was operating off the Moroccan coast, and Italian submarines had travelled as far south as Sierra Leone, attacking traffic in the Freetown area. In general however the range of the Type IX U-boats and of the improved Type VIIs was being translated into patrol endurance time, for they were still concentrated for operational purposes in battle areas at most a few days cruising from their French bases. More and more boats were now located in France, and the 2nd and 7th Uflotillas were fully operational from Lorient and St.-Nazaire.

# FINDING THE CONVOYS  7

At the beginning of 1941 Dönitz had a total of 89 commissioned U-boats, of which 46 were operational. One of the latter was earmarked for the Commander of the new 3rd Uflotilla, due to come on strength in March. First Uflotilla had nineteen boats by then, and was due to operate from Brest in June, after building up its complement. In June 2nd Uflotilla had 21 U-boats, and 7th Uflotilla 26. The training Flotillas (22, 23 and 24) held the majority of the remainder, including the Type II boats retired from Atlantic operations, a total of 43 U-boats. On 7 January another dimension was added to Dönitz's operational command, for a *Geschwader* of *Kampfgruppe 40* was put under his direct command. This was the long-awaited air reconnaissance element, and the CO, Major Petersen, was directly responsible to Dönitz. The aircraft, all Fw 200 '*Kondor*' four-engined bombers, were based at Mérignac airfield near Bordeaux, which was also the headquarters of the *Fliegerführer Atlantik*, Colonel Harlinghausen. Dönitz had already moved his headquarters from Paris to Lorient in November 1940, and so the entire anti-shipping force was concentrated as near to the operational area as possible. Both U-boats and aircraft would save time and fuel to get to their patrol areas.

The unit, I/KG 40, had considerable anti-shipping experience, for it had been formed before the war began, first as a reconnaissance and then as an operational anti-shipping bombing squadron. The aircraft was not really strong enough to carry a heavy bomb load (the original design had a civilian role), but the military C-range aircraft had sunk a total of 360,000 tons of shipping up to February 1941. The range was sufficient to allow a unit of the squadron to operate against Icelandic targets from the Bordeaux base. It was the answer to Dönitz's plea for reconnaissance aircraft, having a range of some 1,000 miles and a duration of fourteen hours. The aircraft could patrol as far out as Rockall Bank.

Operations in January, even with aircraft patrols, did not achieve anything significant until the end of the month. Italian submarines had been out to the west of Ireland, with scattered U-boats further north. Then, on 28 January the Fw 200s on reconnaissance reported a convoy in the approaches to the North Channel. Six U-boats nearby were ordered to close and attack. Only three of them reached SC.19, but they sank five ships. In the course of these early attempts at air–sea co-operation, the aircraft often bettered the U-boat sink-ings, for they sighted many convoys going in both directions, but only two were attacked as a result of the information they transmitted to Lorient. They were of course able to attack as well as find the convoys, and they sank fifteen ships, damaged two more (later sunk by U-boats) and caused some damage to three others. But on four occasions air contact could not be followed up by the U-boats; Dönitz and his staff were untrained in air–sea liaison, and had to learn the lessons the Royal Navy and Coastal Command had spent the last seventeen months practising.

The same thing happened in February, and the aircraft themselves failed to locate a target until the 18th. The U-boats had however found some targets. There were six U-boats patrolling in the North Channel area, and U123 was farther west as weather boat. The Italians were even further out, under their own command. On 3 February U107 sighted and attacked OB.279, but the other boats (U123, U52, U96 and U103) could not reach the convoy. Stragglers from SC.20 were then attacked by U123 and U107. In the meantime U37 had been off the Spanish coast where she located HG.53, which she attacked five times during the morning of 9 February, sinking two ships. U37 then shadowed the convoy, having run out of torpedoes. This enabled the aircraft of II/KG40 to attack during the day with five Fw200s, sinking five more vessels. U37 maintained contact throughout the night of 9/10 February, and sank another ship in the morning. So far there had been air sea co-operation, but now submarine/surface vessel operations took over as Admiral Hipper (cruising in the area) was ordered to attack the convoy on the basis of U37's reports. She found only a straggler, but then fell upon SLS.64 which was unescorted. She sank seven of the nine ships in the convoy, and damaged the other two. She then sailed for her Atlantic base at Brest.

The operation was the result of fortunate circumstance however, not planning, and German air–sea–U-boat co-operation never achieved the level achieved by the Allies. However, the Fw 200s were finding targets. Attacks on OB.287 were made only by aircraft, because the position report sent by them to Lorient was inaccurate. (This problem continued to frustrate air–sea operations throughout the period of U-boat operations from France, and never had a satisfactory solution.) Five U-boats and three Italian submarines spent 19 February chasing around the Iceland–Faroes Gap without success. Then the aircraft got another contact and sent the correct position. Convoy OB.288 was located west of Ireland and Dönitz immediately set up a patrol line on the reported course with U73, U69, U107, U552, U97 and two Italian boats.

U73 got a contact on the morning of 22 February, only to lose it, but the contact was regained the following day by a patrol line of four U-boats and two Italian submarines. U99, U69 and U73 attacked, U96 sinking one ship. The convoy then turned away to the north, and the Fw 200s missed it. Then, just after midnight on the 23rd U95, U96 and U69 attacked again. As the convoy scattered in panic, six ships were lost, bringing the total sinkings (including a straggler) to eight. Not far to the north U97 was attacking OB.289 and sank three ships the same morning, but with no support for U97 the rest of the convoy escaped. It had been located by U552, which had had torpedo faults in her attack; *U95* and *U108* failed to arrive, leaving *U97* alone. Two days later OB.290 was attacked as it approached the north coast of Ireland. *U47* and the ubiquitous Prien had just entered the area, and he shadowed the convoy into the night of 25 February. He attacked just after midnight, supported by the Italian submarine *Bianchi*. He sank four ships, and *Bianchi* added a fifth with one ship damaged.

Again the U-boat campaign was beginning to bite, but the U-boats were slowly but inexorably being pushed away from the immediate area of the North Channel and the Rockall Bank. British air cover and slightly increased escort numbers were beginning to have effect, although not yet in terms of U-boat sinkings. No U-boats were sunk from December 1940 to March 1941, and they had sunk 70 ships in January and February of the new year, 42 of them from five convoys. Thirteen stragglers from other convoys were sunk, high-lighting a problem that was to dog the Allied navies throughout the war. The convoy escort had only one recourse with stragglers – leave them. Any diversion of even a single escort vessel left the convoy that much less protected, and the safety of the majority was paramount.

The first wolf-pack attack in March was planned against OB.292 in area AL. On the 2nd the convoy was located by an Fw 200 which then sank one ship. Six U-boats and two Italian submarines were ordered to form a patrol line across the convoy course and three more Fw 200s were sent to reconnoitre next day. Not until the 4th did an Fw 200 sight the convoy again, and this time a patrol line of five U-boats and the Italian *Velella* was ordered for the 5th. All of this effort was wasted, however, for the large volume of radio traffic led the Submarine Tracking Room to re-route the convoy past the second patrol line. This was an effective method of combating the U-boats, but was dependent upon sufficient radio traffic from the Germans; in this case decipherable *Luftwaffe* transmissions helped the British (slipshod radio procedures frequently presented Bletchley Park with errors which helped decryption; some of the greatest mistakes were made by the *Luftwaffe*). Whenever a U-boat located a convoy, it made every effort to stay in contact with it and with Lorient. The shadower U-boat was the subject of a lot of thought later in the year, and when the Submarine Training School was set up in England in 1942, anti-U-boat tactics and counter-measures centred on it.

Electronic measures could not avoid the next attacks, for they were against convoys located by U-boats and surface vessels. OB.293 was found by Prien who led *U70* and *U99* in on the night of 6/7 March, but they were driven off by the escort, except for *U70* which got among the ships and was sunk after her attack by HM ships *Arbutus* and *Camelli*. *UA* made contact next day, failed to sink anything because of torpedo defects, and was then severely damaged by depth-charges. *U99* made brief contact, but *U37* stayed away. This may have been prudent, for the escort had sunk one U-boat and damaged another when *U47* went once more into the attack. A heavy squall had sprung up and the valuable Prien was surprised on the surface by HMS *Wolverine* which sank the U-boat. If other U-boats had been able to join, the operation could have been successful, but their failure resulted in a net loss to the U-boat Arm, including one of the most able and experienced commanders. The escorts had a lot to be pleased about, having sunk two U-boats (unknown to them, a third had been damaged). The proof of the convoy system was here: the U-boats had to approach the escorts to get at the convoys, and the escorts could destroy them at their point of concentration. Many people remained sceptical.

The loss of Prien was serious for Dönitz for he was one of his top commanders. He had sunk 29 ships, damaged another six, and had sunk HMS *Royal Oak*, the escapade for which he had been lionised. This was in an operational career spanning eighteen months. But the loss of the two U-boats in the action against OB.293 *might* have been counter-balanced by the attack on SL.67. On the morning of 7 March *Scharnhorst* and *Gneisenau* sighted the convoy off the West African coast. The presence in the escort of HMS *Malaya* (the battleship) caused Admiral Lutjens to steer away, but he signalled Lorient.

There were two U-boats in the area, and Dönitz ordered them in immediately. They came up on the night of 7/8 March, and sank five ships. *Malaya* was not sighted, but the U-boats were driven off by two destroyers and a corvette at first light. The next convoy sighting was far to the north, just south of Iceland, where HX.112 ran into a patrol line of five U-boats and six Italian submarines. *U110* reported the convoy and *U37*, *U74*, *U99* and *U100* were ordered in as support. Lemp, in *U110*, had less success against HX.112 than he had had in *U30* against *Athenia*, only managing to damage one ship in the course of three attacks. *U106* sank one ship, but Kretschmer in *U99* did the lion's share of the work. He sank five ships and damaged one before running out of torpedoes; as he withdrew another 'ace', Schepke, took his place. However, the escorts *Scimitar*, *Vanoc* and *Walker* all had radar and *U100* was quickly located and, as she tried to dive, was rammed and sunk by *Vanoc*. Then, as *Vanoc*, screened by *Walker*, went to pick up survivors, *U99* submerged, only to be picked up by Asdic. *Walker* forced her to the surface with six depth-charges and she surrendered, Kretschmer (alone of these 'aces') surviving, with 45 of his men. The escorts were beginning to fight back: Asdic and radar were proving their worth, and Dönitz had lost three top commanders in a few days.

Luckily for Dönitz he was not now wholly bereft of experienced and very able men, but with this action the whole campaign took on a much more serious aspect. More ships were now concentrated in convoy than before, the escorts were getting bloodthirsty, and they had had some real successes to their credit. The balance was shifting away from being almost entirely in favour of the U-boat Arm. Furthermore, operations were now extending to areas other than the 'hunting-ground' of the North Channel. Dönitz had made tentative efforts in other areas to the west and south in the hope of richer pickings and to avoid air patrols. In the south convoys to and from Freetown, Sierra Leone and the Mediterranean via Gibraltar were worth attacking. The move against SL.67 had been the first such attack, the U-boats which located it having been allocated tropical operational areas. SL.68 was also attacked nine days later, after location by *U106* just off the West African coast on 17 March. Oesten reported the convoy, and then attacked with *U105*. In a conflict lasting almost exactly five days they sank seven merchantmen. Unknown to *U106* was the fact that he had also damaged *Malaya*, escorting SL.68 just as she had escorted SL.67. After such a long but successful chase, both U-boats returned to base.

Schultze, captain of *U48*, was an old hand at anti-shipping operations. He was operating in the northern area at the end of the month. His tactics were to locate a target convoy and make one telling attack before the escort could react, and then retreat at best speed. In less than two hours against HX.115 he sank four ships in five separate attacks, whereas when *U46* and *U69* attacked OB.302 they took fourteen hours to sink two ships. Schultze's method was in fact modified and adopted by Dönitz later in the war, for he ordered U-boat groups to assemble at a convoy following guidance from the shadower and to make the most effective use of the first night, knowing that thereafter there was only occasionally an opportunity for further effective attacks. The month, despite the losses of the 'aces', ended on a high note for Dönitz, for the U-boats had sunk more than 70 per cent of their total score of merchant ships in convoy.

It is of importance to take a look at the statistics of the war at this point. There are many critics of the U-boat campaign who argue that in fact Dönitz never came near to cutting the Atlantic lifeline; if one has regard to the raw figures, this can be argued successfully. Sailings in the first three months in and out of UK ports totalled more than 3,000 (ships in cargo and in ballast, in foreign trade only). The U-boats sank 113 ships out of this total of sailings. Furthermore, the total tonnage available to the British merchant fleet was as follows:

| Year and Quarter | | Gains '000 GRT | Losses '000 GRT |
|---|---|---|---|
| 1939 | September | 50 | 149 |
| | 4th | 347 | 312 |
| 1940 | 1st | 295 | 335 |
| | 2nd | 901 | 473 |
| | 3rd | 717 | 892 |
| | 4th | 467 | 956 |
| 1941 | 1st | 558 | 992 |

These figures show a mean loss of 764,000 gross tons. Some authors argue that this loss was compensated by the large tonnages that came under the control of the British in requisitioned ships, time charters and so on. This is quite true, but the net loss against the figure for 1939 stands, and if Dönitz had been able to break the convoy system he would then have had easy pickings and would have achieved Raeder's aim. Had this occurred there has to be some question as to the ability of the Great Britain to survive as the one European country standing out against Hitler, and denied American supplies.

British yards were building ships as fast as they could and repairing damaged ships, and soon there would be a British yard turning out merchant ships in America, but the situation was getting serious. In 1940 British yards had launched 771,000 gross tons of shipping over 1,600 tons, but the Germans in the same period had sunk 2,125,000 gross tons throughout the Atlantic, a high proportion of which was British. Furthermore, not only were the ships lost, but their cargoes as well. Losses were to exceed gains for some time to come.

In April the pace slowed, with the U-boats seeking less dangerous quarry. Of 44 ships sunk that month, only sixteen were in convoy, against two U-boats lost while attacking convoys. On 2 April SC.26 had the misfortune of running into a patrol line of eight U-boats. A number of these had unsuccessfully attacked OB.302 at the end of March; they moved in quickly, U76 having reported the convoy's presence to Lorient 1 April. U76 shadowed and then joined U74, U73, U69, U94 and U98 in the attack. Between midnight and first light on 2/3rd, they sank nine ships, but U76 was sunk by HM ships *Wolverine* and *Scarborough* just before dawn. There then came a respite for the convoys until the end of the month when HX.121 was attacked. In the afternoon of 28 April U65, U96 and U552 made contact and by mid-evening when they broke off, four vessels had been sunk. During the attack, constantly emphasising the danger to the U-boats from the escorts, U65 was lost to HMS *Gladiolus*.

On 26 March the Battle of Cape Matapan had opened. Although not affecting the U-boat campaign directly in any way, the Germans became rapidly aware of the fact that radar had been used during the battle, and very effectively. HM ships *Ajax* and *Warspite* were fitted with gunnery control radar and their accurate night bombardment of the Italian Fleet, during which two cruisers and two destroyers were sunk, was conclusive proof. The sinking of U100 in the Atlantic by *Vanoc* brought the matter closer to home and although Dönitz was not fully aware of the details, a Type 286 radar had brought about the first radar-controlled U-boat sinking of the war. The extent of progress made in the UK was not known to the Germans, but the tactics of the U-boats were soon to be conditioned by it.

May saw increasing U-boat activity on the convoy routes, but there were only two significant attacks. The month began badly for air–sea co-operation; the Fw 200s located a convoy south-west of the Faroes, but once more the U-boats were unable to find it from the position signalled by the *Luftwaffe*. Further contacts with convoys were made by the U-boats, but there was a failure to follow-up by other boats in the area. By 6 May Dönitz finally gave up all ideas of direct air–sea co-operation, and he also directed that the Italian submarines were to operate separately from the U-boats.

The next day, 7 May, a flood of sightings poured into U-boat Command. HX.122 was sighted by an Fw 200, SC.29 was sighted by *U95* off the North Channel, and then *U94* found OB.318 off the west coast of Ireland. OB.318 was accompanied by 3 Escort Group (three destroyers and the AMC *Ranpura*) and part of 7 Escort Group (one sloop and five corvettes). Kuppisch attacked, and sank two ships before being damaged by depth-charges from three of the escorts. 3 Escort Group then left the convoy for HX.123 as the remainder of 7 Escort Group (three corvettes and three trawlers) joined the main body with the convoy. *U110* made contact in the evening, and on 9 May signalled *U201* to join. They attacked this strongly-defended convoy at 1200 and 1400 hours, sinking three vessels and damaging one.

*U110* had just made her attack when she was forced to the surface by HMS *Aubretia's* depth-charges. The result of the capture has already been noted. The intelligence thus provided was to save many convoys from attack, and an estimated total of some one and one half million tons from sinking. The attack on the convoy was resumed on 10 May and Wohlfarth in *U556* sank two more ships and damaged a third. In all the convoy, despite the strength of its escort, lost nine ships of totalling more than 50,000 tons. The engagement showed that escorts were still unpractised in working in such large formations (there were ten ships escorting the convoy), but the size of this particular escort is worth noting. Of greater importance was the fact that convoys were soon to be escorted right across the Atlantic, thanks to US co-operation.

After the relative success of the operation against OB.318, eight U-boats were stationed SSW of Cape Farewell as 'Group West'. Six of them attacked HX.126 which was first sighted by *U94* on the 19th, south-east of Greenland. She sank two ships before losing contact. Re-located next day by *U556*, the convoy was attacked by five U-boats between mid-afternoon and first light on the 21st. Nine ships were sunk and one damaged, and *U94* was damaged on the second day of the operation, just as contact was lost.

During this five month period air reconnaissance and direct *Luftwaffe*–U-boat co-operation was a failure. Incorrect position reports from the aircraft led inevitably to frustration in the crews and exasperation among the staff. There seemed to be no solution to the problem, for aircrews were incapable of plotting exact positions once they were a few hours away from land. Changing drift caused by shifting winds misled them in their navigation (as it did for Coastal Command), and only an inertial or satellite navigation system would have helped – neither of which was available. Considering that the RAF bomber squadrons were similarly inconvenienced in operations against Germany, despite the advantages of having the terrain below them, it is clear that dead reckoning was no longer more than a vague guide.

January had been a quiet month in the battle at sea. This was due, Raeder told Hitler on 4 February, to bad weather and the continuing shortage of operational U-boats. At the beginning of the year there had been 42 operational U-boats, in three flotillas. By the end of May there were to be 87, double the number. Dönitz had had a total of 139 commissioned boats in January, but as he was constantly increasing the training function, not every boat was sent straight to an operational flotilla. In fact he had had 46 training boats in January, and still had the same number in May. The relative strength of the U-boat Arm was increasing. In 1940 reorganisation had reduced the number of flotillas from seven to four. The total reached seven again in January 1941, of which three were training units. A further reorganisation took place in mid-1941, to take account of the increased number of newly commissioned U-boats available for operations. The flotillas and their strengths throughout 1941 were as follows:

| Flotilla | Jan | Feb | Mar | Apr | May | Jun | July | Aug | Sept | Oct | Nov | Dec |
|---|---|---|---|---|---|---|---|---|---|---|---|---|
| 1 (Opl) | 3 | 10 | 18 | 26 | 24 | 23 | 23 | 21 | 22 | 19 | 17 | 13 |
| 2 (Opl) | 17 | 18 | 19 | 19 | 19 | 20 | 22 | 24 | 23 | 23 | 23 | 23 |
| 3 (Trg) | 1 | 2 | 2 | 9 | 24 | 27 | 27 | 26 | 24 | 23 | 21 | 16 |
| 4 (Trg) | | | | | 1 | 2 | 5 | 7 | 12 | 18 | 24 | 27 |
| 5 (Trg) | | | | | | 2 | 13 | 19 | 21 | 18 | 19 | 20 |
| 6 (Opl) | | | | | | | 6 | 12 | 21 | 22 | 23 | 24 |
| 7 (Opl) | 25 | 25 | 20 | 19 | 18 | 22 | 24 | 23 | 24 | 23 | 22 | 18 |
| 21 (Trg) | 19 | 19 | 19 | 17 | 16 | 16 | 16 | 17 | 20 | 20 | 20 | 20 |
| 22 (Trg) | 18 | 18 | 18 | 17 | 16 | 16 | 16 | 16 | 17 | 17 | 17 | 17 |
| 23 (Opl) (only until March 1942) | | | | | | | | | 3 | 6 | 6 | |
| 24 (Trg) | 9 | 9 | 10 | 10 | 10 | 10 | 10 | 9 | 7 | 7 | 7 | 8 |
| 26 (Trg) | | | | 1 | 3 | 5 | 6 | 6 | 6 | 6 | 6 | 6 |
| 29 (Opl) | | | | | | | | | | | 1 | 4 |
| **Totals:** | | | | | | | | | | | | |
| All boats | 92 | 101 | 106 | 128 | 131 | 143 | 163 | 180 | 197 | 199 | 206 | 201 |
| Of these: | | | | | | | | | | | | |
| Opl | 45 | 53 | 57 | 74 | 61 | 65 | 75 | 80 | 90 | 90 | 92 | 88 |
| Trg | 47 | 48 | 49 | 54 | 70 | 78 | 93 | 100 | 107 | 109 | 114 | 113 |

Note: the figures of training boats in the 3rd, 4th and 5th Flotillas represented boats working up for operations and were released to operational flotillas after their training period (about six months). This meant that the operational strength grew extremely quickly and consistently during 1941.

Many other matters had made demands upon Hitler's time during this five-month period. Most important was the preparation of Operation 'Barbarossa', the invasion of Russia. The majority of the Army and the Air Force would be involved actively, but the Navy was little concerned with the operation. Hitler said that as far as western Europe was concerned 'Our position ... is so firmly established' that even if the battle for Africa were lost 'the outcome cannot possibly be to our disadvantage ... The British can hope to win the war only by besting us on the continent.' He continued: 'all attacks [on Great Britain] must be concentrated on supplies and the armaments industry ... Combined raids by the Air Force and the Navy on imports might lead to victory as early as July or August.'

He then discussed other aspects of the international situation, saying, 'If the USA and Russia should enter the war against Germany, the situation would become very complicated. Hence any possibility for such a threat to develop must be eliminated from the beginning.' By this he meant that Russia had to be eliminated, not the threat of war from her. By 4 February plans for the forthcoming operation were at the detail stage, with the Navy being 'concentrated against Great Britain as planned'. At the same conference Raeder noted, 'The growth of Great Britain's sea power ... there is a great increase in the number of smaller vessels, such as destroyers, torpedo-boats, submarines, escort vessels, gunboats and minesweepers, the continuous production of which will have an unfavourable effect on our submarine warfare.' The race was reaching a crucial phase, but Hitler was oblivious to the fact.

It was probably on the basis of the discussion during this 4 February Führer Conference on Naval Affairs that Hitler issued Directive 23, relating to the prosecution of the war against England. It ordered *inter alia*:

Contrary to all our previous conceptions, the strongest blow to the British War Economy was the high figures for losses in merchant ships as a result of the sea and air war ... A further considerable increase in the effects of our war effort can be expected when our U-boat operations are intensified during the course of this year, and this may lead before long to the collapse of British resistance.

He had underestimated the staying powers of the British, but at that time there was little to indicate that he was seriously wrong in his estimate of the situation. British operations against Germany were limited to a mostly inaccurate bombing campaign, and a number of brave but mainly irritating special operations by Commandos, such as the Svolvaer attack in the Lofotens.

The increase in U-boat activity in February continued until May, with a peak in convoy sinkings in February and March. The problem of supply was being felt by the British, and rationing was beginning to bite. The sinkings (in numbers of ships) from the beginning of the war to May 1941 are as follows:

| Year | Jan | Feb | Mar | Apr | May | Jun | July | Aug | Sept | Oct | Nov | Dec |
|------|-----|-----|-----|-----|-----|-----|------|-----|------|-----|-----|-----|
| 1939 |     |     |     |     |     |     |      |     | 48   | 33  | 27  | 39  |
| 1940 | 53  | 51  | 27  | 6   | 14  | 62  | 38   | 53  | 60   | 66  | 36  | 44  |
| 1941 | 23  | 47  | 43  | 44  | 63  |     |      |     |      |     |     |     |

The cumulative total of ships sunk up to the end of May 1941 was 877 of a total gross tonnage of 4,132,502. Of this total 35 per cent had been sunk in convoy, some 267 ships of 1,454,346 tons.

Churchill had seen the submarine threat for what it was – not merely another way for the Germans to prosecute the war against the British Isles, but a way in which they could remove her from the lists. If sinkings achieved a rate that could seriously deplete the available total tonnage for transporting supplies to the UK, despite the much increased new building, the problem of food and material shortages would become acute. Furthermore if sinkings continued at a high rate, merchant seamen might well refuse to sail for fear of their own lives. Any further reduction in tonnage imports would be serious, and increased losses could lead to a cessation of trade.

Churchill later said, of his feelings in 1940, that 'the only thing that ever frightened me during the war was the U-boat peril ... I was even more anxious about this battle [in the Atlantic] than I had been about the glorious air fight called the Battle of Britain.' He considered that the Battle of the Atlantic was fought from July 1940 to July 1941 and that Great Britain had won it. Regrettably, he was wrong about the details. Figures produced by the Ministry of Transport after the war show that cumulative losses during the period September 1939 to May 1941 were 1,374,000 GRT (that is sinkings minus new launches). Arrivals of ships engaged in foreign trade, carrying the supplies needed were:

| Year and Quarter | | Total cargo (,000 tons) |
|---|---|---|
| 1939 | September | 3581 |
| | 4th | 3560 |
| 1940 | 1st | 3475 |
| | 2nd | 3614 |
| | 3rd | 2823 |
| | 4th | 2314 |
| 1941 | 1st | 1995 |

These figures show that imports were cut severely by the combined effects of the various assaults on deep-sea trade; these figures rose slightly for the next three quarters, but fell to their lowest in 1942 and the first half of 1943. The Battle of the Atlantic was nowhere near over in July 1941; it had a further two years to run before the immediate danger was over.

The next U-boat operational phase of the war at sea properly began in August 1941, although the war itself was continuous and relentless for both sides. One significant point was reached, when Dönitz decided that air–sea 'co-operation' could not continue. The element of the *Luftwaffe* committed to the Atlantic campaign remained operational, but in its original anti-shipping role, not acting as reconnaissance for the U-boats. The failure to locate accurately was serious, for at the same time Coastal Command, facing the same problems, was increasing its overall strength and efficiency, and was already a threat to the U-boat Arm. The U-boats sailed to their operational areas as before, but acting on *Luftwaffe* intelligence only if it was felt to be worth the effort.

At the end of May the U-boats had been side-tracked for a moment. *Bismarck* and *Prinz Eugen* had moved into the Atlantic via the Denmark Strait to attack supply traffic north of the Equator for as long as conditions allowed. The Royal Navy set off in pursuit and despite losing HMS *Hood*, *Bismarck* was stalked and cornered, and sunk by gunfire and torpedoes. The only vessels capable of coming to the aid of *Bismarck* were the U-boats, but their effort was badly co-ordinated, and two patrol lines saw nothing as the battle turned away from them. Only *U556* saw some of the large British units in the chase. At 2000 hours on 26 May, Wohlfarth, captain of the U-boat, sighted 'a battleship of the *King George V* class and the aircraft carrier *Ark Royal*'. Wohlfarth was at the time in square BE, returning from the attack on HX.126 in square AJ. He had no torpedoes left. He soon lost contact in a squall and there were no further contacts with the Royal Navy, apart from sightings of star shell on the night of 26/27 May when smaller Royal Navy units were harrying the crippled ship. When *Bismarck* went down she was within air range of France, but there were no aircraft stationed on the west coast of France able to go to her assistance.

After the loss of *Bismarck*, *U74* appeared on the scene at 1900 hours on the 29th and rescued Ordinary Seaman Herbert Manthey. His survivor's report was part of Raeder's presentation of the events at the Führer Conference on 6 June. The loss of the flagship of the German Navy was a great blow. Her presence would have posed a severe threat to US–British communications across the Atlantic. The real enemy of the traffic remained the U-boat Arm, which could not be so summarily disposed of, and whose nadir would not come about until much later.

May 1941 had been relatively quiet on the convoy routes, but June saw operations increase once more. The Italians opened the assault with three of their boats attacking OG.63, from which two ships were sunk. The Italian submariners did not however live up to their illustrious forebears; there were no Pompeys, Octavians or Sullas in this war.

The U-boats were also active, attacking HX.133 and OB.336, sinking nine and damaging two merchantmen. This was immediately followed by a three U-boat concentration on SL.76, from which a further nine were sunk. So far, nine U-boats had attacked three convoys and sunk eighteen ships. U-boat Command suspected at the time that convoys were somehow being routed around the concentrations and patrol lines, and on 20 June Dönitz ordered Group West (22 U-boats) to spread itself in loose formation over the Central Atlantic. In fact the Submarine Tracking Room was using 'Z' (or Ultra) information, backing up intelligence gathered from radio-location. The positions of the U-boats were known, and intentions were deducible from their signals to and from Lorient.

Despite this advantage, OB.336 was extremely fortunate to lose only three ships. *U203* contacted the convoy soon after attacking HX.133, contact with which having been lost after she had sunk one ship. The U-boat returned to patrol and found OB.336 next day, 24 June. *U79* also got within range, and called up *U71*, *U371* and *U651*. *U71* was then driven off, but the last two U-boats sank a ship each. *U111* also joined the attack, but quickly broke off, only to be replaced by two other boats. The shadowing by the five boats proved ineffective however, and they broke away to restart the attack on HX.133. SL.76 was even more unfortunate. Located by *U69* (on passage to Las Palmas to refuel from the *Charlotte Schliemann*), the convoy lost two ships to the U-boat whose report was passed on to *U123* (already refuelled at Las Palmas). *U123* sank two more, and then settled into shadowing, only to sink another ship when it was clear that no other U-boats could get up. The shadowing had a by-product however, for although *U66* failed to make the main body of the convoy, she sank two stragglers whose position became known through Hard-egen's (*U123*) report.

By the end of that month 64 ships had been sunk, 38 per cent of them in convoy. In July German anti-convoy operations were concentrated on the Gibraltar–Sierra Leone traffic. The lack of traffic in the North Atlantic and increasing air and sea patrol activity forced Dönitz to look elsewhere for his targets, preferably outside the range of home-based aircraft of Coastal Command. The move to the Freetown area had been ordered by Lorient after the SL.76 operation, but until 18 July there was little for the U-boats to do except bask in the sun. On the 18th, however, a joint Italian–German assault on Gibraltar convoys began. On the 24th *B-Dienst* located convoys OG.69 and SL.80. Eight U-boats were sent to attack OG.69 and six to SL.80. The convoys were reported by German air reconnaissance (Fw 200s of I/KG40), and fifteen of the U-boats received target information from signals from the aircraft. SL.80 was however lost and never contacted, but OG.69 was sighted again on the 26th and *U68* came within range that afternoon, again using bearings trans-mitted by aircraft. The *Luftwaffe* had got it right – one of the few occasions when this happened.

The convoy was in serious danger, for *U68* took position as shadower, reported to Command, and *U203*, *U561*, *U126*, *U79*, *U331* and two Italian boats were ordered to make best speed to the target. Only *U203* and *U79* had any success, however, sinking two ships at a cost of seven torpedoes. For the next two days the Fw 200 aircraft dogged the convoy, and the U-boats made another attack during the night of 27/28 July. Three boats attacked that night, fired eight torpedoes and sank three ships, and Merten in *U68* also attacked a British corvette with two shots. Although flames were seen, no corvette is listed as damaged that night, and so one must assume error in the heat of battle.

Next day no fewer than five U-boats were trailing the convoy, as well as the aircraft, but only *U203* got into range, sinking two ships. The German operation was untidy, and many torpedoes were wasted. The reason was that the escort was trained and effective. At 0224 hours *U79* was forced to dive by a destroyer heading straight for her. Doubly disconcerting for the captain, for he had fired his four bow torpedoes and after manoeuvring had fired the two stern torpedoes as well. *U203* and *U331* were also forced to dive the same night, having been fired on by the escort, despite the escorts having no radar. In fact a number of the U-boats trying to get into attack positions were driven off by the escorts, but the escorts were unable to sink any of the attackers, nor any of the U-boats attacking other convoys during this month, whereas in June they had sunk two U-boats during the battle of HX.133, and two others were sunk by other escorts.

By the end of the month U-boat Command had comparatively little success to show, however, and so ordered the U-boats to concentrate once more on the North Atlantic convoy routes, with a presence left in the central area. SL81 was located by *B-Dienst* on the first day of August (convoy and Admiralty signals gave the convoy away) sailing in the North Passage bound for the West Coast ports. *U204* found the convoy on 2 August and brought *U559* up, both U-boats shadowing until 3 August when eight more U-boats arrived. That day an Fw 200 was shot down over the convoy by a Hawker Hurricane flown off the catapult ship *Maplin*, and the U-boats were denied both that day and the next, when six U-boats tried to attack. On the night of 4/5 August, however, the escort was unable to prevent the U-boats getting in, although *U401* was sunk by the defenders. Between 0150 and 0542, four U-boats managed to penetrate the screen, fired ten torpedoes and sank five ships.

The U-boats then retired from the action, and U-boat Command now had a total of 21 U-boats operating in the area south of Iceland. Ultra intelligence allowed the traffic routing to avoid the concentrations, but farther east there was some activity. On 17 August OG71 was located by an Fw 200 south-west of Ireland. Kell came up (*U204*) and shadowed for forty-eight hours before attacking and sinking the Norwegian destroyer *Bath*. As if the way had been cleared, *U559* fired four torpedoes and sank a merchantman three minutes later. Kell had resisted several opportunities to attack during his successful shadowing, and was able to take a front seat during attacks by Ju 88 aircraft sent by Air Commander, Atlantic.

Two hours after Kell finally attacked, *U201* (Schnee) sank a ship. Next morning Kell returned and sank another before handing over the shadowing to *U106*. Suhren maintained contact throughout the day and then led a renewed assault on the night of 22/23 August. He sank two, Schnee sank two more, Suhren returned to damage another and to sink the second escort, the British corvette *Zinni*. The ship damaged in Suhren's attack was then finished of by *U552*'s 88mm gun. Losses were eight merchant ships and one damaged; the attackers had once more numbered five, seemingly the maximum capable of operating with success against a convoy. What was to happen when more U-boats got into attack positions was yet, horribly, to come.

What was becoming clear to both sides was that in any anti-convoy operation by U-boats, the first twenty-four hours from the opening of the assault were the most deadly. After that period escort numbers were increased and general vigilance was much greater. Dönitz was only too aware of the value of the shock attack (his tactics always planned that a shadowing U-boat should gather forces around it before the attack was opened). Naturally the Allies were equally aware of the danger of a shadowing U-boat, and the confusion caused by attacks from two or more different vectors. There were still insufficient air and sea escorts equipped with radar. Attacks at night on the surface were still the most profitable tactic, and although this entailed casualties, the losses were not yet enough to cause Dönitz to rethink his overall tactical plan.

The last convoy attack in August was on OS.4, sighted by *U141*, stationed with seven others on a patrol line west of the North Channel. As soon as she had sent a sighting report she came under aerial attack and was forced to dive. That afternoon, however, Paulshen in *U557* gained contact, made a solo attack and sank four ships, and then began to shadow. Three more U-boats came up in the next two days, but the escorts were alert by now, and only one other ship was lost. It was on the day of the air attack on Paulshen that a new element of the battle of the Atlantic appeared. *U570* was also attacked by aircraft of 269 Squadron, Coastal Command. Forced to the surface, she surrendered to the aircraft, and when surface forces arrived, she was taken to England (later to be commissioned as *HMS Graph*). Aircraft were now capable of engaging U-boats, and had become a serious threat. On 28 August, Group Markgraf (fourteen U-boats) was ordered to concentrate south-west of Ireland. Patrolling on a concave course just north of west, on 9 September *U81* located SC.42 off the south-east coast of Greenland. She reported the convoy and began the inevitable shadowing. Five boats of the group were able to get into attacking positions between 0230 and 1719 hours on the 10th. They made two attacks each, sank eight ships and damaged a ninth. The remote position of the convoy meant that reinforcements to the escort were unavailable, and the corvettes attached to the convoy were sent to rescue survivors, making the task of the U-boats easier. *U85* made two attacks late in the afternoon.

Another five boats attacked on the night of 10/11, and then in the afternoon of 11 September they sank eight more ships. Escort reinforcements were managing to arrive, and two Canadian corvettes sank *U501*. Four more escorts joined, and the British 2nd Escort Group was also ordered up from Iceland. Air support was flown from Iceland to reinforce the defences. Speedy reinforcement became increasingly common to the Allies as the reorganisation of the escorts had its effect, and the pure numbers of escorts increased, culminating in the formation of the Support Groups, which had a telling effect. Generally, efficiency too had improved.

The net result of the SC.42 operation was 17 merchantmen sunk and two damaged, for the loss of just two U-boats (*U207* was lost to *Leamington* and

*Veteran* on the 11th.) The attack had lasted for ten days, although the fury of the first two nights was not repeated. Twelve U-boats had been involved altogether, but Dönitz could not get enough of them into the attack during those crucial first twenty-four hours. His tactic remained the same: locate and shadow a convoy until a number of U-boats were available for the assault, and then attack from all points of the compass. This would overwhelm the escorts in the ever-shortening period between the escort commander signalling for assistance and the arrival of air and sea reinforcements. The curtailing of the response time was becoming of significance to both sides.

As a counter to the increasing numbers of escorts and aircraft, Dönitz did have more U-boats at sea, and the group system was now seen to be working. In the six months from June to December 1941 twenty-nine convoys were attacked, 130 merchantmen were sunk and nine damaged. At the same time fifteen U-boats were sunk by sea and, ever increasingly, air–sea escorts.

The construction problem still facing the U-boat Arm, emphasised continuously by Raeder and Dönitz, had been the cause of contention between the three German armed services since before the war. On 22 June 1941 German ground and air units attacked Soviet Russia, in the largest confrontation of forces ever seen. The sheer magnitude of this campaign threw a shadow over other areas of the war, and Raeder expressed fears that Hitler might lose sight of the equally important, extremely gruelling campaign being fought in the vastness of the Atlantic Ocean. Saying he was aware that Great Britain was still an enemy not to be disregarded, Hitler assured his Commander-in-Chief that he had no intention of relaxing the sea and air attacks. He foresaw the Russian campaign taking a matter of months only, and until that was over he wanted the USA kept out of the war. Once Russia fell, Hitler said, he reserved 'the right to take severe action against the USA.' But his strategic thinking was always dominated by the situation on land.

While his forces were driving rapidly through the front line of Russia's defences, there was also the matter of the Italo-German campaign in North Africa, the aim of which was the Suez Canal and beyond. Earlier Hitler had seen this as a side-show, but now he proclaimed that the loss of North Africa 'would mean a great loss both to us and to the Italians; the British are very dependent on supplies by sea in the eastern Mediterranean ... it is very desirable to relieve the *Afrika Korps* with a few submarines'. This heresy alarmed both Raeder and Dönitz who knew that only a concentration of U-boats in the Atlantic would have any strategic significance. One U-boat removed from that area could affect the whole outcome, the situation being knife-edged at that moment. Raeder argued that:

In view of the fact that enemy convoys are more and more heavily escorted, successes can be achieved only if they are attacked, not just by a few, but by a large number of U-boats simultaneously. The transfer of enemy traffic to more distant and remote areas also necessitates use of a very large number of boats merely to locate the enemy convoys, therefore, all available boats will have to be concentrated in the Atlantic.

Despite this accurate appreciation of the strategic situation, Raeder was eventually forced to agree to send some U-boats and set up a base in Italy. The future of these boats would be oblivion, and they would contribute nothing to the important battle. Entry to the Mediterranean, passing Gibraltar, was difficult enough, and the shallowness and translucence of the sea in comparison with the murkier waters of the Atlantic made aerial detection much more likely.

These considerations had an airing of sorts at the conference with Hitler on 22 August 1941. In September, at the time when SC.42 was under attack, Raeder and Dönitz had another conference. The US presence was becoming more marked, and on top of this technical matters were causing some concern. Effectiveness was falling generally for the U-boats at sea, due to increased escort strengths, air patrols and radar being fitted in ships and aircraft. It was also noticeable that the U-boat patrol areas were being avoided, but senior German intelligence officers were certain that the Naval M Code (transmitted by the Enigma machine) could not be broken. The British maintained total silence over their windfalls of intelligence in May and June, and this reinforced the conclusion.

Raeder summed-up, saying:

The latest successes should not be allowed to obscure the great difficulties caused by very strong Anglo-American escorts and the extensive enemy air patrol. In order to be as successful as last year, three to four times as many U-boats are needed in view of the heavily escorted convoys. Reconnaissance to locate the convoys is still the main problem. However, the number of boats becoming available by the end of October permits us to anticipate increased successes, especially if the number of planes available for reconnaissance will increase likewise.

Fortunately Göring, like Hitler, had no interest in or understanding of the needs of strategic economic warfare, and the importance of air reconnaissance against the convoys.

Although Raeder was fully convinced of the strategic need to keep the maximum number of U-boats in the Atlantic, he was ordered to supply some boats to operate east of Gibraltar (from bases at La Spezia in Italy, and Salamis in Greece), and to detract further from the Atlantic effort by sending some U-boats to operate in the Arctic against the convoys to Russia. By 13 November the demands these theatres were imposing on the main effort in the Atlantic caused him to report:

Submarine warfare on British imports in the Atlantic will be greatly reduced for a time after the boats now at sea have completed their missions, as tasks in the Arctic Sea and the Mediterranean are more urgent. The Naval Staff is endeavouring to commit all the remaining boats wholly for the war on merchant shipping.

He added that the forces were tied down in various ways, and that repairs were being delayed owing to labour shortages, the latter caused in part by the enormous manpower demands of the eastern front. The conclusions to be drawn from the shortage of available U-boats to fight the Atlantic battle are simply that:

a. There had been no pre-war planning for what was one of the main strategic elements of the Second World War. As mentioned before, Hitler's inability to see beyond land campaigns left his Navy in an intolerable position, especially when it could have been successful in delaying, or even preventing, the second front in Europe, by denying the USA bases in the UK as a result of an intense and successful campaign in the Atlantic;

b. Events as the war progressed were taking command of Hitler and his strategy, rather than the reverse. His conviction that the economic 'Blitz' method would prevail was to fail in Russia and in the Atlantic.

So, following the attacks on SC.42 the tempo of the Atlantic war died away. Three more convoy operations took place in September, against SC.44, SL.87 and HG.73. Eleven U-boats made attacks, and sank 26 ships. In October five convoys lost sixteen ships and sustained three damaged merchantmen, losses inflicted by another eleven U-boats. Just five U-boats attacked successfully in November, causing three convoys to lose nine ships, and in December only HG.76 was attacked, five U-boats sinking only three ships. Naturally, weather and the increasing effectiveness of the escorts played some part in these figures, but the War Diary shows U-boats being prepared and sent off on side-shows.

US involvement in the activities in the Atlantic, on a so-called 'neutral' basis, were a constant reminder to Hitler of the danger of embroiling the USA in the war, and he made considerable efforts to ensure that there was no provocation offered. However, the attack by the Japanese upon Pearl Harbor on 7 December 1941 changed the global situation. When Hitler declared war on the USA on 11 December 1941 (incidentally the only real act of co-operation with Japan at a strategic level throughout the war), he saved Roosevelt the problem of how to involve his country in the war; the only problem left to the American president was to get acceptance for his 'Europe first' strategy.

Japan made her unannounced attack on the morning of 7 December on US naval forces and aircraft based in Honolulu and the Pacific islands around the natural and strategic harbour at Pearl. Luckily for the Americans (who had had a number of hints, if not outright warnings of the attack, but which had seemingly been ignored), the US Pacific Fleet had sent its aircraft carriers to sea prior to the attack. Still in harbour were a number of battleships which were important strategically, but not as much as the carriers were soon to prove themselves to be. The war in the Atlantic was essentially U-boat versus escort, in the Pacific it was aircraft carrier versus aircraft carrier.

As noted above, Hitler had mentioned to Raeder that he intended to chastise the Americans for their unwarranted intervention in the war in the Atlantic, but he wanted to keep them out of the war until 'Barbarossa' was brought to a successful conclusion. There can be little doubt that he saw the Russian campaign as proceeding smoothly, if a little behind schedule, for German troops were within sight of the towers of the Kremlin. So a declaration of war against the USA would not affect Europe immediately, and when Russia was defeated Great Britain would be next. What could the Americans do, three thousand miles away across the Atlantic, which the German Navy would soon control? On 12 December Hitler met Raeder, and the consensus at the conference was:

> The situation in the Atlantic will be eased by Japan's successful intervention ... light forces, especially destroyers will be needed in increased numbers in the Pacific. The need for transport ships will be very great, so a withdrawal of American merchant vessels from the Atlantic can be expected; the strain on British merchant shipping will increase. This calls for intensified U-boat warfare on British supplies ... [Raeder then outlined the U-boat situation as follows:] At present thirty-six U-boats are en route to the Mediterranean. It is proposed to station fifty boats in the Mediterranean, twenty in the eastern area, and thirty in the western and Gibraltar areas. This leaves thirty-six boats at present, three of which are in northern Norway, and five in the south ... Six large [Type IX] boats are to proceed as quickly as possible to the east coast of America.

The U-boat Arm was not merely stretched, it was operating in penny packets, something that was inimical to success. Albeit with hindsight, cutting down the operational numbers in the Atlantic, which Dönitz had built up painstakingly over two years and more, could only reduce the effectiveness of the German Navy where it was to have its only significant part to play: the destruction of supplies to the only combatant German enemy in western Europe, and the concomitant denial of the United Kingdom to the greatest industrial nation as a base for her military operations against the Fatherland. However, the German Navy was now to take the war across the Atlantic to the North American continent itself.

# TECHNOLOGY AND WARFARE I  8

At the beginning of the war the German Navy had had 57 U-boats commissioned, most of which were the small Type II variants. Production of this class and of the heavier Type I boats had been stopped, as soon as hostilities began. The Type II boats had too limited a range in what was soon seen as an ocean war, and the Type IA had bad diving characteristics. This left Types VII and IX in production, but with other types either on the drawing-board or under consideration. For many months after September 1939 U-boat building had been limited, but production figures improved as the war went on:

| Year | Jan | Feb | Mar | Apr | May | June | July | Aug | Sep | Oct | Nov | Dec |
|---|---|---|---|---|---|---|---|---|---|---|---|---|
| 1939 (Production to end of August 57 U-boats) | | | | | | | | 0 | 1 | 0 | 2 | 3 |
| 1940 | 1 | 1 | 2 | 3 | 3 | 3 | 3 | 5 | 7 | 7 | 6 | 9 |
| 1941 | 10 | 9 | 11 | 14 | 24 | 14 | 19 | 19 | 15 | 24 | 23 | 22 |

This made a grand total of 317 U-boats. Losses, from a variety of causes, were as follows:

| Year | Jan | Feb | Mar | Apr | May | June | July | Aug | Sep | Oct | Nov | Dec |
|---|---|---|---|---|---|---|---|---|---|---|---|---|
| 1939 | | | | | | | | | 2 | 5 | 1 | 1 |
| 1940 | 2 | 5 | 2 | 4 | 1 | 2 | 1 | 2 | 0 | 1 | 2 | 0 |
| 1941 | 0 | 0 | 5 | 2 | 1 | 4 | 0 | 4 | 2 | 2 | 6 | 10 |

Total losses for the period were 67 U-boats, which left 252 at Dönitz's disposal for operations in January 1942. Production had increased to reflect the higher priority the U-boats had been accorded, based on their successes, and while the successes stayed on a par the losses would be acceptable and sustainable.

The war being waged by Dönitz was an economic war; his task was to cause such losses to the enemy that he would lose the will and the way to fight against his stranglehold in the Atlantic, thus removing the life-line that stretched from the New World to the Old. He had had to build U-boats in sufficient numbers, and of the types which could operate within his strategic plan. He accepted losses as inevitable, but he was not prepared to sacrifice elements of his U-boat fleet which was still far below the total strength he had predicated as essential for this type of warfare. He had to probe for enemy weaknesses wherever they were to be found. *B-Dienst* was able to decipher the BAMS code, and even the Royal Navy's own Administrative Code and Naval Codes 1, 2 and the later Code 3. This and other sources provided Dönitz with a great deal of intelligence to help in his strategic planning over the surface of the Atlantic, and in more distant waters.

The majority by far of U-boats built in Germany to the end of 1941 had been of Type VII, with a lesser but still significant production of the larger, longer-range Type IX boats. The Type VII was to stay in build throughout the war, and was the mainstay of the U-boat fleet. It had a range of some 8,500 nautical miles at 10 knots (surfaced), with a crew of four officers and 40–56 men. It carried eleven torpedoes. Its battle effectiveness was limited by two factors:

a. Its range was, in the Atlantic, relatively limited.
b. It carried too few torpedoes.

It was well built, however, and modifications during the war helped keep the boats up to counter-measures, although with decreasing overall success.

Its companion boat, the Type IX, had a longer range of 13,850 nautical miles (at the same 10 knots), and it had an increased displacement of some 1,000 tons surfaced, compared to about 750 tons for the Type VII. The extra tonnage enabled the designers to build in more space for fuel and torpedo stores. The crew was four officers and 44 men. These boats ranged into the Indian Ocean, and were the first boats to go to the eastern coast of the USA when Operation 'Paukenschlag' was mounted at the beginning of 1942.

A number of other designs were being considered for production, and improvements were constantly being made to the Type VII and IX boats when they came into base between patrols. The original Type VII had had 143 tons less displacement than the Type VIIC (the workhorse of the fleet). The VIIC had its range increased by 2,300 nautical miles and replaced the Type VIIB which had gone into production before the war began. The Type VII was an update of the UBIII Type of the First World War. There were five compartments:

a. Forward torpedo room and main seamen's quarters. Reserve torpedoes were stored under the bunks, and food stores pushed into any available space. The lockers fitted were also for food, not for personal effects. At the after end of the compartment was the torpedo loading hatch which penetrated the pressure-hull, and was angled to allow the length of the torpedo into the hull.
b. Officers' and Petty Officers' quarters, with a separate cabin (really a curtained corner) for the Captain. Beneath this lay the forward of the two battery rooms, filled with AFA accumulators. This battery compartment and its twin aft were separately ventilated from the boat proper.
c. The control room, with the attack tower above. The control room held all sailing controls, chart table and main compass. The main periscope

was operated from here. Control when cruising was exercised from here by the Officer of the Watch, but in a submerged attack the Captain controlled the ship from above in the attack tower. The attack periscope was used from the higher position, with repeaters and telephones to all parts of the boat. If attacking on the surface the Captain and First Lieutenant were on the bridge with lookouts, and the attack would be directed from there. This latter method allowed the Captain to use the U-boat as a torpedo-boat. It also gave a better view of the target, which would always be above him and against the sea horizon in relation to any light there might be at night.

d. The after crew's quarters. Here slept (when cruising) the engineer branch seamen, close to the engines and motors. This compartment lay above the second of the two battery compartments. The galley was squeezed in at the rear of this compartment.

e. The engine and motor room. This held the two main diesels, each developing some 3,000 hp, giving a surface maximum speed of about 17 knots. This was enough to outrun a corvette, and to manoeuvre at will in relation to a convoy. The electric motors, run from the batteries mentioned earlier, were, via a gearbox, linked to the main shafts, and provided reduced power to the boat when submerged. They developed 750hp each, and could produce an underwater speed of 7.5 knots for a limited period. When surfaced, the two power systems could be linked to increase range, the batteries being constantly topped-up by the diesels. There was a stern torpedo tube and one torpedo in the compartment which allowed the Captain to maintain the impetus of an attack by using this tube while the forward tubes were being reloaded.

At each end of the pressure-hull, which surrounded these compartments, the steel was rounded to give maximum possible hull strength. The greater the strength, the deeper the dive to escape enemy attack.

The Type VIIC/41 was essentially the same as the Type VIIC with the exception that, in order to increase diving depth, the steel used was Ww grade. This change was forced on the Germans by the increasing effectiveness of depth-charges. The Type IX design was similar, the IXC/40 being the later model. The layout of the boat was similar to that of the Type VII, with the same five main compartments. The increased engine-room space was needed to house two auxiliary electric motors for battery charging when running combined diesel-electric on the surface. The range increased as the Type was improved and went from 11,350 to 16,300 nautical miles. Later developments would increase the range to as much as 30,000 nautical miles without refuelling.

No matter how sophisticated or practical the designs were, the main problem in 1940 had been production. Not until the beginning of 1941 did production per month reach double figures, but thereafter it increased rapidly.

Hitler had stated in 1940 that although U-boat production was not yet high enough, the Army and the *Luftwaffe* had precedence in view of the forth-coming campaign in Russia. The fall of France had ensured certain of the material requirements – steel and copper – and had enabled Dönitz to over-come the shortage of operational boats by moving the bases so much nearer to their operational area. But as the number of enemy sea and air escorts increased, he needed more U-boats to patrol and locate the convoys, and to overwhelm the escorts during the attack.

The occupation of France was of great significance economically to the Navy, apart from the purely geographic advantages. The industrial area of Alsace released much German capacity for the war in the east, and plans were laid for a limited production programme of 25 U-boats per month from January 1942. In mid-1940 Hitler had been preoccupied with France, then Operation 'Seelöwe', and then by preparations for Operation 'Barbarossa'. Dönitz found a loophole: if torpedo-tube production could be stepped up, the boats already on the slips could be launched some four to six months early. The whole future of U-boat warfare then hung upon this one matter. Finally Hitler put U-boats, torpedoes and torpedo-tubes into the same production category as tanks, anti-tank guns and aircraft.

Hitler's preoccupation with 'Barbarossa' was such that he continued to disregard the strategic importance of the Atlantic battle. As he dismissed Oper-ation 'Seelöwe' in 1940 and began to plan his crusade in the east, so too did he lose sight of the threat posed by Great Britain to his dream of a European pan-Germanic hegemony in Europe. Raeder however did not lose sight of the problem, and he was also against the concept of the invasion of Russia from the start. On top of this, although he had a building priority for the U-boats, the yards did not have the workers to fulfil the demands of the programme.

'Barbarossa' began late, thanks to Mussolini's Greek adventure, but initial successes were on a grand scale. Total tactical surprise was followed by the capture of enormous tracts of western Russia and hundreds of thousands of Russian soldiers, as well as the near total destruction of the Russian Air Force. But Hitler did not see that the war of attrition his Navy was waging in the Atlantic was to be repeated on land in the east, and against his Army.

By the end of 1941, although things appeared to be going well, threats were beginning to appear. Moscow was not taken in the winter of 1941/2, and although there were more sweeping operations in 1942, Russian resistance was, like anti-U-boat forces, growing apace.

Mention has already been made of U-boat Types X, XI, XII and XIV. Of these, two Types were built: the Type X long-range minelayer and the Type XIV transport. Experience during the Norwegian campaign had proved the value of a U-boat transporter, and long-range minelaying would be of value if the earlier mine-laying campaign off the British Isles was anything to go by. The first Type X (Type XB) was launched in May 1941, and the first Type XIV (which was to figure significantly in operations in the north-western Atlantic especially) was launched in September of the same year.

The Type X had a range of 18,450 nautical miles and carried 64 mines in its shafts. Only eight were built, and had little effect, despite the prognosis in their favour. The Type XIV boats, however, were far more important. (No plans exist of these boats, having all been apparently lost during the war). Their role was to refuel and re-supply (RAS) operational boats. Ten were built and they were a considerable thorn in the Allies' side, always being searched for, but eventually all were sunk.

Despite every attempt to redesign the U-boats during the war, the Types VII and IX remained at the heart of the fleet at sea. There were however a number of developmental projects, two of which saw fruition. The Types XXI and XXIII were manufactured in limited numbers, and a few saw service. They were not radical designs, but they incorporated refinements which would have made them very serious enemies in the Atlantic had not air cover been so devastatingly effective. Only one 'new' concept was built, and this was the Walter Type XXVI boat. Driven by hydrogen-peroxide, its power cycle was such that it partly replenished itself, and produced vastly increased but short-term power. It failed because of handling problems with a highly volatile fuel, and after the war was replaced by nuclear power.

The manpower problem did not go away. To circumvent the difficulty to a certain degree it was decided to examine other production methods. Under normal circumstances every plate for the hull and the pressure-hull was cut individually and at a high time consumption in the yard of build. Then were added all the relevant tanks, electrical leads, hydraulic pipes, connectors and brackets, and then the part was assembled. There then followed another long period in which through-boat connections were made, external fittings attached, decking put in place and so on. But electrical welding had been developed to such a degree by the beginning of the war that it was proposed that individual sections of each boat could be completed away from the yards, and on delivery the relevant sections could all be joined to make the finished boat. The aim of this was to cut delays in the yards, and turn them into production lines, cutting time wastage and hence manpower requirements in the yards themselves.

The most significant building element of a submarine is the pressure-hull. Designers concluded that the Type VII could be prefabricated in eight sections, and the Type IX in ten. Assembly was easier because the builders had open access to both ends of the boat, except for the forward and aft sections. More simultaneous work could be done. The sections then went to the yards with most of the work already done, the yards now having the responsibility for assembly, fitting out and launch. (This was refined to such an extent that the section building works were able to assemble both pressure and outer hulls for the Types XXI and XXIII, but not for the Types VII and IX.)

When the sections arrived at the assembly yard an entire boat set was brought to where the ballast keel had been laid on the slip. The control room was installed and the tower started. The immediate forward and aft sections were added, engines being installed appropriately, and the operation completed with the welding of the end plates. Longitudinal and vertical accuracy were monitored continuously with theodolite systems. Once complete, the pressure hull was tested internally to 45 pounds per square inch to test the welding. The boat then had external ribs welded on to the pressure hull to support the external tanks and outer hull. Assembly was again from the centre outwards. Bow and stern sections were able to be assembled separately from the rest of the work, and were welded into place when the last tower welding was done. Hand fitting of air and fume trenching followed, after which the decking was laid onto its metal frame. The actual upper decks planks were virtually the last operation on the boat before it went to fitting-out where the last turns on the decks planking screws were taken up.

The largest items for installation were the diesels and the electric motors. During assembly of the engine room a large rectangular section was left open in the pressure hull. The engines and motors were swung above the hole, located and bolted into place. Shaft and other connections were made at the same time, and the shafts were checked for alignment. Once electrical and auxiliary controls and internal trunking had been laid, the rectangle was welded shut with a plate. Although apparently straightforward, some problems arose, which wasted time. Electrical fittings which were through-boat were a nuisance, but experience gained with the earlier boats was put to good use in the assembly of the Types XXI and XXIII, which had exceptionally short assembly times.

The boats were launched as soon as possible, to free the slip for the next assembly. This eliminated another bottle-neck, for the slips had always been such. Decentralisation and section building had two advantages: the speed and accuracy in section building was high, and raw materials could be routed to arrive at the relevant place and time, and secondly enemy bombing attacks on the section yards would be far less effective than on assembly yards. Sections damaged were far easier to replace than whole boats. (In actual fact the bombing offensive had such little effect that the Germans all but disregarded it as far as submarine production was concerned. The *United States Strategic Bombing Survey* reports give ample evidence of this ineffectiveness at the time when bombing might have had a very significant effect.)

By 1942 all Type VII U-boats were being built in this way, and sixteen yards were assembling the sections produced by 24 steelyards. The result was a significant reduction in production man-hours per boat, Germaniawerft cutting total build time from 380,000 to 250,000 man hours, and Blohm & Voss achieved an even lower 180,000 man hours. When the boats went to UAK for pressure testing the future Captain and Chief Engineer were present, no doubt adding to their confidence in the boat. The end result was production at some yards reaching one boat per week; this was the result of workers having specific tasks which were made easier by repetition – the skill of the production line. This also meant that production could be planned almost by the hour, with ancillary services planned around major building tasks, and critical path analysis applied to the whole project.

But despite this potential for streamlining production and increasing output, there were still organisational problems. Dr. Fritz Todt was in charge of the German economy, and he was responsible, until March 1942 when he was killed in an air crash, for a multiplicity of efforts. He controlled not only naval construction, but also aircraft and military manufacture, and the multitude of supply and service organisations to which all three were closely bound. On his death Albert Speer (Hitler's architect) was called in to replace Todt and to re-organise production in the Reich. The effects of his re-organisation began to show in the figures for the period to the end of May 1943:

**U-boat Production**

| Year | Jan | Feb | Mar | Apr | May | June | July | Aug | Sep | Oct | Nov | Dec |
|------|-----|-----|-----|-----|-----|------|------|-----|-----|-----|-----|-----|
| 1942 | 15 | 16 | 17 | 17 | 20 | 21 | 21 | 21 | 19 | 22 | 24 | 23 |
| 1943 | 21 | 22 | 28 | 18 | 28 | | | | | | | |

The failure of the G7e torpedo to fire in certain circumstances has already been mentioned. Although the design was essentially simple, it had refused to explode where it should – under the keel of the target, where it could break the ship's back. The failure had led to the re-issue of the G7a with its more reliable contact pistol, and this situation prevailed throughout the campaign of 1941–2. This torpedo suffered from having less effect, as the explosion took place at the side of the target, and it had a visible track in the water up to the target, showing the vector from which it had been fired.

Development was not restricted to these two models, however, and even they had been tested with different explosive loads and firing mechanisms. The traditional torpedo was only replaced gradually from November 1942 when TIII became available. The TIII or Eto was fitted with the P1 39 H (Pi 2) pistol, which was in effect a proximity fuse that could also function as a contact pistol. At the same time the G7a was modified to be able to change course automatically to port, to starboard and to port again in a menu of pre-programmed manoeuvres selected at the time of firing. This allowed a general shot at a convoy which, if the first target was missed, remained a potential hit for the 12,500 metres (at 30 knots) of its endurance. The TIII and the pre-programmed G7a both proved themselves in trials and use, and Dönitz claimed a 75 per cent hit rate for them. These torpedoes saw continuous service until partly replaced by more sophisticated sound-hunting torpedoes, which will be described later.

The U-boat war was not one merely of chance, despite its apparent character, and other influences than the merely military often made themselves felt. Behind the masses of men actively engaged in the war on and under the Atlantic, there were thousands at work on scientific projects related to all aspects of the campaign. This is not to belittle in any way the sheer courage and tenacity of the men on all sides who went out and fought this war, but the scientific background enabled them to do their jobs more efficiently, and sometimes more safely. From the U-boat sailors' point of view, however, the majority of the successful work was being done by their enemies.

Radar, as already noted, was beginning to have an effect upon the U-boats. The more aircraft and escorts that carried radar, the more the U-boats were under threat of location on the surface. The Americans were also working on reducing the wavelength, and eventually objects on the surface only a few centimetres in diameter could be located. At Bletchley Park every effort was being made (and eventually the Americans helped bring in the '*bombe*' computers in numbers) to decrypt the U-boat codes and get up-to-the-minute information to the submarine tracking room and the other units involved. Perhaps even further in the background, a group of operational research scientists were also looking at the effects of anti-submarine operations by Coastal Command. Their task was to help Coastal Command find more U-boats, and be able to do something about them effectively. These scientists were grouped as the Operational Research Section (ORS), Coastal Command, and their work demands comment.

Their role was to examine the statistics of every patrol and every attack, establishing what equipment, weapons and personnel were used, and to evaluate the success or otherwise of the effort put in to sinking U-boats from the air. Their job was not to design new weapons or equipment, but to state the criteria a new design must satisfy if an improvement to performance was to be made. When the Section was established, in November 1941, U-boats were sinking a great number of merchant ships for few losses to themselves, and the first task was to see if equipment or methods were to blame. The Section benefited from the start in being established on its own, between administration and operations, with a foot in both camps. Furthermore, the Air Officer Commanding-in-Chief had the head of operational research reporting directly to him.

One of the decisions taken, without the assistance or guidance of the scientists, was the changeover from the 250lb depth-charge (aerial) to the 600lb bomb. In fact the aerial depth-charge (it was established by ORS) was by far the better weapon, but this was not then realised. It was a questionable start, but the injection of scientific counsel soon settled the Section into a more integrated position. Their remit later extended into operational areas as well, acting in concert with the relevant staff, and significant reductions in flying hours per U-boat attack were made.

It was never a large organisation, reaching a total of only sixteen staff and a few assistants, but like Winn's submarine tracking room (of which more later), its services were invaluable. It had four fields of study, of which anti-U-boat was the main priority. Each of its studies depended upon two factors:

a. The problem had to be identified.
b. There had to be sufficient data available for the evaluation to be valid.

Every flight in a Coastal Command aircraft had to be logged in detail, and every attack committed to a record card to satisfy the constant demand for more data. Reports were filed with the Section, including negative reports, so that the data base upon which the statisticians could work was constantly updated.

The main difficulty was definition of the problems. When they were asked to look at photographic reconnaissance they had no previous criteria upon which to base their work: they had no existing measure of effectiveness. To establish a basic success rate they had to discuss the whole matter with the producers and the interpreters of the photographs, and from this it emerged that the first difficulty was not the accuracy of the photography but the lapse of time between the initial request and delivery of the positive proofs. The factors involved were analysed, and the process was speeded up. This is an example of practice determining theory; when flying effort was analysed, theory took precedence over practice.

Luckily for the observers the Germans used diesel-electric propulsion systems throughout the war. This meant that the boat had to have air to run the diesels and thereby charge the batteries. Up to mid-1943 (when operational research began to find its feet) the U-boats had to surface at least once every twenty-four hours to recharge batteries. In fact they spent as much time on the surface as possible, and it was operational research that was largely to blame for the increasing amount of time spent submerged, which was forced upon the U-boat captains. What Coastal Command was looking for was a submersible, and operational research had to optimise aircraft usage and crew training to ensure more sightings and more effective attacks.

Dönitz's tactics demanded that his boats travel at maximum speed whenever possible, and this meant on the surface. Their speed allowed their patrols to intercept and attack the convoys. As numbers of available boats increased, so the pack tactic became more efficient, and sighting U-boats stalked convoys until a number of boats were in a position to launch the often devastating 'first night' attack. Submerged U-boats were invisible from the air and, as Dönitz said, had 'no more to fear from aircraft than a mole from a crow'. Not until the end of the war was the sonobuoy brought into service, but even that could only detect a recently submerged boat, and had no general search ability.

But limited underwater speed and reduced observation rendered the submerged U-boat almost ineffective; they had to be on the surface to operate successfully. Furthermore, U-boats travelled on the surface between attacks, and at night. ORS was aware of these habits, and of Dönitz's tactics, especially the value of the surfaced night attack. From this they easily concluded that aircraft were of great value in finding U-boats, because of their height above the sea and their patrol speed, and they could of course be on the lookout from leaving land to returning.

So the first effort was to consider how the aircraft could find their targets. The obvious answer was to patrol as large an area as possible. The entire Atlantic was out of the question, because of range and endurance limitations, and so the next best solution was to patrol in areas where other intelligence suggested a high probability of U-boat presence. Thus aircraft patrolled around convoys at sea, and used Ultra and other sources to identify possible U-boat locations and concentrations.

Navigation over the sea on a long patrol (as noted elsewhere) had proved an inexact science for the aircraft operating out of Bordeaux, searching for convoys for Dönitz. The problem was addressed by the Section, as was an analysis of what happened while an aircraft was where it should be – on station. The search had to be effective, and the answer lay in eyes and radar. Even if the aircraft merely forced a U-boat to submerge, it was immediately restricted in its options, and almost certainly prevented from making an attack or moving fast enough to take any advantage of its submergence. A U-boat forced under was out of the battle for at least half an hour in many cases.

From the beginning of the war Dönitz had operated his boats in areas of traffic concentration. Initially targets were found inshore, near the great harbours of the British Isles, but the Royal Air Force and the Royal Navy soon became too much of a threat in these shallow waters. Dönitz then shifted his attention to the nodal points at sea, where convoys were constrained to pass by the needs of destination and seafaring. The first of these was in the South-West Approaches to the English Channel, which was denied to the Allies by the capture of the French bases. The emphasis then moved north to the North Channel–Rockall Bank area for some time. Escort numbers and the end of invasion fears slowly forced the U-boats to concentrate farther west in the Atlantic (compounded by the increasing effectiveness of Coastal Command). Eventually the U-boats began to zone in on the Central Atlantic area where aircraft could not yet patrol regularly and effectively.

This meant that aircraft patrols were unable to operate in the area of greatest U-boat concentration. Undaunted, operational research proposed that Coastal Command become effective within the range of its aircraft. Until Very Long Range aircraft became freely available (and thanks to Air Marshal Harris this was always a questionable matter), Coastal Command aircraft would have to operate over the transit and other areas around the British Isles. At the time of the first German convoy offensive, operational research was more concerned with aircraft camouflage and attack training (based on *ad hoc* principles) than in analysing U-boat sinkings. However, the system ensured that all experience gained was logged for future reference, and in navigation and Ultra interpretation great strides were made.

Operational research scientists and their staff were still wrestling with the problem of best possible use for their limited number of available aircraft in late 1941. Once sufficient data were available, and the required number of hours required to sink a U-boat were established, operational planning took note of the recommendation in early 1942. From this came the minimum flying effort which could give effective cover to the patrol areas accessible to Coastal Command aircraft. There was still no figure for the number of hours each aircraft should be in the air. There was also the time requirement for maintenance and repair to be put into the equation, and if this factor could be reduced, more air time would result. The Section examined this and the weather problem at the same time. To establish a statistical basis for the study it was decided to spend six months observing 502 Squadron (equipped with Whitley aircraft). The results were revealing and showed that of the number of hours available for flying the following was the actual use:

| Utilisation | percentage of time |
| --- | --- |
| Flying | 6 |
| Serviceable, not flying | 23 |
| Awaiting spares/crews | 41 |
| Maintenance | 30 |
| Total | 100 |

This meant that 64 per cent of every aircraft's time was being wasted by waiting for operational orders or spares or crews. The Section declared that flying time for a Whitley squadron should be increased by a factor of three.

The other aircraft types available to Coastal Command, and those slowly becoming available, were also examined and it was found that in all cases aircraft effectiveness decreased dramatically as distance from base increased. Crew fatigue was significant, and to a lesser extent the effect of long-range operations on the airframe. Coastal Command could not escape the immutable rule that states that the more miles an aircraft flies the longer is the maintenance period before the next flight. One shortcut was found in 1943, and that was to limit the number of inspections of maintenance (but not the maintenance itself), thus increasing operational availability.

Once in the air, navigation became crucial. Even with electronic aids, navigational skills in the services generally were not exceptional. Over the sea the problem was magnified, for there are no physical features to check against a map, often for very long periods. Up to the end of 1941 aircraft met convoys by dead-reckoning, with a success rate close to shore of only 75 per cent, and a far lower rate farther out to sea. The Section established that for every 100 miles off-shore the rendezvous was planned, there was a fall-off of 81–82 per cent in the 'meet rate'. And if a convoy were under attack, zig-zagging and other evasive manoeuvres could result in no aircraft contact, even if wide sweeps were made around the original location.

If one adds to this the error in the convoys' own plotting (with an average error of some 35 miles along course and 15 miles across) and the position which it signalled to Coastal Command, this explains why some 60 per cent of distant convoys were never located by their aircraft. Operational research then suggested that if the aircraft transmitted a continuous signal when it reached 100 miles from the dead reckoning rendezvous point, and was corrected for bearing by the convoy, this would assist the aircraft, and yet not offer the enemy much help, in contrast to the convoy sending a homing signal. This procedure was adopted and reduced the failure rate to about 20 per cent, and the remaining 20 per cent was mainly accounted for in ships which did not, for one reason or another, establish contact with the aircraft.

The first radar location of a U-boat occurred in November 1940, when a Sunderland equipped with ASV-I found either *U47* or *U100* when they were approaching HX.84. Radar was the antidote to Dönitz's tactics, but good equipment in sufficient numbers was slow in coming, regrettably caused to an extent by the constant demands of Bomber Command. Up to mid-1943 the equipment operated on between 170 and 220 megacycles. In aircraft the beam was transmitted (ASV mark II) from three aerials, one running forward to aft, the other two on either side of the fuselage. The aerials were fixed, and although range could be estimated from the A-scope, bearing was found by adjusting the aircraft's course until a match was obtained on the signals on the scope. The Germans installed a receiver on the U-boats as a counter (the Metox), which was crude but generally effective in warning that there was a radar set operating somewhere not too far away. The U-boat then merely dived. Operational research examined the sets, and came to the conclusion that the more the target was abeam of the aircraft, the less were the chances of contact. This problem was eliminated in later radars (Mark III British, Mark V American).

By the end of 1942 U-boat radar detection had improved so much that aircraft were losing contact before they came into visual range, and so although the U-boat had been forced down, it could not be located and destroyed. This was because the German Navy had developed its own search receiver (Metox was a French design), the FuMB set, which identified ASV II emanations at much greater range.

No matter what means were used to find a U-boat, the next function of the aircraft was to attack and sink it. The anti-submarine bomb has been mentioned already; ORS Report 142 of 1941 described the statistical efficiency of the bomb attack as 1 per cent, and said:

It is clear that under such circumstances, the U-boat is in fact in very little danger from aircraft, which must be regarded as moral deterrents, rather than killing weapons.

The main point of the report was that in aircraft attacks the first fifteen seconds were the most important. When the U-boat spotted the aircraft the order to dive would immediately be given. If the aircraft were more than fifteen seconds flying time from the U-boat there was little chance of damaging it, and much less chance of sinking it. Once the boat had submerged so too had almost all chance of causing any damage to it, and no matter what depth settings were put on either bombs or depth-charges there was every chance that the U-boat commander could avoid them. Added to this was the experimentally established killing radius of the 250lb depth-charge – only twenty feet.

In September 1941 the ORS was advising the Admiralty on depth-charge fillings, arguing that if the charge were of a higher explosive yield, the radius of lethality would be improved. The Admiralty asked the RAF if they would supply some RDX, a newly developed high-yield explosive. The Air Ministry replied that it could supply Minol (a lower grade explosive) and the matter would have stalemated there had not the scientific adviser to the Commander-in-Chief been a party to the experimental work and the correspondence. His comments caused Torpex (RDX in a form suitable for torpedoes and depth-charges) to be made available, and was used by the Admiralty for the rest of the war. But the radius of lethality remained at twenty feet, for the ORS scientists were erring on the side of caution. This led to depth-charge settings being reduced from 100 feet to 50 feet in the autumn of 1941, and soon thereafter, again on ORS recommendation, to 25 feet. This improved lethality significantly.

The lethality percentage of attacks in fact bore out the truth of the experimental data, for in the first year of the war it was 1 per cent, whereas by the last months of 1942 it had risen to no less than 7 per cent. The next problem was how to get sufficient depth-charges onto the target as to make it highly probable that the boat was damaged or sunk. Work on this occupied some members of the team until the middle of 1943.

For the Germans' radar became a problem which was only successfully solved by the installation of search receivers, which eventually allowed the U-boat to submerge before the aircraft got within attacking range. This enabled the boats to continue to cruise on the surface, with early warning of danger. The Germans had some success with search receivers, but were always stalled by Allied developments of shorter waveband radar sets, until 3cm radar was brought in by the Americans. Radar in the surface escorts also posed a problem, but one which could be limited in effect by careful submergence and good anti-Asdic tactics. Losses were rising, but were still within the limit that Dönitz accepted as the risk he had to take to succeed, and he was always on the lookout for soft targets whenever they presented themselves.

# 9 'A ROLL OF DRUMS'

With the declaration of war on the USA, Hitler solved the greatest problem facing the western alliance against him: how to get America actively into the war. Churchill's relief was probably the greatest, although he was now to be constantly harangued for a 'second front' by Stalin. Churchill was nothing if not devious, and he managed to postpone Russian requests and American proposals for two years. He had dreamed, as mentioned above, that the end of the U-boat war had been reached; this was utterly wrong, but he may have gained some hope from the HG.76 operation. A return must be made to the last convoy operation of 1941, in which the U-boat Arm suffered a reverse which may have contributed to a number of erroneous decisions made by Dönitz thereafter.

The convoy sailed from Gibraltar for Home Waters on 14 December 1941, with a complement of 32 merchant ships (Commodore Fitzmaurice) and escorted by 36 Escort Group (Commander Walker). In addition to the close escort there was a support group of three destroyers and the 'Q ship' HMS *Fidelity*. As even further support a U-boat hunter group of four destroyers from Force H also sailed, giving a total of fifteen escorts to the 32 ships of the convoy. There was also air support from Coastal Command based in Gibraltar.

German spies reported the sailing, and Dönitz ordered the *Seeräuber* Group to attack it. This was a group of six U-boats (*U67*, *U107*, *U108*, *U131*, *U127* and *U574*). To avoid reconnaissance aircraft and the inevitable U-boat patrol line, the convoy was ordered south along the Moroccan coast initially, and not until midday on 16 December was the convoy first sighted by an Fw 200 of I/KG 40. The position report was relayed to the U-boat Group, but when *U67* and *U108* attempted to get within range they were driven off by the escort. That night *U131* had a similar lack of success.

Next day three U-boats sighted the convoy, and aircraft were flown off from the improvised carrier *Audacity*. Several air attacks were made on *U131* and although she shot down one of the Fairey Swordfish, she was so badly damaged that she could not submerge, and was scuttled when four escort/support group vessels approached. Meanwhile *U434*, the shadower, was detected on the morning of 18 December, forced to the surface by depth-charges, and abandoned by her crew. On the same day two of the Fw 200 reconnaissance aircraft keeping contact with the convoy were shot down by Grumman Martlet aircraft, also flown off *Audacity*.

That evening a further attempt by two U-boats to come into contact was foiled by the surface escort. Then, on the morning of 19 December, *U574*, the third U-boat to be lost for little profit (*Empire Barracuda*, 4,972 GRT on 15 December) was sunk in a ramming attack by HMS *Stork* with Commander Walker aboard. The combined efforts of the sea and air escorts had held the U-boats at bay for two days, and sunk three (*U131*, *U434* and *U574*) as well as shooting down two Fw 200s. Then the *Audacity* Martlets shot down two more aircraft.

*U107* had managed to gain contact, and proceeded to shadow for two more days while five more boats assembled for the attack (*U574*, *U125*, *U751*, *U71* and *U567*). After further abortive attacks two U-boats (*U67* and *U751*) managed a short attack and *U751* sank a merchant ship and, far more importantly, HMS *Audacity* on 21 December. *Audacity*, ironically, was formerly the German merchantman *Hannover*, captured in 1941 off San Domingo and converted to carry aircraft. Although her fighting career was short, the importance of her aircraft, which were on call to the convoy at all times, was proved. They had shot down four enemy aircraft and damaged one U-boat sufficiently to present the surface escorts with the certain kill.

Before the convoy escaped from the *Seeräuber* concentration, it managed to sink one more U-boat (*U567*). So four U-boats were sunk and a fifth (*U127*) was sunk by the hunter group from Force H the day after the convoy sailed. Lost to the convoy were three merchantmen (11,165 GRT); more important were the losses of the escorts HMS *Stanley* (destroyer) and HMS *Audacity*. *U574* had sunk *Stanley* just before being rammed by HMS *Stork*, and *U751* sank *Audacity*. The action was one of the first in which the escort was strong enough to keep a force of U-boats at bay for much of the time, and to strike back at the U-boats and the reconnaissance aircraft. The U-boats were aware of the threat to them of *Audacity*'s aircraft, and she was sunk.

*Audacity* was well known to the BdU, who had made her a priority target for the U-boats; she was the first of three escort carriers to be sunk during the war. Bigalk, Captain of *U751*, must have thought her to be an *Illustrious* or *Courageous* class ship, however, because his sinking report to Lorient reported the destruction of an aircraft carrier of 23,000 tons, rather than the 11,000 tons she displaced. This operation had been the first in which Dönitz ordered his boats to attack a warship, and only after the events of May 1943 did the escorts become prescribed targets for the U-boats.

This action confirmed the Admiralty's conviction that seaborne aircraft and a strong sea escort combined could defeat the U-boats. But this convoy was an anomaly: it was close to Gibraltar initially, had its own aircraft (and so the Gibraltar air gap did not affect it), and it had an escort which was supernormal. But more conversions to escort carrier were being made – grain and oil merchantmen with a superimposed flight deck, carrying aircraft as well as cargo. The more primitive version of this, the CAM (Catapult Armed Merchantman), could merely launch one Hurricane, but could not recover it, consigning the pilot to a swim before his own recovery (if he was near enough).

Numbers were the constant problem, and HG76 was an exception. The new escort carriers were not available then, and the next, *Empire Macalpine*, only came into service a year later. The Atlantic air gap would exist for a number of dangerous months. Although the Americans were now partners, demands from the Pacific were making themselves felt. In reality the convoy routes of great importance – those across the Atlantic – were as little protected as ever. Land-based aircraft were still limited in numbers, range and effect. As Dönitz surveyed the scene at the end of 1941, his situation seemed much improved. Now he could attack merchant traffic in the soft target area of the immediate east coast of the USA, and he had Type IX U-boats to do it. When the Type XIV boats were ready he could add the Type VII boats to the assault force, their range being extended enormously by refuelling from the Type XIVs. The Atlantic was target area for U-boats from the moment they sailed, for they could attack convoys en route to the east coast, refuel and rearm, and then attack the traffic off the US coast. A further refuelling and re-arming would then make the homeward passage profitable too.

Until the end of 1941, the refuelling programme was based on surface supply ships positioned in the Atlantic at various rendezvous. The Canary Islands had been available until July 1941, but the Spanish Government then withdrew this facility, so he again positioned his ships at sea; the *Egerland* was the first such supply vessel, but she was soon located and sunk. Further attempts to ensure re-supply by surface ships were thwarted by British action, based in part on Ultra intelligence. Finally Dönitz was convinced that the only remaining, and potentially successful, means of RAS (Re-supplying At Sea) was by using the Type XIV tankers. At the end of 1941 six of them were launched, and two were commissioned.

The Type XIV U-boat could carry four torpedoes in external, pressure-tight containers, for re-arming other boats, and 432 tons of diesel fuel in internal tanks, as well as 203 tons for its own use. The RAS fuel would completely refuel six Type VII boats, or top up a much larger boat. Their range was 12,350 nautical miles, and their strategic significance was incalculable. *U459* and *U460* were launched in September 1941, and went, with the boats that followed, to 4th Uflotilla to work up before transferring for operations to 10th Uflotilla which was established at Lorient in February 1942.

This was to enable Dönitz to follow up the initial assault off the US coast by Type IX boats with further waves of Types VIIs able to undertake RAS. The greater time spent on passage was planned to be put to good use, and once off the coast it was expected that defences would initially be minimal. Defences on the east side of the Atlantic had forced the U-boats into the central area of the ocean, and even there the boats could no longer reckon on impunity in their patrols, with more escorts becoming available, especially in view of the reduced U-boat activity during the last quarter of 1941. Patrol Groups had been set up to come to the aid of the close escorts, and also be able to stay behind to continue anti-U-boat operations without weakening the close escort.

Up to now, the desire to send U-boats into prohibited waters had been denied to Raeder and Dönitz by Hitler, for fear of precipitating active US involvement in the war. This had been generally successful, the only exceptions being the incidents involving *Greer, Kearny* and *Reuben James*. Now the German Navy had a free hand, and the pickings promised to be more prolific than ever before, until US defences came up to strength and efficiency.

The results were actually such that Dönitz himself was astonished. From January to June 1942 there was virtually no organised opposition to the U-boats, which ranged freely along the eastern seaboard. They avoided local concentrations of anti-submarine forces, and took the battle into the Caribbean Sea and the Gulf of Mexico. In fact the effort was a strategic mistake, but events will need to be studied before they can be analysed.

The boats were despatched in waves from the French Atlantic bases and by 11 January 1942 eighteen were operating in the coastal waters. There were only five Type IX boats, however, the rest being Type VII, with much lower endurance and only half the torpedo armament of the larger boats. They set to with a will, nevertheless, only a few days after *U130* had fired the first two torpedoes in this phase. The first operational area ordered was between Cape Race and Cape Hatteras, and *U130* sank two merchantmen just south of Placentia Bay on 12 and 13 January. There was no need for pack attacks in this area – there were no convoys – so the U-boats were in a similar situation to the first halcyon days of the war. For the U-boat men, this became the second 'happy time'.

The US Navy had been helping the Royal Navy in the Atlantic for months, and was fully aware of the value of convoy, yet seemed strangely uninterested in that institution in their own coastal waters. To an extent this was a product of the problems of a two-ocean war, but the attitude was very slow to change, even when the U-boat successes became painful. Furthermore, the Americans had had five weeks (the time it took for Dönitz to get his boats to the US coast) to prepare; the conditions that greeted the U-boats were far from the grim realities of mid-Atlantic. Hardegen (*U123*, and by now a veteran) wrote in his War Diary:

> [on the night of 18/19 January, 1942] ... I saw about twenty steamships, some undarkened; also a few tramp steamers, all hugging the coast. Buoys and beacons in the area had dimmed lights which, however, were visible up to two or three miles.

Hardegen commanded a Type IXB, and he sank three ships on the 19th, and damaged one; the last three attacks all took place after sunrise, against individual ships. The damaged ship (the US steam tanker *Malay*) was even engaged with the deck gun, which was a rare occurrence elsewhere. The prospects for the U-boats seemed unlimited. The author of the official American history of US naval operations during the Second World War called this time one of 'merry massacre', but before it is examined Germany's overall strategic position should be considered.

The Russian campaign was held up by Generals *Janvier* and *Février*, and Hitler's insistence that the German units give no ground in the face of a Russian counter-attack. The General Staff had asked for a withdrawal to consolidate the main defended locations, and to eliminate bulges in the line. Hitler adamantly refused. He was proved right (unfortunately for the German soldiers) because the Russians had not yet got their breath back after the reverses of 1941, and had no large-scale counter-attack planned. But in the north-west of Russia Leningrad maintained a stubborn and heroic resistance to all German attempts to capture the city. This also meant that Russian troops were still within striking distance of Finland, and, through Finland, Sweden and Norway.

The UK appeared to have been bypassed, like a beleaguered fortress, whose fall had been postponed until Russia was conquered, expected during the 1942 campaign season. But the British were still receiving supplies from the Americas and the Commonwealth. British forces were facing Germans and Italians on the coast of North Africa, and although that too looked promising for the Axis, the British and Commonwealth troops were going to be a tough nut.

From the UK the phenomenon of small raiding parties appeared, especially in Norway. Commandos had attacked German positions on the Norwegian coast, returning after disrupting or destroying *Wehrmacht* installations and killing or capturing the troops stationed in them. These raids, mere pinpricks intended to sustain a weak morale at home, weighed heavily on Hitler's thoughts for his future strategy. If Sweden joined the Allies (more a pipe-dream than a prospect, bearing in mind her geographical position) not only would Germany lose vital iron ore supplies, but she would be caught between the Russians in the east and the other European nations in the north. The effect upon the Navy's operations would be significant, for the Baltic would be open to attack, and transit of the North Sea made this more hazardous. The U-boats needed the Baltic for training and working up, and the North Sea to get to the French bases. Hitler decided that he must pre-empt any chance of invasion of Norway.

His problem was how to man the proposed defences. The campaign in Russia was yielding large areas of land and more than three million Russian soldiers had been killed or captured, but the *Wehrmacht* too was suffering, having lost more than 800,000 officers and men. The needs of this war, which was to bleed Germany's manpower reserves dry, were not yet appreciated, any more than the potential strength of the Russians, but Hitler could not reduce his forces in Russia. His decision was to leave the task of guarding Norway to Raeder and Göring.

The Mediterranean was also a problem; Italian forces were not the equal of their opponents, and the gradual stiffening with German units was one more drain upon reserves. Then there were the campaigns in Yugoslavia and Greece, forced upon Hitler, followed by the campaign for Crete. The campaign for the Adriatic was more than it seemed, for it cost lives but more importantly time, delaying the start of '*Barbarossa*'. He also saw some of his best soldiers – the paratroops – decimated in Crete to such an extent that they were never again used in battle.

The Middle East campaign was no side-show: if German troops took Suez, eastern access to the Mediterranean would be denied to the Allies, leaving Malta and Gibraltar only, and they could wither away for lack, then, of strategic significance. German troops from Suez could look towards the Caucasus and the Middle East, the loss of which would have disastrous consequences for the Allies. German possession of the Middle East oilfields, when added to Romanian production, would eliminate one of Hitler's strategic weaknesses – his sources of oil.

So, although Hitler's gaze was almost permanently fixed upon Moscow, and then the Ukraine (that strange volte-face), he could not fail to glance occasionally at the situation in Norway and North Africa. The *Kriegsmarine* and the *Luftwaffe* had almost total responsibility for the northern flank, and all three Services were involved in the Mediterranean. The demands upon the Navy were for both surface forces and U-boats. Surface units were to be concentrated in the north, where they could be expected to deny the Norwegian coastal waters to the Royal Navy, and thereby also tie down large naval forces desperately needed elsewhere.

While the U-boats were opening the attack on the US coast, Hitler and Raeder had the further problem of how to employ *Scharnhorst*, *Gneisenau* and *Prinz Eugen*. They were lying in Brest, having been used to keep much larger Royal Navy units in home waters, and to divert some of the Royal Air Force attacks from German cities. Raeder did not agree with Hitler's premonition of danger in Norway, although he saw clearly the strategic importance of that country. He wanted to leave the three ships (all heavy cruisers, *Scharnhorst* and *Gneisenau* mounting nine x 11in and *Prinz Eugen* eight x 8in guns) where they were. Despite their potential they were manned by untrained crews whose efficiency was low. There was little hope of them being able to transit the northern route around England and Scotland to reach their proposed Norwegian bases. The only hope was a Channel dash, which no warships had successfully completed in British maritime history. That they managed to escape from Brest and reach Germany (albeit damaged) is a tribute to the daring of the project, which the British considered most un-German in concept.

But while Hitler, Raeder and Göring were concentrating on the mainly continental aspects of the war, Dönitz was suffering from a stream of demands which were steadily reducing the overall Atlantic U-boat strength. U-boat production began to increase significantly in 1941, and Dönitz had increased his training numbers at the same time. Initially this meant a reduction of boats operating, but by the end of the year the benefits of the new production were being felt.

Losses at sea and diversions of U-boats away from the Atlantic were seriously affecting his strategic plan. Hitler wanted U-boats sent to Norway and to the Mediterranean. For Dönitz U-boats based in Norway would not be able to sink as many Atlantic ships as those based in France, and boats that succeeded in passing the Straits of Gibraltar would be entombed in the Mediterranean for the duration. So, every U-boat posted away meant a loss to the main campaign in the Atlantic, long recognised by Dönitz as the decisive theatre of naval warfare.

Dönitz estimated success by the tonnage sunk per day, and his War Diary shows his analysis of performance based upon this formula. His aim was to increase the daily sinking total by getting every available U-boat to operate in the Atlantic. But his aim had undergone a subtle change. Prior to the US involvement, he was rightly engaged in stopping convoy traffic from reaching the UK. In January 1942 he wanted to sink Allied shipping at a rate that would exceed the replacement rate possible in the Allied shipyards.

The question now arises as to whether Dönitz had been more influenced by events at the end of 1941 than he was willing to admit. In his memoirs he wrote, in relation to the operation against HG.75:

The results were very disheartening ... we ... lost five U-boats ... once again among our casualties was one of the best and most experienced of our U-boat Commanders ... After this failure and in view of the unsatisfactory results of the preceding two months my staff was inclined to voice the opinion that we were no longer in a position successfully to combat the convoy system ... It was an opinion, however, which I was not prepared to endorse ...

and he goes on to give sound tactical reasons for his comment. However the real truth may lie in his lament for Kapitänleutnant Endrass (U567, sunk by the Royal Navy). The loss of his U-boat commanders always seems to have hit Dönitz too hard, and his reaction when presented with the opportunity of attacking the US coast – a soft target – might well have been to heave a sigh of relief, and put his mind to creating a justification for sending his remaining boats into less dangerous waters.

Up to 11 December 1941, the Pan-American security zone delineated the western limit for U-boat operations. The Germans had not accepted further expansions eastward to 26° and then 22° West, but they had stopped at the original line. Also, Allied air cover could not extend that far, and so the U-boats could operate on the surface at night. Once the USA was in the war, all restrictions were dropped, and the U-boats could operate freely off the coast until the Americans devised means of stopping them.

As noted above, the conditions Hardegen and his companion commanders met were very similar to peacetime. What further forces could Dönitz throw in to make Operation 'Paukenschlag' the 'massive shock' he intended it to be? Total operational strength was 94 U-boats. Only nineteen of these were Type IX, capable of operating in those far waters without too much of a fuel problem. The main body of Type VII boats seemed incapable of reaching and operating off the US coast; only when the Type XIV re-supply boats were available would they add significantly to the weight of forces for the operation. Two Type XIV boats were on trials at that moment, and more due to commission.

Operationally, Dönitz was hamstrung. The Type IX boats he needed were not even all under his command, four being attached to Northern Command, operating in the North Sea and against the Murmansk convoys, and no fewer than eleven were lost to him forever in the Mediterranean. In the Atlantic on 1 January 1942, Dönitz had just six operational boats, with sixteen others at sea either en route to other mid-Atlantic operations or returning to base. Fifty-four boats were at bases under repair or with crews on leave. His effective forces were risible in the face of such an opportunity. There was one positive factor, however, if time was on his side. More than 100 U-boats were under-going trials and working-up. Of these, two were Type XIV, three Type XB and 27 Type IX, all essential to a campaign in distant waters. There were also 68 Type VII U-boats to bolster the mid-Atlantic operation, if he chose to use them.

Dönitz despatched a scratch force, five Type IXs, closely followed by a number of Type VIIs, to the east coast area; their task was to reconnoitre the prospects for a much larger operation. U123 was, as mentioned, among the first to arrive, and soon reported, together with U130, U66, U109 and U125. Twelve VIIC boats went to the area off the Newfoundland Bank and as far south as Nova Scotia. Although close to their maximum range (if there was to be an operational fuel reserve) they also had some successes, but it was the Type IXs that convinced Dönitz that prospects were phenomenal, to be exploited as soon as possible with the maximum force available.

By 27 January four boats (U123, U130, U66 and U109) had sunk 24 ships (157,355 GRT). On 11 January reports of traffic and defences reached U-boat Headquarters, showing that ships were sailing independently, and that there were assembly points off New York, Baltimore, in the Straits of Florida, and off Aruba and Trinidad. There was a quantity of shipping, but as yet no sign of convoys, virtually no defensive surface vessels, and air patrols were totally inexperienced and posed no threat to the U-boats. Dönitz planned expansion immediately, knowing that the Atlantic bases would now earn their keep, and that he had a reserve of boats capable of replacing foreseeable losses. He would be able to maintain a constant presence off the US coast with the new boats (unless diverted to other areas), so that when the Americans introduced convoy he could use pack tactics as he had in mid-Atlantic.

He planned a disposition to as far south as Trinidad and Aruba, with the shorter-range Type VIIs concentrated nearer to home in the north. Once he could refuel the boats he would be able to extend operations to cover the entire Atlantic seaboard of North and Central America. This would give a tremendous potential to his 'tonnage war', if the first sinkings were a yardstick. He intended to maintain a small number of boats off Central America, to harass convoys and attack targets of opportunity, and by so doing extend the defences still farther. In the Central Atlantic again, some U-boats would remain, with the same role. In the War Diary on 20 January Dönitz reported that the success of U123 'justifies sending boats to this area and the future is hopeful for other boats'. His enthusiasm had increased by 24 January, when he noted that all boats stationed to the west of England (in the North Channel and farther west) were to be recalled, because attacks on the US east coast would be more profitable than elsewhere until defences improved and convoy was introduced. In support of this he mentioned weather conditions (one of the reasons, he wrote, for the relative failure of the attack on HG76) which were bad in mid-Atlantic compared to those off the US coast.

The bases in France were, he continued, well suited to repairing and refitting the boats, and could complete the supplying and arming of the recalled boats before the first wave returned from US waters. New boats, as they came out from Germany, could do one operation in the area Rockall–Greenland–Newfoundland before docking in France for the first time, where, already blooded, they would join their operational flotillas.

By the end of January Dönitz had an adequate picture of what his boats might achieve. Fifty-four ships had been sunk during the month, of which 48 were sunk off the US coast (total 263,913 GRT). Nine of the vessels lost had been in convoy and were attacked further off the coast than the main operation, but the net result was a tonnage sunk comparable with that of the autumn and summer of 1941, when British concern at the rate of sinking had been at its highest. The future of this campaign looked promising to Dönitz, and would have been more so if problems had not arisen.

The first was a recurrence of torpedo pistol failure; a number of boats reported G7e failures, adding that there was a serious pressure build-up in the balance chambers of the torpedoes, even after only a day or two at sea. This was very important, because the balance chamber regulated the depth at which the torpedo travelled under water. The problem was caused by the screw's drive-shaft passing through this chamber via an imperfect pressure seal. The pressure inequality resulted from the slight increase in pressure in the boats caused when diving. When fired, the pressure in the balance chamber was supposed to be that at sea level. The torpedo, on firing, related that pressure to the water pressure around it. With an increase in the balance chamber pressure the torpedo would travel deeper to achieve the pressure differential of the depth setting put on by the torpedo yeoman in the boat.

This was probably a more important cause of torpedo failure than the pistols, as well as the reason for many torpedoes taking a direct course to the bottom. The problem took time to solve, and this delay was one of many factors which contributed to the defeat of the U-boat Arm. At the end of January 1942, however, no such thoughts occupied Dönitz's mind.

As far as the operational boats were concerned, events were constantly changing. Their number had increased by seven, and 53 boats were in the Atlantic. But there were nineteen boats in the two flotillas in the Mediterranean now, with four still in the Arctic. On 6 February Hitler demanded that the northern boats be reinforced to six, with two more to be on stand-by at Narvik, Trondheim and Bergen, and eight more to be available for operations in the Iceland–Hebrides area. This would cut the Atlantic fleet by 37 boats. Dönitz was unable to withstand the demand, although disapproving. He planned, if possible, to transfer U-boat training to Norway, to bypass the real effect of Hitler's demands; unfortunately for him the practical problems were too great to overcome.

As a palliative, Dönitz had the pleasure of greeting Hardegen, back from his Atlantic crossing. As was his habit whenever possible, he interviewed his captains personally. (This practice was only discontinued when Headquarters moved to Paris later in the year.) Hardegen confirmed his first impressions, adding that there was an abundance of targets, and said that three times as many boats would have had their share. Dönitz noted that the original plan to send twelve boats would have enjoyed considerable success, and the decision to concentrate operations off the US coast was justified, especially with his revised terms of engagement.

He would have had more boats had Skl had a less continental approach. In December 1941 five Type IX were operating under Skl control off Gibraltar, their great range being wasted sitting about. Skl would not release these boats to Dönitz for 'Paukenschlag', and he had to make do with what he could scrape together. The results of the first-wave operation finally injected some reality into Skl, and the Type IXs were released for the Atlantic.

With the growing emphasis on 'Paukenschlag', there was little other activity in the Atlantic. In January individual boats attacked ON and SC convoys, but these attacks were accidental rather than planned. Strangely, however, the total of ships sunk in convoy was the highest for the first half of 1942, the figures falling to nothing in March. In April they rose again, reflecting increased American effectiveness off their own coast. Almost all attacks were concentrated on the continental shelf of the Americas. Despite the fact that all

U-boats were operating on one load of fuel and ammunition, they were achieving results which were much greater than had been expected.

The long-range boats enjoyed great success, but the Type VIIs operating off the Newfoundland Bank and Nova Scotia were met by extremely bad weather. One U-boat, as a result of heavy seas and icing, and while trying to escape the attentions of a destroyer east of Cape Breton Island, shipped eight tons of water and hit the bottom, the air inlet valve to the diesel (normally closed on diving) having frozen in the open position. Two hours later the boat surfaced and proceeded, noting in her log that the destroyer had not attacked, presumably because 'their depth-charge throwers must have iced up'. Range limitations and cold and stormy weather meant that little of note was achieved by these first Type VIIs; eight of them sank only nine ships (62,847 GRT). Range limitation forced *U564* (operating 300 miles south of Nova Scotia) to refuel from *U107* (Type IX) before she could return to base. Some crews however circumvented the fuel problem, as Dönitz noted in his biography:

> In their eagerness to operate in American waters the crews sought every means to help themselves. They filled some of the drinking- and washing-water tanks with fuel. Of their own free will they sacrificed many of the amenities of their living quarters in order to make room for the large quantities of stores, spare parts and other expendable articles which an increase in the radius of action demanded. The German submarines even in normal circumstances were very much less comfortable to live in than the submarines of other nations because they had been built on the principle that every ton of their displacement must be used solely in fighting power ...

Apparently, morale was not a problem at this time, although one must ask if the extra fuel was merely to ensure a homecoming, rather than a totally avid expression of willingness to fight. Sailors the world over are practical men.

A fundamental problem Dönitz tried to overcome was the inability of his peers in the German Command structure, as well as Hitler, to understand what his U-boats represented, and his concept of their strategic role. Before the USA became involved, Dönitz repeatedly stated that the U-boats' task was to sink ships carrying goods and equipment, as well as men, *being conveyed to the British Isles*. With the inclusion of the USA he changed that aim to one of sinking the maximum tonnage for the minimum U-boat losses. (It is a basic principle of war that the aim, once selected, is maintained to the bitter end.) To achieve this he needed every U-boat he could get from the training flotillas in the Baltic. He was constantly frustrated in this by diversions of U-boats to areas of lesser immediate strategic importance – the Mediterranean and Norway.

By 15 February the demand for ten more boats for Norway had been increased to twenty; to add to this burden was a proposal that four U-boats be modified to act as transports for all three services in Norway, should the need arise. Dönitz argued with Skl on this: he could not agree with the idea of an Allied invasion of Norway, and further argued that in any case any shipping he sank in the Atlantic would automatically reduce the available shipping for such an enterprise. He wrote:

> The more shipping sunk – anywhere in the world – and the more the enemy's vital supply lines across the Atlantic are threatened, compelling him to take measures for their immediate protection, the less likely it is that he will be in any position to divert tonnage and escort duties for a landing.

Skl continued to argue, saying: 'The amount of shipping required by the enemy for a landing in Norway could be made available, despite the losses he has so far sustained.' This, and the weakness in Dönitz's argument caused by the shift in aim, made a strong case against him.

But Dönitz did try; he resumed the offensive in May, and this time he was on slightly firmer ground. The argument and its conclusion will be examined later, especially in the light of the impact of Type XIV refuelling, which first became available in March 1942. Sinkings off the US seaboard increased in February, and extended to the Aruba–Trinidad area. From 16 February sixteen boats were attacking shipping there, and even shelling shore oil installations at Aruba, the main target being the oil tanker traffic, taking crude oil northwards to the USA.

The significance of these targets brought a more marked reaction than to operations off the US coast. Air patrols were increased and shipping routes were altered to avoid the U-boats. However, *B-Dienst* had little difficulty reading the radio traffic, and the U-boats were diverted to the new concentration areas. Dönitz also allowed a greater degree of freedom of operation to these boats, to counter the Americans' defensive measures.

A bombardment of Aruba by *U156* was a total failure. A premature detonation in the barrel of the deck gun forced Hartenstein to retire. Any further hope of repeating the operation more successfully were denied when the Americans switched off coastal lights and alerted a naval patrol. The opposite was the case in Port of Spain and Port Castries, Saint Lucia, where *U156* (Korvettenkäpitan Achilles) attacked shipping with torpedoes and gunfire in the third week of February.

The eastern seaboard was not, however, the sole operational area, despite limited boat numbers. Two Type IXs were sent south to the Freetown area of West Africa, where they operated from March with some success. The aim was to divert escorts wherever possible, and to try to stop the British lending escort ships to the Americans. Dönitz did not want the protean crop of independent sailings on the east coast to dry up, or to group into convoys, until he had taken every advantage he could.

This meant, of course, that convoy traffic in mid-Atlantic enjoyed a respite from attack throughout the first half of 1942. However, one convoy was subjected to a severe onslaught in February (the month in which the new four-wheeled Enigma code 'Triton' was introduced, and not read for months). The operation was reminiscent of the earlier heyday of summer 1941. Convoy ONS.67 (36 merchantmen, escort four US destroyers and one RCN corvette) was located by *U155* on 21 February, about 600 miles north-east of Cape Race.

The rescue ship attached to the convoy was equipped with a new anti-submarine device: HF/DF (high-frequency direction-finding), but although *Toward* managed to get a fix on *U155*'s transmissions, USS *Lea* did not have radar and the U-boat avoided her attack. By 0700 on 22 February *U155* was in position to attack, firing a forward tube spread at 0703-0704. Two ships exploded simultaneously. Headquarters was signalled (using 'Triton') and *U155* took up as shadower; *U587, U558, U94, U588* and *U158* were directed to the convoy by Dönitz.

They were to make a standard group attack during the early morning of the 24th, and they did. *Inverarder* was sunk at 0428 in *U558*'s first approach, and the inexperience of the American escorts favoured the U-boats from this moment on. They attacked successively until 1540 hours, and five more merchantmen were sunk. Eight of the convoy were sunk for no U-boat lost, but this was exceptional; no more group attacks took place until ONS.92 was engaged on 12 May.

From the Allied point of view, things were looking even worse than they had in late 1941. Sinkings off the US coast were mounting, and if convoy attacks were resumed after some delay there was the added problem of the precious loss of precious intelligence from Ultra by the introduction of the four-wheel 'Triton' cipher. Something was known of the wiring for the fourth rotor at Bletchley Park, but there were no four-wheel synthesisers ('*bombes*') to help in the mammoth task of decipherment. The airwaves were rich in intelligence, but the key was lost. The war in the Far East was proving to be disastrous; stalemate existed in Africa with Rommel and Auchinleck facing each other, exhausted, at Bir Hacheim. In Russia the counter-attack launched to everyone's surprise by the Red Army was having no success against the German hedgehog defence. Spring was coming, and with it the German forces would have rested and been re-supplied to begin offensives which Hitler hoped, and the Allies feared, would end resistance to the Germans in Europe and Africa. Once more Great Britain might be left alone, for the Americans might be forced to turn their attention to the Japanese in the Pacific.

Certainly Dönitz seemed to have few worries apart from the perennial shortage of U-boats and delays in the shipyards, the latter caused by many skilled workers being called up for Army service. The losses of 1941 had to be made good, yet the conscripted shipyard workers were the very men Dönitz needed to build his U-boats and maintain them between patrols.

**Above:** A Type VII U-boat on the slips. The boat is ready for launching, after which she will for fitting-out and will be equipped with war stores and guns.

**Below:** A flotilla of Type VII U-boats sets out to sea for exercises. In all, ten U-boats can be n as well as a trawler, often used to recover practice torpedoes. The scene is the Baltic.

**Above:** A U-boat and a surface patrol vessel 'somewhere in the Baltic'.
**Below:** A single 2cm anti-aircraft gun. This mounting was seen on surface vessels; a simpler mounting was issued to U-boats.

**ght:** What the
**r** in the Atlantic
**s** about – a
**erchant** ship
**ks,** her back
**oken,** while a U-
**at** crew member
**tches** the results
the attack.

**low:** The layout
the Type IX U-
**at.** With longer
**nge** than the
**pe** VII, this boat
**uld** operate in
**e** Indian Ocean.
**owever,** it
**ffered** from
**oblems** with
**ngitudinal** stress.

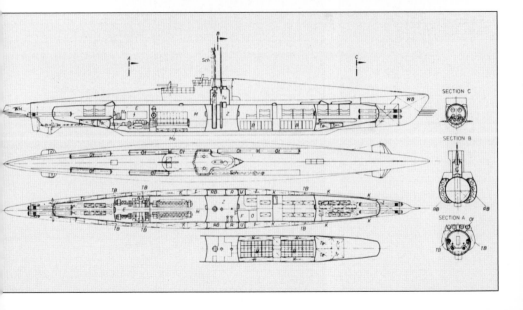

**Above:** A Type VII U-boat in dry dock. The clean lines of the boat are visible, as is the port saddle tank, the screws and rudders.

**Below left:** The moment of emergence as an early Type VII U-boat surfaces.

**Below right:** The attack periscope and its tell-tale track in the water. The still waters in these two pictures indicate that the U-boat is in the Baltic, not at sea in the Atlantic.

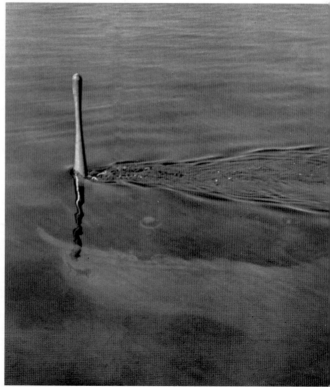

...assage through U-boats was via the bulkhead doors, which were watertight. The hand-grip ...bove the opening shows how they were negotiated. This hatch leads from the control room ...o the captain's and crew spaces forward. Note that 'BBC' stands for Brown, Boveri and Co., not the broadcaster.

**Above:** The bow deck of a U-boat. The housing on the right contains the dismounted Schnorchel tube. The open hatch and the loose items on the decking indicate the boat is in a quiet haven, not on the high seas.

**Left:** The 8.8cm deck gun fitted to early U-boats. Once surface gunnery attacks became too dangerous, these guns were withdrawn, to be replaced with anti-aircraft cannon.

**ght:** The diesel room of a
pe VII U-boat. Diesel
gines provided surface
opulsion for all standard
boats and were used to
arge the batteries that
ovided underwater power.

**elow:** A Type VII U-boat
rly in the war proceeding
a good rate of knots en
ute to the North Atlantic
om her home base in Kiel.
te the 8.8cm forward deck
n and the single 2cm FlaK
the tower rear.

Photographs from the German magazine *Signal*, which recorded events during the war and was published in many occupied countries as well as in Germany. **Above:** A meeting at sea – here two Italian submarines make a rendezvous. **Below left:** A swell covers the fore end of the boat. **Below right:** Constant vigilance was necessary to spot convoys and aircraft.

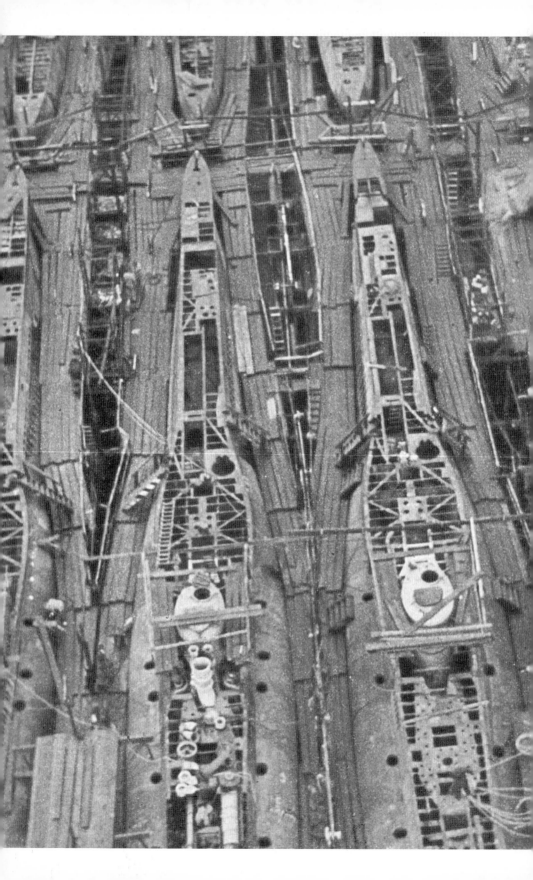

**above:** A U-boat under attack from an aircraft. The splashes around the U-boat slick show that the attack is on target. The attacking Sunderland aircraft of Coastal Command can be seen just to the right and above the depth-charge splashes. (IWM C3880)

**opposite page:** Mass production was not only an American phenomenon: here eight Type II boats are under construction. The pipes and tubes for air, compressed air and drainage are clearly seen on the two central boats.

**below:** Two escort carriers at sea. The escort carriers were a major factor in defeating the U-boats. Sailing with the convoys, they provided air reconnaissance and attack power throughout the convoy's passage. (IWM A12574)

**bottom:** A depth-charge attack on a U-boat very close to a convoy. The power of the depth-charge is witnessed by the plume of water, but in fact depth-charges had to be exploded very close to their target to cause damage, let alone sink a U-boat. (IWM A12022)

**Above:** Ships in convoy protected by a patrolling aircraft. The mere presence of aircraft was enough to force U-boats below the surface, where their speed was even less than a slow merchant ship.
**Opposite page, top:** A close-up of a gun and bomb attack on a U-boat. (IWM C4605)
**Opposite page, centre:** A view of the fleet carrier HMS *Furious* from one of its aircraft. Astern is an escorting destroyer.
**Opposite page, bottom:** A flying boat flies over two escort vessels in harbour. The air element of escorts proved to be fundamental in defeating the U-boats.
**Below:** A Type VII U-boat returns to base early in the war. The swordfish design was the flotilla emblem of the 9th U-Flotilla.

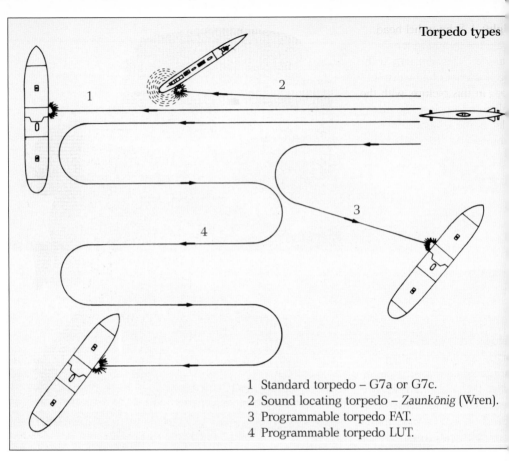

1 Standard torpedo – G7a or G7c.
2 Sound locating torpedo – *Zaunkönig* (Wren).
3 Programmable torpedo FAT.
4 Programmable torpedo LUT.

**Below:** The Walther Type XVII experimental U-boat, powered by a revolutionary hydrogen-peroxide drive system. The smooth lines reflect later design work in the Types XXI and XXIII

**right:** A Schnorchel head, coated with anti-radar material. The similarity with the household ball valve is clear in this picture, with the ball rising to close the air inlet as the U-boat submerged.

**below:** The *Neger* – two torpedoes linked togther, the earliest of the *Kleinkampfmittel* of the German Navy. *Neger* did not submerge and was of no significance apart from being a German version of British and Italian designs.

**Left:** The bow section of a Type XXI U-boat seen befor assembly with the forward compartment to the rear. Th section assembly process meant fewer man-hours spe per U-boat and allowed prefabrication of sections at various yards before the ind vidual sections were brough to the final assembly yard.

**Below:** Eight Type XXI U-boats can be seen in this photograph of the Blohm and Voss yard at the end of the war. Some bomb damag is evident, but the boats we still being assembled right u to May 1945.

*All images courtesy of Chrysa Images*

On 25 February Dönitz made a Diary note, writing that convoy attacks were only to be made when the U-boats were at maximum strength in the area; it seems that the memory of HG.76 had not faded. He also continued the fight for priority of allotment of new U-boats, for now there were twenty-one in the Mediterranean and twenty-four in Norway. He wrote another report to Skl: 'It is well worth considering whether the protection of Norway cannot be achieved indirectly by using submarines against merchant shipping', *in the Atlantic war zone* being implied. In fact the U-boats in Norway were contributing nothing, even though Churchill had considered (and dropped) the idea of an invasion in April 1942.

March saw the organisation completed for a resumption of operations off the US coast, and on the first of the month twelve boats were in position and twelve more en route from a total of 51 boats in the Atlantic. Another 51 were in harbour being refuelled and provisioned or being repaired. No fewer than 104 boats were working-up, but they were not getting to the operational flotillas fast enough, work in the Baltic being slowed by ice. But U-boat Command had done its best, and got as many U-boats as was physically possible out to the US coast.

In March, 81 ships were sunk in the Atlantic, 78 of which were lost in the western area. Only one was sunk in convoy, and only three U-boats even came close enough to convoys to attack. The War Diary records convoys by consecutive serials, and convoy 16 was sighted on March 20, number 22 not until 11 May. By the end of the year the total had risen to 72.

The March total in GRT was more than half a million tons, making the first quarter's sinkings more than one million tons of Allied and neutral shipping sunk. Of equal importance to Dönitz, however, was the arrival of *U459* on the strength of 10th UFlotilla: the first of seventeen supply boats to become operational. Her role in the western and southern Atlantic would be fundamental to the operations of the Type VII boats. Her first operational patrol was in the area south of Newfoundland and west of New York – Cape Hatteras, some 300–500 miles offshore. She refuelled no fewer than fifteen U-boats, including two Type IXs. The effective patrol length of the Type VII had been doubled, and was now dependent upon torpedoes rather than diesel fuel. Before they had had only ten days (or less if bad weather had interfered with their Atlantic crossing) to operate before returning.

The arrival of the Type XIV boats meant that U-boats could now stay longer in their effort to destroy 700,000 GRT each month. The IXC boats were even able to penetrate the Gulf of Mexico as far west as the mouth of the Mississippi, as well as operating off the north-east coast of South America. The Type VIIs now extended their patrols to include the Cape Hatteras area.

There was a fall in the rate of sinkings in April, caused by a reduction in traffic in the area, and a general dislike by ships' masters of sailing in U-boat waters. Neutrals were almost absent. Defences in March were generally regarded as small, badly-led and untrained, except in the Halifax–Cape Race area, where the Royal and Royal Canadian navies were in action. There was no convoy system and it seemed to Dönitz that when traffic stopped for a few days it was not because of defensive measures coming into force, but fear of the threat in inshore waters.

In April, when *U459* was beginning her re-supply operation, the defences off the east coast had begun to improve, with warship patrols running along the continental shelf. There were also escorts in the most dangerous places, especially Cape Hatteras, but they seemed either unable or unwilling to press home attacks on U-boats, preferring to go on their way once the U-boat had submerged. Air activity was most pronounced now, and U-boats were obliged to submerge by day and at night during full moon periods. They were also being pushed away from the most productive target areas in the inshore traffic lanes. Successes were still high enough, however, to allow the operation to continue, especially as one by-product of *U459* was a greater stretching of the defences as U-boats stayed longer, and more of them appeared in the battle zone.

At this time, Dönitz was faced with the question of whether he should be operating off the US coast, rather than in the Central Atlantic against convoys bound for the UK. The point made, a valid one, was that hitting US domestic traffic was a contribution, but was on a different plane from the previous avowed aim of the U-boat campaign, the strangulation of Great Britain. Dönitz's answer was that the 'enemy powers' shipping is one large whole', so that what he was doing was attacking the entity, and sinking as much of it as he could.

A decision would be forced, he maintained, if enemy shipping losses exceeded, and continued to exceed, shipping built. His argument rested upon the fact that the USA was the production centre for the Allies, and so attacks on her traffic had more significance than elsewhere. In retrospect the error of the argument can be seen, for ships sunk in convoy had two disadvantages to the British – they lost the ship and they lost the goods. Further sinkings were a deterrent to the merchant fleets of the world to sail in waters where U-boats patrolled. Dönitz lost sight of these factors in his attempt to achieve a high 'head-count', a characteristic not unheard of since.

In a rare moment of literary flight he described the United Kingdom at this time as the 'outpost and postern-gate of the enemy powers in Europe'. He had begun to think less of Great Britain's importance in the war, and had moved the USA into the first rank. Her industrial and military potential was enormous, but it was of no value for or against Europe if Great Britain fell. No UK meant no bases, and all plans for the invasion of Africa and France would be void.

However, Dönitz justified the attack on the Americans as an attack at the root of Allied power, particularly economic power. He argued that all losses in the US area would reduce the British will to fight, and simultaneously cut the amount of shipping available from the UK in any proposed invasion. As a bonus, sinkings in the western Atlantic would assist in the defence of Norway as well. In his opinion, he wrote, 'it is much more important just to sink than to sink in a certain area and reduce the total sinkings.' This was allied with his assertion that 'Supply traffic to the United States is equally important as that from the United States to England.' His final remark was that he would continue to attack in the west until no more profit was to be had. The thesis is invalid, and an examination of this and other errors made follows in Chapter 12.

Of course there was an abundance of profit still to be had. Attacks in April cost the Allies 65 ships of 376,836 GRT. In May in western Atlantic waters alone there were losses of 120 ships of 551,120 GRT. The War Diary comments that sinkings had deteriorated since 20 April, but no-one seems to have told the U-boat commanders. May was a remarkable month for the U-boat Command, for some 75 per cent of all operational boats had been at sea on patrol (compared with a still respectable 55 per cent average). In fact May 1942 was the pinnacle of success for the Germans in terms of effort and success, and in itself this would mean a fall in effort in June, because of rest and refitting when the patrols returned to base. Nevertheless in June some 109 ships were sunk, for a total some 40,000 GRT greater than in May.

The entire operation seemed a success. The inclusion of a first U-boat Group (*Pfadfinder* in the Caribbean and the Gulf of Mexico) had increased sinkings again, and the entry of the USA into the war seemed to have brought none of the threat originally feared. The U-boats lost amounted to just 21, and only six of those were in US waters. But the Allies were beginning to find real answers to the U-boat threat, and as convoy was introduced in US waters, there was another assault on the very doorstep of the Atlantic bases in France. Aircraft of Coastal Command, their strength greatly increased, opened the offensive against U-boats in the approach lanes in the Bay of Biscay. These two problems were added to the central need to restart operations against the convoys in mid-Atlantic.

How, then, did Dönitz see these momentous six months? The presence of the supply boats made '*Paukenschlag*' potentially even more of a decisive operation, if indeed it were decisive. By June there was a second Utanker operating (*U116*) and six more were to become available in June and July. Operations in the western Atlantic would be able to apply more pressure on the escorts and the convoy planners, and might thereby bring about the fracture for which Dönitz had seemed to be striving. It is quite possible that for Dönitz the real danger to come in the Atlantic war had been hidden behind the still considerable successes of the Army in Russia. In 1942 the whole world wondered not if, but when, Russia would capitulate. This heady stuff of success would have reduced the grimy economic factors of war in the Atlantic to a secondary position, although there is no real evidence to support this conjecture.

Churchill saw the matter clearly, and said that 'The Battle of the Atlantic was the dominating factor throughout the war. Never for one moment could we forget that everything happening elsewhere ... depended ultimately upon its outcome ...' It was clear to Churchill at least that the western Allies could not defeat Hitler until after the invasion, and then only with the help of enormous Russian sacrifices; but the Germans could remove the British from the race, and the USA indirectly, by making it impossible for Great Britain to continue. As has been seen, however, Dönitz was being frustrated in his need of all available U-boats to be operating in the Atlantic, and indeed, even by his own strategy. Local superiority of force does not always lead to a decisive battle when one considers the wide view necessary in looking at the events of this war.

# THE GREAT BATTLE I  10

During the months from July 1942 to May 1943, the Battle of the Atlantic was decided. The effort put in by both sides led to amazing successes for the Germans up to March 1943, and an equally amazing reverse in favour of the Allies just two months after that. There are many historical parallels, but none with quite the same significance for the outcome of a war as all-encompassing as this.

The stakes were so very high, for if Dönitz were to win, it could mean that the USA would be isolated between the two Axis powers, and isolated from all her east and west trade. The besieged Americans would then be put into a position of glowering impotence for many months, while Germany and Japan continued their empire-building. The strategic importance of the British Isles had never been so great as now, for the loss of the islands would mean 'no land, no bases'.

Dönitz now had to make his greatest effort to break the spirit and ability of the naval and merchant crews by destroying their ships in convoy at a hith-erto-unsurpassed rate. To do this he had 331 U-boats commissioned, of which 108 were operational, 91 of them in the Atlantic, and he had no fewer than 132 working-up, to augment the total and replace losses. Furthermore, U-boat production was now averaging about 20 boats per month, and increases in launchings were soon to come. By the end of the year he was hoping for more than 300 operational boats. An independent assessment in July 1942, based upon the military situation at this point, could only conclude that victory in the Atlantic was odds on in Germany's favour. In Europe the same conclusion seemed to be drawn.

The German forces for the forthcoming battle were:

| Flotilla | Location | Operational boats |
| --- | --- | --- |
| 1st | Brest | 16 |
| 2nd | Lorient | 26 |
| 3rd | La Rochelle | 16 |
| 6th | St.-Nazaire | 10 |
| 7th | St.-Nazaire | 6 |
| 10th | Lorient | 17 |

Plus 23 boats with 11th UFlotilla in Bergen, available to a certain extent. This gave a total of 91 boats operational in the immediate battle area.

There was little in support of the boats themselves, however, for the air–sea co-operation exercise had, as noted above, ended in failure. Nevertheless the U-boats were fresh from a highly successful operation off the US coast, morale was high, and the boats still had the advantage of surprise. They could concentrate their forces against specific targets at will, whereas the convoys had to wait to be attacked before they could react, and hope to employ the new weapons which were gradually becoming available. For the Allies there was one further drawback: no Ultra intelligence was available during this crucial summer, GCCS having yet to break the four-wheel 'Triton' cipher.

Ranged against the U-boats in the Allied Order of Battle were the surface escorts, the support groups, the aircraft of Coastal Command and the now growing numbers of other aircraft (many of them American), and the new centimetric radar. Behind these forces were the improving anti-submarine techniques being developed by the Royal Navy from the reasoned scientific researches of the ORS and other sources.

Escort forces had increased during the period of 'Paukenschlag', and were, at the end of July 1942, as follows:

| Base | Destroyers | Sloops | Corvettes | Others |
|------|-----------|--------|-----------|--------|
| Londonderry | 24 | 19 | 24 | 8 |
| Liverpool | 18 | 4 | 33 | – |
| Greenock | 12 | – | 10 | – |
| Gibraltar (local) | 7 | – | 6 | 9 |
| Freetown | 7 | 3 | 20 | 23 |
| W Atlantic | 29 | – | 74 | 14 |
| Totals | 97 | 26 | 167 | 54 |

These 344 vessels had to escort the convoys everywhere in the Atlantic, and still fell short of the January 1942 target, but it was nevertheless a significant increase on the position of only seven months previously.

Coastal Command was of course also available, and again its main role was anti-submarine warfare. Despite attempts by Bomber Command, its strength had again increased, and at 1 July stood at:

| General Reconnaissance | Aircraft Squadrons | Aircraft |
|------------------------|-------------------|----------|
| Very Long Range | 1 | 16 |
| Long Range | 1 | 12 |
| Medium Range | 19 | 370 |
| Flying-Boats | 10 | 91 |
| Totals | 31 | 489 |

Short-range aircraft had been phased out, but there was still an increase in aircraft over the past twelve months. The real, and qualitative, increase was in fact 165 when all short-range aircraft were disregarded.

Numbers alone, however, were not enough, for the U-boats were still able to roam much of the Atlantic at will. There was still an enormous need of accurate intelligence, not yet forthcoming. refuelling at sea increased both the range and the threat of the U-boats, which could now proceed to the Atlantic direct, only returning to base after a patrol. In mid-Atlantic these U-boats still had enough range for a curtailed patrol. The RAS meant that Dönitz could now extend his operations to waters previously out of range, where escorts would be thinner on the ground and less experienced. With the Type VII boats able to operate throughout the Atlantic, the long-range Type IXs could be committed to the South Atlantic and even the Indian Ocean.

Thus, more than numbers were needed to beat the U-boats, and there seemed little hope of being able to drive them away from the convoy routes. The secret weapon, Ultra, had been silent on U-boat plans since 'Triton' (GCCS name 'Shark') had been introduced on 1 February 1942; the cipher brought with it a total signals blackout, which the cryptographers at Bletchley Park were struggling, so far unsuccessfully, to resolve. Seamanship and statistical analysis alone would not be enough.

Skill is a basic element of military training, and without it the best of plans can come to nought. In the anti-submarine war, the British had one advantage: the Germans had a lot of submarines at sea. This meant that a lot of experience in everyday operations against them could be gained, and if this experience were recorded and evaluated centrally, and then passed out to sea again in training, it would be valuable in the fight. It might even help to sink U-boats, and this was the reasoning behind the appointment, in January 1942, of Commander Gilbert Roberts to the new Anti-U-boat School of Western Approaches Command.

Roberts's brief was simple, but all-embracing: examine everything to do with U-boats in order to, as Churchill put it, 'Find out what is happening in the Atlantic, find ways of getting the convoys through, *and* sink the U-boats'; This was, of course, an extension of Commander Winn's task (to locate and avoid U-boats), and made the underlying change towards an offensive policy, rather than the present purely defensive attitude forced on the Allied forces. When Roberts took command of WATU (Western Atlantic Training Unit) there was little anti-U-boat work going on in any organised or planned way. Asdic enabled a contact to be attacked with some accuracy, but this depended upon individual escorts getting on with their own job, not co-operating with others in the common aim. But the most experienced of the Atlantic commanders at the time was Captain Walker, who had devised one counter to U-boat attack, the gentle sounding 'buttercup' manoeuvre.

Walker had trained his escort group to react within a pre-ordained plan when attacked. They each turned outwards from the convoy without orders as soon as an attack began. At night (and it normally was) they then fired starshells away from the convoy for twenty minutes. This did two things: it put U-boats on the surface under illumination, and it back-illuminated any U-boat caught between the escort and the starshell, enabling it to be attacked. It was crude, but simple, and it surprised the U-boat captains, and it was responsible for the loss of two U-boats in the battle for HG76, yet another reason for Dönitz to regret that attack. The U-boats lost their immunity of darkness, and if they then submerged, Asdic, which was improving as were the operators, could pick them up. If they stayed on the surface they were at the mercy of the escorts' guns. It was a start upon which Roberts could base his experiments, and was easily taught in the war-gaming situations that he used.

His first task was to interview as many of the escort commanders as possible, to establish what they did when attacked; only Walker had anything positive to recommend by way of reaction. Roberts also spoke to one of Walker's subordinates from the escort to HG76, Lieutenant-Commander Higham, who told him that escort commanders were taught that U-boats would fire from outside the escort line around the convoy. As is known, the U-boat commanders were actually penetrating convoys (although this had fallen off somewhat of late). This would invalidate Walker's tactic, and the starshell would actually help the U-boats. Dönitz had trained his men before the war to get in close, and when Roberts established that escorts were stationed some 5,000 yards from their wards, he knew that the U-boats must be inside this radius when they fired their torpedoes.

He then tried to imagine what he would do, if he were the U-boat captain. A U-boat could be anywhere in relation to the convoy when running in to a firing position. If ahead a high-speed, but rather dangerous approach could be made, firing when close enough, then diving to avoid the mass of ships. Alternatively, the U-boat might submerge ahead of the convoy, and surface in its middle. This was perhaps the most risky of all methods, having the dual dangers of position on surfacing and the surfacing itself, making a splash for all lookouts to notice. The flank approach, thought Roberts, was most unseamanlike, in view of the danger of collision with the escorts, and so this left but one safe and effective way of getting into the convoy. This was by approaching from astern, using the speed advantage of the surfaced U-boat, and once inside attacking and then submerging to avoid retribution, traffic and escorts. A subsequent similar manoeuvre was then possible. He was not completely right, but near enough to make a start on the solution to the problem.

In fact the U-boats used a number of methods, none of which was as cold-blooded in its reasoning as Roberts supposed. Nevertheless, some boats did approach as he had suggested, and this gave him an opening. His theory was supported by the fact that convoys often experienced sinkings inside the convoy before ships were attacked at the edge of the group. (He was not aware of the erratic performances of many German torpedoes.) He spent time listening to captured U-boat crews, and this added to his store of information when they mentioned the silent running technique used after an attack. All he then had to do was evolve a counter-measure, which he did.

One escort group commander used a series of code words to initiate night action, and the manoeuvres were simple enough to be performed even without the individual captains being on the bridge. Roberts borrowed this idea, combined it with others, and called his first anti-U-boat tactic a 'raspberry'. As soon as a ship was torpedoed all escorts executed a turn aft, and formed up in a straight line some two miles to the rear of the convoy. They then did a line abreast Asdic search. If a U-boat was identified ahead of the convoy the forward escort fired starshell to put the U-boat down. The more timorous U-boat commanders would make an escape immediately, but the more resolute were also catered for. The forward escorts made full ahead for fifteen minutes, passing over the last known position before turning and making rendezvous at the estimated point of resurfacing for the U-boat, which would now be under attack.

Many sightings of U-boats were made either ahead or astern of the convoy, and they were often seen diving. The natural conclusion was that the U-boat had seen the escorts; Roberts concluded that it meant that some U-boats were shadowing convoys.

The mass of information furnished by the escort commanders gave Roberts a good idea of tactics used by the U-boats and he devised set-piece antidotes, but there was one situation in which only weight of escort numbers would be of any use – the pack attack. And Dönitz was about to do everything he could to ensure that when attacks were made on convoys, they were made in large numbers, to outnumber and outmanoeuvre the escort. But before he could do this, he still had to find the convoys.

Air–sea co-operation had been tried at the beginning of 1941. Whereas it worked for Coastal Command a lot of the time, it was far harder in the reverse situation where a fast moving aircraft was trying to give comparatively slow-moving boats a position to move to. To an extent the problem had been resolved, as it had been with Coastal Command. The *Kondor* would transmit a homing signal on one of the U-boat frequencies, and the U-boats would home on that. At the same time all U-boats picking up the signal reported their bearing to Headquarters, to allow a position plot to be made. Headquarters then transmitted a dead-reckoning position for the rendezvous to boats coming up. This was still dependent upon the aircraft being reasonably accurate about the course and speed of the convoy.

Most of the time, however, the U-boats had to do their own searching. Operational areas were being pushed farther west, beyond the range of the Fw 200, by the ever-strengthening Coastal Command Very Long Range aircraft. All boats had to report any convoys or other traffic seen, and after the first few months of the war had to wait for permission to attack. As has been seen, when a U-boat sighted a convoy it was often ordered to take up a position astern to shadow while Dönitz assembled an attack group, or ordered an established group to the attack. Once a number of boats had short-signalled 'Yes' to Headquarters, showing that they were in sight, the order to attack was given. Dönitz always hoped for a minimum of five boats, but he was not always successful.

Once the boats went in, Dönitz's control was over, and it was every boat for itself. After the first attempts, local tactical control at sea was dispensed with, as no U-boat commander had a suitably high viewpoint for physical control of the U-boats around him, and no other way of knowing dispositions. If there were collisions (actually very few), they would have to be accepted as part of the risk. The numbers for attack and reconnaissance were rising, however, and in one assembly for attack two boats did collide, but this was a rarity. The War Diary records the search for each convoy in detail, and demonstrates that even when Dönitz was aware of a sailing, and of the port of origin, he often only managed to get the U-boats into position to attack with some element of luck. Some were also lost even when contacted because the shadower was forced off station. Roberts's tactics were important in this, which was nearly as important as sinking the U-boats.

If a convoy had been lost, either by the shadower being forced away or by weather or whatever cause, there had to be a search. The same method was used if contact had been lost after an aircraft report, and the first thing was for Headquarters to issue a 'known last position' report on the convoy. Dönitz would then order his boats to a rendezvous calculated from that report and the course and speed observed. At the rendezvous the U-boats would then have individual orders to comb the track of the convoy from there, the calculated courses being on either side of the projected target course. Each boat would be a finger in this search, moving at maximum speed on the surface and meandering from side to side in the hope of re-contacting the convoy. Once contact was regained standard attack tactics took over.

In cases where a convoy was expected, the U-boats were put into patrol lines, sometimes sweeping the expected track of the oncoming ships. At other times they stayed in place, especially when intelligence had reported an oncoming target on a specific course. At yet other times all boats could be ordered to a fixed point, but this, as well as the static patrol line, could be avoided, as was the group at rendezvous waiting for HG.76 earlier. The advantage of the static patrol line was that a number of boats would be immediately available if the convoy appeared. Invariably, after contact, the standard procedure came into play: assemble and attack. But in all cases when the U-boats were on the surface, they were becoming more vulnerable to aircraft, and it was for this reason that Dönitz operated whenever possible in the aircraft-free 'gaps'. The Allies knew that until these gaps were closed convoys were at high risk, and not until the escort carrier became available were these gaps sealed tight.

One area into which Coastal Command aircraft could easily penetrate was the Bay of Biscay, where U-boats could be found near their bases. There was always a chance that the aircraft would catch a U-boat in transit, and once the Bay Offensive patrols started, Dönitz wrote that the Biscay area was becoming the 'playground of English aircraft'. He needed fighter cover for the U-boats to contest the command of the air so easily won by the British. On 27 June 1942 he was in conference with Göring who promised him aircraft: 24 twin-engined Ju 88s, under the command of the *Fliegerführer Atlantik* at Mérignac. They were of no assistance whatsoever.

Dönitz then decided that his U-boats would stand a better chance against aircraft if they could fight them on the surface. This would make the aircraft's depth-charges relatively ineffective, even if set for only 25 feet. Dönitz had been impressed by the results when the U-boats stayed up to fight aircraft, and a number had been shot down or damaged in this way. He admitted that in the Bay 'the enemy had tactically gained the upper hand with his (anti-U-boat) measures'. The technicians now had to come up with an antidote to aircraft anti-submarine weapons as well as the radar they carried. The long-term plan was to bring the Walter submarines into service (of which, more later), but for the moment existing weapons and equipment had to be made more effective.

Radar could be detected; the Germans were aware of this, for they too had operational radars, although their development had lagged behind that of the Allies. The cavity magnetron was the answer to the short wavelength problem, but German scientists refused to believe it possible until the *Rotterdam Gerät* (an H2S set fitted in a captured Bomber Command aircraft and examined, but not until March 1943) told the story. To counter the threat of airborne radar the Germans first used the French Metox-Grandin R-600 search receiver, with a low wavelength limit of 130cm. This crude device (supported by a cross of wood, and hastily dismounted when diving) was sufficient to reduce the first Bay Offensive to near ineffectiveness by October 1942. This in turn brought Coastal Command the bonus of new, shorter wavelength radars, usually the prerogative of Bomber Command.

What the U-boats really needed was their own radar, to locate aircraft and especially escort ships whose own radar enabled them to use their guns freely in bad weather, fog or at night. With a location radar the U-boats could fight back, or disappear. The parallel between Bomber Command and the *Luftwaffe* appears once more: Göring was unwilling to release active radars to the Navy, because he wanted them for his anti-aircraft guns; the RAF wanted every set for the bombers. Some sets were eventually fitted to U-boats, but they came too late to affect the outcome of the battle.

The next move was to make sure that the FlaK armament on the U-boats was capable of shooting down the surprise attacker, especially if the British managed to shorten the frequency of their radar. The first expedient was to add a platform aft of the bridge (the *Wintergarten*) equipped with a twin 2cm C38 gun. This was purely defensive, but in September 1942 *U256* returned from a patrol badly shot up after an aircraft attack. It was decided to turn her into a floating FlaK battery. Conning-tower and pressure hull were armoured, and she was fitted with a greatly increased FlaK armament (including two quadruple 2cm *Flakvierling* units). Her purpose was to shoot it out with attacking aircraft after being 'caught'. It was a trap that really did not work.

Metox plugged the gap for the immediate future, and in July Dönitz had been well pleased with the situation. He was, as noted, also thinking to the future, with planning now going ahead for the Walter Type XXVI boats, as well as the Types XXI and XXIII. Also in mind were experiments which had been carried out on acoustic torpedoes and some remote-controlled torpedoes, all of which would be of great value if they were available within a reasonable time. Unfortunately, Dönitz had no idea of what 'reasonable time' was. Development of the acoustic torpedo reveals that Dönitz was thinking of attacks on the escorts themselves, because they were beginning to present an increasingly dangerous threat. An acoustic torpedo was the U-boats' remedy when needing to attack an approaching, fast-moving, target. A standard torpedo was of little use, for a hit on the bows of a destroyer was extremely difficult to achieve, but an acoustic torpedo could miss but still turn to attack its target once more. Of course, on the front of the torpedo there had to be an effective pistol, and this problem was still unresolved.

On the Allied side, although still faced with increasing numbers of U-boats and a U-boat Arm whose morale was high, there was some cause for limited optimism. Still short of the means to provide constant escort and air cover to all convoys in the central and eastern Atlantic, efforts were being made to use what was available to its maximum potential. There was still a delay in instituting convoy in the Caribbean, the Gulf of Mexico and on the eastern seaboard, and the U-boats were still active in those areas. The Royal Navy lent warships experienced in escort work to the Americans, and the interlocking convoy system came into being in about the middle of 1942.

This meant that U-boats could no longer enjoy easy pickings; it was time to go back to work in the more dangerous waters of the Atlantic, but to the still aircraft-free zones. Air cover was not ubiquitous in the Atlantic, and south of Greenland there was a large area with no air patrols. Further gaps open to exploitation were situated around the Azores and the Canary Islands. But Dönitz had to find the convoys in those areas before he could commit his U-boats to the attack once more.

He maintained a significant presence in the Caribbean, where he left his IXC boats, but he also moved forces on to the convoy routes established by intelligence work. U-boat patrol lines and *B-Dienst* had established that the main traffic concentration lay along the great circle (and shortest) route between Nova Scotia, New York and the west coast ports of the British Isles.

The months of May and June 1942 had been most profitable for Dönitz, and the U-boats sank 246 ships (8.4 per cent of the war total) in those two months. American introduction of convoy reduced the figures in July, as did the need to regroup in the central Atlantic area and the leave requirements for the U-boat crews. With Type XIV tankers at sea, a Type IXC U-boat could now be at sea for three months, and the strain upon crews was enormous, especially as the Bay Offensive ensured no rest for them until they came ashore in France.

July saw few convoy actions, the emphasis returning to independents. With only a few boats at sea, Dönitz had to wait to get the anti-convoy operations started again. Many boats were still operating off the US coast, but losses inflicted by the Americans were forcing Dönitz to pull his boats away. Farther south the attacks continued, as they did off Freetown on the other side of the ocean.

On 1 August Dönitz recorded that there were 152 operational boats in the U-boat fleet, 113 assigned to the Atlantic (in fact there were 121, but some were under repair or refit). A further 131 were working-up. The most experienced crews were now ready to put to sea again, having spent July recuperating from the extended trans-Atlantic patrols. The majority were to sail for the air-gap zones, and some were bound for the waters off Cape Town, to disrupt traffic and keep the escorts spread as thinly as possible. These latter were to be accompanied by a Type XIV Utanker to increase their range, and they were to sail farther from base than any U-boat had done before.

The great circle route from Halifax was the main target area, and U-boats ordered to this area were directed to that line. *B-Dienst* was still reading the BAMS code, to help locate the convoys, but Dönitz remained shaken by the effects of the HG.76 operation. The War Diary for August begins in a despondent manner in respect of the prospective convoy operations, and the results of the attack on SC.94 were recorded as an apologia.

SC.94 had been attacked after an assault on ON.115, in which four ships were sunk out of 41 in convoy, and of twelve U-boats attacking, one was lost. Eight of these boats were then ordered into a patrol line, but heavy mist caused the ON.115 operation to be broken off. While patrolling off the Newfoundland Bank they sighted SC.94 on 5 August. The convoy consisted of 36 merchantmen and Escort Group C1 (one destroyer and five corvettes). Nine U-boats opened the attack, and although joined by eight others, they sank only 11 ships, and damaged one. Two U-boats were lost to the escort, and seven were damaged, three of them so badly that they had to return to base.

Dönitz explained this poor performance by noting that only one of the U-boat commanders had any real experience, and that bad weather for the first three days of the attack had hampered it. He also noted that the already heavy escort had been reinforced, and that the convoy had had good air cover. In fact the surface escort was only increased to seven, one of which left after ramming *U379*. Furthermore, the escort (with one exception) remained behind on the night of 8/9 August to fight the attacking boats, leaving only HMS *Primrose* to accompany the merchant ships for many hours.

Even with air cover on the afternoon of 9 August and the following day, five U-boats got into firing positions, but not one of them scored a hit. This time, however, it was not the torpedo pistol at fault, but bad fire control. These U-boats had spent more than six months without group experience of any sort, and this was the root cause of the relative failure of the attack. Dönitz did not record this in the Diary, probably unwilling to admit that the free-for-all that had been '*Paukenschlag*' had taken the fine edge off the U-boats' fighting ability.

Some boats were still operating alone, taking advantage of the inexperienced escorts and air patrols attached to the newly-created American convoy system. In the Windward passage a number of WAT and TAW convoys were attacked to good effect by a small number of Type IX boats. Farther west, off the Guyana coast, there was still some good hunting, and off Bahia, still further to the south. In the central Atlantic, in the area where independents were routed (higher speed ships) there was a crop of sinkings, extending into the Freetown area. To the north, off the coast of Spain, more convoy attacks were made without loss against the south- and west-bound traffic.

Dönitz and Hitler met at the routine FCNA on 26 August 1942. At the previous meeting, on 15 June, Dönitz had had to argue forcefully that U-boats could not stop invasions (in connection with the Azores, Cape Verde Islands and Madeira), another of Hitler's distractions. The August meeting was, however, of more importance, and examined the war situation in general. It was said that 'It is urgently necessary to defeat Russia and thus create a *Lebensraum* which is blockade-proof and easy to defend. Thus we could continue to fight for years.' This was Raeder speaking, who knew that he would get his way if he started out with something with which Hitler could readily agree. His second point was:

> The fight against the Anglo-Saxon sea powers will decide both the length and the outcome of the war, and could bring Great Britain and America to the point of discussing peace terms.

By this time, this was wishful thinking, but Hitler agreed explicitly. One must wonder however if he saw the real point behind Raeder's statement, which was simply that the Battle of the Atlantic had to be won, or the war would inevitably be lost. He was no longer saying that the war could be won in the Atlantic.

Further matters were then discussed, including the strategic necessity for holding Norway. Its position across the convoy route to Russia had helped in the virtual destruction of PQ.17, and the failure of PQ.18 to sail on schedule.

The presence of U-boats, aircraft and surface units restricted Allied supplies to Russia, considered in danger of total collapse. The Home Fleet of the Royal Navy was being kept at home, and the surface units doing that were better based in Norway than in German waters because air mine-laying was making those waters too dangerous for the pocket battleships and cruisers.

In the Baltic, Raeder reported, mines were the main weapon, and only two or three Russian submarines had been able to take advantage of the melted ice and penetrate that sea. If the Army were to take Leningrad it would release a few naval units, but would make the Baltic mine-free, allowing its full use for training purposes. Again, if Leningrad were taken, there would be another advantage: the shipyards would be available to increase building capacity. The conference also agreed that although the Black Sea had no real strategic importance as yet, six Type II boats from the training flotillas would be transported there overland to attack Russian traffic and influence Turkish opinion.

The conference then turned to the main area of discussion, the Atlantic. Raeder, speaking for Dönitz as well, said that even when the war against Russia was finished, the naval war there would continue, and the only hope for success lay in 'constant successful attacks on their sea routes'. He described the results of 'Paukenschlag', and the reasons for the withdrawal of the U-boats from the east coast of the USA. He attributed the rearrangement of operational areas to the new convoy system, and increased air patrols. The increased rate of U-boat production, and the large monthly numbers arriving at the operational flotillas, now allowed Dönitz to renew anti-convoy operations in the sea lanes used by the enemy. Off the US coast attacks would continue, but in areas unprotected by aircraft, and especially where unprotected sailings could be expected. As far as the renewal of the anti-convoy battle was concerned, he reported that 'opportunities for attack are not much worse than before as long as the convoy remains beyond the range of aircraft protection'.

He then showed Hitler a chart showing the operational range of enemy aircraft flying from the mainland, and commented that they were equipped with 'superior location-finding devices' which had caused the loss of four U-boats in the Bay of Biscay and three damaged. He added that the Metox R600 could detect the transmission of radar waves, and would be able to protect the U-boats since installation had begun on 8 August. Much too was expected from 'Bold', an Asdic deception device which was being fitted. On release from the submarine 'Bold' created a large gas bubble, which caused a false echo on Asdic receivers, and enabled a number of boats to make their escape from attacking escorts.

Raeder then outlined the Skl plans for the future of the U-boats. The aim was to attack simultaneously in a number of target areas – quite feasible with the strength of the U-boat Arm being so high. There was to be an operation (noted above) off the Horn of Africa, perhaps extending as far as the Natal Passage, with four boats. In the Arctic the PQ convoys were to be attacked as soon as they made a reappearance, and in the Mediterranean there were boats available to assault the Malta convoys; the capture of Malta was, Raeder observed, of prime importance, and Gibraltar should be next. He rounded off the U-boat discussion with a report on losses, which he said had increased due to the air activity in the Bay of Biscay. (Appended to the original notes of this conference is a summary of losses to date, presumably prepared by Dönitz's staff, giving a total loss of 105 U-boats since the war started, with 3,803 men killed, of whom 360 were officers and 1,386 of warrant rank.)

The U-boat war was becoming one of increasing technological importance, as was noted in the War Diary. The side with the best equipment was going to win. Radar was of prime strategic importance, although its actual use was, of course, tactical. Allied efforts were giving escorts and aircraft the means to find U-boats on the surface, where before they had been safe, at least at night. The freedom to travel at night on the surface had had three advantages: batteries could be charged, high speed could be maintained and the crew could enjoy fresh air. The Germans now had need of more, and better, search receivers. If they did not have them, or they were ineffective, the balance in this battle would pass to the Allies, for U-boats submerged were slow, almost blind, and vulnerable within Asdic range, if they ever got so near to a target.

Operational plans for September, therefore, were designed to put the U-boats into 'soft' areas where there were no air patrols, operations in the northern Atlantic and off Africa and Spain. There were 171 operational U-boats altogether, of which 147 were in the Atlantic flotillas. In the Arctic U-boats fought battles against two Murmansk convoys (the delayed PQ18 and QP 14), and off the coast of Guyana and Freetown mainly independents were attacked. In the main area of the North Atlantic the U-boats began to make their presence felt again, and Dönitz commented on the help the British route planners were giving him. On 9 September he said:

> It is astonishing with what persistence the English have plied the routes immediately north and south of the great circle during the last few months in spite of several large-scale attacks by U-boats. For several weeks boats have been disposed in the same area to pick up west-bound convoys.

As will be remembered, Dönitz was now equating west-bound traffic with the value of east-bound, but felt sure that the west-bound convoys would be a softer target. The U-boats were being concentrated on the great circle route, and B-Dienst had reported on 9 September that the convoys were being routed only just south of that shortest route. In fact outward-bound convoys suffered from the fuel shortage affecting all British naval operations, and from the lesser status they enjoyed in comparison with the goods-laden arrivals to the UK.

Dönitz's problem, as ever, was how to get the maximum number of U-boats to attack the maximum possible number of convoys. He wanted the northern operation to reflect in its success the importance it had with respect to Great Britain's survival or fall. One major opportunity arose when ON.127 was located on 5 September by *U584*. Contact was lost at nightfall, and not regained until the 10th. The escorts were suffering from radar failure, and thirteen U-boats directed to the convoy all made attacks. Six ships were sunk, six damaged. The *Vorwärts* Group attacked during the first night, and again on 11/12 September, and *U96* attacked alone in daylight on the 10th. The convoy consisted of 32 ships, escorted by Escort Group C4 (two destroyers and four corvettes). One remarkable event was the attack made by *U96* which went in as soon as she arrived, sinking two and damaging a third ship – not notable until one realises that the attacks were made *submerged*.

Dönitz, perhaps in relief, proclaimed the attack a great success, and noted that the weather had been a great help. Of the thirteen attackers, he noted, eight had been on their first patrol, and the convoy had been severely mauled. The Diary claims (erroneously) nineteen ships sunk, and six damaged. In the confusion of the action, some commanders had claimed hits that were actually hits by torpedoes fired by others, but the action put Dönitz into a better frame of mind. He reported that convoy operations were still possible, 'and can be successful outside the range of the enemy air force, providing a sufficient number of boats are [sic] used and the weather is fair'. But the number of ships damaged bothered him, and would have been an even greater concern if he had known the true ratio between hits and sinkings. He once more commented: 'It is regretted that torpedoes with impact firing still have such small effect'.

By the end of the month, however, he was committed to the renewal and continuation of the assault on the North Atlantic convoys, and he had had some reasonable successes. Since the tentative attempts of July, and including convoys attacked in the Caribbean, no fewer than 34 convoys had been attacked, and there were also the operations outside his control in the Arctic to add to these totals. In the Atlantic battle 90 ships had been sunk from the convoys contacted, more than 40 per cent on average of all sinkings during those three months. Furthermore, sinkings were maintaining a satisfactory level, as the following shows:

| Month | Total sunk (Ships GRT) | | Total sunk in convoy (Ships GRT) | | Total damaged (Ships GRT) | |
|---|---|---|---|---|---|---|
| July | 75 | 365566 | 16 | 88219 | 8 | 67739 |
| August | 105 | 547146 | 45 | 236713 | 9 | 70052 |
| September | 85 | 419902 | 29 | 143617 | 18 | 18879 |
| Total | 265 | 1332614 | 90 | 468549 | 35 | 156670 |

On 30 September Dönitz made his first official report to Skl on the 'Submarine situation and intended operations'. In it was noted the following:

1. In the North Atlantic the convoys were once more beginning to scatter, although not as widely as in 1941. He added that the west-bound convoys were easily located by *B-Dienst*, and that the weather element was extremely important for his operations. He said that the best U-boat type for the anti-convoy operations was undoubtedly the Type VII, of which he had 136 operational (actually 147).

2. Three U-boats had been very successful in the area of the St Lawrence river and the Belle Isle Straits, where defences were weak. He thought that operations should continue there until such time as support groups were operational.

3. Off the east coast of the USA operations were not so profitable, as the convoys there were strongly escorted and had continuous air cover. Mining operations, however (the only resort when active attacks were impossible), were to be planned involving individual patrols.

4. In the Gulf of Mexico and the Caribbean the situation had changed from the halcyon days of the high summer. Now U-boat losses were high due to air attack and radar. Although the U-boats were protected to an extent from air cover at night, if they were to attack they had to accept the dangers of radar-equipped escorts. In the Old Bahamas Channel and the Windward Passage only single U-boats would be used from now on, with most boats concentrating in Trinidadian waters, where convoys were to be found. Morale too was at risk if the boats stayed in these far-off waters too long; this meant that refuelling from Utankers was no longer of such benefit to these operations.

5. So far as Trinidad was concerned, conditions for the U-boats were best to the east of the island, where there were still no convoys, and little air activity. Otherwise conditions there were similar to those described in paragraph (4). He said that the main problem for the boats was finding independents to attack, and that Type IX boats were better suited to patrols in these waters.

6. On the Sierra Leone route air patrols were prohibiting the U-boats from making extensive pursuits northward. Aircraft based at Gibraltar were the cause of this problem, and air cover was almost continuous from the west coast of northern Morocco to the North-Western Approaches. A further problem facing the U-boats was the ten-day delay between convoys, which could mean the operational loss of three weeks if one convoy were missed.

7. On the Freetown route there were still ships to be sunk, and, as in the Trinidad area, convoy route changes were impossible.

8. Operations off the coast of Guyana were still at an experimental stage,

with two Type IXs being bound for the area, in the distant company of two Italian submarines.

9. The operation off Cape Town was under way, with the boats en route under strict radio silence.

10. In view of the successes gained by the boats operating from Norway on the PQ/QP route in the waters east of Iceland, Dönitz was planning to operate his boats there too. Although group attacks were ruled out by the light nights of the summer, individual operations would be organised and a number of boats sailing for Germany from the Atlantic could be ordered to the area when reports of sailings were received.

11. Finally, Dönitz commented on the situation in his home waters – the Bay of Biscay and its approaches. There was still a danger from mines and aircraft patrols. The Metox device, however, was reducing the effect of the offensive against the U-boats in the Bay to manageable proportions, but he repeated his request for more air cover for them while in transit, and he added a request for more surface strength as well.

The tone of the report is cautiously optimistic, even though his operations were being curtailed in some areas. Although the War Diary notes his continuing disquiet over air patrols in Atlantic waters, he did not allow this to pervade the report: no doubt in the hope that optimism brought reinforcement. He still had the ever-increasing problem of radar to face, and his torpedo pistols were still not 100 per cent reliable.

The fourth year of the war began in September 1942 in a business-like manner; Dönitz's report had assessed the overall picture accurately, and without bias. He was aware that he would need even greater numbers of U-boats from now on to combat the effect of growing numbers of escorts, aircraft and weapons. To divert an escort now would need his numbers as never before. The days of the devastating 'first night' were past, and he would have to grind away at every convoy for as long as possible if he were to achieve his targeted sinking rate. His options were, of course, severely limited by having to be outside effective Allied air cover range.

To make the most of the remaining air gaps, Dönitz had to position the U-boats on either side of the Atlantic, picking up convoys when they were beyond air cover. The U-boats would then have to harry their targets through the gaps, releasing them at the edge. The plan hoped for a repetition in the opposite direction. The refuelling problem, sure to be significant with all the movement inherent to the plan, was met by having five Type XIV and three Type XB boats available in relays. To avoid unwelcome inshore air attention, or combat it, he decided that boats would henceforth leave the French bases in groups, thus affording each other protection from air attack. This proved less effective than he had hoped, and the concept of U-boats fighting off aircraft resulted in so many losses and damage that the idea was eventually discarded.

He also had to determine whether he had sufficient U-boats to sustain operations in nine areas within four main zones of the Atlantic: the Atlantic routes to and from America, off Freetown, off the north coast of Guyana and the central Atlantic independent route. A fifth zone, off South Africa, might be added once reports were received from the first boats sent there. There were 182 operational U-boats nominally under Dönitz's command, but 35 were based in Norway, leaving him 147, which he thought adequate. There were also 105 more boats working-up in the Baltic and elsewhere, soon to reinforce the Atlantic flotillas. Operations could continue so long as losses did not rise significantly.

To the Allies the U-boat threat was even more menacing than before. The first Bay offensive had been moderately successful, but was now losing effect. Escorts were more efficient, but as the tempo was stepped up more areas were being opened up to U-boats, and counter-measures were stretching the limit of the defences. Furthermore, Ultra was still holding on to the secret of 'Triton', despite every effort at Bletchley Park.

October saw, in fact, a reduction in the success rate, despite the increase in strength of the Atlantic flotillas. In the North Atlantic, the central area and in the far west the sinkings fell, and boat losses rose to twelve in the northern sector. Off Africa things were easier, as the *Streitaxt* Group demonstrated in their operation against SL.125, located by *U409* of the group on the morning of 27 October.

The tactics were standard, and *U203* shadowed during the day, while the others came up. *U509* was the only boat to attack on the first full day, the 28th, but she sank two ships. Next day *U134* maintained contact, while waiting for the others to arrive; that night four U-boats attacked, sinking three ships and damaging three others. On the 30th two shadowers held on to the target until nightfall when five boats sank four more ships and damaged yet another. Dönitz then broke off the operation upon the arrival of extra escorts and air cover.

Farther south still, Group *Eisbär* went into action against the Cape Town traffic, and was very successful. The boats had been refuelled south of Ascension Island towards the end of September, and started their onslaught during the night of 7/8 October. So confident had Dönitz been of this success that he had already despatched a second group, before the first had arrived. The gamble was to pay off, despite the loss of one Type IXD2 to HMS *Active* on 8 October. In all, during the month the Type IX boats in this area sank 23 ships of 156,244 GRT, and the next month a further 29 ships of 160,633 GRT. All of these were unescorted individual ships, and only *U179* was lost.

In the northern area, as mentioned, U-boat losses were higher in comparison with the other operational areas, but were still only average for this particular area. Sinkings had fallen to 66 ships of 427,948 GRT, but the accumulated total of all ships sunk by the U-boats had now exceeded the 2,000 mark, and the total tonnage lost in the war so far was no less than 10,114,720

GRT. The year 1942 had been an exceptional one, for the figures at the end of 1941 were approximately one half of what they were now. If only Dönitz could maintain the momentum, perhaps he would achieve his aim.

The winter of 1942 was to see the 'end of the beginning' (to borrow Churchill's famous phrase). In Russia the summer attacks on Moscow had suddenly been diverted to a drive upon the Caucasus where it had bogged down, especially in front of Stalingrad. By 19 November Soviet forces began the counter-attack that would erase the Sixth Army from the German Order of Battle. The Battle at El Alamein was soon to take place, with a break-out by the British Eighth Army, balanced by the landings in Morocco and Algeria, Operation 'Torch'.

During Group *Streitaxt*'s operation against SL.127, much of the other traffic in the area was connected with the invasion plan, but signs of great shipping movements were missed, probably because U-boat Command was concentrating hard on this attack. The Germans were completely surprised by the 'Torch' landings, and Dönitz's own comments, made after the war, were that:

> The German intelligence service [the *Abwehr*] under Admiral Canaris failed completely, just as it failed throughout the war, to give the U-boat Command one single piece of information about the enemy that was the slightest use to us.

Skl had been misled too by the continued presence of French troops and naval personnel in North Africa who, they felt, would defend the coast against any such invasion, so deterring the Allies from the outset from a hazardous undertaking, especially bearing in mind earlier action against the French Fleet in North Africa at Mers-el-Kebir.

The landings do show how tenuous command of the sea can be; it is virtually impossible to have complete control, even with the most powerful navy, and Dönitz did not have that. He had but occasional local control at any one time, and he was in danger of losing even that. A similarity occurred during the Channel dash after the break-out of the surface units from Brest: the Royal Navy could not even control one of the nearest of the seas it supposedly commanded. The success of Operation 'Torch' was due to consummate skill in security, which was becoming a byword of Allied operations.

The month of November was remarkable in another respect: the U-boats sank more shipping in this month than in any other month of the war, a total of 125 ships of 784,885 GRT. This may have been due to the demands for escorts to the invasion ships, and rounded off a period of five months in which the U-boats sank no less than 20 per cent of all the shipping they destroyed during the entire war. Even 'Paukenschlag' results were overshadowed by this success. Dönitz was still on track, although he had little success as far as the mass of shipping around the landing beaches was concerned.

As soon as he heard of the landings, he positioned 40 boats (nineteen U-boats and 21 Italian submarines) from the Mediterranean in the area west of a line from the Balearics to Algiers. They could not stop the invasion forces, and in subsequent operations five U-boats and one Italian boat were lost. Twenty-five boats in the Atlantic were ordered to the area.

Their task was to harass the transports maintaining the troops ashore, and *U173* was the first boat to penetrate the defences, causing some damage in the Fedala roads. The next was *U130* (Kals) who, driven off earlier, made a second, more successful approach. His log records:

> November 12. 1321. 20 miles north of Fedala. My intention is to go inshore until I reach the fifteen fathom line and then to proceed along the coast to the Fedala roadstead and attack. The patrols will hardly expect a U-boat to approach so close inshore.
>
> 1440. Grazed bottom. Depth 70 feet. [The shallows were another danger the U-boats had to face, somewhat different from the depths in the North Atlantic.]
>
> 1600. Some 20 vessels observed lying in the roadstead, among them an aircraft carrier at the extreme southern end, a cruiser with a tripod mast close inshore, and two tankers. Remaining ships consist of large freighters and troopships. A few escort vessels to the west and in the vicinity of the warships. Proceeded with great caution on account of completely unruffled surface. Periscope only used for brief glances. Decided to go for the ships nearest me.
>
> 1828–1833. Fired four single torpedoes from bow tubes, then turned about and fired from stern tube VI. Tube V out of action. Hits observed on three large modern freighters. Heavy explosions and clouds of thick smoke over the whole formation ... As I thought the enemy would certainly expect me to head west or north-west and make for deep water, I clung to the 10-fathom line and proceeded north-east along the coast without any difficulty.

These notes show the operational difficulties quite clearly. In this attack *U130* sank three US ships: *Edward Rutledge*, *Tasker H. Bliss* and *Hugh L. Scott*. All were troop transports, totalling more than 42,000 GRT. Considering the waters *U130* was in, and the local defences, this was a considerable coup.

Operations in the area continued for some days, but the U-boats were unable to affect the lodgement in any way, either the US forces in the west, or the combined forces in the east. They were soon withdrawn to safer, deeper waters off Gibraltar. One can only speculate what might have been the result if U-boats had established the significance of the invasion force as it sailed through waters so close to their bases. The various ships moving south had been reported four times by separate U-boats, and once by an aircraft, but the significance of the movements had not been realised. The paucity of German military intelligence combined with Allied security measures led to a strategic success for the Allies.

The aim of the invasion had been to show Anglo-American co-operation, and to put Germany in a strategic quandary. There was a new fear that the Allies would also land in Europe, and Raeder and Hitler met to discuss the situation as soon as the initial shock had passed. Various other areas were discussed and then discussion turned to North Africa. There seems to have been little reaction by the German staff, and the fact that the Allies could raise the ships for the enterprise seemed more important than the effects of the land-ings themselves. Then Hitler was told that the key to North Africa was Tunisia, and that German troops held that country. All the enemy had done, according to the notes on the conference, was to gain 'the advantage of moving his air bases closer to our North African positions and Italy. This is offset, however, by disadvantages due to vulnerable supply lines and the large numbers of troops needed.'

The reality of the situation had not, or could not, penetrate the inner circle of the Nazi hierarchy, and only Raeder voiced concern about future Allied operations in the Mediterranean, which might lead to the invasion of either Spain, Italy or the Balkans.

The conference then looked at the U-boat situation, and Dönitz said that the strength in the Arctic was to be kept at 23. Of the 24 boats originally in the Mediterranean, five had been lost in the attacks on 'Torch' ships, and were to be replaced by boats from the Atlantic. There was to be an increase in the number in the western Mediterranean, with some others transferred to form a reserve. In the Atlantic at this time there were 57 boats operating, with two Utankers. A further 33 U-boats were en route to or from base. Three boats were off the Cape of Good Hope, four in the Gulf of Guinea to Freetown area, and seven off Trinidad. There were 25 concentrated off Gibraltar, with orders to attack supply convoys to North Africa. A further fourteen were in the North Atlantic. The plan was to leave a number of boats in the Azores–Gibraltar area, and for the rest to operate against Atlantic convoys, as escorts would have been reduced by Operation 'Torch'.

One other significance of 'Torch' was that it caused a disruption once more in Dönitz's plans for the North Atlantic, where the true strategic battle was being fought.

# 11 THE GREAT BATTLE II

November 1942 was not merely the month in which the Allies landed in North Africa, however, for the U-boats on the North Atlantic routes were now benefiting from their experience, as was U-boat Command. At the beginning of the month, on the great circle patrol area, Group *Veilchen's* thirteen boats were patrolling, together with five independent boats that had been positioned in the area. *U522* located a convoy, SC.107, south of Cape Race. The convoy had just joined up with feeder convoys from Halifax and Sydney, and the rendezvous with Escort Group EG C.4 had been made. There were 42 ships in the convoy, and the escort consisted of a Canadian destroyer, one British and three Canadian warships and two destroyers of the Western Local Escort Group. The rescue ship *Stockport* also sailed, and was equipped with HF/DF.

*U552* located and immediately attacked one of the destroyer escort, but the attack failed. But *B-Dienst*, having deciphered convoy radio signals, had ordered Group *Veilchen* to move south from its original position. On 1 November the convoy was sighted by *U381* which quickly called up two other boats. All three were located by HF/DF and forced off by the two corvettes. Then, just after sunset, when the U-boats were surfacing to use their better surface speed, *U71* was radar-located and also driven off. But other boats were approaching, and *U402* opened the account at 0200 on the 2nd with an attack which missed, but which frightened the ship in position 5.3 in the convoy, and then sank another vessel.

When the last torpedo of this attack was fired, at 0255, four merchant ships had been sunk and two damaged. The second attack, starting at 0650, saw five more merchantmen sunk when it ended at 0743. Seven U-boats were involved in this phase of the assault. On 2 November the U-boats maintained contact, but in the evening a heavy sea mist caused them to lose sight of their target. Contact was not regained until the following day, when no fewer than nine U-boats were able to get a sight of the convoy. Despite losses the convoy did not change course, but made more pronounced zig-zags. At 1139 on the 3rd *U521* managed to sink a tanker, but was then driven off with all the other U-boats. That night five boats sank four ships, and damaged a fifth. On the 4th only a few attacks were made, but the convoy lost another of its complement. In all the convoy lost fifteen ships, and four others were damaged.

The attack on ONS.144 was not so successful; eleven boats managed only six sinkings. Many U-boat commanders were so new to the business that they were claiming depth-charge detonations as torpedo hits. The confusion was compounded for these tyros by the fact that the Norwegian corvettes *Mont-*

*bretia* and *Potentilla* between them dropped 60 depth-charges in just over ninety minutes.

Further attacks during the month helped add up to a grand total of sinkings for the month of 125 ships of 534,049 GRT. Obviously the effects of 'Torch' were being felt by the convoys, because 81 destroyers were needed as part of the warship complement for the landings, plus 66 smaller naval vessels. The question must arise, however, as to whether SC.107 *may* have been left to its own devices to act as a decoy away from the naval activity to the east.

At the FCNA during which 'Torch' and its effects were examined on 19 November, Dönitz also had to face a demand for more U-boats for the Arctic station. Raeder managed to side-step this order, saying that U-boats could be directed there at any time by diverting outward-bound boats from Germany, and he could also divert boats at will from the Atlantic. Dönitz was, of course, committed to maintaining maximum strength in the North Atlantic, and after the war, he wrote:

> At that time I did not believe that a continuation of U-boat operations off Gibraltar was justified, nor could I accept Naval High Command's [Skl's] opinion that the very sharp decline in sinkings in the Atlantic would 'be more counter-balanced by the infinitely more valuable sinking of ships carrying supplies and reinforcements to the Mediterranean'.

One should bear in mind again the caution raised earlier: that Dönitz seemed wary of putting his U-boats in areas of high danger, especially when there was little strategic return to show for the inevitable losses.

Sinkings in November were the highest for any month of the war, and the U-boats had fared far better on the convoy routes than they would ever have done in the defended areas around the landing beaches. That they achieved far less in December was due to a combination of factors, one of which was the enormous successes of the previous month. The U-boats that had been engaged around Gibraltar and farther north in the Atlantic had to return to base, to rest, refuel, repair and re-arm. But Dönitz had been arguing in the interim against any of them being transferred to the Mediterranean, to support Skl's continental attitude. Skl thought that the U-boats would be best employed attacking convoys to North Africa, demonstrating their subservient attitude to the demands of Hitler and the Army, rather than taking a strategic view, which would place the centre of effort where Dönitz wanted it, on the convoy routes.

Dönitz said (again) that more transfers to the Mediterranean would 'have disastrous effects on the war against shipping in the Atlantic' and went on, almost as if to paraphrase the later writings of Winston Churchill:

> The war on shipping is perhaps the one contribution that the U-boat arm can make towards winning the war. This is clearly recognised by the

enemy, and his main preoccupation remains the Battle of the Atlantic and the unceasing drain on his strength which he is incurring in it ... if sinkings in the Atlantic decline as a result of the transfer of U-boats from that area to Gibraltar ... no one will be more pleased than the enemy ...

Then, borrowing a leaf from Raeder's more oblique approach, he suggested that the twelve U-boats stationed off Gibraltar be used to attack US reinforcement far to the west, beyond the Azores, and this request was approved.

U-boat operations against Allied landing areas in North Africa came to an end on 23 December 1942, and on Christmas Eve the new Group *Spitz* of eight U-boats took station in a patrol line on the eastern side of the North Atlantic (areas AL/BE). To their south *U664* was patrolling independently, and she sighted ONS154 on Boxing Day. The convoy consisted of 45 merchant ships and a Canadian escort of one destroyer, five corvettes and the HF/DF-fitted rescue ship *Toward*. Group *Spitz* was ordered to the convoy as soon as Dönitz knew of it, as was Group *Ungestüm*, which was also in the area. This second group was eleven strong, and made contact in the afternoon of the 26th. The first attacks were made that night by two boats, which sank four ships and damaged one. *U356* was lost to four corvettes when making her second attack, and this caused the group to lose contact, which was not regained until the afternoon of the 27th. *U225* was now the shadower, attacking alone that night, damaging a steam tanker.

Contact was lost again until *U260* sighted the target and brought twelve boats up in support by transmitting beacon signals. Thirty firing runs were made and twelve ships were sunk and eight more damaged. The convoy, once 45 strong, was reduced to 29, and only nineteen of these were undamaged. The U-boats then withdrew to refuel from *U117*. This, said Dönitz, was a normal tactical attack, but one he could not have mounted the week before. Up to Christmas Eve weather in the Atlantic had been impossible, and he had only just started to build up the numbers on patrol.

In view of the fact that the Americans had been participating in the convoy system since 1941, it is remarkable that they had taken so long to bring it into effect. It seems, however, that even when they were operating in the same way as the British, Dönitz was, due to the continuing lack of escort warships, able to operate wherever air cover was sparse or non-existent. The Utankers had pushed his French bases some one or two thousand miles further west; the IXC boats were free to cause havoc, first in the Caribbean and the Gulf of Mexico, and later even further west, with little or no interference. The Type IXD2 boats could range farther still, and operate for two or three months, with the aid of a Utanker, in areas previously considered safe from U-boat attack: in the Cape of Good Hope area and even in the Indian Ocean. The U-boats had sunk more than 1,000 ships at a cost of 92 boats in all theatres. Losses in December had been high because Dönitz's boats had to operate where they were least safe: off shore, near high concentrations of warships. There were plenty of them left for operations in 1943.

The Official Historian writes of this period as follows:

During the closing days of 1942 the Admiralty reviewed yet again the problems and prospects of the Atlantic battle. 'Our shipping situation,' reported a senior member of the Naval Staff, 'has never been tighter'; and our surface and air escorts were still far too few. In spite of the success of the North Africa landings, grave anxiety was felt that future offensive plans might be delayed or even frustrated for lack of shipping. In particular fuel stocks had fallen to a very low figure. In mid-December there were only 300,000 tons of commercial bunker fuel in Britain, and consumption was running at 130,000 tons a month ... As to the losses we had suffered during the year, it was beyond question that the enemy had done us great damage ... a further deficit of about a million tons of shipping had been added ... British imports fell below 34 million tons, one third less than the 1939 figure. To the British Admiralty it was plain that the Battle of the Convoy Routes was still to be decided, that the enemy had greater strength than ever before, and that the crisis in the long-drawn struggle was near.

The decision was yet to come, but no-one could be optimistic on the British side. In January 1943 Dönitz had 393 U-boats in commission, of which 212 were operational, 168 of them in the Atlantic, 21 in Norway, 24 in the Mediterranean and three in the Black sea. Working-up, were no fewer than 89 Type VIIB/C boats, 27 Type IXC/D1/D2, two Type XB and one Type XIV. With an additional seven foreign boats, he had 400 U-boats, 53 per cent operational, and a further 30 per cent to be operational within the next six months. Prospects looked good from the German point of view. Against him, the surface escorts had increased too, and the following were available:

| Base | Destroyers | Sloops | Corvettes | Other |
|------|-----------|--------|-----------|-------|
| Londonderry | 20 | 14 | 47 | 7 |
| Liverpool | 25 | 2 | 31 | – |
| Greenock | 10 | – | 11 | – |
| Gibraltar | 23 | 9 | 23 | 12 |
| Freetown | – | 4 | 15 | 24 |
| Western Atlantic | 30 | 2 | 60 | 14 |
| Totals | 108 | 31 | 187 | 57 |

In addition were the escort carriers which were now becoming available, as well as US Navy vessels when they could be spared from duties in coastal waters and the Pacific. The total of Royal and Royal Canadian Navy ships available was 384, just 40 more than six months previously.

Air cover, provided by aircraft of RAF Coastal Command comprised:

| Aircraft type | Squadrons | Aircraft |
|---|---|---|
| Very long range | 3 | 52 |
| Long range | 5 | 66 |
| Medium range | 13 | 278 |
| Flying-boats | 11 | 111 |

The VLR and LR components had increased greatly, compensating for the reduction in MR aircraft, for range was now more important than mere numbers. The aim was, where possible, to close gaps with shore-based aircraft, covering those left with carrier-based aircraft.

But the U-boats still had the edge, because they could choose where to operate, and even the areas covered by air and sea patrols were initially vulnerable to attack. The seven Type XB and XIV supply boats were worth many times their own numbers in terms of continuing operations in the vastness of the North Atlantic. The battle was all set to be fought in one area, however, the transport route from Nova Scotia to the west coast of England, especially in the area south of Greenland where the air gap was still marked; and aircraft were often unable to fly off the escort carriers by day because of weather, and at night because of the problems of returning to the mother ship.

The general strategic situation in the war as a whole was, unlike in the Atlantic, showing vague signs of a turn towards the Allies. The Japanese were adopting a defensive posture in the Far East, but this was in fact part of their strategy, and aimed at consolidating gains and building up defences to ensure that their possessions could not be retaken. Their greatest disadvantage was loss of so many aircraft carriers at the Battle of Midway. In Africa, Rommel was apparently trapped, although he was soon to attack the US II Corps at Kasserine and inflict great losses on them; the Mareth Line defied penetration by Montgomery. In Russia it was winter again, although the situation at Stalingrad looked promising from Stalin's viewpoint.

In the evening of 6 January Hitler and Raeder conferred at *Wolfsschanze*, Hitler's headquarters. The Chief of Staff, OKW, was also there. The minutes record that Hitler spoke for about an hour and a half 'about the role played by the Prussian and German Navies since they came into existence'. He said that the German Navy had been patterned on the Royal Navy, but had no strategic role in the wars that had brought into existence Bismarck's German national state of 1871. The first weapon the Navy perfected was the torpedo-boat, on which special care was lavished. He went on: 'Submarines constituted the most important branch of the German Navy in the last war and must be considered equally important today.'

He then 'explained' why the High Seas Fleet in the First World War had not taken a greater part in that war: it was because the Navy 'lacked men of action who were determined to fight with or without the support of the Kaiser ... the Navy has always been careful to consider the number of their own ships and men as compared with the enemy before entering an engagement. The Army does not follow this principle.' But this quasi-historical peroration was not to criticise the U-boats, but the surface units, tested in the action against convoy JW.51B. Admiral Kunmetz had gone to sea under strict orders to retire should his force be exposed to serious danger; his force consisted of two heavy cruisers and six destroyers. When they were engaged not only by Captain Sherbrooke's seven destroyers, but by the close escort, two light cruisers and two destroyers, the German Admiral turned away. Göring got the news first, and used it to slander the Navy. Hitler was ready to break up the surface fleet entirely.

He demanded that once naval forces were engaged, they fight to the finish. The capital ships could not be left idle, at anchor, for months; of course he was disregarding (at that moment) what they were doing, even in their idleness, in tying down much superior forces. The destruction of the German surface forces would have benefited the Allies considerably. Raeder during Hitler's peroration 'rarely had an opportunity to comment'; he could, said Hitler, easily do away with the planned aircraft carriers, main guns for other large units could be better installed in concrete on land, and he ordered Raeder to write him a report on the whole matter.

Raeder went away, wrote his report and presented it on 15 January. In it he gave his plans for decommissioning the big ships, and he also wrote a 'child's guide' to sea power for the Führer. Raeder was Navy through and through, and he resisted Hitler's plans for the destruction of the surface navy. He was a sound strategist, and had he had the time would have presented Hitler with a balanced Navy. But Hitler, the politician and opportunist, had failed to give him the time he needed to build it. Hitler saw Army divisions raised by the post office, and lost patience when it took three years to commission a battleship. The matter ended with Raeder doing the honourable thing. He presented his resignation to Hitler on 30 January, and Dönitz was appointed Commander-in-Chief of the Navy. He came to the same conclusion vis-à-vis the big ships as had Raeder.

Amid the machinations and recriminations at Führer Headquarters, a convoy attack of strategic significance took place between Trinidad and Gibraltar. Mention has been made already of the Official Historian's comment about the shortage of bunkering fuel reserves held by the British. Convoy TM.1 was to alleviate this problem for the Mediterranean forces, and consisted of nine tankers, escorted by Escort Group EG B5 (one destroyer and three corvettes). It sailed south of the usual route in an attempt to avoid U-boat concentrations.

Unfortunately the convoy was soon located by *U514* which damaged one of the tankers at 2252 on 3 January (later sunk by *U105*). U-boat Command had already established that convoy comprised tankers, and orders were given to stalk at maximum speed, 'because of the pressing need to attack convoy traffic to Gibraltar'. Group *Delphin* (six boats) was ordered in to attack. Only *U514* and *U125* were close, but they soon lost contact and the convoy was not sighted again until 8 January. Then, *U381* spotted the ships and called up reinforcements. Two boats attacked on the night of 8/9 January, sinking a second tanker and damaging one. The morning of the 9th saw the assault renewed, and Dönitz commented later that 'the escort ... was inexperienced and not very dogged'. Three more tankers were damaged or sunk in the afternoon. Finally, after midnight on the 10th, three U-boats administered the *coup de grâce*, leaving the convoy with only three tankers afloat, with damage only to *U134* in return. ·

There was little other activity in the Atlantic this month, and even on 8 January Dönitz was writing 'the submarine situation in the North Atlantic is far from satisfactory ... the thirteen boats of Group *Falke* form the only operational group in the area' (Group *Delphin* was in the central area). The build-up of another group had been hindered by the weather, and there was little information about convoys from *B-Dienst*. Dönitz was constantly reiterating his plea about 'the crying need of more submarines'. He was unable to find convoys simply because his patrol lines were far too thin to be effective, and only by chance did the U-boats fall upon a target.

By the end of January the U-boats had sunk only 32 ships (200,646 GRT), of which eighteen had been in seven other convoys, and in TM1 which was so badly mauled. February saw some increase, however, and a total of 54 ships were sunk (320,856 GRT). Of these 38 were sunk in convoys, two of which were particularly heavily engaged: SC.118 and ON.166.

SC.118 consisted of 61 ships with escort EG B2 of three destroyers and four corvettes, plus the USCGC *Bibb* and the faithful *Toward* as rescue ship. The convoy had been identified by *B-Dienst* and through POW statements. There was now a new BdU, Admiral Godt (previously Dönitz's Chief of Staff, Operations), who ordered Group *Pfeil*'s eight boats to set up a patrol line on 2 February. The convoy ran into the line on the 4th, and *Pfeil* was reinforced by five more boats on the 6th. *U184* reported the sighting to U-boat Command, and was immediately located by *Toward* and *Bibb*. Two of the destroyers promptly sank the U-boat. No fewer than five attacks were driven off during the night of 4/5 February for this was a much sterner escort than TM1 had had.

Further attempts were made to get in to the main body of the convoy, but most were unsuccessful until *U465* sent her contact report. In a bombing attack soon after that the U-boat was damaged by a B17 flying from Ballykelly. Five boats responded to the signal, three approached, but only one managed to fire, and missed. The operation was beginning to assume a farcical character, but then *U402* penetrated the defences during the night of the 6th, sinking five merchantmen and damaging one. This was in addition to the intermittent but erosive earlier attacks that had sunk six ships. One vessel damaged was *Toward*, fitted, as may be remembered, with HF/DF. Stung by this loss the escort managed to sink *U609* and kept all but two of the group, *U402* and *U456* at bay. Both were forced under in the afternoon by *Bibb* and another Flying Fortress from Ireland, which also removed *U624* permanently from the battle.

During the night of 7/8 February more attempts were made to penetrate the escort cordon, but only two boats got near and, again, only *U402* was successful, with one more sinking. This operation had been a dour struggle, and the convoy had lost eleven ships, for three U-boats sunk. This escort had proved to be a far more formidable opponent than before, and long-range aircraft were showing how effective they were to be in combating the U-boat threat.

St. Valentine's Day in 1943 saw Group *Ritter* poised for what they hoped would be the massacre of HX.226, but the trackers re-routed the convoy to avoid the twelve boats. They were then ordered to attack ON166 which was sailing in the central area of the North Atlantic. They received *B-Dienst* intelligence about the convoy and were informed of its location on 18 and 19 February, as were Group *Knappen*'s four boats to the south. On the 20th the 40-ship convoy was sighted by *U604* of the southern group. The escort was commanded by an American, and consisted of two Coast Guard cutters, and one British and three Canadian corvettes. Before the rest of the U-boats could respond to *U604*'s signal this shadower was radar located and attacked, and the next day the rest of the U-boats were kept at bay by the escort and a friendly flying-boat. However, as always happened once the U-boats got inside the escort, on the night of 21/22 February *U92* damaged two ships (sunk later), but no other boat got in. Next day two of the remaining eight attackers penetrated the cordon, *U606* sinking two ships and damaging a third, only to be sunk herself soon afterwards.

At first light on the 23rd a further effort to close was made, aided by the fact that the escort was depleted. Two ships had been detached to help *Campbell* which had been so damaged in a ramming attack that she had to be taken in tow. This attack, lasting until 0740, sent one more merchantman to the bottom, and damaged three others. Two U-boats shadowed for the rest of the day, assembling six more for the evening onslaught. They surfaced in an empty sea: a course change had taken their prey from them. Located in the early hours of the following day, the attack resumed and one more vessel was sunk. During the day things got even harder for the U-boats, and shadowers and the other boats were driven off by the escort and by aircraft flying from Newfoundland. Escort reinforcements arrived that night, and attacks by three boats towards first light on the 25th sank one ship but *Spencer*, one of the US Coast Guard cutters, which were so useful in the battle, was missed by torpedoes from both *U600* and *U628*. The operation ended with both sides exhausted as fog came down.

Three main points arise. The first is that Dönitz was still forced to use the same tactics that he was using eighteen months previously. He had to find the convoys, and so put out patrol lines in the general path of them. On sighting, the U-boats assembled and attacked. There was no alteration to the U-boat tactics because they had no means of changing them. Unlike the Allies, they were stuck with the single option of getting in to a firing position and then hoping to escape. The new FAT torpedo was not such a departure that U-boats could lie off the convoy and fire in its general direction, and *Zaunkönig* was not much of an improvement on that, nor were any other torpedo developments capable of bringing about a fundamental tactical change. What the U-boats now needed was the ability to patrol and attack while submerged, in daylight as well as at night. The Type XXI U-boat might have forced a radical change in the battle, but it was as yet too far away from the field. Time was running out for the U-boats.

The second point is that the Allies now had the advantage of being able to fly aircraft from Newfoundland, albeit only in small numbers. In all, throughout Canada and Newfoundland there were only 128 aircraft, and this total was of course not fully operational at any one time. It meant, however, that the last air-gap in the North Atlantic was now closing, and the U-boats were subjected to air patrols and air attack throughout the whole convoy route across the North Atlantic. On the whole of the western Atlantic an enormous training and aircraft production effort had resulted in no fewer than 820 aircraft available for reconnaissance and anti-U-boat work, and there was an almost continuous line of air cover from Greenland to Brazil. On the eastern side there were 230 more aircraft from Iceland via Gibraltar to Morocco, and 38 more in West Africa and 32 in the Union.

Regrettably, in the eastern sector there were only eighteen VLR aircraft to be found, and none at all on the western side. This was due to the US Navy claiming the lion's share of the Liberators for reconnaissance work in the Pacific. The matter was resolved at the end of March 1943, when 255 Liberators were transferred to anti-U-boat operations. They were not all immediately available, but the 20 that were by the end of that month were to have an enormous effect upon the battle, as were the Catalinas, Fortresses, Halifaxes and Sunderlands now ranging over the convoy routes.

Finally, the escorts were proving their worth. The nightmare that had been HG.76 for Dönitz was now becoming an everyday reality, and was soon to get worse. Tactics were changing, and the escorts were beginning to benefit from technological developments of weapons and search equipment which were soon to swamp the U-boats, which were looking more and more what they were: merely slightly improved U-boats of First World War vintage. The tenacity of some U-boats was notable (such as *U402*), but the days of a fast night attack on the surface followed by an easy escape were gone. Now they had to work extremely hard to get a sight of a convoy, and to get into a firing position was even more difficult and hazardous.

That the U-boats continued to have success was due solely to their numbers. With some 60 in the operational areas daily, five groups of twelve could easily be maintained and directed to a target almost at will. The numbers were important not only for reconnaissance purposes, but to overwhelm the local escort during the first night of an attack. After that the well-trained and highly aggressive escorts made life extremely hard, and losses were mounting for the U-boat Arm.

Losses during February reflected the increasing effectiveness of the escorts and air patrols: fourteen U-boats sunk in the month, seven to air patrols and seven to sea escorts. In return the U-boats sank 54 ships in the Atlantic, of 320,856 GRT. Ten convoys had been attacked, which lost 38 ships, but the return per U-boat loss seemed to be swinging in favour of the Allies. In March the reverse seemed to have happened; the U-boats made such serious inroads into convoy traffic that there were doubts at the Admiralty as to whether the convoy system could survive in the face of such an onslaught. Only after the war can it be seen as the product of circumstance, and what is nowadays termed a 'blip'.

Seventeen convoys were attacked in March, and 67 merchant ships sunk of 422,919 GRT. Three of those convoys were exceptionally heavily mauled: SC.121, HX.229 and SC.122. Dönitz's wolf-pack system, *Rudeltaktik*, worked well. At 0210 on 7 March 1943, *U230* opened the assault on SC.121 by sinking the British steamer *Egyptian*. The attack on SC.121 lasted for twelve days, until *U333* fired the *coup de grâce* into the Greek steamer *Carras*, last of the ships to be lost from that convoy. During those twelve days the highest losses in convoy during the entire war occurred for the loss of a single U-boat.

Thirty boats were in the path of SC.121 which was taking the northern route to the UK. Originally of 59 ships, the convoy had lost a number of stragglers in recent gales. Accompanying the remaining ships was the escort, EG A3, of one US Coast Guard cutter, the USS *Greer*, of earlier fame, three corvettes (two Canadian and one British) and a rescue ship. When *U405* sighted the convoy on 6 March the BdU had more than enough boats to send in, and so he ordered seventeen for the immediate attack, and positioned nine more on the convoy's mean course, farther to the east.

The escorts employed the anti-submarine tactics then being taught by Captain Roberts to get rid of *U405*, but were not numerous enough to cover all points of the compass, and two boats slipped into watching positions from which *Egyptian* was sunk. U-boat tactics were standard, but they worked well against this relatively weak escort. The boats shadowed and made night attacks, and when bad weather caused radar and radio equipment failures they managed daylight assaults as well. The convoy lost twelve ships in all, of 55,661 GRT. The operation was finally broken off by the BdU when escort reinforcements arrived and the last contact-keeper had been driven off.

While the above battle was in progress, another started against HX.228, in which four merchant ships were sunk and three damaged, and five other convoys were attacked by individual boats or pairs. Then came the confluence of two very large convoys, HX.229 and SC.122, attended by the largest assembly of U-boats ever brought together in one battle. The convoys comprised some 100 merchantmen, the U-boats totalled half that number. The battle that ensued brought fear to the hearts of many at Allied Headquarters on both sides of the Atlantic. For the BdU it was to be the single greatest success of the anti-convoy war.

Ultra intelligence (once more available to planning and routing staff since 'Triton' had fallen to the decryption effort in December 1942) had warned the convoy routing staff of the presence of a U-boat group shadowing ON.170, due to arrive in the western Atlantic at about the same time as HX.229 and SC.122 were due to sail, and so the two departing convoys were re-routed to the southern track across the ocean. However, B-Dienst in its turn (is it not strange how both sides were doing the same thing to each other?) intercepted and deciphered the re-routing instructions and the BdU was able to put eight of the U-boats then shadowing ON.170 on to the line of SC.122's course for 15 March. In anticipation of the convoy's arrival in the eastern Atlantic, eighteen more boats, including some from the SC121 operation, were assembled on 14 March.

A gale then blew up from the west, and before the U-boat patrol line was aware of the fact, the convoy had passed by, and HX.229 had also passed to the south. Then, on the 16th, U653 found HX.229 (now 38 ships and escorted by only three destroyers and two corvettes).

Although U653 was driven off, her attackers were forced to return westwards for lack of fuel, and the U-boats stationed earlier in the west joined forces with thirteen others, eleven of them from the eastern patrol line, giving a total of 21 boats. HX.229 was then repeatedly attacked on the night of 16/17 March. That same night U-boats from the northern end of the reception group, together with boats from the group formed to intercept SC.122, joined forces and these 29 U-boats were directed against SC.122. This convoy was escorted by three destroyers, a frigate and five corvettes, and had a rescue ship. The escort managed to repel six separate attacks that night, thanks to HF/DF, but during the morning of the 17th Godt learned of the relative positions of the two convoys.

He ordered a total of 50 U-boats against the two convoys. As they drew closer a Liberator flew over which, with the escorts' efforts, drove away those nearest, and only one daylight submerged attack was possible, by U338.

HX.229, still desperately short of some of its escort, was attacked, but the shadower was forced away by a Liberator in the afternoon. The escorts performed some prodigious feats of defence when contact was re-established. Air patrols had increased by then, and the escorts reinforced, so that the mass attack of the nights of 16, 17 and 18 March could not be repeated. The operation ended on the 20th, although the last torpedo had been fired at the straggler *Carras* at 2128 on the previous day.

The mass night attacks had been made easier by the enormous concentration of merchant vessels in a comparatively small area, and by the amount of light the burning ships, escorts' star shells and tracer produced. The U-boats had a beacon on the skyline to guide them. The escorts themselves were too small in number to have any hope against this mass of U-boats, and were weakened by the ammunition expenditure and fuel consumption of the first night of the operation.

On the first night nine ships were sunk and five damaged; in daylight on the 17th six more were sunk. That night six more were sunk, and four damaged. The last two ships (both stragglers) were taken on the 19th. In all 22 merchant ships of 167,283 GRT were sunk, and a further nine of 48,978 GRT were damaged.

The March figures were staggering, especially when considered against Allied improvements in strength, training and equipment. All major convoys that month were attacked, and many of the lesser ones, and nearly 82 per cent of ships sunk by the U-boats had been in convoy. At the end of the month the Admiralty saw that 67 ships (422,919 GRT) had been sunk, at a cost to the U-boats of just fifteen. Godt noted in the War Diary: 'As in so many convoy operations, this surprise attack by many boats in the first night was the most successful ... counting boats arriving and leaving there could have been an average of about 20 boats per day in the vicinity of the convoy.' This was in accordance with the Dönitz doctrine, clarified more than three years before, but at a time when he had only a few boats. That early paper Dönitz wrote was prophetic, and his theory was proved during the four days of this operation. Unfortunately for him, he had the numbers now, but it was too late.

The resistance shown by the convoys was rising, as were losses. The losses were acceptable so long as the reward continued at the same level as in March. But in April losses were fifteen U-boats, fourteen in the Atlantic, and sinkings were low: just 38 ships of 223,076 GRT. In March, by comparison, twelve U-boats were sunk in the Atlantic for 490,326 GRT of merchant vessels sunk. There were changes too, in the way the Allies were conducting the defence, changes which were detailed by Dönitz after the war. In his Memoirs, he wrote:

We now know how very greatly the enemy had increased the strength of his escort forces at this time. The escort carriers, which the enemy had been preparing for a long time, came into action in March. Their advent finally closed the air gap in the North Atlantic, one of which, HMS *Fidelity*, had flown such effective local air cover for HG.76. Another, HMS *Avenger*, had been in the escort to PQ.18 and had taken part in Operation 'Torch' before being lost to *U155* when escorting MKF1 returning to the United Kingdom from North Africa on 15 November 1942. Their contributions had shown what even a few aircraft were capable of, if they could follow the convoy throughout its transit of a trans-Atlantic route. [Note the reference to HG.76.]

The arrival of the escort carriers into the escort strength for trans-Atlantic convoys had been delayed by the demands of Operation 'Torch', just as the introduction of Support Groups had been deferred by the same operation. HX.230 and SC.123 were the successors to the badly mauled convoys of March, and SC.123 benefited from the presence throughout its transit of the USS *Bogue*, which ship was to make its mark on the battle in the most definite manner. Indeed, the arrival of *Bogue* also marked an increase in the activities of the US Navy in Atlantic convoy operations at a time when all was yet to be won or lost.

Dönitz continued:

> At the same time more 'Support Groups' appeared on the scene. A Support Group consisted of four to six anti-submarine vessels and was generally commanded by a Captain of the Royal Navy. These groups were highly trained in tactical co-operation in anti-submarine warfare, and their task was to reinforce convoy escorts as soon as the U-boats delivered an attack. *Once they located a U-boat they were at liberty to pursue it without regard to the distance which such a pursuit drew them away from the convoy.* Hitherto the actual escort vessels of a convoy had frequently been compelled prematurely to break off a pursuit, because they would otherwise have been drawn too far from their charges to perform their primary function of immediate protection. [My emphasis.]

In March 1943 five of these Support Groups were set up, and their Order of Battle was:

| Group | Captain | Anti-submarine destroyers |
|-------|---------|:-------------------------:|
| 1st | Commander Brewer | 6 |
| 2nd | Captain Walker | 7 |
| 3rd | Captain McCoy | 5 |
| 4th | Captain Scott-Moncrieff | 5 |
| 5th | Captain Abel-Smith | 4 |

These destroyers were supplementary to the destroyers and corvettes of the local escorts to convoys, having a freedom of operation (as noted by Dönitz) unless directed to the extra support of a convoy by the Admiralty. The third decisive factor [wrote Dönitz] which turned the scales in the enemy's favour in the U-boat war was the increased number of very long-range aircraft which became available for operations in the Battle of the Atlantic.

The establishment of an air base in Greenland had been one half of the air expansion that took place in the early months of 1943. But in mid-March the Admiralty was beginning to wonder whether the convoy system had lost its effectiveness, and this view was being very seriously considered by the British Naval Staff. It had become automatic to think in terms of convoy, so long had it been in force, and there was no contingency plan if it should fail. It seemed possible that the wolf-packs had broken the convoy system, and they were growing in strength almost by the day.

In fact, although neither side knew it, the tide had just turned in favour of the Allies. The newly introduced land- and sea-based aircraft, and the Support Groups, and recent developments in technology and weaponry had all arrived together, giving the anti-submarine forces all the necessities to change the pattern of the Battle of the Atlantic once and for all. The losses sustained up to April 1943 by the U-boats were not unacceptable, and it would have taken an age to sink the whole of the U-boat Arm, even without its reinforcements. At the same time, Dönitz and Godt had received assurances that supplies of the new Pi39H (Pi2) contact *and* proximity torpedo pistol would be maintained, and new torpedoes were also on issue: the G7a FAT and the G7e FAT. Some U-boats were being fitted with active radar, and these improvements might have spelled further disaster for the Allies if the effectiveness of their counter-measures had not increased so dramatically.

The proof of the Allied improvements would only appear when the U-boats were once more out in the Atlantic, making attacks on the convoys again. After the heady days of March many of the boats had been forced to return to France for repairs, rest and re-supply. For two to three weeks those crews were out of the battle, resting against the further dangers to come. By the middle of April Godt had managed to assemble the 21-boat Group *Meise* north-east of Cape Race. Only HX.231 had been attacked earlier that month, losing six ships to torpedoes, and leaving one damaged straggler behind.

The general intention of the Admiralty, formulated at the end of March, was that as Ultra information was less informative than it had been, although still reliable when decrypted, the convoys would just have to fight their way through the U-boats by which 'the Atlantic is now becoming so saturated'. The severity of the attacks had lessened in the first half of April for the reasons already given, but Group *Meise* was now ordered in to attack HX.234 which had been located by *B-Dienst*.

This convoy of 42 ships, escorted by EG B4 (eight ships), was located by *U306* on 21 April, and an immediate attack sank one ship. In approaching the convoy five other boats were side-tracked by ON.S4 and then by ON.178. Only three boats came up to HX.234, but they sank two and damaged one vessel. ON.S4 was attacked, unsuccessfully, by von Bülow in *U404*, who used the new torpedoes. He fired two FAT (programmed course torpedoes) and two of the very latest *Zaunkönig* (sound-detecting) torpedoes, all to no avail as they exploded short of the escort carrier HMS *Biter*. ON.178 was lost soon after contact was made.

The weather had its effect upon the HX.234 operation, with mist and then driving snow cutting visibility on the surface so that the U-boats were totally vulnerable to radar detection. Wisely they broke off, only to renew the attack for a short while when *U306* found the convoy despite rain, hail, fog and snow squalls. *U306* and *U954* attacked on 23 April, but sank only one ship and damaged another. For a total of three ships out of the convoy two U-boats were lost: *U189* to Liberators of 210 Squadron, RAF, and *U191* to the new Hedgehog anti-submarine mortar on HMS *Hesperus* during the abortive assault on ONS.4.

The air cover for HX.234 was also operated over another convoy in the area, ONS.5. The arrival of the VLR patrols helped HX shake off the last of its pursuers, and a B17 of 206 Squadron sank *U710* as she was approaching. But the HX convoy was virtually home, and assured of protection. Convoy ONS.5, was on the outward leg of its long voyage to the USA. The convoy sailed on 21 April with 42 merchantmen and an escort (EG B7) of two destroyers, HMS *Duncan* (Commander P. W. Gretton) and HMS *Vidette*, the frigate *Tay*, corvettes *Sunflower*, *Snowflake*, *Loosestrife* and *Pink*, and two trawlers, *Northern Gem* and *Northern Spray*. This convoy was to be the focus of the deciding engagement in the Battle of the Atlantic.

The convoy sailed on the northern route from the North Channel, setting course to rendezvous with a feeder convoy from Iceland, ONS.J-5, just north of 60° N, and to the south of Iceland. With no enemy detected, the convoys rendezvoused at about 0800 on 26 April, and the combined convoy headed westwards towards Cape Farewell. The air cover flown from British bases was replaced by air patrols from Iceland soon after the ships joining from Iceland had taken up their positions. Their next navigational point was WESTOMP (West Ocean Meeting-Point) off St. John's, scheduled for daybreak on 7 May.

At about midday on 27 April ONS.5 had passed the westernmost point of Iceland. On its course Godt was assembling a group of sixteen boats in a patrol line lying north to south at 39° W. *B-Dienst* and experience had given the BdU just enough data to establish this patrol line, just as Ultra warned the Admiralty of the dangers into which the convoy was sailing. To reinforce the escort the 3rd Support Group was ordered from St. John's, after having given support to HX.233 some ten days before. It left port on 29 April, but it would take three days to reach the threatened convoy.

In deteriorating weather, *U650*, at the northern edge of the patrol line, made the first sighting on 28 April, some 500 miles off Cape Farewell. Despite frequent dives forced on her by Catalina flying-boats of USN Patrol Squadron VP.84, she signalled contact, and *U386* and *U378* arrived during the day. Then the weather closed in completely, but Godt managed to assemble some U-boats directly in the path of the oncoming convoy.

The U-boats reported their evening positions to U-boat Command, and Gretton's HF/DF sets picked them up; conditions were bad, but Gretton decided to take the offensive. Knowing the approximate positions of the U-boats from fixes obtained by *Duncan* and *Vidette*, the escorts fanned out to use 'scare' tactics to force the U-boats away. They made all the noise they could, and lit up as much of the area as possible with star shells, and the U-boats were forced down as the escorts cruised down their HF/DF bearings to the enemy.

During the night *U386* was driven off, by *Sunflower*, and *Duncan*, *Tay* and *Snowflake* spoiled attack chances for various boats. *U650* and *U532* were damaged by depth-charges and forced to withdraw, but *U532* had managed an attack. At 0514 on 29 April she fired four torpedoes at the convoy. After a running time of seven minutes the U-boat heard two explosions (faulty fuses again); *Snowflake*, tracking back from the detonations, then delivered the attack to damage and drive off *U532*.

*U258* managed to score the only success of the attack; after firing a salvo the Captain radioed that he had hit three freighters, one each of 4, 5 and 7,000 tons; once more, an example of over-confident estimation. One ship had been hit, the American steamer *McKeespor*, of 6,198 GRT, which was sunk. The other two detonations heard by *U258* had actually been outside the far side of the convoy. But this attack had taken place as dawn was breaking, and Gretton had anticipated this. The defences thrown at the U-boats by this relatively small escort had saved the convoy from all loss the previous night, although *U650* had managed to maintain contact long enough to guide *U258* in.

The weather got even worse, building to gale force, but the first part of the battle was not yet over. On the 29th HMS *Oribi* was detached from SC.127 to join the escort of ONS.5, and Catalinas and Liberators from Iceland continued to fly cover despite the terrible conditions. Towards evening one of the Catalinas drove off a shadower, and after nightfall *Snowflake* succeeded in driving *U192* away. The first shadower, *U258*, was so badly damaged at the bow by an aircraft bomb that she was forced to return to base.

On 30 April the weather was no better, although *Oribi* did manage to refuel, and air cover responsibility passed at 0600 to the shorter-range aircraft flying from Ivigtut in Greenland. The aircraft from Iceland continued on station for the rest of that day, and two Liberators from there were radio-homed to the ships. That day and the next the U-boats could not get into firing positions, and after *U192* made an unsuccessful attack during the night of 1 May, contact was lost. Ominously for them, the U-boats had reported to Godt that during the night of 30 April / 1 May a Mitchell aircraft (from Greenland) was seen on 'continuous patrol ... carrying a light like a planet that went on and off'. This, presumably, was a Leigh Light or the American equivalent.

The convoy had been severely dislocated by the storm, and on the morning of 2 May Gretton was using up a lot of the escort's fuel shepherding stragglers back into line. By 0900 only ten ships were missing, but a snow-storm blew up from the south-west, lasting for three hours, when it was replaced by fog. To give stragglers some form of protection he detached *Tay* and *Pink*, each of which was to form a mini-convoy and lead it back to the main body. The Support Group, which had left St. John's three days previously, had forced its way through to the convoy by 2000 on the 2nd. But in the meantime Godt had put 30 U-boats ahead of the convoy, in an eight-mile patrol line, and backed them up with eleven more; and yet ten more were on their way. The effects of fuel consumption by the escort group was felt by 3 May, and *Duncan* was detached to St. John's to refuel, as one of the Support Group destroyers had been forced to do the day before. Command of the escort now devolved on *Tay* (Lieutenant-Commander R. E. Greenwood, RNR) and the stage seemed set for another disaster.

During the forenoon watch on the 4th, two more of the Support Group destroyers left to refuel, so that the escort was now reduced to seven warships (*Tay, Vidette, Sunflower, Snowflake* and *Loosestrife* from the original escort, plus *Oribi* from SC.127 and *Offa*, last of the Support Group ships) and radio interception indicated a large concentration of U-boats ahead. The convoy had 31 ships in the main body, with the addition of *Pink* and *Northern Spray* astern with five stragglers, and the 1st Support Group (sloops *Pelican* and *Sennen*, frigates *Jed, Wear* and *Spey*) was ordered from St. John's to reinforce. But for the next few days the convoy was on its own.

The U-boats were drawn up in two groups. The first, of 30 boats in Group *Fink*, lay across the path of the convoy in latitude 55° N, while 21 boats, in sub-groups of five or six, were positioned to catch ONS.5 or any other convoy in the area. Catalinas flew air patrols during the day, and two attacked approaching U-boats; *U630* was sunk. The other boat, *U438*, fought with the Catalinas and escaped, for the aircraft were not equipped for shooting it out with a surfaced U-boat.

But the real battle was yet to begin, and to facilitate the German plan the rough weather slackened, sea state a moderate swell. The attack began, after midnight on 4/5 May, and there were just 30 ships in the main body of the convoy, protected by an indomitable seven warships. The escorts were totally outnumbered: conditions were almost perfect for the U-boats. The Northern Lights provided illumination, the sea was just rough enough to provide perfect cover, and the U-boats were in a perfect tactical position, enveloping the convoy from north, west and south.

Following the standard tactical technique, the first attack was made after midnight. At 0243 Hasenschar in *U628* fired all four bow tubes, turned about and fired one stern torpedo (keeping torpedo six for any escort) and reported to U-boat Command. He claimed one sinking, and a probable, and a third ship left burning; in fact he had only damaged the British steamer *Harbury*. *U628* was one of five boats that attacked that night, but they did not have it all their own way. *Tay, Offa* and *Oribi* did sterling work during the night, and prevented a number of attacks, and *Vidette* damaged *U270* with depth-charges before she could attack. But the weight of the attack, and the slender nature of Sherwood's resources, meant that there had to be some losses.

At 0251 *U952* came in and fired a T-3 *Zaunkönig* torpedo, with a magnetic pistol, which hit and sank the steamer *Lorient*. The new MZ (*Magnet-Zünder*) pistols were being issued then, and to ensure detonation they were ordered to be fired at a depth less than the draught of the target. There was little chance of failure, especially as there was a fail-safe mechanical pistol fitted as well, but this also meant that the torpedoes were not being used properly. After that single shot *U264* went in and at 0320 fired at two targets, both of which were hit. The *Harperley* sank after twenty minutes, but *West Maximus* needed a *coup de grâce* torpedo from *U264* at 0659.

Then *U358* came in, to make the final approach of the night, and at 0424 and 0428 fired on two targets, and claimed two sunk. He was partly correct, for *Bristol City* went down immediately, but *Wentworth* had to be sunk later by *Loosestrife*. *U628* made another approach, and sank a damaged ship which was heaved to. Hasenschar claimed another sinking, but in fact this was the earlier damaged *Harbury*, the only ship damaged in his previous attack.

On the morning of the 5th, then, there were 26 ships left in the main body, but the weather was good enough to allow the escorts to refuel. The escort was spread so thinly that the U-boats decided that they could also attack during the day, and *U192* also found the *Pink*-escorted straggler group. Before she could attack *Pink* got an Asdic contact and promptly sank the U-boat with a Hedgehog attack. Other U-boats were more fortunate, and after *Northern Spray* had been detached to St. John's to land survivors, the escort was too weak to be everywhere. At 1634 on 5 May *U584* sank the *Dolius*, and claimed two other ships sunk. The same afternoon *U707* damaged *West Madaket* which had to be sunk by *Pink*. Then at 2150 *U266* sank no fewer than three ships in one attack.

*Offa* managed to exact a penalty by damaging *U266* in a retaliatory attack, but then had to return to her station with the convoy without making sure of a kill; night was falling and the merchant ships were under-protected. Mist came down before last light, and the U-boats closed in once more under its cover, having been urged by Dönitz to make greater inroads into the remaining ships. The boats were also *ordered* to fight on the surface, something which had never been needed before.

Fifteen U-boats were waiting for the convoy when the fog came down, and as they were making very little way in the obscure conditions *Tay* could be heard firing all over the place following up every radar or Asdic contact, and depth-charging merrily. *Sunflower* located four boats in succession, and attacked *U267* with gun fire. After an initial miss the U-boat was hit and damaged. *Loosestrife* was similarly engaged with *U267*, and drove her down. Then she found *U638* and sank her with depth-charges just as she was about to fire her torpedoes. At about midnight *Oribi* was ordered to assist two corvettes battling it out with yet another U-boat, and *Vidette* succeeded in driving three others off. *Snowflake* then found three more U-boats almost simultaneously, one of which, *U531*, attacked her and missed. *U531* was promptly smothered with depth-charges and forced to the surface; en route to help in this action, *Oribi*, having expended all her depth-charges, rammed *U125* which was later sunk by *Snowflake's* guns.

In this insane chase around the convoy, *U533* was next to fall foul of *Sunflower* which rammed her. Furthermore, after the first attack by *Snowflake*. *U531* had managed to submerge, only to be sunk by *Vidette*. Then *Offa* attempted to ram a U-boat, while *Loosestrife* began the first of three depth-charge attacks. The night was described (most laconically) by Commander Sherwood as one in which 'All ships worked hard, capably and with intelligence and considerable humour.' It is tempting to see the arrival of 1st Support Group just after dawn as the arrival of more 'correct' naval reinforcements, looking down their noses at such frenetic activity. The significance of the action however belies any such light-hearted treatment.

The agony was now piled on for the U-boats. *Pelican* and *Jed* proceeded upon arrival to sink *U438* after radar contact, and *Sennen* attacked, but failed to sink the gunfire-damaged *U267*. With these losses, daylight approaching and with it air cover the moment the fog lifted, BdU called off the operation. This was the first time the U-boats had been called off in the middle of an attack due to the defences being too strong for them at that time, rather than the fear of improving defences as a convoy neared the coast. It was not simply the end of just any U-boat operation, it was the end of the U-boat threat to the convoys across the North Atlantic.

No fewer than 51 U-boats had faced the seven escorts of ONS.5. The convoy had lost twelve ships and two damaged, but it had caused the loss of five U-boats sunk by the escort and another one sunk by shore-based aircraft. The fog, rain and generally evil weather had not been enough to shield the U-boats from the Type 271 radar, and a combination of good tactics by the escort, and its obvious willingness to get stuck in had brought about the reverse of fortunes for which so many had prayed, yet despaired of on both sides of the Atlantic.

The losses during the rest of the month resulted in Dönitz sending the following signal to all U-boats stationed on the northern convoy routes, at 1752 on 24 May 1943:

The situation in the North Atlantic now forces a *temporary* shifting of operations to areas less endangered by aircraft ... It is intended to attempt attacks on a convoy only under the most favourable conditions. [Emphasis in the original]

# 12 TECHNOLOGY AND WARFARE II

Data available to Dönitz at the end of May 1943 revealed that the causes of U-boats losses were:

| Year | Sunk by Sea escort | Air escort / patrols | Air/Sea co-operation |
|---|---|---|---|
| 1939 | 5 | | |
| 1940 | 12 | 1 | 2 |
| 1941 | 25 | 3 | 2 |
| 1942 | 35 | 32 | 8 |
| 1943 to end May | 30 | 45 | 7 |

It was the disturbing increase in sinkings by air escorts and patrols that concerned him most up to that time. Until 1942 aircraft had neither the range nor radar to be a force to reckon with, but the arrival of long-range aircraft fitted with metric and later centimetric radar, and improved depth-charges and anti-submarine bombs, led to a greater part being played by aircraft in the Battle of the Atlantic. The air patrols in the Bay of Biscay were also having increasing successes, partly because more U-boats were crossing the Bay than ever before.

As a counter Dönitz decided on a novel tactic, hoping that the aircraft could be forced off the Bay patrol by their losses. The tactic depended upon an augmented FlaK capability fitted to the U-boats, and for the boats to sail in groups of two to five across the most dangerous areas. The actual results are discussed in the next chapter, but the FlaK equipment of the boats is of interest at this point. The idea of remaining on the surface and fighting it out with attacking aircraft was based on the fact that most of the time only one aircraft was available to make an attack, and its weapons were limited to machine-guns if the U-boat remained on the surface – depth-charges were of much less danger to a surfaced boat.

The U-boats were originally fitted with the standard 8.8cm deck gun, and either a 2cm FlaK or perhaps a 3.7cm weapon. The FlaK weapons were auto-matic. The 2cm fired a 132gram shell at 900m/sec; the 3.7cm the much heavier 623gram HE tracer at 820m/sec to a height of 4,800 metres, the same upper limit as the lighter 2cm gun, but with far greater hitting power and effect on target. But the weapons were originally designed for use only when the boat was caught on the surface unavoidably, or when protecting a Type XIV that was refuelling it. The Type XIVs were under orders to dive as soon as they could for their own protection, while the boats refuelling from them were to remain on the surface to cover the dive no matter what the cost to themselves.

However, when *U256* limped into harbour in September 1942, very badly damaged by bombs, there seemed to be no alternative but to scrap her, until it was proposed using her as an anti-aircraft vessel in the Bay of Biscay and as an anti-aircraft escort for boats in the same area that might be damaged or otherwise temporarily incapable of submerging. The most noteworthy point was that U-boats were to be used to perform a task which should have been done either by surface vessels or aircraft. Surface vessels were unavailable for the job, the majority of destroyers being elsewhere. Aircraft were only available occasionally, and the Ju 88 CIV of Atlantic Command was too limited in action radius to be of any real value. Thus the U-boats had to protect themselves against air attack, which they were singularly ill-equipped to do. Even when fitted with increased FlaK, the role was not suitable for them. But the need for protection meant that U-boat Command had to improvise. The table below shows the various forms that the FlaK up-arming meant for the U-boats. The sequence was as follows:

| Bridge modification No. | Date. | FlaK weapons (mounting) |
|---|---|---|
| Normal | to 1943 | 1 x 2cm C/30 (LC 30/37) |
| II | 1943 | 2 x 2cm C/38 (LC 30/37) |
| III | 1943–5 | 2 x 2cm Twin 38 MII (double LM 43U) |
| | | 1 x 3.7cm M42U (LM 4211)or 1 x 2cm Quad 38/43 or 1 x 3.7cm Twin M42 (Twin LM 42U) |
| U-FlaK I (IV) | 1943 | 2 x 2cm Quad 38/43U (with shield) |
| | | 1 x 3.7cm SKC/30U (LC 39) V |
| V | 1943–5 | 4 x 2cm Twin 38 MII |
| VI | do. | 3 x 2cm Twin 38 MII (one forward of bridge) |
| VII | do. | 2 x 3.7cm Twin M42U (one forward of bridge) |

The modifications V to VII were fitted only to FlaK U-boats, which were so designated before completion, and carried only five torpedoes, compared with the usual Type VIIC boats.

The Type IX boats were not modified as FlaK U-boats, for they were far too susceptible to even minor damage. In addition to the upgrading of the weapons, the upper part of the pressure-hull was armoured, as was the bridge itself. But all these external protuberances led to a lower underwater performance; although this was unavoidable, the fact was noted, and the Type XVII and Type XXI boats benefited from streamlined, internally controlled, twin 3cm gun turrets forward and aft of the bridge.

This increased protection was necessitated, of course, by the effectiveness of the enemy's anti-submarine devices, especially radar. From February 1943 the 10cm radar set was being installed in Allied aircraft, in addition to the increasing number of sets already at sea in the surface escorts, and this meant that the early anti-radar measures were rendered useless. The Metox-Grandin and FuMB sets were unable to discern the higher frequency, so many more boats were being surprised on the surface. The aircraft were attacking at night especially, using the Leigh Light or the newer starshell or Snowflake illuminants, and the U-boats were unable to dive fast enough to go deep before the aircraft was able to drop its depth-charges. The stop-gap measure was to stay on the surface, and hope to shoot the attacker down. The real answer to airborne radar would be a counter-set, which could identify centimetric transmissions, and ideally give the vector of the attacker as well.

The combination of attacks by night, and the exceptionally high losses of May, caused the replacement of Vice-Admiral Maertens (Chief of Naval Radio Services) by Rear-Admiral Stummel; it was assumed that the Metox device was being used to locate the U-boats. It was established that even passive radar receivers emit waves and the German scientists were sure that these emissions were being picked up by patrolling aircraft, and used to locate the U-boats. The capability of H2S radar, which had been found in a crashed aircraft in Holland, was being exaggerated to such an extent by the Germans that this alone would explain the high ratio of sightings. In fact, German disbelief that radar could operate on a frequency as low as 10cm was being perpetuated. The German scientific advisers could not themselves design such a radar set, and being unaware of the cavity magnetron, thought the Allies equally unable to deliver such equipment; so they devised the Metox-radiation hypothesis to cover up their ignorance.

Glad of any suggestion that might alleviate the pressure on the U-boats, U-boat Command ordered all Metox sets to be removed from the boats in August, anticipating a renewal of the Atlantic campaign as soon as new location sets were installed in the boats. The new device was the FuMB 9 search receiver (also called the *Wellenanzeiger*) code-named 'Cyprus' or 'Wanze'. This was an automatic frequency-searching set, but its general performance was too low for it to be the answer – it had neither the range nor the sensitivity now needed. But U-boat Command thought it the answer when *U161* made the passage across the Bay of Biscay safely at the beginning of August. This euphoria was soon dispelled when *U386* was attacked in September, although also equipped with FuMB 9. Once more fears arose of detectable emissions, and the more secure WAnz G2 was thought to be the antidote until NVK/Telefunken could produce their new FuMB 10 set, the 'Borkum', which had a frequency range down to 20cm, and was completely secure from the point of view of the much-feared (but never used) tell-tale source emissions from the other devices.

The discovery of an H2S set in the bomber near Rotterdam had certainly altered the German attitude. Unfortunately for the U-boats, testing and evaluating the H2S set took time, and its 9cm wavelength became significant too late to save the May boats. Once more NVK/Telefunken were charged with finding the antidote in the form of a search receiver, which they did in June 1943 with the first unit of the FuMS7 Naxos being produced. This was a simple device which benefited from an impulse amplifier, but it had two drawbacks: it had a very short range (about 5 kilometres) and would not be available to the U-boats until the end of the year.

The weakness of the FuMB 7 led to further development work which was complicated by the Americans' introduction of 3cm wavelength radar. This problem was not solved until mid-1944 with the introduction of FuMB 26 'Tunis' which could detect both wavelengths up to a range of 70 kilometres. Like the Metox device the aerial was not immersible, and had to be installed on the bridge by hand once the boat had surfaced. No doubt the rush to install the aerial on coming to the surface was worth it, as it gave the U-boats effective warning of radar sets at a range which left them outside the range of attack radar, and they could submerge if the signal got closer, with little danger of attack. By the end of the war the aerial problem had been solved in the most sophisticated way – by making them pressure-tight and installing them on an extendable mast controlled from within the boat so that a radar listening search could be made before surfacing. Furthermore, the set was upgraded to the FuMB 35 'Athos' which was a coarse radar direction receiver, which could receive all frequencies (hence 'coarse') and give a bearing on the transmitting station.

Enemy radar detection of U-boats began the 'electronic counter-measures' battle of which so much is heard today. The Germans were not content merely to know if they were being observed on a radar screen, but they also attempted to reduce the size of the echo produced by the reflection of the radar waves. They experimented with absorbent coatings initially for the entire boat, later just for Schnorkel heads. The aim was to absorb some of the energy of the incoming wave so that the return wave would not be obvious to the searching set until much nearer to the target than before. This electronic camouflage was achieving some limited success in the latter half of the war, but suffered from the abrasive effects of sea water, which often stripped the 'Alberich' coating from the hull and superstructure; it also fared badly when subjected to temperature changes and to pressure. The first boat to be fitted with 'Alberich' was *U480* which operated in the English Channel in August 1944 despite the frantic activity attendant on the follow-up to Operation 'Overlord', and had a successful patrol, sinking two merchant vessels, a corvette and a fleet minesweeper.

Other ECMs, which are still in use today, were the reflection devices evolved by German scientists. These were 'Thetis', which was a floating device, and 'Aphrodite', an aerial deception device. 'Thetis' was a tube filled with porous cork, coated on the outside with tin-foil, which has high radar reflective characteristics. It was to be released when a U-boat was attacked and served as a decoy while the boat got out of range of the attacker. 'Thetis' was designed to absorb water at a fixed rate, sinking soon after the U-boat escaped. In fact the cork filling did not do its job properly every time, and this decoy was soon known to the Allies for what it was. 'Aphrodite' was another decoy – an oxygen balloon coated with tin-foil – which had the same function as 'Window' (Düppel). The reflectivity of the tin-foil, which was cut in length to half the wavelength of the transmitter, caused sets to be flooded with returns so that the real target would escape as just one more 'blip' on the PPI. But trained operators soon learned to look for the blip that moved, for the other echoes would not have the same rate of movement as the U-boat making best speed to get away from the area.

Once submerged the U-boats' problems were still not over; originally many had seen Asdic to be the answer to the U-boat, but for some time the underwater locating device had been negated by U-boats remaining on the surface to attack.

This was no longer possible, and Asdic, especially since it could establish depth as well as range, came once more into its own. To confuse searching operators the U-boats were issued with 'Bold', which enjoyed considerable success. The Allies frequently referred to it as 'Pill' from Pillenwerfer which was the alternative German name for the device. It consisted of a cylinder which could be fired from within the U-boat, containing a calcium carbide compound. When sea water came into contact with the compound it produced a hydrogen bubble which returned an echo to Asdic sets. While the hunter above was dropping depth-charges on to the gas bubble, the U-boat could often make an escape, and many U-boat crews were glad of the device. In addition the crews could load a torpedo tube full of oil, clothing and other matter, firing the contents when hard pressed by an attack. The arrival of the detritus on the surface might convince a novice crew that the U-boat had sunk. But experienced Asdic operators knew exactly the sound of a U-boat breaking up beneath the surface and without hearing that sound, the attack would continue, any doubts as to whether there was a U-boat below handily dispelled by the target itself. A further decoy was designed, a mini-torpedo, which had the sound characteristics of a U-boat running below the surface at some 6 or 7 knots, but this does not seem to have caused the hunters any real problems during the war.

Despite all the various and ingenious devices thought up by the German scientists, they had forgotten one basic factor: U-boats did not maintain strict wireless silence when they were on patrol, and refinements in ship-borne

High-Frequency Direction-Finding equipment undoubtedly led to many of them being located by this means when they were out of range of shore installations and ship-borne radar. The prime example of 'chatting' of which Dönitz was so proud occurred between him and Korvettenkapitän Mohr of *U124* on 17 June 1942, when Dönitz 'rang' Mohr to ask him if he had ever personally encountered a surface-location device. Mohr's reply would have taken at least thirty seconds to transmit, which would have given an indication of U-boat activity in the area at least. The next month Dönitz remarked, 'I ... exchanged a series of cipher signals with Topp, the most experienced of the captains engaged' (against ON.113); what Dönitz needed was a weather report! Admittedly weather was a decisive factor, but to spend time 'chatting' over the air when the enemy was bound to be listening was criminally negligent, and a total breach of security for which Dönitz alone was responsible. His original plan to control operations from shore was valid, and the short signals provided much very valuable information, including a brief summary of the weather, but Dönitz's over-free use of it was a vital contributing factor to the Allies' campaign against the U-boats.

All the measures discussed so far have been either passive, or defensive, and one may wonder whether the attitude taken by U-boat designers and crews was essentially also defensive in terms of the various escorts which protected the convoys. In fact, active radar had been installed in two U-boats as early as 1939. In that last peaceful summer NVK put two of their radar sets into *U3* and *U41*. These were 80cm wavelength Freya sets with a range of some 120 kilometres. However, Dönitz was not in favour of such equipment, and they were removed, because he felt that the U-boat silhouette would be increased greatly, and the aerial was not water- or pressure-proof. Also the range was limited in U-boats to some 6–7,000 metres. Another problem with early radar was the space requirement, which would have been difficult to provide in the Type II boats.

Then, in 1942, when aircraft became more than just a nuisance, Dönitz raised the matter again, and in the autumn of that year the first very limited sets were installed on an experimental basis in a few U-boats. Some sets had fixed aerials, fitted on the forward part of the bridge (FuMO 29), some had two dipole aerials (FuMO 30), but the results were not at all satisfying. It was thought that the situation would improve if the Navy could obtain some of the *Hohentwiel* sets developed for the *Luftwaffe*, for this was a ship-search radar of 56cm wavelength (FuMG 200). The dipole aerials necessary for operation had been concentrated into a 1m x 1.4m rectangle, and the naval version was coded FuMO 61 or *Hohentwiel U*. By 20 September 1944, 64 operational boats had been fitted with this set, and 32 more sets were to be fitted to Type VII and IX boats. *U862*, which was then operating out of Penang, reported that the set had performed well up to 17 September 1944, and that its range was 7.2 kilometres against a loaded freighter. But this was not of value against aircraft, and so sixteen boats were fitted with a modified radar for that purpose.

By that time, however, there were virtually no surface operations by the U-boats, and very few occasions when the sets could be tested operationally, and so the use of anti-aircraft radar was never fully tested. Nevertheless, the idea persisted, and the Type XXI boats were designed with the developed anti-aircraft radar (FuMO 65 *Hohentwiel Drauf* ) as a standard fitting. The final development in U-boat radar came right at the end of the war, only in time to be of benefit to the victors: this was the Berlin UII set which could operate at periscope depth. It was of centimetric wavelength, and the aerials were fitted in a pressure-tight housing at the top of an extendable mast (FuMO 84), which could be used for navigation. In conjunction with that set there was also the *Lessig* (FuMO 391) anti-aircraft radar, of 2.4m wavelength, which had a telescopic aerial and could look vertically above the boat. This too became part of the spoils of war in May 1945, for it was intended to be installed into new U-boats produced from the middle of that year.

If all the above measures proved successful to a degree, there would be some hope that the U-boats would once more be able to attack the prime target – surface vessels. Up to 1943 the main torpedoes had not had a happy history, and many ships had escaped sinking and even damage because of the erratic performance of the detonating pistols and depth-keeping equipment with which they were fitted. These problems had finally been resolved at the moment when new torpedoes were being issued for war use for the first time. Much of the history of these earlier torpedoes has already been recounted, and so now the new types and the modifications to the originals can be considered. Note that all standard German naval torpedoes for U-boats were 7m in length, hence the type ('G' *Gefechts* – HE warhead '7' metres long in 53.3cm calibre 'a' proximity pistol) – G7a. The Pi (*Pistole*) 2 (or Pi 39 H) was the replacement for earlier firing pistols, and was initially a proximity, electrically fired detonator, but it had a secondary contact detonator in case of failure of the primary circuit. This pistol was fitted to all further torpedoes during the war. However, whereas the method of detonating the torpedo was fixed, many delivery methods were now tried out.

During the war torpedoes were usually driven by electric motors, fuelled by internal batteries. What the Germans now developed were pre-set programmable torpedoes. These no longer merely proceeded in a straight line to (and often past) the target, but had the ability to alter course, returning to a general convoy course line; a further development was the target-seeking torpedo. The first type of course-changing torpedo was fired parallel to the course of the target, and after a pre-set distance it turned towards the target and made a course at right angles to it. After travelling a pre-set distance if the torpedo had not struck a target, it reversed course and crossed the target course once more. This meant that ships had to fear the torpedo's return as well as its outward travel, which made life more difficult. But this was merely the dumb version of the pair of torpedoes the Germans now introduced.

The active torpedo did far more, for it actively searched for its target, and then homed on it – in this case the noise of the ship's screw, which is quite distinctive, especially between merchant vessels and warships, for it was warships that were to be the target of the *Zaunkönig* (Wren) torpedo. Attacks on escorts with a torpedo of this kind would have been many times more effective three years earlier when the convoy system was in its infancy, and the number of escorts available so low as to be ineffective; had they been attacked then the effect upon Merchant Navy morale would have been disastrous. Now the main target of these target-seeking torpedoes was to be the higher tone of a warship's screws, easily distinguished by the receiver which could be tuned to eliminate vessels proceeding at lower revolutions.

Tactical considerations reduced the anti-convoy torpedoes to a minor role, for few convoys were located after May 1943, and then rarely by more than one or two boats. The first of this type to be issued was the G 7ES (electric drive, target seeking) or *Falke* torpedo, but it was incapable of seeking targets whose surface speed was greater than 13 knots, and so was used generally against merchant ships. The increased weight of the target-seeking equipment meant that the warhead had to be cut down to 274kg. After the very minimum of testing (which seems typical of this aspect of the German Navy's efforts), it was on general issue to boats from 1 July 1943. This hybrid was quickly followed by the more effective acoustic torpedo, with a higher speed, but fitted with a contact pistol only because of insuperable technical difficulties in fitting a proximity fuse. This was the *Zaunkönig* itself, planned to be issued from the beginning of 1944; there were a number of problems inherent in this new design, some of which were never solved during the war, and the hit-rate was not as high as Dönitz and Godt had hoped. (Inflated claims by U-boat commanders once more disguised the less than satisfying performance of the type.) This was compounded by Dönitz's not unnatural reaction to the losses of May in insisting that *Zaunkönig* be available to the operational boats by 1 August 1943.

Eighty of the torpedoes were on issue by that date and they seemed to be the answer to the problem of how to hit the escorts. Due, however, to the inability to distinguish friend from foe, once fired the U-boat had to go deep, which limited possibilities of observation of the effects of the torpedo. In fact the Allies found the answer very quickly, for they had been expecting the acoustic torpedo before it arrived. 'Foxer' was developed to counter the 'Wren', which it did by the ludicrously simple system of having their warships trail two iron bars which banged together in the water. The Wren failed to distinguish this noise from that of the ship's screws, and exploded harmlessly against some very profitable scrap iron. A further development of Foxer (to cut interference with Asdic) included only one iron bar, making the device even more cost effective. There were a number of variations of these two types of torpedo issued, and many more designed, but none of them had the really dramatic effect on the tactics of the Battle of the Atlantic, which now seemed to be dominated by the Allies' defensive systems and anti-submarine tactics.

What was needed, as Dönitz, as well as Raeder earlier, and Hitler now appreciated was a new type of boat – the true submarine. Whether such a possibility existed or not depended essentially upon one man: Hellmuth Walter. It was he, of all submarine designers, who had come upon a theoretical solution to the problem of U-boat propulsion, which would allow the boat to become a true underwater weapon, never needing to surface while in its tactical operational areas and having sufficient submerged speed to get to its target, engage, and then evade counter-attack. To understand the revolution of which Walter was one of the first practical instigators, one must look back to the first of Germany's submarine designers, Wilhelm Bauer. The greatest problem facing submarine designers was the underwater power source. Manpower was the first prime mover for submarines, but eventually, and quickly most of the time, his air supply ran out. Electric motors might have been the answer if the batteries had not needed recharging so frequently. Bauer had stumbled on the solution theoretically, although his method was impracticable. After the relative success of *Brandtaucher* he had come up with a far more sophisticated design, the *Küstenbrander* (coastal fire-ship). He said that battleships were no more than *Eisenkolosse*, 'metal monsters'. His foresight was amazing in this field. So too was his concept for the *Küstenbrander*. He argued 'on the assumption that the same protection is given by armour plate from enemy shell as by earth-works, and by being under water, if total destruction of the enemy is the sole sign of victory'. This destruction could be achieved without spending the millions that battleships required. The *Küstenbrander* would do the job of a battleship at a fraction of the cost and the risk.

The specification for the new design continued with a general description, followed by the details of the power source Bauer planned to use. The propulsion was to be supplied by a petroleum engine producing high-pressure water to a turbine. The system was to be enclosed and circulating so that the water performed the task continuously, being cooled between turbine and re-pressurisation. To keep the engine running below the surface Bauer proposed to extract oxygen in sufficient quantities from magnesium oxide, which would mean that the crew's air supply would be independent of the oxygen supply to the engine and so not be lost to that engine. This re-circulating and self-contained engine, equally functional on and below the surface, was exactly what the submarine designers needed to turn the submersible into the submarine.

Walter, half a century later, in 1917, was doing his practical year as part of his degree at the Reiherstieg Schiffswerft in Hamburg. His subject was mechanical engineering, in which he was capable both practically and theoretically. The practical year for Walter gave him what Bauer had not had, practical experience and the realisation of the limitations of heat engines; Bauer's proposal to extract oxygen from $MnO_2$ was theoretically possible, but apart from other drawbacks would have produced extremely high, probably intolerable temperatures in the *Küstenbrander*. By the time Walter had started work in Hamburg an important milestone in submarine building had been passed – the cruise of the U-boat *Deutschland* to the USA.

*Deutschland* was a submarine freighter, and the profits from this remarkable voyage virtually paid for the cost of construction. As a result six more boats of the type were ordered, three of them to be built by Reiherstieg, Hamburg (*U152–U154*), which were all launched towards the end of 1917. The magnitude of the exercise clearly impressed Walter, but he saw through the glitter to the nub of the problem – the boats had to have two separate forms of propulsion if they were to submerge at all.

By 1923 Walter, having taken his degree, had joined the famous yard of Vulkan at Hamburg. He was installed in the turbine shed under another Bauer – Dr. Bauer, working on the applications of gas-turbines. As before he soon saw the crux of the problem, and set about finding out whether a turbine could be driven by gases as was the internal combustion engine. In 1925 he applied for his first patent, for a preliminary design for a re-circulating gas-turbine engine which was self-contained. His idea was to re-circulate the exhaust gases, thereby using their latent heat, adding oxygen to regenerate them, and feeding the enriched mixture into the combustion cylinder again together with more combustible fuel. Support was soon forthcoming from the Navy Office under the control of Laudahn, who personally encouraged Walter to continue his work.

In 1930 Walter's design for a pre- and post-compressor received naval approval, whereupon he moved to Kiel to continue his work. While applying himself to turbine development he also designed the interim engine – a re-circulating, enclosed diesel system with the ($CO_2$ filtered out) exhaust gases being enriched by oxygen from a hydrogen peroxide tank. The idea of using $H_2O_2$ had come to Walter at the beginning of the year, and it was one which he was to develop to a high degree during the rest of his lifetime, before and during the war in Germany, post-war briefly in England, and then at Westinghouse in the USA, where he died in December 1980.

He formed his basic ideas in 1933, and chose as his aim the practical production of an internal combustion engine to power U-boats when submerged; the power of the diesel engine, as modified by Walter, would increase submerged speeds by a large factor, bringing the submarine to a new strategic position, as well as giving it superiority over surface vessels in a tactical situation. He had recognised that the U-boat could perform the role of fleet submarine only if its underwater speed were sufficient to keep up with the rest of the fleet – something that the American fleet submarine designers never managed to solve during the war. In sum, Walter realised that until underwater speeds equalled or exceeded the surface speeds then available, the submarine would not be more than a submersible torpedo-boat; that it was such at that time is shown by Dönitz's training methods and the emphasis on surface attacks for the first part of the war. Walter now began his search for a means of providing the U-boats with high underwater speed, calling the end result the *Unterseeschnellboot* or High Speed Submarine (HSU-boat).

By September 1933 his ideas were formulated to the extent that he wrote to the Navy Office with an outline specification for a 300-ton surface displacement boat with a submerged speed of no less than 30 knots. His engine, he claimed, would develop no less than 7,500hp under water, and would allow for an underwater range of 500 nautical miles at 15 knots. To say that this was an improvement over previous designs would be to call the nuclear reactor a mildly interesting power source. The next thing he had to do was to find a suitable hull into which he could put his engine. He solved the problem quite simply by designing it himself. He described it to the Navy Office in his letter of proposal in October 1933 as being 'fish-shaped'. He emphasised that the hull would have to be as smooth as possible externally, having no protuberances that would affect adversely the boat's hydrodynamic value. (The design of submarines and aircraft began to assume the same criteria from this point, Walter bringing hull design right up to date with this proposal.)

His first design was included with the letter. The engines drive separate screws, and there is an extendable air-shaft above the boat for use at shallow depths, saving $H_2O_2$ for deeper diving. The engine circulatory system had a basic simplicity. The hull design was revolutionary; Walter proposed to do away with the encumbrance of a conning-tower, and to maintain the inner boat (apart from the crew's area) at between 2 and 10 atmospheres, cutting the weight overall of the boat yet again. The boat was to proceed awash when on the surface, and be able to dive to ten metres in just a few seconds. All Walter needed was naval approval, and somewhere to build the first experimental boat.

On 10 April 1934 he got both; Raeder's office gave him approval to continue the experimental and development work, and suggested that Germaniawerft, Kiel build the first trials boat. Furthermore, it authorised the continued examination of the gas-turbine as the next generation of engines for U-boats. In fact Walter soon decided to put all his efforts into the turbine unit, considering that the results to be obtained from the re-circulating enriched exhaust system were not as great as the gas-turbine system promised to be.

The next thing he had to do was build an experimental version of the turbine and install it in a test boat. He also had to ensure a ready supply of $H_2O_2$ and to have it as rich in oxygen as possible. ($H_2O_2$ can be either very rich, producing say 80 per cent by volume of oxygen, or low, producing perhaps only 20 per cent oxygen by volume; in the latter case more $H_2O_2$ has to be carried to perform the same task as a smaller amount of richer $H_2O_2$.)

By 1935 Walter had sufficient support from the Navy for his ideas that he was able to set up his own firm – H. Walter, Engineer and Designer, Limited – in Kiel; the stories of his early days as a rising inventive engineer have an air of romanticism, but he did get on with the main task of producing a viable test design, and at the same time started work on designs for small Walter turbines to drive torpedoes. Naval support soon allowed him to expand, and he was soon looking for bigger premises, for his factory in the old gasworks at Kiel-Wik was too small for his 300 employees. At the same time, he was able to use research facilities at both Germania yards and the Navy's Physical Chemistry Research Establishment. By 1939 building was under way of a 1,000-worker factory on the side of the Kaiser Wilhelm Canal, and Walter was nearing completion of the design and construction of a model turbine as well as other $H_2O_2$ devices, now intended for use by all three services of the Wehrmacht.

The first of the test boats, VB60, proved the turbine to be workable, but Walter then had to build a more practical version, and test it in a larger boat; the reason for this was that the VB60 proved the engineering to be on the right lines, but left questions of practical, and above all, military application still to be answered. So, the next experimental boat, V80, was built by Germaniawerft in Kiel. The design for the boat was again entirely by Walter. The form of this boat was very similar to that of the 1933 design and VB60: above all, the boat had a high length-to-beam ratio. This is fundamentally important in all military vessels: it allows for higher speeds, which cargo-carrying hull designs do not. The length-to-beam ratio of the V80 design was approximately 11:1, which is ideal for a high-speed warship. To enhance underwater performance the outer hull was tested in a wind tunnel to ensure that the drag coefficient caused by the necessary protuberances was reduced to a minimum. The submarine had begun its transformation into the second generation – the generation of which the most modern nuclear submarines are merely the most adult at present.

Many of the ideas that Walter incorporated in V80 were later to be incorporated in the nuclear boats, but the heart of the boat lay in the turbine room. By 1939 Walter had succeeded in reducing his turbine to an extremely practical size, which could be built into the boat as Germaniawerft built the hull. To reduce the high revolutions of the turbine drive, the recently invented epicyclical train gear system was used, bringing the turbine speed of 20,000rpm down to 1,000rpm for the propeller shaft; the turbine system was capable of delivering an enormous amount of power, and by careful arrangement of the gearing and the selection of the most effective form of screw Walter aimed to transfer as much as possible of the output power to driving the submarine underwater.

In 1940 V80 was complete, and started trials in a roofed dry-dock where an underwater speed of 14 knots was easily achieved. But Kiel was felt to be too dangerous a place for continued research, and she was moved to Hela in the Danzig Bight in the autumn. Despite some minor teething problems, the boat proved herself, and by the end of 1942 some 100 test cruises had been made. The maximum underwater speed was no less than 28.1 knots, from a 2,000hp turbine (compared to the Type VII C/40 electric motors rated at 1,000hp which produced an underwater speed of just 6.9 knots). Although V80 did not complete her test programme until the end of 1942, Walter had not fallen into the trap of 'wait and see'. He had the initial design for a sea-going U-boat – that is, a turbine boat with torpedo tubes – off the drawing-board by September 1940.

This was V300 Type II, and the Type III was designed by the same time in the following year. The V300 was a sophisticated medium-size boat which would have had a similar tactical use as the earlier Type II boats, with the added advantage of very high underwater speed – some 19 knots. In addition the submerged range and duration was a far cry from the one hour at 4 knots of those boats: V300 could travel 205 miles underwater at 19 knots before needing to surface. But the boats were still not much farther advanced from engineers' test models, and the design had to be sold to the Navy as practical boats for the future at a time when the conventional boats were having enormous successes (October 1941), and were about to enter their most profitable phase of all with the opening of Operation '*Paukenschlag*'.

On 14 November 1941, Walter had his chance. He had arranged for Grand Admiral Raeder to come to a presentation of the new boat when the present and future work was explained to him in some detail. Raeder was completely entranced by this concept, although Fuchs, who was also there, was inclined in favour of the Engelmann design, which was an exhaust re-circulating system design. Following this success with Raeder, Walter now had to convince Dönitz, who had already shown great interest in his work. In January 1942 Walter went to Paris with Waas, his chief designer, to see the BdU. Dönitz came down firmly on Walter's side, and rang Berlin to ask that the work continue, having as an ultimate, but early, aim the production of an ocean-going Walter U-boat.

The work was to take some time, obviously, and in early 1942 Dönitz did not feel too pressed by events to ask for an accelerated development programme. Nevertheless he did not want any more time wasted, although he saw the need for the further testing of the design test boats in what was now the Type XVII range of U-boats.

U792 and U793 (or Wa 201) were laid down by the end of 1942, with U794 and U795 (both Wk 202) laid down the next year. The first of the Type XVII boats were also laid down in 1943 (U1405–U1416 – Type XVII B, and U1081–U1092 – Type XVII G. The same year U796 and U797 of Type XVIII were also put on the stocks at Germaniawerft, which were the first of the ocean-going boats that Dönitz wanted. And by the time they were laid down they were more than a pleasant thought for the future: they were by then a dire necessity to overcome the overwhelming superiority gained by the escorts in the first five months of 1943.

It was at this point that the demands for immediate innovation overtook Walter's work; his Type XVII and XVIII boats could not be ready for two years at least, but the problem of the escorts was immediate. New boats had to be brought into the Atlantic battle, having above all the ability to stay below the surface when within tactical range of convoy targets. Radar was far more to be feared than Asdic, a weapon that was only slightly improved in 1943 over the versions with which the Royal Navy had started the war. They were a risk the U-boat Command could accept, whereas radar was not. Furthermore, in view of the failure of the supply boats, once radar and other intelligence sources had been brought into play, the new boats needed to carry a larger number of torpedoes than the Types VII and IX. All these requirements bespoke a larger boat with increased submerged endurance and enhanced submerged speed; as the Walter turbine was not yet available, the designers had to find a means of upgrading the electric motors in any new design, to approximate Walter boat performance, even if for a much shorter duration.

The earlier history of the U-boats at the beginning of the war has already been recounted, and it may be remembered that one of the design-concepts had been the U-cruiser. By 1943 the use of U-boats on the surface had been denied by the Allies, but the idea of a large, long-range U-boat had not disappeared entirely. In the years since the war had started conventional boats had proved their worth, and Walter's ideas had received only token support from the K-Amt.

Dönitz's backing for Walter's ideas had its effect however, and from 1942 the pace quickened, so that by 1943, when the need for the new boat type was most acute, Walter had a design available which with modification could fill the gap between the conventional boats and the second generation Walter turbine boats. Further support had come from Hitler following a conference with Raeder, Dönitz and their staffs on 28 September 1942. Hitler examined and approved the design of the pre-Type XVII test boats and wanted to know when they would be ready. He foresaw the conventional boats being driven from the surface by radar and aircraft, and hoped that the Navy was ready with an answer to this change of fortunes. The net result of the conference was the decision that development and building of the Type XVIII U-boat should go ahead immediately. This was an ocean-going boat of 1,485 tons surface displacement, designed by the Glückauf engineers to Walter's specifications. It had twin 12-cylinder supercharged diesel engines, twin Walter turbines and twin electric motors; a 'belt and braces' submarine. The turbines produced 15,000 effective horse power, enough to propel the boat at 24 knots submerged for 202 nautical miles. However its building suffered from bureaucratic interference, and although it was started at Deutsche Werke Kiel in

January 1943, it had to be transferred to Germania at the end of the year because of lack of skill at the yard chosen by the K-Amt.

Dönitz was so convinced by the prospects held out for the new type that he ordered the changeover to new boat production on Walter's word alone. Luckily for him the design of the Type XVIII had also been examined by Marinebaurat Oelfken, who was subordinate to Bröking (chief engine examiner for the Navy). Oelfken saw that because the electric motor of the Type XVIII produced only 198hp (being intended as a stand-by or auxiliary motor only, and doing duty as a creep motor if in extremis), when the H2O2 was exhausted, the design had no reserve performance worth mentioning. But, thought Oelfken, the hull form was so elegant that it might be amenable with modification to produce a highly effective type of standard boat, but fitted with extra battery space.

He recommended to Bröking that this could be achieved by extending the Type XVIII design vertically in cross-section to produce the now well-known 'figure eight' design, with battery space set below the main operating hull. If this hull form were extended for about half the full length of the boat, the battery capacity compared to previous boats could be increased some three times. This in turn would mean greater submerged duration and speed, and he recommended this modification to the K-Amt at a conference at which he said:

> When we can build such a large boat, and have so much room to fill, then conventional machinery can be used to achieve much higher performance than up to now. And when underwater characteristics are more important than those on the surface, we can naturally lay out conventional machinery in different ways than heretofore.

By April 1943, aware that the conventional boats were at the end of their useful tactical life, Oelfken, together with Schürer and Bröking, presented the leader of K-Amt with plans incorporating these ideas. Fuchs was competent enough to recognise the value of these stop-gap proposals, and ordered the immediate continuation and development of the primary design study. Within the month Dönitz had been informed, and had also approved the idea, ordering the new design to be put into production as soon as possible.

This new boat, the Type XXI, was a perfect replacement for the Type IX boats, and bridged the gap between the two generations admirably from the tactical point of view. Like many good ship designs the lines of the Type XXI were pleasing even to the non-sailor's eye, and the ship was soon nicknamed the Electro or Hertha boat, the latter from the manufacturer of the electric motors. It was the electronics of these boats that was one of their most important characteristics.

On 2 March 1943 Walter had a conference with Dönitz to consider the proposed modification to his design, and he not only endorsed the idea but proposed that a Schnorkel tube be added to increase the use of the diesels. Walter showed in this instance that he was utterly unselfish with regard to his own designs, and quite able to accept the ideas of others when they were practicable, as this proposal of Oelfken's undoubtedly was. What is even more remarkable is the speed with which the basic requirements had been settled; no doubt the worsening situation in the Atlantic contributed to this, but the flexibility of the German shipbuilding industry was such that the new designs were accepted as being capable of construction, the only question being how soon could it begin.

The Type XXI design, with Walter's advice incorporated, was ready on 19 June 1943. The increased batteries would, it was thought, allow the boat to make 18 knots for one hour, and 12–14 knots for 10 hours, which would get almost any boat out of trouble. Furthermore, the surface range of the 1,621-ton boat was 15,500 nautical miles, nearly 1,700 miles more than the IX C/40 which it was replacing. This would mean that the Type XXI would have the freedom of both North and South Atlantic without the need to refuel, which had plagued the Type VII and the earlier Type IXs. In a sense, the Type XXI had now become a hybrid boat because Dönitz clutched at its potential in the aftermath of May's events, seeing it as the replacement for both types of ocean-going boat, despite its size. But in one sense he was correct, for the Type XXI was to be the last of the conventional submarines, serving until the Type XXIII Walter boat could come into service.

U-boat production up to mid-1943 had been based on standard methods: the boat was built from keel to tower in the same place, and this meant that if supplies of steel and other materials necessary were maintained at present levels, the first of the Type XXIs would be ready to launch in October 1944, and production per month might be eight in January 1945, rising to a maximum of 20 boats per month in that summer. This meant that Dönitz should have just thirty of the new boats ready for operations by early 1946, which he considered to be too long to wait. The problem he faced in June 1943 was how the conventional forces at his disposal could continue to operate against the increasingly sophisticated anti-submarine techniques of the Allies, and at the same time be effective against merchant shipping, even if in a much more limited way than in the heyday of the U-boats.

Many commentators criticise Dönitz for his argument that the U-boat would 'tie down' vast numbers of men and ships by continuing to find methods of attacking despite the opposition, even if the results were by no means encouraging. British and American historians tend to pour scorn on the holding tactics that Dönitz was forced to employ at this time, but he had no alternative, unless he were to withdraw altogether, and he was assured that the new boats would re-assert the superiority of the U-boat when submerged even though the conventional boats had lost the battle for the surface. Thus he had to continue operations and take the increasing losses (which he certainly felt grievously) until such time as the new tactics could be put into practice. Critics seem to have lost sight of the fact that in 1943 Germany was still very much a contender in the war, despite setbacks; Hitler was constantly promising many innovative strategic weapons, and in many spheres he backed his promises with action (i.e. the V1 and V2 guided missiles, jet aircraft, the Type XXI and XXIII U-boats, and the Tiger tank). Unfortunately for all the Services, the ideas often came too late, and in too small quantities to affect the outcome of the war, but the time-scale was not known to the Allies in 1943 and the new U-boat types were greatly feared by the naval forces involved in the Battle of the Atlantic.

But Dönitz was looking for a means of increasing U-boat production even before he was promoted to Commander-in-Chief of the Navy. After 30 January 1943 he had increasing access to Hitler, and now he was able to ask for more steel and increased yard availability for U-boat building. By the end of March 1943, with the help of Speer, Minister of Armaments, Dönitz had his wish. Speer was to have overall control of naval supplies, and Dönitz had Hitler's blessing for his other requirements. Speer was now able to co-ordinate supplies for the Navy, and the Board for U-boat Construction (under the chairmanship of the Managing Director of Blohm & Voss, Hamburg, the largest single U-boat contractor) was a party to the general scheduling of construction. This meant that every U-boat that was built was fitted into a main plan, from the time when the steel for it was ordered to the time that it was handed over to the Navy after its acceptance trials.

In the process of reorganising U-boat building, Speer formed a new committee, the Central Shipbuilding Committee, which was answerable to Speer for all fitting-out and modifications. A personal appointee to this committee by Speer was Otto Merker, a specialist in production-line car-assembly, a skill that had its roots on the other side of the Atlantic. Merker, rather like his counterpart Kaiser in the United States, had no detailed knowledge of naval vessels, but he had a clear idea of how to slim down production times. Being in character very like Kaiser, he was both unconventional and energetic, and he presented Speer with an idea which he said greatly cut down U-boat building times.

After Speer, himself a man of considerable ability, and Merker had worked on this idea, they presented Dönitz with a sensational rethink, just as he was beginning to despair of getting the new U-boats to sea in time to be of strategic value. The idea came from observation of the traditional U-boat building methods referred to earlier. Once the hull was finished and the diesel and electrical power units installed, the only access the workmen had to the interior of the boat, where the majority of the rest of the finishing work was done, was through the restricting hatches in the pressure-hull. This slowed the finishing process considerably. As an answer to this problem, and as a means of combating the air-raids which were expected to stay at the level of the 1943

Hamburg three-day fire raid, Merker and Speer proposed that the Type XXI be built in sections.

This method would allow constant access from both ends of all but two sections, and would also allow individual sections to be built away from the coast, with only final assembly being done in the launching yards. By this method the final assembly yards had no more to do than fitting sections together and linking controls and electric cables. The old scheduling problems for order of installation of the myriad of equipment, cables and pipes and the slowness of the work would be removed at a stroke.

This matter was one upon which Dönitz needed more than a sailor's eye; he put the whole plan to Schürer, who was chief hull examiner at K-Amt, with the instruction that if Schürer agreed, Speer and Merker could go ahead. Schürer did approve of the idea, and on 8 July 1943 Dönitz informed Hitler of the plan, and emphasised his own feeling of urgency. Hitler put the final seal of approval on the plan, and it swung into motion. The rapidity of the changes that took place in just six months must be emphasised once more: the new plan brought about a complete change in methods of submarine construction, and introduced mass-production commercial methods into an area which was traditionally conservative, especially in view of the service that was involved – the German Navy. That Dönitz and his staff were able to fall in with the plan shows their willingness to adopt new methods, and it would be facile to comment that the change was merely a result of necessity. (Furthermore the methods laid down by Merker are still used today to produce nuclear submarines.)

Once the plan in outline was accepted, the next task was to set up the overall control organisation for is implementation, and draw-up a first construction schedule for the Type XXI boats. However, work was in progress on no fewer than 180 VII C/42 boats which were scheduled to be built under pre-Merker programmes. The planners decided to continue to build these boats until the Type XXI sections came on stream, when there would be a complete change-round to building the Type XXI. The Type VII C/42, a more advanced Type VII, was to continue to build at Stülckenwerft, Hamburg and Nordseewerke, Emden, to replace losses as they occurred, but the Type XXI programme was to be concentrated on the three largest and most experienced yards: Blohm & Voss, Hamburg, Deschimag, Bremen, and Schichau, Danzig.

Sectional work was to be done inland in many cases, with specified feeder routes to the coast. All the planning was concentrated on producing the first Type XXI at the earliest possible date, and the production of 33 boats of this type per month from the autumn of 1944 – only eighteen months from its conception. Naturally there were some engineers unwilling to accept the pressure of a pre-set completion date, but Merker had his way in the end, and Skl issued the first production order for 170 boats on 6 November 1943. The steel mills began production of the plate for the pressure-hulls and other preformed steel at the end of the month. On 8 December the plans for fitting-out the boats as well as for the section assembly had been completed, and on 1 January 1944 the final assembly programme was issued.

The plan called for assembly in three stages. The first was the production of plate by the decentralised inland iron foundries. The curved plates were then transferred by road, rail and inland waterway to the section yards which were all chosen for their ship-building experience; there were many quality tests applied as the sections moved towards completion. To ensure complete understanding of what was to be done, a number of pre-production boats was assembled and installed in the three final assembly yards; this gave the builders a completed example which they could compare with the plans they were given and the sections as they arrived from the section yards.

Merker's plan included every known method of avoiding mistakes during all stages of construction, until all the personnel involved were fully aware of the problems that would arise if pre-production of, for example, steel plate did not conform to the strictest tolerances. The actual building time was also important, for every man-hour saved on one boat meant more time spent on the next, and the wastage rate was much lower in mass-production. Workers could go from completing their job on one boat to the same job on the next in line, cutting their down-time considerably. Despite criticisms levelled after the war that most of the boats were delayed by ill-fitting pressure-hull sections, on-the-spot modification was used and the building times were remarkable when compared to the traditional methods. The figures given by Rössler are:

|  | VIC | IXD2 | XXI | XXI |
|---|---|---|---|---|
|  | Autumn 43 |  | Dec44 | Final target |
| Steel | 35000 | 45000 | 80000 | 64000 man hours |
| Yard | 180000 | 405000 | 252500 | 202000 |
| Total | 215000 | 450000 | 332500 | 266000 |
| Man hours |  |  |  |  |
| per ton: | 280 | 278 | 205 | 164 |

The man-hours per ton show how Merker's plan reduced building time, and is a vindication of the method. After the war the rapidity with which the victorious navies took control of numerous Type XXIs shows the technical interest the boats aroused, and the continued service of two Type XXIs (the *Wilhelm Bauer* of the Federal German Navy and the *Roland Morillot* of the French Navy) until the 1960s show that the design had much to recommend it. Nevertheless on occasions there were problems which required drastic solutions.

In view of the complexity of the operation, it would be well to look into the building process and also examine some of the problems caused both by the programme itself and by Allied activities. The War Economy was not running at full stretch at the beginning of the war, and the slack began to be taken up only when the war turned against Germany. This meant that the Type XXI programme would not overburden shipbuilding capacity if it were well planned, and the completion targets were not set unrealistically high. But everything needed for the new boats had to be ready for installation in a very short time, including new, higher output electric motors, which SSW and AEG were to build jointly.

The pace of the programme initially resulted in delays, and this, plus the strict completion date of the first of the Type XXIs, led to her being unseaworthy, gaps in welding having wooden plugs: according to Merker's plan the boat was to be launched on 30 April 1944, Hitler's birthday. The Type XXI programme had approximately 50 per cent of German steel production devoted to it; the general priority in all matters was one which would have delighted Dönitz four, or even three, years before, but was now a priority of desperation. Risks were being taken to get the Type XXIs to sea, and even the Army found itself in second position for steel; the balance between unacceptable risk and complete safety was difficult to maintain, but had there been more time available there can be little doubt that the new boats would have made their mark, and been a very able successor to the Type IX and Type VII C/42 boats.

The entire system was co-ordinated to produce the finished boats, with each element having fixed completion dates to ensure that final production was possible with no delays due to shortage of sections. There were three types of building yard involved. The first built both the pressure and external hull of each section, fitted bulkheads, and certain hull equipment. These yards received plating and frames ready cut from the steel suppliers and fashioned them to the designed profiles. These sections were then transported (mainly by canal, river or sea) to the fitting-out yards where all piping, wiring and the fitting of main and some auxiliary power units was completed. The third stage took place at the three main building yards on the coast where the batteries were installed, the eight sections welded together automatically, and the boat finished.

The boats were then painted and launched, followed by final fitting-out at the piers; within eight hours of a launching the sections for the next boat were being lined up on the recently vacated slip. The first boats suffered from badly fitting sections, but the problem was eased initially by the judicious application of the cutting torch, and later by familiarity with the task, which led to greater accuracy of finishing at each of the stages. Merker's programme caused the problems, but also had the solution – familiarisation.

Once the boat had left the fitting-out piers it went for sea trials where everything that could be tested was put under examination. All electrical and mechanical equipment was tested to the maximum, pressure testing ensured the homogeneity of the welding, and dive and trim tests established seaworthiness. If the UAK accepted the boat, it went to a training flotilla for commissioning.

The early boats did, however, suffer from the insistence from Merker that they be finished no matter what the delays; and delays there were. The first steel plates delivered to the section building yards were not milled to the correct tolerances, and could not be returned to the suppliers, so corrections had to be made on the spot, which strained the already tight schedule. This meant that not all the work scheduled for the section building yard could be done there, and had to be passed up the line to the section fitting-out yards. When the early sections arrived at the main assembly yards, they were often either unfinished or so badly finished that in normal circumstances they would have been rejected, or torn apart and rebuilt.

Under the Merker plan this was impossible, and so every feasible method of forcing a fit, or bending pipes or cutting out ribs was used to get the whole boat looking like a submarine. Unfortunately this led the directors of Deschimag AG and Blohm & Voss to launch incomplete boats without reporting the fact. The tension between Merker and the yards even continued when Dönitz appointed Rear-Admiral Topp as his mediator, for, as the General Director of Blohm & Voss realised, the early completion dates were settled on by Merker and his team to impress Hitler and the Navy Board. There was an external factor too; the bombing offensive against Germany was having an increasing effect on the delays. Although rarely specifically aimed at the U-boat industry, side-effects of the bombing were felt from the huge 1943 raid on Hamburg. Although the yards were virtually undamaged, the workers were prevented from getting to work by damage to the town, or were killed in the fire-storm or otherwise affected by it. The production rate at Blohm & Voss fell drastically after this raid, and never fully recovered. Furthermore, as the concerted attack on Germany's transportation system went on, more delays were caused to section deliveries at all stages of manufacture, thus prolonging the completion dates.

Nevertheless, during the period between the birth of the idea in February 1943 and the end of the war, 120 Type XXI boats were commissioned, and a number more were building and nearly finished. In addition the prefabrication of 62 Type XXIII coastal boats had been possible, as well as considerable work to conclude the Type VII and IX programmes; extra to all this was the construction of significant numbers of small underwater craft intended for inshore work. Delays caused the below-maximum performance in the ship-building industry, however, rather than actual bomb damage, and the air offensive had only a 10 per cent effect upon production as a whole.

The speed with which the work was done ensured that problems would arise. That solutions were found is remarkable, but the solutions also brought to light factors which had not been considered before the mass production of these boats was thought of. One phenomenon was the increased magnetic field created by the boats, which would make them easy prey for magnetic mines if not corrected. It was found that the electric mains of the boat was designed (for simplicity) to go stern to bow up one side of the boat, returning on the opposite side. This was rapidly corrected, but it was one of the few occasions when the needs of the fighting men were part of the design – albeit belatedly. Normally reports of good and bad points of the boats came from the flotillas as well as from engineer officers and other sources, but the speedy production time meant that there was no time for testing them at sea and modifying them before others were built. Many of the purely mechanical problems were both recognised and been eliminated by April 1945, when the fruit of the labour was available to the Allies.

Once the boats had been taken over by the German Navy there had to be a training and evaluation period before the boats could go on operations. In fact the first boats of this type were at sea by July 1944, but teething problems extended the training period initially from three to at least six months with the early boats. The most serious effect of these recurrent snags was that training was constantly being broken off while the boat was returned to dry dock or even to the yard so that faults could be corrected. This even happened with some of the first boats after they got to UAK at Kiel for acceptance trials, for although UAK was allowed to modify boats (the only naval unit so authorised), some of the problems were beyond that unit's capabilities. But even considering small modifications only, there were 150 of them on the list for every boat by September 1944 – only two months after the boats first came under scrutiny.

After the boats had passed through the hands of UAK they went on to the technical training school at Hela where training under battle conditions was carried out. There were diving trials and Schnorkel manoeuvres, as well as damage control and repair, and all the other elements of submarine training, including anti-escort and escape techniques which were then an integral part of every submariner's stock-in-trade. The training may be encapsulated as beginning with a straightforward attack at periscope depth, and ending with a crash-dive under the most arduous simulated battle conditions. Only when all the technical training officers were completely satisfied with the state of the crew's training would the boat be allowed to proceed to its first operational posting.

While some of the boats were actually at sea, prior to operational sailing, others were held by UAK for technical training and more intensive evaluation. They were subjected to every test the sailors and engineers could conceive, and it was soon proved that the designed submerged speed of 18 knots for 1 hour could not be maintained, and that the maximum speed would be nearer 15.8–16.2 knots.

This was too near the average speed of an escort for comfort, and various attempts were made to increase it, including blocking up some of the flooding slits in the casing to reduce the drag they caused. Another method was the grinding down of all welding protrusions on the outer casing, which gave the test boats a maximum speed of 17.2 knots, but production boats levelled out at 16.5 knots for a 1-hour submerged sprint.

The boats did not prove to be an abject failure; at lower submerged speeds they were easy to handle and fulfilled the designed performance. Furthermore, and exceptionally important to every German submariner at this stage of the war, the diving time of just 20 seconds was much lower than conventional boats, and even when some of the flooding slits had been blocked, diving took only 25 seconds, again lower than ever before. When it was discovered that the time taken to get under the surface could be shortened by putting the stern hydroplanes into the 'up' position when 13 seconds into the dive, the news was received with joy. The general buoyancy of the boat was such that the main diving tank when flooded in emergency only took five seconds off the time taken, whereas on the Types VII and IX it was unthinkable to try a crash-dive without flooding that tank. Boats that were properly constructed, the Navy soon realised, were very good boats indeed, and the diving times were eventually so good that the crash diving tanks were rarely used.

Compared to the earlier types, the boats had a great deal of electronic equipment to counter the Allied counter-measures, and BdU issued directives for its tactical use. These were tested by the training units. An experimental tactical unit was set up in August 1944, which was to evaluate the boat and new anti-convoy tactics.

Type XXI boats were to approach the operational area submerged, at an economical speed, using diesel-electric drive in conjunction with the Schnorkel. The boats had to Schnorkel for three hours daily to recharge batteries, sailing at 5–5½ knots, and this allowed a daily range of 120 nautical miles; they could transit the route from Norway to the area South of Iceland in 4–6 days, thus only needing a maximum of 5 nightly Schnorkel sessions. Of course the new boats were relatively immune to interference while Schnorkelling because they could switch to full electric drive and escape rapidly, then travel at creep speed and put a good distance between boat and attacker before resuming recharge again. This would reduce the chances of boats being lost on their outward passage to the Atlantic, the only zone where the new boats could achieve their full effect.

Once a ship, or preferably a convoy, had been located by whatever means, including the boat's sound-location equipment (superior to previous sets), the Type XXI could attack from any angle because of the high submerged speed. Using the special equipment of the GHG (*Gruppen-horchgerät*) and predictor equipment, the captain could attack without using periscopes, at night, or in fog, while submerged, or in similar conditions on the surface using his search radar. A salvo of six LUT torpedoes followed by six more twenty minutes later at the same convoy was expected to have a 95 per cent hit rate, meaning that at least ten ships could be hit by one submarine in less than an hour.

If this had been only half correct, the effect of these boats would have been considerable, and could have prolonged the war to a considerable degree, had the land situation not been so critical to their operational use. To aid the captain further, TEK (*Torpedo Erprobungs-Kommando*) had developed a computer which linked the GHG sound-locator and the torpedo-setting equipment, and the boat was to be equipped with the H11 torpedo, which was capable of out-foxing Foxer and finding the decoy's host.

Initially the boats were to operate as they had at the beginning of the war – individually. But the time would come when there would be enough operational Type XXIs to form packs again, when the hope was that whole convoys, including their escorts, could be sunk in one attack. And at last the Navy's enthusiasm caught up with the *Luftwaffe*'s, whose performance in 1944 was being limited by the Allied air escorts for their bombers. The latest and fastest piston-engined aircraft, the Dornier Do 335, was to operate with the new boats. It was to overfly the British Isles at night at 700km per hour and to patrol the western sea lanes, but the grandiose nature of the plan was brought down to earth by Admiral Godt, who believed there would never be enough aircraft anyway.

But problems so delayed the trials and testing of the Type XXI boats that hardly any got to sea on an operational patrol, and they did not sink a single ship, although U2511 did manage an undetected dummy attack on HMS *Norfolk* en route for Bergen to surrender. One other Type XXI, U3008, went operational, but she too achieved nothing militarily. Another, smaller new boat, the Type XXIII, was more of a success, although fewer of this class were actually built.

The Type XXIII had a similar start in life as the Type XXI, and grew out of the technical impossibility of getting the Walter turbine into operational use after the defeat of May 1943. The smallness of this design did at least allow extra building of U-boats to go on where otherwise there would be none taking place, and the construction of the boats would be part of the development programme of both conventional boats, and later of the Walter boats. Dönitz said that the Type XXIII was designed for operations in the shallow waters off the British Isles and in the Mediterranean. These boats were also sections-built, final assembly being carried out at Deutsche Werft, Hamburg. The first fifty were officially ordered on 20 September 1943, and the first boat went into service on 21 June 1944. Actual building time for this type was approximately five weeks from laying the keel to launching, followed by some two months' fitting out and acceptance tests (later cut to some three weeks only).

The two types (XXI and XXIII) were to be the interim answer to Allied escort supremacy, although only the Type XXI was to compete with the escorts on the high seas in the Atlantic. The Type XXIII was to engage in hit-and-run tactics. The Type XXI was designed to retake supremacy of the sea lanes by virtue of its much greater submerged endurance and its ability to sprint submerged from both an attacking position and from where it was initially attacked. Unfortunately these boats were too late to make any impact, and their real capability remains unknown; against them would have been the weapons ranged against the Types VII and IX, as well as the more advanced equipment that was becoming available from the US.

Before looking at the existing weapons and tactics available to the Allies for the remainder of the war, the building programme of the old and new boats should be briefly examined, to establish the Germans' planned time-scale. The new weapons can then be put in the context of the ships against which they would be used. The table below shows the way the building programmes for the conventional boats were linked with the production of the stop-gap boats, and the expected production of the Walter boats:

(Figures are actual production except where Walter boats are concerned.)

| 1944 | Jan | Feb | Mar | Apr | May | Jun | July | Aug | Sept | Oct | Nov | Dec |
|---|---|---|---|---|---|---|---|---|---|---|---|---|
| VII | 17 | 15 | 17 | 15 | 15 | 11 | 8 | 3 | 6 | 1 | 2 | 2 |
| IX | 4 | 4 | 4 | 6 | 4 | – | – | 1 | – | – | – | – |
| XXI | – | – | – | – | – | 1 | 3 | 7 | 8 | 10 | 14 | 20 |
| XXIII | – | – | – | – | – | 1 | 3 | 4 | 6 | 4 | 7 | 6 |
| Walter | | | | | | | | | | | | |
| XVIIB/G | 2 | 3 | 4 | 8 | 8 | 9 | 9 | 9 | 10 | 9 | 9 | 10 |
| XXII | 1 | – | – | 1 | 6 | 6 | 6 | 6 | 6 | 6 | 6 | 6 |
| XX | | | | | | | | | 1 | 2 | 3 | 3 |

(Figures after May, and for Walter boats are the planned production)

| 1945 | Jan | Feb | Mar | Apr | May | Jun | July | Aug | Sept | Oct | Nov | Dec |
|---|---|---|---|---|---|---|---|---|---|---|---|---|
| VII | No further production of Type VII boats | | | | | | | | | | | |
| IX | – | – | 1 | No further production of Type IX boats | | | | | | | | |
| XX | 3 | 3 | 2 | 2 | 3 | 3 | 2 | 2 | 1 | – | – | – |
| XXI | 25 | 9 | 19 | 4 | (10 | 9 | 11 | 12 | 10 | 8 | 5 | 4) |
| XXIII | 12 | 7 | 7 | 4 | 1 | | | | | | | |
| XVIIB/G | 9 | 9 | 10 | 8 | 5 | 1 | | | | | | |
| XXII | 6 | 6 | 6 | 3 | | | | | | | | |

There was also provision for a rebuild of eight Type XIV supply boats, as well as the new Type XX boats included above, and the production of the Type VII C/42, but much of this work was either cancelled to allow the Merker programme a free rein, or because of the deteriorating situation. But the general trend towards the Type XXI as the main battle boat can clearly be seen, and actual production began to outstrip the programme quite quickly as the new methods of construction became more familiar to the workers at the various stages of building. The problem that eventually became insuperable was the damage to the internal transport system in Germany which the Allied bombing achieved. This meant that sections already built could not be moved on to the next stage. Direct bombing had almost no effect whatsoever, although the final result in terms of boats not produced because of delay was some 10 per cent in the last eighteen months of the war.

Having said a great deal about the loss of offensive ability in the Atlantic in May 1943, and having examined the German plans to regain the initiative, the Allied tactics and weapons that had brought about this reverse should be considered. To sink a U-boat the scientists of the Operational Research Section had established that a suitable charge of explosive (the weight of the charge in the Mark VII depth-charge) had to be exploded within fifteen feet of the hull of the boat. The force of the explosion would be enough to rupture the pressure-hull. If this happened when the boat was already deep, the result was immediate flooding by ultra high-pressure water, and a total loss. There was no escape if the boat went deep to escape attack, and was then hit, because every additional foot below the surface increased the water pressure significantly. Only if the boat were within reach of the surface could it survive damage to the pressure-hull: then it could surface and hope to make its way home.

Some boats did this, reaching base despite cracks in the pressure hull, but many more reached the surface only to be attacked from the air by machine-guns, and later airborne guns, or shot at by the waiting destroyers, corvettes, frigates, and any other vessel that had a gun capable of firing a round. The U-boat is ill-designed to operate against surface gunfire, especially in calibres above cannon-shell size, for any further penetration of the pressure-hull would increase the chances of destruction. Many U-boats did fight on coming to the surface, but very few lasted for more than a few minutes. The high-velocity guns carried by all escorts were more than enough to ensure their destruction, and in many cases only a few of the crew survived.

Another weapon which made its debut in the latter part of the war was the anti-submarine acoustic torpedo, affectionately code-named 'Fido', which could be dropped by an aircraft or a sea escort. It had an acoustic head which, like the *Zaunkönig*, homed-in on the sound of the target's screws. There was no counter-measure, for the U-boats could not trail a Foxer-type device for fear of it fouling their screws, and it could not be retrieved. Thus the U-boat had the unintelligent depth-charge to fear, the more so later in the war because dropping patterns were now of up to 24 charges whereas before they had been perhaps two or three or four. In addition there was this intelligent depth-charge, quite capable of following them wherever they went. This form of anti-submarine torpedo is still being used today, although it is now somewhat more sophisticated.

On the surface, bombs, shells, and anything else available was fired, thrown or dropped on them, and there was a further danger – the ahead-throwing weapon. The British had developed the first of these in a bid to cut out the 'dead' spot which occurred when Asdic could no longer pick up the U-boats at short range (within some 200 yards of the transmitting head). Captain Walker used the creeping attack, the searching escorts using Asdic and lying motionless while another escort was directed to a position over the target, when she would be signalled to drop a depth-charge pattern. But the resultant explosions deafened the Asdic for some time, perhaps allowing a U-boat to get away.

Ahead-throwing devices obviated the need to direct others in the attack, because they could be fired at a target still on the attacker's Asdic, and the bombs themselves only exploded if they hit the submarine target. Unfortunately, as the Operational Research Section noted, this type of detonation did suffer from the drawback that the U-boat would not be damaged by a near miss and the morale effect on both sides of a considerable explosion was missing.

The 'Hedgehog' fired (in standard form) 24 bombs arranged to fall in a statistically calculated pattern around the target to cope with both the boat that did not try to avoid the bombs, as well as the one that did. A number of U-boats were lost to this weapon, as well as to the larger version, 'Squid', an anti-submarine mortar firing a much larger projectile. In addition to Asdic the Allies were installing radar and high-frequency direction-finding equipment in the escorts to warn of U-boats as well as to attack them, and airborne radar and land-based direction-finding stations completed the picture of Allied electronic anti-U-boat techniques.

Early efforts had now developed into sophisticated and readily available equipment, and a large number of escorts were fitted with both radar and HF/DF (high-frequency direction-finding, or 'Huff-Duff'). HF/DF could locate a U-boat's transmissions at a greater range than radar, and thus give early warning to one escort and a fix on a U-boat to two or more; this ability, coupled with the results of the expanded land-based direction-finding equipment, led to the Submarine Tracking Room and its American counterpart knowing the approximate position of many of the U-boats at sea. But direction-finding could also be used to home an aircraft in on a target, as well as the surface escorts, and once within radar range the U-boat had to submerge or almost certainly perish. Once located on the surface, even if the U-boat did submerge it had insufficient speed to avoid an Asdic search, and now that depth could also be established it was usually the escorts who won the guessing and waiting game that ensued. Until the U-boats were independent of the surface to some practical, tactical extent, they would continue to be destroyed. It was to this end that Walter recalled the earlier Dutch use of the Schnorkel, and the installation of this device is dealt with later.

Much has been said of the code war that went on between the two belligerents, and of the successes they both had up to May 1943. The GCCS team tackling the U-boats' 'Triton' code had achieved their breakthrough in December 1942, and despite a momentary loss of intelligence due to the Germans issuing orders for this code to go on to 4-wheel Enigma, the almost current reading of the code was restored after a gap of only a few days in March 1943. The German U-boat code remained readable from then until the end of the war, apart from a short break in 1943 as noted, and certain individual U-boat codes which could not be deciphered. Merchant shipping also benefited from the changeover to more complex ciphers during 1943, and *B-Dienst* lost its value as an intelligence source.

It is of interest to note that whereas the U-boat Arm up to the final defeat of May 1943 had been a coherant but flexible operational doctrine, the Allies had pursued as many policies as there were navies and air forces involved. But once the Battle of the Atlantic had reached the stage when the U-boats were denied their previous advantages, and forced beneath the surface, the Allies at long last began to plan an economic use of their forces to ensure that the U-boat menace could not again raise its head, for the ultimate planning effort was being devoted to the long-awaited invasion of Western Europe, Operation 'Overlord'.

Before looking at the developments of early 1943 in the anti-submarine war at sea, it is important to make a brief note of the situation in the air over Europe. The RAF failed in virtually all of its aims in the Strategic Bombing Offensive, as is evidenced by the United States Strategic Bombing Survey (despite some palliative comments on RAF accuracy later in the war). The attack on morale simply failed; furthermore, although the Germans were glad the bombing had stopped once the war was over, during it they were more affected by the worsening military situation and the sudden drop in reported U-boat successes that they had been accustomed to hear daily up to the month of May 1943. But the US Eighth Army Air Force (in particular) made a contribution that needs to be firmly acknowledged.

On 19 October 1942, General Eisenhower wrote to General Spaatz (Commanding VIII USAAF) that as far as he was concerned the target status of the U-boats (previously an intermediate target, as were German aircraft) was undoubtedly too low, and he put U-boats at the top of his and the VIII AAF's list for the foreseeable future. This policy was more than welcome at the Admiralty, but caused the Air Ministry to protest that their area bombing of ports would do the job more effectively. What the Air Ministry could not and would not see was that the U-boats at the end of 1942 and the beginning of 1943 were such an immediate danger to the Allies and their plans for an invasion of Europe that long-term attrition programmes were simply inadequate to meet the constant danger that the Germans might still win the western war by closing the lines of communications between the United Kingdom and the New World.

With typical American forthrightness Spaatz agreed that his aircraft would begin an all-out attack (within their capabilities) on the one target they could reasonably be expected to deal with – the massive U-boat pens which protected the U-boats when in base. They used five main ports on the French Atlantic coast, Brest, St.-Nazaire, Lorient, La Pallice, and to a lesser extent Bordeaux. Of these bases, three were extremely busy (Brest, Lorient and St.-Nazaire), and it was against these targets that the main effort was made. The RAF had dropped some 396.1 tons of bombs on the combined targets in 33 night raids in 1941, but policy had then become almost exclusively dedicated to bombing Germany in 1942, and there had been no further attacks on the pens by Bomber Command after 1941.

General Spaatz felt that attacks on these targets might be a waste of effort, but he was willing to try, appreciating as he did the immediate threat the U-boats represented, Unfortunately for the Americans, the Organisation Todt had made the roofs of the pens so thick that no Allied bomb existed that could penetrate them. An OSS report of late 1942 commented that even armour-piercing bombs could only go five feet into the twelve feet of ferro-concrete that formed the carapace of the shelters. This resulted in the effort spent by the American bombers being largely wasted, although the towns of Lorient and St.-Nazaire were rendered uninhabitable for the French, and so utterly unsuitable for R & R for the Germans. American losses too became an embarrassment, but the dogged pounding of the bases was planned to go on until a decision could be reached. Luckily events farther out in the Atlantic relieved the VIII AAF of its dangerous and unprofitable task.

The events of the first five months of 1943 proved, in fact, what the Admiralty had been telling the Air Ministry and everyone else (who generally refused to listen) since 1939, that the U-boat could be defeated most readily in the area of his target – the convoys. The Admiralty had learned the hard way. As shown earlier, anti-submarine patrols had sunk a number of U-boats (36 up to the end of December 1942) but a far larger number had been sunk by the convoy escorts (87 during the same period). What was significant about the figures of U-boats sunk during the first 40 months of the war was that only one had been sunk by Bomber Command (11 March 1940, *U31* was sunk off Heligoland Bight by HMS *Antelope* and a Coastal Command flying-boat). The Admiralty had learned from this experience, and from the affair of *Courageous* in 1939, that anti-U-boat patrols were far less likely to have any real effects compared with convoy protection, especially if the shortage of suitable escorts was also taken into account.

The question of 'protect or patrol' came up again in late 1942, when the US Army and the Navy were at loggerheads as to who should command aircraft attacking U-boats at sea. This was a direct repeat of the Air Ministry–Royal Navy conflict over Coastal Command. The Air Ministry rather smugly spoke of Admiralty control of Coastal Command aircraft as a 'polite fiction', although the Admiralty did not see the matter that way. But by the middle of 1943 the problem had been solved in fact, if not on the organisation charts.

Leaving this controversial subject requires just one summarising comment: the RAF contributed nothing of import to the defeat of the German U-boat Arm in May 1943 except for allotting begrudged aircraft to Coastal Command. These latter aircraft did sterling service, and eventually became masters of their art. The US bombers contributed nothing of consequence, but it must be said that this was not for want of trying.

In 1943 efforts were being made, especially by the Americans, to speed up the whole process of the war, and of course the invasion of North Africa had been a direct result of their insistence on some tangible and effective large-scale action. The invasion of Europe was the next major step which had to be carried out by the Allies, but Churchill and the War Cabinet seemed to be dragging their feet. To ensure that the U-boat menace did not appear again to hinder increasing trans-Atlantic traffic, the Americans (benefiting all the time from consultation with their more experienced counterparts in the Royal Navy and the Royal Canadian Navy, as well as Coastal Command), decided to establish the 10th Fleet, whose sole role was to be anti-submarine warfare.

Originally the Americans had decided that the one sure way of keeping the U-boats under control was to have a single Atlantic anti-U-boat Command, controlling all forces of all nations, but for political reasons they were aware that the British would never accede to this proposal. Rather than remain on the same organisational basis as hitherto, with a multitude of small commands (the United States Sea Frontiers) all clamouring for men and equipment, it was decided not only to unite these commands, but to expand the force to include offensive action against the U-boats wherever they might be found.

In March 1943 the Atlantic Convoy Conference (a child of the Casablanca Conference) met for the first time in Washington. Among the participants were Admiral Sir Percy Noble, Vice-Admiral Sir Henry Moore and Rear-Admiral V. G. Brodeur (RCN) as well as representatives of the Royal Air Force and the newly formed US Army Air Force Anti-submarine Command. Surprisingly they were addressed by Admiral King, who had earlier advocated switching all American forces to the Pacific theatre after Pearl Harbor. However, ordered to continue support operations for Great Britain, he had backed this decision with all his efforts, and no trace of his earlier position remained. The address began with the assertion that convoy was both the best method of getting things across the Atlantic and the easiest way to attract U-boats. The concept of the hunter-killer group was once more raised, but now with two important differences. The first was that now that the UAS was a participant, more ships were available for such duty, and eventually some could be spared; secondly, the groups were to operate on the convoy routes, rather than undertake intuitive patrols with little or no chance of success. The EU Committee sat for twelve days and its final recommendations were:

1. That the RN and RCN should have charge of North Atlantic Convoys. This reflected the growing status of the RCN in the conflict and the part the RN had played in the battle so far. It also solved the problem of mixed operational procedures which caused confusion.

2. The United States Navy was to have control of all convoy operations in the Caribbean, the tanker convoys to the UK, and the Central Atlantic convoys to Gibraltar and North Africa.

The RAF units affected were also moved, and Coastal Command left the enviable base in Trinidad for one further north. There were other organisational changes recommended and implemented, one of the most significant for anti-U-boat warfare being the setting up of American Escort Carrier Groups. There were still too few very long range aircraft available (for bombing or anti-U-boat patrols) and the air gaps that had plagued convoys for so long had to be filled if the U-boats were to be beaten. The American solution was that if land-based aircraft did not have the endurance for such operations, they would send out well-protected aircraft carriers with short-range anti-submarine aircraft aboard to do the job. The results of this policy far outstripped expectation, for the various carriers had made a total of 47 anti-submarine patrols by the end of 1944, sinking unaided a total of 47 U-boats and assisting in the sinking of a further sixteen. This closing of the air gaps was as important as the actual battle of 1943, for it kept the U-boats below the surface after their efforts had been moved south after Dönitz's order of 24 May 1943.

As with all things American, ideas must lead to action, and Admiral King appointed Rear Admiral F. S. Low to command the new US 10th Fleet on 6 April 1943, and ordered him to come up with a solution to the vexing problem of the U-boats as quickly as possible. After intensive study of every relevant document he could lay hands on, his report was submitted to Admiral King two weeks later. He wrote:

> The prosaic answer to the problem is enough escorts and aircraft, recognition of fundamentals, and pressure to make them work.

What the Royal Navy had been trying to bring to the attention of the War Cabinet and the Air Ministry was encapsulated in those few words. Needless to say, the War Cabinet in London had been under heavy, unrelenting pressure for a long time, and the entry of the USA into the war did not alleviate its problems at a stroke, but it is true to say that it had failed to act upon its own appreciation of the facts – that the single most dangerous menace was the U-boat.

Although Admiral Low suggested that his command be turned over to Admiral Ingersoll, who was Commander of the US Atlantic Fleet, and the most experienced officer in the navy, Admiral King and Admiral Ingersoll demurred. King's reason was that Admiral Low was to have overall command of the anti-submarine effort and was of sufficient rank and experience to resist the combined pressure of Mr. Churchill and President Roosevelt, both of whom were charismatic men, well aware of the persuasive ability of charm – or of anger when needed.

On 1 May 1943, the month in which the battle was to be decided and when convoy ONS.5 was waiting for the inevitable attack from the massive force of U-boats, Admiral King announced the formation of the 10th Fleet, and that he was to command it personally, with Admiral Low as Chief of Staff. The importance attached to the U-boat war was fully acknowledged by this. It encompassed, as a command, operations, operational research and tactical development, convoy and routing control, as many scientific advisers as necessary. It was the American answer to the much more compartmentalised arrangement in operation, which centred on Liverpool and the North-Western Approaches Command of Sir Max Horton.

The height of the Battle of the Atlantic was reached suddenly, and in retrospect, seemingly without warning. As noted earlier there was no hint at the beginning of May that by the end of the month the U-boats would have been forced off the northern convoy routes into the safer waters of the southern sector of the North Atlantic. That this happened was to an extent a combination of good fortune which could not have been foreseen by the Allies, but which had been a fear present in all Dönitz's calculations for many months, indeed since the operation against HG.76. Even without the aid of escort carriers, the battle of May was lost because the U-boats had been simply too old-fashioned to compete with the newly developed counter-measures.

# 13 THE LAST TWO YEARS

The situation in June 1943 was that the Allies had gained the upper hand in the Battle of the Atlantic, and Dönitz had ordered the U-boats to make a covert withdrawal to more southern waters where cheaper pickings might had. Hoping for the rapid arrival of the new U-boat types, he had in the meantime with the help of Admiral Godt to ensure that the Allies' forces were kept extended, and that his boats could operate without suffering losses on a par with those of May.

Initially, U-boat operations for the remainder of 1943 suffered a relatively high loss rate, but towards the end of the year Allied successes were diminished by the introduction of the Schnorkel. Given the scale of their operations, U-boat losses up to May were acceptable. It has been suggested that the higher losses of February to April were part and parcel of the May defeat. This was not so, for the U-boats were still capable of a full offensive, despite morale problems that were slowly creeping in, culminating in the disastrous losses of May. The immediate answer was the change of operational areas, but the message transmitted to the U-boats on 22 May at 1752 hours included the following comment:

> The situation in the North Atlantic now forces a temporary shifting of operations to areas less endangered by aircraft ... It is intended to attempt attacks on a convoy only under the most favourable conditions.

Seemingly words of defeats until one reads on:

> These conditions comprise a temporary deviation from the former principles for the conduct of U-boat warfare. This is necessary in order not to allow the U-boats to be beaten at a time when their weapons are inferior, by unnecessary losses while achieving very light success. It is however clearly understood that the main operational area of U-boats is, as it always was, in the North Atlantic and that operations must be resumed there with every determination as soon as the U-boats are given the necessary weapons for this.

The War Diary continues to note the weapons considered to be effective against the enemy – quadruple 2cm FlaK guns, the *Zaunkönig* torpedo, and an improvement in location devices. Once the quadruple FlaK had been fitted it was the intention that convoy attacks in the North Atlantic would be resumed.

Until that happened, however, the U-boats were under strict orders to remain submerged where previously they had travelled with impunity on the surface. Unfortunately for Dönitz his U-boats would never regain their previous freedom, and even the Schnorkel allowed them to achieve only very limited success. As will be seen, the new *Zaunkönig* torpedo was so readily countered that it never achieved any status as an anti-escort weapon; German naval opinion was misled by the U-boat captains' reports.

At the beginning of this next phase of the U-boat war, the boats were still to be found ready for action in their bomb-proof shelters on the French Atlantic coast. There the eight operational flotillas had the following strengths up to the end of 1943:

| Flotilla | Jun | July | Aug | Sept | Oct | Nov | Dec |
|---|---|---|---|---|---|---|---|
| 1st (Brest) | 20 | 19 | 22 | 21 | 14 | 18 | 19 |
| 2nd (Lorient) | 21 | 18 | 17 | 16 | 15 | 15 | 16 |
| 3rd (La Rochelle) | 22 | 21 | 20 | 18 | 18 | 19 | 15 |
| 6th (St.-Nazaire) | 22 | 18 | 18 | 18 | 20 | 16 | 18 |
| 7th (St.-Nazaire) | 21 | 19 | 19 | 17 | 18 | 19 | 20 |
| 9th (Brest) | 21 | 17 | 17 | 17 | 14 | 17 | 15 |
| 10th (Lorient) | 23 | 16 | 14 | 13 | 13 | 14 | 14 |
| 12th (Bordeaux) | 15 | 13 | 12 | 11 | 14 | 11 | 12 |
| Totals | 165 | 141 | 139 | 131 | 126 | 129 | 129 |

The numbers were falling month by month, but there remained a force which, if it could get back into action, would be capable of causing considerable damage to the increasing traffic across the Atlantic. Ranged against them were the increasing strengths of Allied sea and air escorts. At the end of May 1943 the aircraft were disposed in the following numbers:

| | USN Air Arm | | | USAAF | | | RAF & RCAF | | |
|---|---|---|---|---|---|---|---|---|---|
| | VLR | LR | MR | VLR | LR | MR | VLR | LR | MR |
| Iceland | | 9 | | | | | 12 | | 18 |
| Greenland | | 5 | 1 | | | 8 | | | 8 |
| Newfoundland & Nova Scotia | 6 | 23 | | 24 | 15 | | 13 | 86 | 50 |
| US E. seaboard | 15 | 36 | 3 | 15 | | 65 | | | |
| Mexican Gulf | | 10 | 2 | 5 | | 32 | | | |
| Caribbean | 3 | 42 | | | | 8 | | | |
| Bermuda | 8 | 8 | | | | | | | |
| Brazil/Guyanas | | 35 | | | | | | | |
| Morocco | | 23 | | 15 | | | | | |
| Gibraltar | | | | | | | | 25 | 36 |
| UK | | | | | | | 216 | 139 | 15 |

Ranges to the battle zone were 900 miles from Newfoundland, 500 from Iceland, and 900 miles from the British Isles; the air-gaps were soon to be filled on a permanent basis as well, by the escort carriers, meaning that there was to be a continuous air umbrella over the trans-Atlantic convoys. (By October even more cover would be available by the agreement of Doctor Salazar in Portugal to British use of the Azores as an air base against U-boats operating in the Central Atlantic.)

Naval construction was supplementing the escorts available to all the navies in the Battle of the Atlantic, and British shipyards alone built 127 escorts of the Bird, Hunt, Flower and River classes, which were in commission by 1 January 1943; these figures were to increase. In addition to the standard escorts, no fewer than 21 escort carriers had been built by 1 June 1943, and there were 59 in service on 1 January 1945. They proved their worth as did so many of the purpose-built convoy escorts produced both in the UK and in the USA.

So, despite various inter-service rivalries among the naval and air forces of the Allies, there was a great number of ships and aircraft available to ensure that Dönitz's U-boats would never regain the upper hand; against all this, Dönitz and Godt had the untried *Zaunkönig* and the Schnorkel which was now being fitted to the boats under an accelerated programme, aided once more by the ubiquitous Professor Walter. The Schnorkel had originally been developed by the Royal Dutch Navy and some of its submarines had this underwater breathing-tube fitted before the war. When Germany invaded Holland, among the many spoils were five Dutch O-Class submarines. For the Germans, the Schnorkel was no more than a curiosity at that time, but it was remembered in 1943 when the U-boats were forced into submerged operations. What the U-boats needed was a device to enable them to travel underwater while using their diesels, because the electric power of the batteries (even in the Type XXI) was severely limited, as was submerged speed for the Type VII and IX U-boats. Walter soon came up with a design for a Schnorkel for the standard U-boats and the new boats, and installation went ahead rapidly. Some earlier boats had already been fitted with test installations, and the experiences gained at the time ensured that this stop-gap device would be serviceable. It would allow the boats some freedom of movement and enable them to operate to a certain extent against shipping. The Schnorkel has often been termed a defensive device, it being no more than a breathing tube to enable U-boats to approach their hunting-grounds at a reasonable speed without too great a danger of air-attack. This being so, it could be classified as an offensive device.

However, the Schnorkel did not help the U-boats that were having to cross the Bay of Biscay, where anti-submarine aircraft from Coastal Command and the USAAF based in the UK were stepping up their campaign. It has already been mentioned that U-boat Command had ordered the boats to travel in groups of two to five for mutual protection, and FlaK-trap U-boats had been tried as well. Some but not much *Luftwaffe* help had been available, generally in the form of the outdated Ju 88, which could nevertheless hold its own against the bombers that the Allies could send on such patrols.

The original Bay Offensive had started in 1942, and was at its most effective from July to October, when a total of five of the six U-boats sunk there were lost. A much enhanced campaign was mounted by Coastal Command and the USAAF in 1943 and that year saw a total of 34 boats sunk and a large number damaged. What bombing of the pens had failed to achieve, attacks on the boats at sea managed: an increase in the turn-round time for operational boats, and the added advantage that some boats were being sunk by the aircraft involved.

Attention must now turn again to the Atlantic to see what the results were of the German concentration in the Central Atlantic, and the anti-escort campaign that Dönitz was now forced to mount. *Zaunkönig* had been expected and feared by the Royal Navy and was a deadly weapon if there was no defence. The first U-boats to carry this new torpedo did not sail until September; in the meantime the boats had to do what they could against superior odds. Needless to say the now outdated, virtually First World War designs were hard pressed to achieve anything against vastly superior weapons.

Dönitz himself set the scene when he reported to Hitler on the war in the Atlantic on 31 May 1943. He attributed the present situation to the substantial increase of the enemy air force. He supported this with the results of a sound survey which proved that 'as many planes now pass through the narrows between Iceland and the Faroes in one day, as only recently appeared in the course of a week'. He added that 'In addition aircraft carriers are being used in conjunction with North Atlantic convoys, so that all convoy routes are now under air protection'. But the aircraft alone were not the real cause of the sudden and dramatic change of fortune in the North Atlantic:

> The determining factor is a new location device [in fact centimetric radar on 9cm and 3cm wavelengths, which had come into service fully in March 1943] evidently also used by surface vessels, by means of which planes are now in a position to locate submarines.

Dönitz said that the aircraft and surface vessels were able to find U-boats on the surface even when weather conditions were bad, and at night, and the U-boats could not get advance warning from Metox any more. He made specific mention too of the foggy conditions during the ONS.5 attack, and the fact that the escorts had been able to locate the U-boats despite almost zero visibility. In an analysis in the War Diary, which formed part of the report to Hitler, Dönitz added that some 65 per cent of U-boat losses occurred 'while the U-boats are en route or lying in wait; only 35 per cent occur near the convoys themselves'.

The sudden change was undoubtedly due to the increased efficiency of Coastal Command and the new, regrettably (for the Allies) short-lived US Army Air Force Anti-submarine Command. The combination of aircraft escort for convoys, together with the offensive Bay of Biscay Air Patrol and other patrols was beginning to have effects in direct contrast with the efforts of Bomber Command and the Eighth Army Air Force attacks on the submarine pens and the manufacturing industry in Germany.

Dönitz admitted to Hitler that the enemy forces had caused losses to the U-boat fleet which were too high; he argued that 'We must conserve our strength, otherwise we will play into the hands of the enemy.' To continue the assault on the North Atlantic convoy route at that time would indeed have been folly, but he had missed too many chances earlier on for a later resumption (which he planned) to have the effect he was hoping for. He continued, saying that he had withdrawn the U-boats from the North to the sector west of the Azores, in the hope of encountering less air reconnaissance there. Interestingly, if an Army General had proposed a withdrawal, Hitler would have forbidden it; in naval matters however he was an ingenue. Here Dönitz once more emphasised the problem that had bedevilled the U-boat Fleet for almost the entire war – the lack of adequate, effective air reconnaissance by the *Luftwaffe*.

The resumption of the attack in northern waters depended upon further factors. The first was the installation in the U-boats of an efficient radar interception set, which:

> will show the frequency used by the radar-equipped plane and will warn the U-boat of an impending attack. We do not have such a set. We do not even know on what wave length the enemy locates us. Neither do we know whether high-frequency or other location devices are being employed.

Here Dönitz confirmed that the Allies had well and truly won the electronics war that had been waged for the last three and a half years: Allied radar was working efficiently at sea and in the air and the Germans could not find out if it was being used, and the 'Ultra' secrecy was being maintained, with no real suspicions being voiced as to the security of German U-boat codes. This latter point was no doubt reinforced in Dönitz's mind by the recent changeover to 4-wheel Enigma operation. Unfortunately for him, GCCS had overcome this problem almost effortlessly, and the messages to and from the U-boats were being read virtually on a current basis.

Until the new electronic equipment was ready, the U-boats had to operate on just one electric motor at night, so that the sound of the diesels would not blot out the sound of an approaching aircraft: the U-boats were reduced to the 'Mark One Eardrum' against the burgeoning array of electronic equipment mounted by the Allies. Dönitz went on to mention that 'Aphrodite' was soon to be used, subject to Hitler's approval; this was one of the very few counter-measures available to the hard-pressed U-boat crews. Further electronic counter-measures and improvements were being intensively researched, but they were crude and relatively ineffective against the aircraft that were hunting the boats down. One remedy, the four-barrelled 2cm FlaK, was available in limited numbers, and this was to be fitted as soon as possible to as many boats as there were guns, but this was a purely defensive measure, and none too efficient in the event of attack from more than one aircraft. As the Commander-in-Chief of the Navy then said:

> It will not do the U-boats much good to fight off the planes with the four-barrelled machine-gun unless they have the anti-destroyer torpedoes at the same time.

These torpedoes were the *Falke*, and later the *Zaukönig*: both optimistically called *Zerstörerknacker* (destroyer killers). Steps were to be taken jointly by Dönitz and Speer to try to get the anti-escort torpedoes to sea as soon as possible and in fact the first issues were made to boats departing for operations from September onwards, but results against the escorts were extremely disappointing from the German point of view.

Returning to the problem of air support and reconnaissance, Dönitz first asked for some air cover for the U-boats in the Bay of Biscay, where they were forced to concentrate en route to and from the French bases. The locations of these bases could not be altered, and they certainly could not be abandoned just because of the continual presence of enemy aircraft. The Admiral asked Hitler for newer types of aircraft, for the Ju 88 was unable to operate except in formation against Allied aircraft, otherwise 'it would in turn become the victim'. What Dönitz wanted was a few squadrons of the new twin-engined Me 410 fighter, which had already been requested for this purpose by both the 3rd Air Fleet and the Commanding Officer of Naval Air Atlantic.

This enabled Hitler to begin a soliloquy on the failings of the aircraft industry, although as usual he agreed with Dönitz when he said that the air and submarine forces that were to work together in his original plan should have been built and trained at the same time, much earlier in the war. Even then Dönitz said 'it is not too late to give our naval forces an air force'. Hitler's agreement was noted, but as always, the Führer's agreement did not mean action. Göring (who, despite his constant failures, still had Hitler's ear) continued to block any move that threatened his air empire, and his method was the most effective of all – inactivity. The Reichsmarschall had fallen from favour to an extent over the Battle of Britain, and his reaction was virtual withdrawal from the day-to-day conduct of the war especially where the Navy was concerned. His presence at conferences did not mean that he would act on decisions made, and his massive inactivity consigned the U-boat Fleet in particular to defeat; he was one of the architects of the Allies' victory in the Atlantic. (Incidentally, his counterparts in Bomber Command were trying almost as hard to nullify the effects of his laziness and insularity.)

Promises were made to Dönitz which were not to be fulfilled, but there can be no doubt that whatever he thought of these promises, he was determined to get back into the most significant area of the battle – the North Atlantic. He knew that if he were to have any further strategic effect upon the war, he must resume the offensive against the convoys bringing the necessary *matériel* for Operation 'Overlord'. The invasion of Europe was the final act which, in conjunction with massive offensives on the Russian front, would spell disaster for Germany. The fear of *Zweifrontkrieg* was now ever-present.

Dönitz knew only too well that the U-boats could not stop an invasion while it was under way, but they could have a delaying effect at least on the preparations. However, when he spoke to Hitler on this occasion, the seeds of doubt were in his mind. He said 'it is impossible ... to foretell to what extent submarine warfare will again become effective'. The circumstances showed, he said, 'the growing effectiveness of anti-submarine defence, and the diminishing effectiveness of submarines'. His attitude was that no matter what the results, the U-boats had to continue, and Hitler went even further, finally showing some appreciation of the real situation in the Atlantic. He replied to Dönitz:

> There can be no talk of a let-up in submarine warfare. The Atlantic is my first line of defence in the west, and even if I have to fight a defensive battle there, that is preferable to waiting to defend myself on the coasts of Europe. The enemy forces tied up by our submarine warfare are tremendous, even though the actual losses inflicted by us are no longer great. I cannot afford to release these forces by discontinuing submarine warfare.

These comments set the tone of the U-boat war from now until the end of hostilities. The attempt to return to the convoy routes was frustrated by the increasing numbers and growing efficiency of all the air and sea forces concerned. The assault against the escorts, which came far too late, was a failure supported for a long time by false and erroneous reports from the U-boat commanders (not entirely their fault). When the invasion came in June 1944 the U-boats were prevented from having a major effect upon the enormous shipping presence in the Channel by constant air and sea patrols. The move to Norway, forced upon the U-boats by the investment of the French Atlantic bases, led to constant air and sea patrolling off Norway, and a containment that the U-boats never managed to escape. By the end of the war Dönitz was happy to allow the German broadcasting service to announce sinkings of 50,000 tons of shipping, when once the totals had been averaging ten times that amount. The new boats saw only limited services with equally limited results and only one Type XXI U-boat actually completed a war cruise. Small battle units of coastal attack craft achieved slender local successes, but the U-boat Fleet of 1 May 1943 became a defeated and hunted force which had no real strategic significance once Dönitz ordered it south on 24 May. All the work that went into U-boat building and new technology after this period was wasted because it was too late.

# 14    ANALYSIS OF A FAILURE

The historian, by virtue of his profession, is often able to arrive at answers which were not possible in the heat of the moment for the subjects of his work. In the case of the U-boat Arm and its loss of the battles of May 1943, there are no new discoveries to be made, for the facts were plain to see, had Dönitz sat back and looked at them. Only one factor remained unconfirmed to him – loss of security in the U-boats' code – and had he had less self-interested security advisers that error could have been avoided rather than compounded. But for all the other errors that led to the U-boats' loss of freedom of action, two men were to blame – Hitler and Dönitz himself. Hitler because he was the decision maker in the Nazi state, Dönitz because he was in overall charge of virtually all U-boats. A little help came from the Allies, in the form of the US Navy and the Royal Air Force, but the help they gave to the Germans was in the form of inaction, or too little action, and was not in itself decisive.

It is time now to look at the mistakes that were made, so that the failure of May 1943 can be readily understood. Then the efforts of both sides in the second part of the battle of the sea lanes can be examined, to see if either side made any progress after this setback for the German Navy. In the political maelstrom of the pre-war years, the government had managed to get the London Naval Agreement past the Royal Navy, to ensure that Germany could once more build surface ships and submarines to certain limits. This agreement was now to be seen as a double-edged sword; it had allowed construction, but only to 45 per cent of the British fleet in terms of submarines. How had this affected the wartime building and use of the U-boats? The London Agreement had been signed in 1935, with the full approval of the Commander-in-Chief of the German Navy, Grand Admiral Raeder. It permitted Germany to start re-arming officially, naturally using the know-how gained from the clandestine experiments carried out before then; as far as U-boats were concerned the chief source of information and ideas was Igewit.

Once Raeder had international approval from the largest naval power in the world, he decided that the first priority was to build a number of ships as quickly as possible, so that the new Navy had some actual strength, rather than a lot of plans. The only way to get into production and commissioning was to build submarines, and small ones at that. So he authorised the completion of the first batch of Type II U-boats. *U1–U6* had been laid down under conditions of the strictest secrecy in 1934, with the authority of the Reichstag emergency powers granted to Hitler's new government on 4 March 1933.

This meant that only three months and nine days after the Agreement had been passed across the table in London, Germany's first U-boat Flotilla had six boats, and a flotilla Chief – Dönitz. As Raeder noted in his biography, written after the war, the construction programme had been carefully thought out, with three basic designs (Ia, IIa and VII) ready for issue to the building yards. All that could be done to make the task easier and the building quicker had been done, so that Germany's new fleet should be seen as soon as possible after the signing of the Agreement. This was a partly political and partly military decision. Hitler agreed because he wanted the world to see that Nazi Germany could do things very quickly; Raeder wanted some ships at anchor, if not at sea, so that the German Navy could begin to regain its old pride, and there would be training facilities and recruitment prospects to ensure manning of the later U-boats, and of the surface fleet.

The surface fleet was not merely an exercise in public relations. Raeder was an advocate of the balanced fleet concept, and wanted the German Navy to have a fleet capable of coming to battle with France or Poland. He was not ambitious enough, nor so foolish, as to think that he could build a fleet to take on the Royal Navy generally: time alone was against that. The surface fleet plans were carefully detailed in the years that followed and especially in the Z-Plan of 1939. The main elements of the fleet were to be completed by 1944, and the fleet would have:

6 battleships
4 heavy cruisers and four more building
4 light cruisers (with thirteen more to complete in 1948)
2 aircraft carriers, and two building
126 U-boats (of all types) with another 95 planned

This would be supplemented by a number of destroyers and the auxiliary craft which are a necessary part of any balanced navy. These craft were to be in addition to the fleet in being, which on the eve of war comprised:

Three 'pocket' battleships (*Deutschland, Scheer, Graf Spee*)
Two battleships (*Gneisenau, Scharnhorst*)
Two battleships still completing (*Bismarck* 1940, *Tirpitz*1941)
Two heavy cruisers (*Blücher, Hipper*)
Four new light cruisers (*Königsberg, Köln, Leipzig, Nürnberg*)
Two modernised light cruisers (*Emden, Karlsruhe*)
One heavy cruiser building (*Prinz Eugen*)
Two aircraft carriers building (*Graf Zeppelin*, 'B')
57 U-boats due for completion by September 1939
In addition, the following were building:
Two battleships ('H', 'J')

Four proposed conversions to aircraft carrier (*Europa, Gneisenau, Potsdam, Seydlitz*)
Three light cruisers ('M', 'N', 'O')
34 destroyers with 30 building
U-boat production monthly of some 2–3 per month, rising in the second half of 1940

The large majority of the initial plan was either built, or close to being built; the end result was to have been thirteen battleships, 33 cruisers, four aircraft carriers, 267 U-boats and a commensurate number of destroyers and other smaller craft. By comparison the Royal Navy in 1939 had the following strengths:

Twelve battleships (and five building)
Three battlecruisers
Six aircraft carriers (and six building)
25 heavy cruisers (and nine building)
32 light cruisers (and ten building)
Six anti-aircraft cruisers
184 destroyers (and eight building)
69 submarines

It is clear that although the modernity of the German ships would carry some advantage, in terms of overall strength the German surface fleet would, even when completed, have been no match for the Royal Navy, especially as in the years taken to build the German ships, other and newer ships would have been completed by the British. The balance of the fleets would always have left Germany as a purely European naval power, that could never aspire to world rank. Only four navies could lay some claim to that: the Royal Navy, the growing US Navy, the Japanese and the Italian fleets.

But Raeder, as noted above, saw France and Poland as Germany's naval enemies, France because she held the Atlantic ports and the coast of the English Channel and could deny passage on the southern route to the Atlantic, Poland because of her position on the Baltic. The Baltic was the training ground for the German Navy, but the Poles controlled the strategic access to the rich trade routes of the Atlantic and beyond. The fleet that Raeder wanted to build was to face at most the combined French and Polish naval forces, of which only the French was of any consequence. Furthermore, Germany stood between the two, and could prevent any amalgamation of those forces.

The threat of war with England was anathema to Raeder, who had made every effort to gain the friendship of the Royal Naval officers at all levels. The presence of Royal Naval officers at German Naval social functions in

1938 was part of this effort. The Royal Navy had shown that it was quite willing to give its friendship to the new German Navy even as early as 1935, when the then First Sea Lord, Sir Bolton Ayres-Monsell, announced the U-boats' building to the House of Commons. He added, to take any threat from the announcement, that Germany was willing to 'subscribe to the international agreements relative to submarine warfare, one of which prohibits the sinking of merchant ships without warning'. This allayed fears of submarine warfare of the kind practised during the First World War, which had damaged the Merchant Navy so much. Indeed, the German Navy was even willing (before the London Agreement) to forswear U-boats if that meant British agreement on other matters in their proposals. The German Navy wanted, above all, a surface fleet which would reflect the new status of Germany of the new era; more pride can be lavished on a battleship, aircraft carrier or cruiser, than an unattractive and definitely lower-rated vessel like the submarine.

This attitude persisted in 1936 too, when Germany became a signatory to the London Submarine Protocol, which meant that submarines could only sink merchant ships after complying with the rules of that protocol. In the agreement, Article 22 read:

*Art. 22. Les dispositions suivantes sont acceptés comme règles établies du Droit International.*

*1. Dans leur action a l'égard des navires de commerce, les sous-marins doivent se conformer aux règles du Droit International auxquelles sont soumis les bâti-ments de guerre de surface.*

*2. En particulier, excepté dans le cas de refus persistant de s'arreter après sommation régulière ou de résistance active à la visite, un navire de guerre qu'il soit bâtiment de surface ou sous-marin, ne peut couler ou rendre inca-pable de naviguer un navire sans avoir au préalable mis les passagers, l'équipage, et les papiers de bord en lieu sur. A cet effet les embarcations du bord ne sont pas considérées comme un lieu sûr, à moins que la sécurité des passagers et l'équipage ne soit assurée, compte tenu de l'état de la mer et des conditions atmosphériques, par la proximité de la terre ou la presence d'un autre bâtiment qui soit en mesure de les prendre à bord.*

Signing such an agreement effectively took away the threat of U-boat warfare. The U-boat was designed to sink ships, and in a war against England espe-cially it would be engaged in sinking merchant ships. If crews had to be taken off merchant ships into the submarine before a ship could be sunk, apart from the dangers of delay caused by being on the surface in the first place, the crowding resulting from such an action would reduce the U-boats to buses for dispossessed merchant seamen. One sinking per cruise would be the maximum achievement.

But signing this agreement signalled that Germany did not contemplate war with England, and that the U-boat Arm was not regarded as anything more than one part of the balanced fleet that Raeder was hoping for. The treaties themselves were to constitute a drawback for the U-boat Arm; not until 1940 were all the regulations dispensed with in areas pre-declared to be war zones, and even then the problem for the U-boats persisted over what to do against the increasingly aggressive US Navy as well as the neutrals problem. Hitler waited nine months before allowing Dönitz freedom of action, at a time when every sinking counted. Furthermore, the 1935 Agreement limited the number of submarines that could be built; this was a defect that only came to light in September 1939 when a somewhat crestfallen Hitler informed Raeder that he had failed to avoid war with Great Britain. The U-boat arm was then the only part of the German Navy that had any real prospect of waging the war at sea that had become a strategic necessity.

The British, with their fleet, would immediately impose blockade; there was some hope that a small number of blockade runners might get through with strategic materials. This would be a defensive measure but very restrictive; how was the German Navy to take the offensive? The only way would be with the limited ships of the surface fleet and the U-boats. But both parts of the fleet were limited in numbers, and the balanced fleet concept which Raeder had tried to bring about now lay in ruins, with little or no hope of ever seeing realisation.

Raeder had to evolve a means of using the German fleet against the British in a way that would optimise its limited potential, and allow its use with minimum loss. The only way of doing this would be by attacking the supply routes. This was both the tactical and strategic aim of the German Navy when the war started. The problems facing them in 1939 were not limited to a shortage of the means to carry out its aim. It also suffered from a lack of co-operation with the *Luftwaffe*, the service which could have supplied some form of reconnaissance effort had it been so minded. The matter was so important that Raeder devoted a chapter of his biography to it, beginning with the observation that in the First World War the German Navy had its own air component. Originally there were airships for reconnaissance and bombing, but naval aircraft were being developed, and 2,500 were built during that war. These aircraft were used for scouting, combat and torpedo work, but their real worth was in the reconnaissance field. In 1918, Raeder adds, the German Navy was testing a four-engined long-range reconnaissance aircraft, but this and all other developments were swept away by the punitive restrictions of the Treaty of Versailles.

The aircraft story between the wars mirrored that of the U-boats: they were developed abroad with the ubiquitous Lohmann spreading funds in this field as well. The Dornier firm designed the Do-Wal, Super-Wal and Do-X while Germany was still subject to the treaty provisions. By the early thirties both aircraft and their necessary radios were well designed and ready and 'the technical basis for a regular naval air force was ready'. The speed of development, and its sophistication was such that by 1932 'we had completely designed, and had in model form, a multi-purpose plane for dropping bombs, mines and torpedoes, as well as a pursuit fighter plane. Also the Navy had developed a promising dive-bomber design to be flown-off aircraft carriers, which was being tested for its future use.'

But then the Nazi party took control of Germany, and the new German Air Force was put under the control of Göring. His attitude, Raeder commented, was that if it flew it belonged to the *Luftwaffe*, and not only the aircraft but the navy's air functions as well; Göring said that his airmen could support the army, engage in strategic bombing, fight the RAF Spitfires and support the navy, including aerial mine-laying and shipping attacks. In the end the *Luftwaffe* managed to support the Army, fight the bombers and precious little else – they were asked to be multi-purpose in an age of specialisation. Göring could have allowed the specialisation, because he had enough aircraft, but his airmen seemed to spend more time adding to the personal glory of the *Reichsmarschall*, or detracting from it, than performing the everyday support tasks which they could have fulfilled extremely well.

It is of interest at this point to look very briefly at the two aircraft carriers that were laid down by the Navy. They were *Graf Zeppelin* (official design date April 1934) and 'B'. They were to be built by Deutsche Werke, Kiel and Germaniawerft, Kiel; in doing so they tied up much of the available space there, but even in 1939 Raeder thought Hitler would be true to his word, and not involve Germany in a war of opportunity. *Graf Zeppelin* was accordingly laid down in 1938. She was to displace 33,550 tons on a length of more than 800 feet and a draught of 26 feet. The designed 200,000shp gave her a design speed of 33.8 knots. Her range, however, was surprisingly limited at 8,000 nautical miles at 19 knots. She had eight 15cm, ten 10.5cm and 29 original FlaK cannon (later increased to 50). She was designed with two hangar decks and two catapults to launch twelve Ju 87D and 30 Me 109F aircraft (later increased to 30 dive-bombers and 42 fighters). By 1940 she was 85 per cent finished when building was stopped. More building was done later in the war, but her practical function during the war was as a naval precious woods store under the code-name 'Bird of Passage'. Had Raeder had more time she could have been a formidable ship, especially if backed up by a building programme which included more such vessels.

No doubt had she gone to sea the aircraft would have been under Göring's command, while the ship was controlled by Raeder. It was this question of control which dogged German naval aviation after 1933, but unlike the RAF and the Royal Navy there was no hope of compromise. Raeder, and more importantly Dönitz, never got autonomous control of reconnaissance aircraft. At the time Raeder argued that all the larger navies (which definition was to include the German) had the opinion that all naval components – ships, submarines and aircraft – had to be under one command, and that naval air units had to be under the command of the Navy. The system was perfectly demonstrated by the US Navy and Army air forces, which even encouraged an exceptional rivalry between the two entirely separate air arms. As well as being under naval command, the air element also had to be trained in the methods and demands of the navy. The problem of navigation has already been mentioned, and it is interesting to note that similar problems arose in Coastal Command units in England, which were of course under the control of the RAF. Coastal Command and its relations with its parent body will be looked at in some detail later; but the Fleet Air Arm/Royal Naval Air Service was autonomous by 1937, whereas there was no such provision in Germany. In fact because *Graf Zeppelin* was never completed, the problem only arose in theory, but in practice as far as control of all reconnaissance aircraft was concerned, only once did Göring relinquish control of a few aircraft (I/KG 40, already mentioned above).

The problem could have been solved to the satisfaction of both sides had Göring been willing to attach some pilots and long-range aircraft to the Navy for training. As Raeder said, 'the element of water is so utterly different from the element of earth. The resulting tactics and methods are so different that only airmen trained in the tactics of naval warfare and trained in the ways and idioms of the sea can be really useful in naval operations.' (The truth of this was shown by the 1982 Falklands conflict, where, despite intense professional naval air training, things still went wrong.) As Raeder noted: 'One of the distinguishing features of naval forces is their great range and mobility and vast range of operations, so that they can exert force in the most unexpected places in the minimum of time. Far-ranging reconnaissance is a necessity.' This was as true in respect of the U-boat Arm, if not more so, for good air reconnaissance could have established convoy routes and ships present far more economically than the U-boats themselves. But the accuracy which naval reports demand is confounded by the miles of featureless seas only intersected by lines of latitude and longitude on a chart: without really accurate navigation a bad report is worse than no report. The Commander-in-Chief went on to say: 'Up to 1933 our naval airmen had especially been trained with these things in mind, and had become familiar with naval doctrine by living constantly with the navy.'

The *Luftwaffe*, through Göring, refused to alter its stance, and could not see the growing importance of naval aviation, despite signs from the USA and especially Japan of this shift in emphasis. Raeder wrote: 'In fact, the issue [of naval co-operation] was often decided from the standpoint of prestige alone, the Commander-in-Chief of the Air Force often seeming to think this was the all important factor.' In 1935 the Navy had plans for 25 squadrons of 300 aircraft in the naval air arm, and increased this to 62 squadrons a year later;

Göring's response was that he would be glad to set up the Air Command (Sea) and put it under the tactical command of Raeder, but the restriction to tactical command meant that he would only have the aircraft when there was absolutely no other call upon their services, and in all events they would be airmen untrained in naval flying.

In an attempt at compromise Raeder transferred all naval airmen into the *Luftwaffe*, only to lose them for good. There was in fact no change in the situation until the war had begun, with the sole exception of I/KG 40, and that unit was only transferred to Dönitz when Göring was away from Führer Headquarters on leave. (He later begged Dönitz to let him have the aircraft back, but Dönitz refused.) The end result, as war approached, was, Raeder said: 'The Navy's original naval air arm was completely wrecked ... but ... we hoped that, as in the British Navy, this carrier's [*Graf Zeppelin*] requirements for air squadrons would point up the absolute need for the Navy for its own air arm.' Unfortunately for Raeder and Dönitz, Hitler was influenced out of all proportion by Göring, and both of them had the continental attitude that had been the downfall of others who had taken on an initially weak Great Britain in war.

It was this continental attitude that brought war in 1939, despite the Navy's studiously maintained attitude against such a war. Hitler felt that if he did not strike there and then he would have to face a reorganised and re-equipped French Army that would be able to defeat him. The *Blitzkrieg* methods brought success in Poland, but brought both France and Great Britain into the war at a time when the Navy was unable to do anything helpful in the strategic field, apart from tie down some units of the Royal Navy. The then rapid successes of 1940 led Hitler to believe that he would not need the Navy and its long-term strategic plan or the increased U-boat numbers for which Raeder continually asked. The small numbers of U-boats in September 1939 would have been immaterial from the point of view of the Navy if there had been a U-boat construction plan that would have increased numbers significantly.

It is here that the threads from 1935 appear once more. The U-boat Arm had been limited to a maximum of 100 per cent of the Royal Navy's submarine strength, and in September 1939, when Hitler had abrogated the London Naval Agreement unilaterally, the German Navy had that 100 per cent. But the situation was that more could have been built, and an immediate increase in general naval building would have had important strategic effects. Hitler had constantly told Raeder that the Fleet would not be needed until 1945 or 1946, and Raeder had cautiously planned to have everything ready for 1944, but that was five years ahead when the disastrous invasion of Poland took place. Raeder said that if he had had any warning, he could have ensured that his fleet 'would be a serious threat to the UK's ocean-borne commerce, the very lifeblood of the island kingdom. Such a fleet would have restricted use, however, as it could not offer battle with the stronger British forces.' But Raeder took Hitler's preference for a strong, balanced fleet as a firm indication that he would not engage in anything likely to bring the Royal Navy out to sea for some years.

Another product of the continental attitude produced in Hitler was a total lack of understanding of the use of strategic naval power. Battleships were a symbol of political power to Hitler, not a valuable strategic force that required many times their individual strength to remove them from the battle scene: the very point that the sinking of *Bismarck* would demonstrate, but Hitler's reaction was one of rage, not realisation. Raeder however was the more astute man, and a good sailor. His view of the Navy's role, in accordance with the Z-Plan, was: 'In the event of war with England, major emphasis should be placed on operations against her commerce, using all the means at our disposal – U-boats, surface ships and naval aircraft. England's economy required an annual import of 50 million tons of goods and materials, and she was absolutely dependent upon getting those cargoes through ... Great Britain's overseas trade would be attacked by groups of battle and light cruisers, as well as by U-boats and surface raiders.' With hindsight it is easy to see what the effect of the Z-Plan Navy would have been, even with the Royal Navy at sea, for more than 200 U-boats alone would have wreaked a havoc with which the Royal Navy could not have coped.

The general errors committed by the German leaders as far as the Navy was concerned may be summarised so far as:

1. Lack of strategic understanding by Hitler and Göring of the role of the Navy in war.
2. Failure to provide for, or allow the Navy to develop, the naval air arm, and no provision for it when it was strategically vital.
3. No initial provision for wartime requirements for an increased naval building programme, and not setting up such a programme once the war had started.
4. Depleting the shipyards of shipwrights and other essential workers.

The Navy was responsible for:

1. Accepting torpedoes that had been insufficiently tested.
2. Not setting up a means of checking U-boat claims of sinkings.

However, these two mistakes were as nothing compared with the breach of two of the fundamentals. All trainee officers throughout the world are taught the Principles of Warfare, and given examples of breaches of these principles during warfare throughout the ages. The ten basic principles are headed by the most important of them all which states that the fundamental of any action, campaign or war is that an aim must be selected, and adhered to – in military parlance this is its 'Selection and maintenance of the aim'. The others are:

| | |
|---|---|
| Maintenance of morale | Economy of Effort |
| Offensive action | Flexibility |
| Security | Co-operation |
| Surprise | Administration |
| Concentration of Force | |

At the risk of repeating some matters already mentioned, each of these principles will now be related to Dönitz's conduct of the campaign up to May 1943, to establish his particular responsibility in the matter. It may be remembered that he maintained after the war that the errors already mentioned plus Allied radar and long-range aircraft had brought about the re-concentration of U-boat forces in 1943.

The German High Command and the *Seekriegsleitung* had agreed about the aim of the *Kriegsmarine* in a war against England. That this aim was known to Dönitz is beyond dispute, because it forms part of the first paragraph of his memorandum of 1 September 1939, and reads:

The Building up of the U-boat Arm.
The state of the U-boat Arm at the present time of tension, and the impossibility of producing the desired results with the numbers of U-boats now available, make it my duty to express my views on the relevant questions, and draw the necessary inferences.
1. The task of the U-boat Arm – The Navy's principal task in the war, is the struggle with England. The focal point of warfare against England, and the one and only possibility of bringing England to her knees with the forces of our Navy, lies in attacking her sea communications in the Atlantic. So long as we do not have sufficient numbers of surface forces which are suitable for this task, it will fall chiefly to the U-boat Arm.
2. Even if our surface forces are equal to the task, the U-boat has the decisive advantage that it can reach and remain in operational areas in the Atlantic without support, and does not have to undergo the same dangers as surface forces. I therefore believe that the U-boat will always be the backbone of warfare against England, and of the political pressure on her.

The target of the U-boats were the convoys to England. Dönitz writes in his autobiography that Churchill wrote to Roosevelt, in that fateful letter of 8 December 1940, that 'The prime need is to check or limit the loss tonnage on the Atlantic approaches to our island.' At the end of 1941 after the débâcle of HG.76, Dönitz wrote:

After this failure and in view of the unsatisfactory results of the preceding two months my staff was inclined to voice the opinion that we

253

were no longer in a position successfully to combat the convoy system because of recent experiences. It was an opinion, however, which I was not prepared to endorse – despite our heavy defeat, though this had been due to exceptional circumstances.

Dönitz did not interpret the action clearly: the convoy had sailed with an escort of one aircraft depot ship, *Unicorn*, three destroyers and several corvettes, as well as a submarine. Thus he knew that the escort was greater than usual, but it was not greater than his U-boats were facing in the Arctic. Also the operation he planned against the convoy was standard – a patrol line to intercept, followed by attacks by all available boats. But the War Diary records that the 'enemy had great success against the U-boats; new U-boats and inexperienced commanders were not a match for Gibraltar area escorts.' So he ordered that all new U-boats would sail from Germany direct to France to refuel (previously they had carried out one operation before docking with their operational flotilla) and were to operate off the Newfoundland Bank. New U-boats were not to be posted to operational areas off Gibraltar as the waters were too dangerous for them. This in itself is not enough to support the argument that HG.76 had a great effect on Dönitz's thinking, but when, on 24 December, Dönitz asked for and got Skl approval to withdraw boats from the Mediterranean approaches and to move their concentration to the Azores, farther to the west, the real effect of the convoy battle can be seen.

In isolation, the convoy result could be considered merely a protective measure by a compassionate commander, although that in itself does not win wars. But when Operation '*Paukenschlag*' followed, Dönitz showed that he much preferred the exploitation of soft targets to maintaining the aim which he personally had endorsed – the campaign against supplies for the UK. He adds to his previous comment that: 'This one isolated case was no reason for making any fundamental change in my views with regard to attacks on convoys, and I was to be proved right by subsequent events. Indeed it was to be in 1942 and the first months of 1943 that we were destined to fight the biggest of our convoy battles.' But the convoy battles occurred after the hiatus of six months during the height of the attacks on the US seaboard.

The question of the USA coming into the war had been the subject of much discussion at top level by the Germans before the events of December 1941. Dönitz was not particularly afraid of the consequences, merely saying that 'I should like to be given timely warning, to enable me to have my forces in position off the American coast before war was declared. It was only in this way, I pointed out, that full advantage could be taken of the element of surprise to strike a real blow in waters in which the anti-submarine defences were still weak.' The Japanese, however, did not make Hitler and his leaders party to their plans, and the attack on Pearl Harbor was as much a surprise to the Germans as to the Allies.

The War Diary records the attack on 8 December, and Skl gave permission for freedom of action in the Pan-American security zone; previously U-boats had been banned from those waters. Despite problems over the numbers of boats that he could send to this new attack area, there is little doubt that by 17 January 1942 Dönitz was in two minds about whether to continue convoy operations, and that on 20 January his mind was made up. The results of patrols by two U-boats had been above expectation, and he decided to commit his forces to a major effort. The arrival in the area of the supply boats in March 1942 made the operation more widespread, and of even longer duration, especially coupled with the slowness with which convoys and anti-submarine measures were put into effect in those waters. He stated that his aim was 'to sink as much shipping as possible in the most economical manner. In other words, the sinkings per U-boat per day-at-sea had to be maintained at the highest possible level.'

Had Dönitz operated at full strength for a shorter of time, perhaps two months, or three, he would have achieved far more in the long run than by indulging in easy pickings for six or even seven months (the Official History suggests the second convoy campaign began in August 1942). By operating at strength in those waters for six months, to the exclusion of the traffic passing across the Atlantic, he allowed vital supplies to reach the UK, and he allowed the escorts six months of working together, generally unmolested. The supplies that arrived during this six-month period allowed a small reserve to be built up in the UK, so that when the U-boats returned to the convoy routes there would be some slack before the attacks began to bite.

There had now been a fundamental change of aim; from sinking ships in convoy to the British Isles the main aim was sinking ships. When the convoy campaign was resumed the all-important statistics still held sway. On the return to the northern route the U-boats were to sink ships in any convoy, and Dönitz regarded ships in convoy to the Americas as having the same importance as those sailing for the UK. Instead of continuing his attack on the primary target, he had switched to a 'tonnage war', which he was soon to realise he could never win. It was this shift from an aggressive campaign against convoys to the 'sink everything' oceanic part of their war: the part in which, had they been successful, they might have had a chance of winning against Great Britain and the USA.

The Admiralty was fully aware of the effects that the convoy campaign of 1940–1 had had. The Board was not fooled by the reduction in losses of the last three months of 1941, being aware that Dönitz had been forced to send boats to other sea areas rather than maintain his concentration in the Atlantic convoy zones. 'Any suggestion that the corner has been turned is not supported by facts,' wrote one of the Assistant Chiefs of the Naval Staff; this was not lightly said, for the U-boat Arm was at last beginning to grow significantly, passing its pre-war strength for the first time in July 1941. Thereafter, the Admiralty felt, its gains would exceed its losses for a long time, as Dönitz's demand for increased production was being met in part at last. (In fact operational strength of the U-boat Arm continued to rise significantly until May 1943, when it was reduced for the first time.)

Then came the relief of the operation against the USA, which proceeded for much longer than expected. There was even some disquiet about the real value of these operations at U-boat Headquarters and at Skl. The first problem had arisen in February 1941 when the operation was put in question by Hitler's intuitive decision that Norway was a place of destiny. Dönitz was forced to send some boats there, arguing that they would be better employed in the Atlantic. Here he attempted to use the original aim as camouflage for his real purpose, saying (on 25 February) that the threat to the supply lines across the Atlantic would obviate any Allied hope of having the shipping for an invasion of Norway. 'The greater the success achieved by the U-boats in the Atlantic', he wrote, 'the less likely will the enemy be even to think of making preparation for such an enterprise.' But the following tell-tale words evidence his real aim; the words were:

> The more shipping sunk – anywhere in the world – [and] the more a threat to the enemy's vital supply lines across the Atlantic compels him to take measures for their immediate protection, the less likely it is that he will be in a position to divert tonnage and escort vessels ...

In May he criticised the continued disposition of those boats for operations in Arctic waters, saying that they would be better employed in the Atlantic, and that 'the twenty boats stationed in northern waters mean much more than a decrease of twenty boats engaged in the war on shipping in the Atlantic.' Dönitz's biography was written after his release from Spandau prison, where he had been sent for ten years after the war; that the decision in his case was unjust can hardly be argued, but his biography is partly a historical account of his actions during the war, and partly a justification. One thing that he justifies continually is his decision to change the aim, when there had been no immediate hope of achieving the initial aim – to cut the convoy routes. It seems from the biography that Dönitz himself was no longer fully convinced that his decision had been the right one.

The level of concern at Headquarters in Germany came to a head in April when the question was asked as to whether the traffic to the UK was not more important than the US eastern seaboard and the waters to the south. Dönitz argued, as a preamble to his meeting a month later with Hitler, that the enemy shipping had to be considered as an entity, and that they should thus be sunk wherever they could be found. The ratio of sinkings to U-boat losses was uppermost in his mind; no doubt this was due to a combination of the purely military need to conserve his strength and yet maintain the offensive, and the patriarchal attitude he had to the U-boats, their commanders and crews.

He saw England then as no more than the European end of a massive arma-ments industry, the centre of which was the USA. His U-boats, he argued, were attacking the very root of Allied military and economic power, and every sinking achieved damaged enemy shipbuilding and armament production. He also expanded the earlier idea that the defence of Norway from invasion was best carried out in mid-Atlantic. Now he said that to prevent England being a base for operations and the stepping-stone into Europe, the centre of attack must be the American coast. His 'profit margin' theory came into play, and he stated in the most simple terms that 'it is much more important just to sink, than to sink in a certain area and reduce the total sinkings'. He went further, adding that 'supply traffic to the United States is equally as important as that from the United States to England'. (The whole tenor of this argument recalls the attrition theory used on the Western Front during the First World War.)

This attitude was reinforced when Dönitz presented his strategic concept to Hitler on 14 May. He used the same argument as before, crystallising it in saying to the Führer 'sinkings are a race with merchant shipping construction'. The USA, he said, was the world's biggest shipbuilder, therefore ships sunk off the US coast were even more important than those sunk en route to the UK laden with war supplies and essential foodstuffs. He also commented upon the high number of tanker sinkings off the US coast, saying that the effect of this attack would be to reduce industrial potential. This last point had some validity. On 20 May, six days after Dönitz and Hitler had met, President Roosevelt addressed the Speaker of the House of Representatives with the following request:

> As a result of the recent study by the special subcommittee on petroleum investigation ... Chairman Cole has transmitted to me for consideration a proposed measure 'to facilitate the construction, extension or comple-tion of interstate petroleum pipelines related to national defense'. This measure is concerned with one of the vital phases of our national defense program.
>
> The vast concentration of industry, population, and military bases on the Atlantic coast is now dependant for petroleum on tankers plying between the Gulf Coast and the Middle Atlantic ports. Not only is this water route long and potentially dangerous, but even present demands upon these transportation facilities make restriction of oil consumption to essential uses a distinct possibility within a few months. The imme-diate construction of pipelines to augment the supply to the Atlantic coast is the one means available to us to relieve the situation.

Dönitz had told Hitler: 'The Americans will be directed to ship their oil by sea at least during the next year'. In this he was utterly correct, and had stumbled on to the one strategic reason for attacking coastal shipping in American waters. Much of the shipping lost there was of limited importance, but the tankers were far more important because of their complexity of construction, and the very fact that they were losing large amounts of crude oil when sunk. The tanker sinkings off the east coast area were as follows:

| 1942 Month | Number | Total tonnage | All tonnage sunk in US waters | % of sinkings represented by tankers |
|---|---|---|---|---|
| 1 | 16 | 127157 | 263913 | 48 |
| 2 | 28 | 209451 | 393593 | 53 |
| 3 | 29 | 242304 | 401809 | 60 |
| 4 | 20 | 159411 | 376836 | 42 |
| 5 | 26 | 190713 | 551120 | 35 |
| 6 | 19 | 143877 | 554611 | 26 |
| 7 | 7 | 55135 | 220349 | 25 |
| 8 | 12 | 95533 | 354316 | 27 |
| 9 | 8 | 62325 | 245776 | 25 |
| 10 | 3 | 29983 | 169944 | below 18 |
| 11 | 7 | 51046 | 348421 | 15 |
| 12 | 1 | 8194 | 113409 | 77 |

The average for the year was that 34.5 per cent of sinkings were of tankers. The long-term effect of this was dramatic, but Dönitz failed to see that this alone of all operations in the western Atlantic had a strategic value, and should have been treated as a special operation in addition to maintaining the assault upon the convoys; the combination of the two efforts would have had an overall strategic effect which the Allies would have found extremely hard to withstand.

Oil transportation on the US seaboard was by tanker almost exclusively (1940, 98 per cent so carried), with pipelines carrying a minimal amount. A large proportion of the oil came from the Gulf coast areas, the rest coming from California and foreign countries. The increasing danger to the continued movement of oil stocks, and the reduction in the numbers of domestic carriers due to U-boat sinkings (119 tankers sunk by the end of May), led Roosevelt to take steps to alleviate the problem. Even in 1941 he had written to the Chairman of the House Committee on Interstate and Foreign Commerce on this very subject, fully ten months before war broke out. He pointed out that the main manufacturing and population centres of the United States were dependant upon these seaborne supplies, and urged the ending of the competition between other oil carriers and the pipeline companies, which latter were losing the battle. The situation was worsened by the transfer of 50 American tankers to Great Britain in mid-1941, and stocks of crude oil on the east coast were reduced accordingly by some eleven million barrels.

Congress acceded to Roosevelt's request for the improved and lengthened pipeline system, but while it was building a number of expedients were pressed into service, including the railways. Steel shortages affected the construction, but the pipeline, from Beaumont, Texas, to Lincoln, New Jersey, was completed in December 1943. 'The completion of these pipelines ... was accomplished just in time, for Axis submarines and the general shortage of shipping had reduced coastwise tanker shipments from 1,472,000 barrels daily in June 1941 to 57,000 barrels daily in January 1943.' Had Dönitz been able to continue the exploitation of this weakness in the fuel situation as well as keep up a damaging level of sinkings in the convoy areas, the result of the war in the Atlantic would have been far more in the balance than it was.

What then of the time when Dönitz was forced to return to the main campaign? He had argued successfully against Hitler's request for a further diversion of U-boats in the anti-invasion role (this time for the protection of the Madeira–Azores area) arguing that the most important role for the U-boats was sinking ships, and defeating the Allied ship-building programme. He went on to say:

In view of the small numbers at present available, any diversion of boats may well have grave consequences, particularly at this moment, when it must be assumed that the still exceptionally favourable conditions in the Caribbean Sea will soon deteriorate, as soon as the enemy holds up or re-routes his shipping, introduces a convoy system and strengthens his anti-submarine defences. This means, in effect, that we shall be unable, even with greater forces, to achieve the same measure of success later, as is being achieved now with a smaller number of boats. Logically, therefore, we must strike now and with all the forces at our disposal.

This comment was made after the traffic in the Atlantic had had nearly eight months of respite. From November 1941 until the end of June 1942 there was a minimum U-boat presence in the old operational areas of the northern shipping lanes to and from England. The new campaign however was to be directed against traffic to and from the New World. During the period from July 1942 to May 1943, when the battle was finally decided, 101 convoys were attacked of which just 30 were HX or SC convoys. Of that 30, fourteen were attacked by three or more U-boats. Thirty-one ON and ONS convoys were also attacked, fourteen by three or more boats. But the attacks on the outward bound convoys could not have the same strategic value for the UK as the inward ships, and the outward attacks may be regarded as a waste of valuable resources.

It is quite clear from both the events, and Dönitz's own writings and entries in the War Diary, that HG.76 had had a much greater effect upon him that he was prepared to admit. It seems certain that he had realised his mistake while in prison, but was unwilling to admit it. The arguments he made for random sinkings do not stand up under examination; had he continued to maintain pressure in the main area, at the same time mounting the many operations that he did at the one time but assigning the other operations to a subsidiary role, he could have maintained the aim of which he approved for so long. In the few months from the disaster of HG.76 to May 1942 his attitude underwent a radical change, and he was unwilling to lose U-boats in pursuit of the original aim. To cover up the fact that he had changed the aim, he disguised the alteration by a smoke-screen of statistical flummery which does not stand up to analysis. However, the device stood his argument in good stead, probably because he was an Admiral, and Admirals armed with statistics are difficult beasts to argue with. Fortunately for the Allies, no one said anything about lies, damned lies, and statistics.

This major error lead to the pursuit of a misleading aim and one that was incapable of fulfilment. The two official historians differ on when the new building exceeded shipping losses (Morrison gives either August or December 1942 at the latest, Roskill July 1943) but the fact is that cumulative losses were flattening out from the last quarter of 1942, and March 1943 was an exception to the general decline in U-boat successes, due mainly to the improved anti-submarine techniques and equipment then available to the Allies, rather than to massive increases in the number of escort vessels available for convoy work.

It is now important to look at the other factors which are encapsulated in the Principles of War. They will be dealt with in the order of importance felt to apply to this particular battle, for they all, with the exception of selection and maintenance of the aim, have varying weight according to the type of campaign being waged. The factors contributing to the eventual defeat were:

1. Lack of concentration of force
2. Lack of co-operation
3. Lack of security
4. Lack of administration
5. Insufficient offensive action and insufficient use of resources, leading to lack of economy of effort
6. Falling morale
7. Lack of flexibility
8. Lack of surprise

The whole campaign was so complex that the factors are frequently so intermingled that separation is impossible. However the examples given will, it is hoped, show how individual principles were violated. The sum of the violations led to the situation of May 1943 and the U-boats being forced to change their operational theatre.

The lack of concentration of force is most noticeable in relation to Hitler's demand that U-boats be stationed in Norway in addition to the previous demand for U-boats to be operational in the Mediterranean. The figures of dispositions recorded in the War Diary of BdU prove this, and show that Dönitz was basically right to argue against such deflection of forces from the one decisive theatre. The figures were:

| 1941 | Jan | Feb | Mar | Apr | May | Jun | July | Aug | Sept | Oct | Nov | Dec |
|---|---|---|---|---|---|---|---|---|---|---|---|---|
| Atlantic | 22 | 32 | 29 | 33 | 40 | 47 | 58 | 70 | 73 | 71 | 80 | 68 |
| Mediterranean | | | | | | | | | 3 | 6 | 6 | |
| Norway | | | | | | | | | | | 1 | 4 |
| **1942** | | | | | | | | | | | | |
| Atlantic | 74 | 83 | 92 | 80 | 85 | 88 | 101 | 113 | 133 | 160 | 162 | 156 |
| Mediterranean | 7 | 7 | 6 | 20 | 20 | 19 | 16 | 16 | 15 | 15 | 19 | 24 |
| Norway | 12 | 12 | 12 | 20 | 19 | 21 | 23 | 23 | 17 | 20 | 26 | 23 |
| **1943** | | | | | | | | | | | | |
| Atlantic | 164 | 178 | 193 | 194 | 207 | 183 | | | | | | |
| Mediterranean | 24 | 23 | 19 | 17 | 18 | 18 | | | | | | |
| Norway | 21 | 18 | 14 | 21 | 12 | 12 | | | | | | |

Dönitz remarked after the war that in the first six months of 1942: 'Of the sixty-nine boats which entered the service ... twenty-six or nearly 40 per cent were diverted to Norwegian waters and two sent to the Mediterranean.' His argument against the piecemeal dilution of his force might have had more merit however if he had not been in the throws of the US operation. But at the time when the U-boat campaign had one of its great successes, in May and June 1941, there were too few boats to sustain that level of success. In the last two months of the year there was the transfer to the approaches to the Mediterranean, and 'Paukenschlag' followed. There was never a real concentration of force in the Atlantic, however, for Dönitz himself was too prone to diverting boats from the main effort. He continued to maintain U-boats in the Caribbean and the coastal waters long after the real weight of the attack had been transferred. He also sent boats to the Freetown area, the central Atlantic and to South Africa. As already mentioned, had these been part of the overall plan all could have served their purpose – to divert escorts from the north. As it was, in the north after July 1942 there was the general 'sink ships' attitude in his command rather than a firm policy of concentrating the forces available where they would do the most damage. Thus both Hitler and later Dönitz himself were guilty of not concentrating what forces they had in the most effective area. Of the two, Dönitz must bear the major share of blame, for he should have known the sea and the enemy better.

The lack of co-operation which dogged the German Navy throughout the war has already been looked at in some detail. It is sufficient to note that when the second campaign against the convoys began, Dönitz remarked that the biggest problem he faced was finding the convoys, for which purpose he was glad to have a larger number of boats for the task. Luckily for him the oil situation had meant that convoys were in the area he expected – along the great circle route – and this saved him a lot of time. That there was no air co-operation was simply and solely due to Göring's stupidity and total lack of strategic acumen. He demonstrated this inability to understand strategic concepts throughout the war as well as before it when he did not continue General Wever's work on a four-engined strategic bomber. One good long-range bomber/reconnaissance aircraft in some numbers would have increased the strategic value of the *Luftwaffe*, and if he had released some to the Navy, or allowed them to go their own way in aviation, the results would have been significant. In 1942, after Dönitz had told Raeder and Hitler about the 'tonnage war', the Führer and his naval commander spoke together for a little on the subject of aircraft carriers. It will be remembered that *Graf Zeppelin* and 'B' were no longer building, but proposals had been made to re-activate them, with Hitler's approval.

Hitler even spoke now of four aircraft carriers to be completed, with a production run of carrier aircraft to be built. The plan was not to be during this war concluded Hitler, but aircraft carrier work should continue. Raeder replied, probably holding his temper well in check, that 'a naval air force with excellent personnel and aircraft existed at the time the Air Ministry was established'. This jibe against Göring was, however, virtually the last word on this vexed subject, and soon the Navy was left almost entirely without air support or cover. This lack of co-operation compounded a wasteful use of U-boats, for they had to find their own targets, and also to losses of U-boats, unprotected when in the vicinity of their bases in the French ports.

The next matter is that of security. Here, although the breaches were not in themselves the cause of the loss of the battle, they contributed a large amount of valuable information which helped the Allies decide upon dispositions and convoy movements, undoubtedly saving many ships from being sunk. An interesting situation arose during the war when each side was reading the other's naval codes, and neither side did anything about it for some time. Much space has already been devoted to the solution of the problem of Enigma, especially after February 1942 when the 'Dolphin' code was changed for 'Triton'. 'Dolphin' was read from 1 August 1941 as far as the U-boats were concerned, until the changeover to 'Triton'. This took place on 1 February 1942, and the decryption of that code was not effected until December 1942, when it was read until withdrawn in May 1943. This meant that orders to the U-boats were being read by their enemy for the five months of 1941 when the campaign was falling-off in the North Atlantic, and again in 1942–43 when the battle was reaching its climax, although the general effectiveness of the boats was decreasing. If the U-boats had used the February to December period of

1942 to better effect on the convoy routes, the lack of admission to the orders and reports could have had a much more serious effect than it did.

Security was suspect on a number of occasions, despite the fact that the *Beobachtungsdienst* had had some marked success in cracking the Administration Code of the Royal Navy, and had made significant inroads into the secrets of naval cypress. Most important of all, after May 1940 *B-Dienst* was reading the Merchant Navy and merchant ships' codes currently, and did so with complete success until after the convoy battles of May 1943. Dönitz was nevertheless constantly advised by his signals experts that there was no breach of German signal security, even after the Allies had invited such a conclusion after appearing uninvited at several refuelling rendezvous, and the surface tankers for the U-boats had been driven from the Atlantic. This was a serious error which detracted from the overall effectiveness of the U-boats, for the Submarine Tracking Office was able to re-route some convoys which were otherwise sailing directly towards a U-boat concentration. The penetration of the U-boat code was, however, of a sporadic nature, and was not a major factor.

Surprisingly, administration failures led to an erroneous picture of the campaign being promulgated at U-boat Headquarters. Dönitz wrote that:

> In Section 3 at Naval High Command were collated all the reports which we received regarding enemy shipping losses and the extent to which he could replace them by new construction. Under war conditions it was only to be expected that information on both these subjects reached us after a fairly considerable lapse of time; indeed there were some facts which we did not learn until after the war had ended.

This was true of the breaking of Enigma too, for security on the British side maintained the secret until 1977, when the true meaning of the term 'direction-finding' was revealed. U-boat Command, however, relied upon the boats' own reports, made after attacks and while the boats were at sea. Whereas the Allies were loath to credit escort commanders with the sinking of a U-boat unless there were ample proof, Dönitz and his staff took the reports as being only slight exaggerations. Although the inability to check on the U-boat claims had no great effect upon the conduct of the war at sea up to May 1943, it was to have a much greater effect when the U-boats undertook the anti-escort campaign with the *Zaunkönig* sound-seeking torpedo, and there arose a false impression of the success rate with this weapon which was not supported by the facts. That the Germans should be so lacking in the meticulous examination of evidence can only partly be explained by the slowness of arrival of the confirmatory information at U-boat Headquarters and Skl. The rest of the lapse was caused by the lack of an administration network to supervise claims and analyse them. Many U-boats commanders were to claim hits of four separate ships by a salvo of four torpedoes; knowing what he did about the unreliability of his torpedoes, Dönitz should have realised that this was an impossibility. Instead the matter was rarely referred to and, as with the *Luftwaffe*, a sense of enhanced prowess grew up, which certainly concealed the fact that torpedoes were running too deep for nearly two years of the war – the two years that were vital to the success of the campaign.

Economy of effort means the use of the correct units or the correct numbers of units in a campaign or battle, so that unnecessary troops are not wasted. At the beginning of the war Dönitz had no unnecessary troops, and could have done with many more U-boats to perform the task they were set. Then, as his numbers rose so did the successes, until a plateau was reached where the U-boats and the escorts were equally balanced. This point arrived during the battle over convoy ONS.5, and on other such occasions, where the U-boats did battle with the escorts, suffering heavy losses as did the ships in convoy. Such occasions were initially rare – HG.76 was another example – but after ONS.5 there followed the sudden slide over the edge of the plateau, when U-boat losses suddenly rose and ship sinkings fell to almost nothing. But this particular type of warfare was so complicated by other factors, and the constantly changing balance, that it is difficult to establish any formula that would represent the true economy of effort; above all the weather played such a vital and often perverse part in the fortunes of war for all the participants, that any analysis would be invalid. However, Dönitz was right when he frequently said that he would have filled the Atlantic with U-boats, and that he needed a standing force of 100 boats in the Atlantic when war broke out. If he had had so many boats, there is no doubt that the convoy trade would have ceased within months (despite torpedo failures and lack of reconnaissance) because the sheer numbers would have overwhelmed the inexperienced and thinly spread escorts until capital ships would have been used and lost in the defence of the merchant ships. Great Britain would have been forced to surrender for lack of food. This would have been the reverse of economy of effort (but is concentration of force), but it would have had the desired effect, and had Hitler given the Navy more time Dönitz would not have been too far from the desired total by 1944.

Offensive action is required to win any battle, for no conflict can be determined simply by defence, unless the attacker is so foolish as to wear himself out by attacking the defender. Dönitz started the war with an aggressive, offensive campaign which bore fruit immediately; but the campaign did not end swiftly, because he had not the forces to maintain the offensive at a constant level for long. The fluctuations in sinkings partly reflect this, and the withdrawal of boats for other purposes compounded it. Boats could only spend so much time on active patrol before the crews had to be rested, and the boats repaired and re-supplied. Inevitably this would mean occasionally that a large proportion of the boats would be non-operational at the same time, giving the escorts a rest. After July 1942 the Atlantic operational strength rose dramatically, but the real offensive spirit was by then somehow lacking in the U-boat commanders. Instead of sending the boats in to attack the convoys bound for England, Dönitz spent half of their effort in attacking west-bound convoys.

To have any chance of gaining a decision in Germany's favour at this time, Dönitz had to make a maximum effort against these convoys, and sustain it. The supply situation was not secure in Great Britain, despite the six months respite granted by Operation 'Paukenschlag', and oil stocks were low. If the 108 ships that the U-boats had sunk in the ON and ONS convoys had been sunk when inward-bound to the UK the situation could still have changed in the Germans' favour. As it was, from July 1942 Dönitz had boats spread all over the Atlantic in the soft spots, rather than concentrated where they would contribute the most. The lack of offensive action in the real sense exhibited itself in side-line operations off South Africa and in the Indian Ocean where sinkings were relatively high but where the effect was virtually nothing in the strategic sense. Again, the continued campaign in the far west, although still sinking ships, had no relevance to the main campaign which was being fought at less than total effort in the northern Atlantic.

In general terms the morale of the U-boat crews can be said to have been relatively high. Only in the northern area did it falter, and even Dönitz was despairing enough to castigate the U-boat commanders when time after time in 1943, just before ONS.5, they failed to find convoys despite their numbers. The mounting losses which the escorts were beginning to inflict were having effect, and the commanders were less than eager to walk into the danger zones around the convoys. This led to a lowering of offensive spirit, which was heightened by the actions of May 1943, which took away the submariner's faith in the boats they were operating. It is this factor above all that sapped the morale of the U-boat captains and crews. For almost four years they had been at sea fighting an increasingly powerful enemy whose methods of submarine detection had improved out of all recognition from the rudimentary Asdic of 1939. Detection methods and anti-U-boat weapons and tactics had undergone a complete change, and the spirit of the escorts' crews was rising as the losses they inflicted mounted. The U-boats had had defective torpedoes for three full years of war, and their only defence against radar had been the Biscay Cross, the rudimentary search receiver to detect metric radar waves. A few FlaK guns had been hurriedly installed, but the Luftwaffe virtually never came to their aid. And the boats themselves were outdated in technique, all having been designed at least a decade before. It is a tribute to the U-boat men that despite these problems and the continuing high losses after May 1943, they continued to fight. This was in major part due to the relationship that Dönitz retained with his crews, even after his translation at the end of January 1943, but his charisma was not backed by the determination to win whatever the cost, and so the lives that were lost were frequently wasted in areas where the endeavour and sacrifice was in vain.

Flexibility is partly a command requirement, partly an administrative talent. In a commander it is demonstrated by a willingness to change the direction of approach to the primary aim (but not by a change of aim); in his staff it is shown by the speed with which troops or equipment can be moved about the battlefield. Dönitz's U-boat Arm showed a general lack of flexibility. When the Americans came into the war by invitation from Hitler, it took a month to get the first U-boats into operation off the US coast. Again, when the campaign returned to the northern convoy routes it was not with a smashing attack, but rather by a campaign reminiscent of the early days of the war. The first mass attack by U-boats was in August when SC.94 was attacked by seven boats. And the tactics used by Dönitz never changed.

Dönitz had advocated the 'wolf-pack' and trained the pre-war crews in it, believing that the idea would overcome the effect of convoy. In the First World War, in which Dönitz had commanded a U-boat, the boats had independent targets until 1917 when convoy cut their effectiveness almost completely. The convoy system had beaten the early U-boats because any boat that saw a convoy had to attack on its own with no land-based command to report to. Dönitz determined to beat the convoy system by controlling his U-boats from land, and assembling his boats into a group before releasing them in attack. For some time this tactic remained supreme, and sinkings of ships in convoy by groups became very serious, and even threatened to force the Allies to rethink the convoy system. But the March 1943 situation was not followed up by continuous aggressive action regardless of cost. Then, two months later, the initiative was lost. But Dönitz stuck to his previous tactics, instead of looking at what had been learned in the years of anti-convoy experience.

On most occasions the most successful attacks on convoys were carried out by either one U-boat, or a few. Thus in February 1942 *U155* sank eight ships of ONS.67 (the highest single performance of the war), and on numerous occasions three U-boats against a convoy produced consistently good results. Surely he could have developed this concept, especially with the increasingly large fleet he had? When overall strength began to decrease after May 1943, small U-boat groups continually attacking convoys might have achieved as much as the enormous groups which took time to assemble, were unwieldy, and above all easy to identify by radio, and observed in their approach by aircraft. Here flexibility might not have been enough, but in January 1942 it would have paid dividends, for then the U-boat fleet could have been profitably organised both off the US coast (the Type IX boats) and in the northern area of the east-bound convoys (the Type VII boats).

Surprise is an element which the U-boat should possess *par excellence* and in the tactical sense the U-boats maintained their surprise ability throughout the war. But the overall effect was lost because of lack of security. Radio traffic was the sole culprit for this and Dönitz the prime mover. His tactical disposi-tions were only possible with the aid of constant ship to shore radio contact. Efforts were made to cut down the amount of time on the air and, as noted, 'Shark'/'Triton' caused problems in deciphering at GCCS. But mere levels of radio traffic and direction-finding (in the real sense, not Ultra now) could indi-cate some idea of U-boats' strengths at sea, and U-boat concentrations. Many convoys were diverted by the Submarine Tracking Room on this evidence alone, and when Ultra was coming through currently, Commander Winn knew as much as Dönitz about the day-to-day events, and probably earlier in the day. The surprise value of the submarine in the strategic sphere was gener-ally lost, although on the tactical level it still existed until radar, when the cloak of surface invisibility was removed to be replaced by that of submerged move-ment – but not entirely secretly.

This then has been a short analysis of the failures that contributed to the U-boats losing the initiative at sea which are attributable to the German side. Now it is important to look at the Allied side to see whether all they did was in accor-dance with the principles of war or if there were also some lapses there.

The aim selected very early on in the war was to destroy the U-boats by all means. The Royal Navy, the Royal Canadian Navy, the US Navy and all other navies involved maintained this aim throughout the war, and were successful. So too did the many airmen directly involved in the conflict, so that by May 1945, when hostilities ended, they had sunk 723 U-boats. But the effort was marred to some extent by the attitude of the parent body of Coastal Command which maintained throughout that the war could be won solely by bombing Germany. It was this lack of co-operation, which was fundamental to the campaign against the U-boats, that spoils the picture on the British side; unfor-tunately the airmen were proved wrong by the results of their efforts, and it must be said that many were lost over Germany who would have better served the Allies by staying alive over the Atlantic.

Before looking at the complexities of the argument that raged over the distribution of aircraft between Bomber Command and Coastal Command, one must see if the claims made as to the effectiveness of the night bombing campaign are borne out by the surveys carried out after the war. Such was the interest raised by this controversy that both the Air Forces involved – the RAF and the USAAF – assembled teams to comb Germany and German records to find out what had been the result of their efforts. One man very much concerned was Reichsminister Albert Speer, who was interrogated in depth after the war. He had this to say:

Question: Which forms of attack at various periods of the war were most effective in weakening the German war effort?
Answer: Only the mass attacks by day, because these were based upon economic considerations and inflicted heavy damage on precise targets.

He said that the American daylight raids were by far the most effective against the armaments industry, and had 'caused the breakdown of the German armaments industry'. The night bombing campaign was ineffective and utterly failed in its stated aim of breaking the will to fight of the German people. He did say that the fire-raid on Hamburg caused great fears of further such attacks, adding that 'We were of the opinion that a rapid repetition of this type of attack upon another six German towns would inevitably cripple the will to sustain armaments manufacture and war production'. But the raids were not repeated, and the civilian population adapted itself to the general pattern of the bombing, which was a gradual increase, rather than the surprise shock tactics against Hamburg which caused so much fear in 1943.

But the bombing offensive did not start until 1943; until then Bomber Command aircraft had made frequent operational sorties over Germany, and had had little or no effect upon war production and none of import against the U-boat industry. From September 1940 onwards the first campaign against the convoys was having a serious effect upon the transport system across the Atlantic. It was at this time that shortages of aircraft in Coastal Command combined with the similar shortages of escorts came to a head with an upsurge in the sinking figures. The Navy was lucky that the Prime Minister was able to obtain the 50 ex-USN ships to add to the escort strength, but there was still a great need of aircraft as well. A request by the Admiralty for aircraft to operate out of Icelandic bases had had to be refused because of those very shortages. Not only were there shortages, which had persisted since the war began, but the aircraft types were not suited to the operational role.

Then Air Chief Marshal Bowhill handed over command of Coastal Command in June 1941, when his nominal strength of 582 aircraft represented about 290 operational aircraft, mainly Hudsons, Blenheims, Whitleys and Wellingtons. These aircraft were all twin-engined, of limited range and capacity, and were no more than the aircraft being phased out by Bomber Command – their 'hand-me-downs'. The new commander, Sir Philip Joubert de la Ferté assessed Coastal Commands needs then at 818 aircraft for local and Atlantic operations. But in October the Prime Minister proposed that the bombers on the strength of his command were to be transferred to Bomber Command for operations against Germany. The Prime Minister was suffering from a feeling of false security because the sinking figures in the Atlantic had gone down. The First Lord of the Admiralty promptly demurred, but all Churchill would do was postpone the question until the New Year.

Because of the Prime Minister's being convinced of Bomber Command's claim that the bombing offensive would have a great effect, he was all in favour of their demands for a 4,000 bomber force by 1943; there was to be no diversion from this. Added to this problem was the refusal of the Air Staff to accept the planned expansion. The clash between the Admiralty and the Air Staff had to be resolved, for, as the First Lord said in March 1942, 'If we lose the war at sea we lose the war'.

In early 1942 the Secretary of State for Air sent a report to the War Cabinet, in which he commented upon the anti-shipping operations that Bomber Command had mounted against Brest and the capital ships there. He stated that 40 per cent of the bombing effort was being expended there, and that the targets were extremely difficult to hit. That this was so is shown by a paper of the Directorate of Bomber Operations of 5 April 1941. It said:

Bombing of *Scharnhorst* and *Gneisenau* at Brest:
2,870 bombs have been dropped on the two warships at Brest between 30th March and 21st April. 2 hits are at least claimed ...'

The aiming error planned for by Bomber command in daytime was at least 1,000 yards! Like all papers that involved statistics during the war, the authors were on extremely dangerous ground, but the import of the paper was that aerial bombing of oil plants would give a better yield. But the Air Staff accepted such papers without question, and a comparison may be drawn between them and Hitler and his High Command. A second paper caused some intense activity at the Admiralty for they had, they thought, a good case for Coastal Command to expand, and certainly not to be depleted when it was already far short of its needs. As Roskill puts it:

The strains from which we were suffering at sea, and the heavy anxieties about the future, focused the Admiralty's attention on the one direction from which it seemed that some fairly prompt easement might be obtained. This was considered to lie in the diversion of more long-range aircraft to Coastal Command, and in accepting the inevitable decline in our bombing offensive against Germany. Ever since 1940 we had been losing ships all over the world for lack of air cover, our losses of merchantmen had been particularly heavy in the waters where aircraft could not reach out to our convoys, and the Ministry of War Transport had several times warned the Admiralty and the War Cabinet that losses above a certain rate were bound to affect the morale of the Merchant Navy. It was, in the Admiralty's eyes, hard to believe that all these troubles could best be cured by bombing German towns ... the heavier bombing of Germany would be warmly welcomed. But before such a programme was embarked upon, the Admiralty had two outstanding and urgent needs which the Air Ministry might be able to fill.

The two demands were for air patrols in the Indian Ocean / Bay of Bengal, and in the Bay of Biscay. The Admiralty now requested the transfer to Coastal Command of 6½ Wellington squadrons and 81 B17 bombers.

This had not been the first occasion for a conflict between the naval and air staffs. The previous year Lord Trenchard had written a paper in which he expounded the philosophy of the Air Staff:

> At sea, although we have an infinite naval superiority, there is no point at which we can strike decisively with our navy, and the German submarine is a very powerful weapon.

He argued that the sea had become a weakness as far as Great Britain was concerned, and there was no way that naval forces could turn the tables by an attack on the enemy weak points, for they were internal land communications. He continued describing what he felt was the enemy's greatest weakness, morale. He painted the accepted picture of the totalitarian regime, which was readily acceptable to men such as the Prime Minister, easily swayed by emotive arguments and the rhetoric of others.

The paper continued with the quotation that 'taking all in all, the percentage of bombs which hit the Military Target at which they are aimed is not more than one per cent'. The answer then, according to the Marshal of the Royal Air Force, was that

> This means that if you are bombing a target at sea, then 99 per cent of your bombs are wasted ... If, however, our bombs are dropped in Germany, then 99 per cent which miss the military target all help to kill, damage, frighten or interfere with Germans in Germany and the whole 100 per cent of the bomber organisation is doing useful work, and not merely 1 per cent of it.

Unfortunately the mathematics of the paper do not stand up, and in any event up to 1943 very few bombers were getting within five miles of their targets, and many of the night targets were not in any sense military.

Of course, the aircraft to carry out this work of bombing, said the paper, was the long-range bomber, and training of these bombers should have priority over all other pilot training, including Coastal Command work. When the paper was read by Sir Dudley Pound, Chief of Naval Staff, his comment was terse, and he described it as 'a complete overstatement ... Read literally, it would seem very unlikely that we should get adequate air forces for the Battle of the Atlantic ...' but his opinion might be said to have been biased. An almost unbiased commentator was Sir John Dill, CIGS at the time. He wrote:

> There is, I think, general agreement that the Battle of the Atlantic must at present remain our chief preoccupation ... The arguments in favour of attack on morale are set out in Lord Trenchard's paper. It is however, essential to take into account the huge bomber effort needed ... With our

existing strength, and allowing for inevitable diversions of effort onto other targets, it is unlikely that we could achieve results on a large enough scale to justify selecting morale as our primary aim at present.

Sir John came down firmly on the side of Coastal Command and using heavy bombers in the Battle of the Atlantic. The clinching point of his argument was that before Bomber Command started the morale offensive, or the Army got observation aircraft, the 'security of this country and of those areas overseas which are essential for the maintenance of our war effort' was of paramount importance. It is a pity that the Air Staff could not see this point clearly, and the Prime Minister's attitude seems to have been curiously ambivalent. By 11 June the Air Staff were absorbing the shock by planning air raids on German ports to help the effort in the Atlantic.

Let us return now to the demands for aircraft proposed by the new chief of Coastal Command. By March 1942 the argument was not simply that Coastal Command should have more aircraft, but that the Navy should have a hand in training the crews, and in controlling their operational use. Coastal Command of course was an RAF operation, and flew reconnaissance for the Navy on request, as well as mounting its own anti-U-boat sweeps. Like Dönitz, the Navy wanted to have the say in what its aircraft did, and where and how they did it; Coastal Command, the Navy felt, was not well-enough trained, and it had been difficult to convince RAF crews that it was not a simple matter to attack a U-boat. Until they realised this fact, and evolved and practised tactics to deal with the situation, the crews were less than fully effective in their naval support role.

There was no question of Bomber Command transferring aircraft to Coastal Command. They argued that the shortage of radar sets limited the number of aircraft that could be supplied, in that for Coastal Command to use aircraft without radar would render their work ineffective. The view the Air Ministry took was once more that the greatest contribution they could make with Bomber Command was by bombing Germany. On 1 April the matter went before the Defence Council, with the RAF arguing that it was threatened with a *de facto* division into three separate services. The RAF argued that the Air Ministry could with American help establish air superiority over Germany, but at the present moment it would not help the later achievement of that aim by the dispersal of the meagre forces at its disposal. They also argued that aircraft used in the anti-U-boat role were being deployed defensively, but as the offensive value of the few aircraft that were able so to operate was apparent, the argument is fallacious.

The Defence Council agreed to transfer four squadrons of Wellingtons and Whitleys to Coastal Command to work against the U-boats in the Bay of Biscay and over the North-Western Approaches, but this was a mere sop, and the Admiralty and Sir Philip agreed, especially when most of Coastal

Command's striking force (the Beaufighters and Hampdens) were either sent abroad or proved worthless in the strike role.

The Air Ministry continued to maintain that the air offensive against Germany would inevitably wear down the German armaments programme and their will to resist; the counter argument by the Admiralty was that in the present situation in the war in the Atlantic, every ship and cargo that was lost was an immediate loss, and such losses were rising to such an extent that Great Britain was in direct danger of being defeated (the Admiralty did not quite say this, but it was what they meant). There had to be an immediate response to the U-boats, rather than a campaign that was yet to get into motion, let alone start to achieve its aim.

It was at this point that the Operational Research scientists made a great contribution to the effectiveness of Coastal Command by putting 'Planned Flying and Maintenance' programmes into use; these schemes reduced the grounded time per aircraft, and optimised every useful component available to Coastal Command, so that with the same number of aircraft, they achieved greater numbers of hours on operational patrol. But this was not the complete answer, for Coastal Command was still well short of what it needed merely to do its job. The Chief of Bomber Command was now Air Marshal Sir Arthur Harris. He was asked by the Prime Minister to prepare a note on the role and work of Bomber Command, and his paper, issued on 28 June 1942, began:

> Those who advocate the breaking-up of Bomber Command for the purpose of adding to Coastal and Army Cooperation Commands and overseas requirements are like the amateur politician who imagines that the millennium will arrive through the simple process of dividing available cash equally between all ... our only offensive weapon against Germany would be destroyed.

In view of the minimal effectiveness of Bomber Command at the time, and the losses it was suffering for little return, and in view of the dire situation in the Atlantic, a commander of greater stature would have allocated all the aircraft he could to an offensive against the U-boats (no matter how ineffective) in the attempt to defeat the danger by weight of numbers. In the Atlantic sheer weight of numbers would have helped, for no U-boat commander was prepared to risk staying on the surface in the face of a four-engined bomber on the off-chance that its crew were totally inexperienced. But the Air Marshal was so single-minded that he would not release a single aircraft, relying upon the added weight of the American bombers to help him bomb Germany into submission.

Sir Arthur went on to say that a great deal of Bomber Command's effort had gone into attacking German sea power. That aircraft did attack Brest when *Scharnhorst* and *Gneisenau* were there is true, but the results were such that the raids would have been less costly if they had been omitted. But Sir Arthur claimed that bombers alone kept those two ships in Brest, and when they left they hit air-laid mines. The truth was that Bomber Command dropped so many bombs that they managed, by the law of percentages, to damage the ships in Brest, but when they broke out, repeated errors by the Navy and the Royal Air Force combined to allow them to make most of their passage up Channel unscathed. He further claimed that Kiel was heavily damaged as a naval base, and that workshops had been destroyed 'with all that that implies with regard to delay in naval supply and repair work.'

In fact, examination of when bombing repair work became a factor in the German shipyards results in the conclusion that Bomber Command caused almost no damage to production in 1942, an increasing amount in 1943, and more in 1944. But the offensive only got under way after February 1943, when the effects on the Battle of the Atlantic of bombing Germany would not be felt for months. The matter had to be decided without any really effective support from Bomber Command. The Air Marshal made claims in his paper that were unsubstantiated, or downright lies. He claimed for instance that the bombing of Cologne helped in the anti-U-boat war, and that

> While it takes approximately 7,000 hours of flying to destroy one subma-
> rine at sea, that was approximately the amount of flying necessary to
> destroy one-third of Cologne, the third largest city in Germany, in one
> night, a town of vast industrial import. 250 of its factories were damaged
> or destroyed.

He also claimed that 'considerable damage has been done to the submarine building yards at Hamburg, Kiel, Rostock, Emden and other ports.' His statements demand belief, but were unsupported by facts then, and directly contradicted by the results after the war. Bomber Command was unloading many of its bombs on the countryside miles away from its targets, and its aircraft would have been better employed in the Atlantic where the crews would have contributed far more, and sacrificed far less, to the victory to come; Bomber Command was responsible for delaying that victory by its parochial attitude to its aircraft.

Figures released after the war show what Bomber Command achieved up to April 1943. Aircraft losses during this period were 62 per cent of all aircraft lost in day raids during the war, and 39.5 per cent of those lost at night throughout. The tonnage of bombs dropped totalled 13.4 per cent of the total wartime tonnage dropped by Bomber Command. If the aircraft, or at least some of them, had been transferred to Coastal Command until Bomber Command and the US Eighth AAF were ready to mount their combined offensives, those aircraft would have turned the tide in the Allies' favour much

273

earlier. As it was they suffered great losses for minimal returns. The survey unit reports show that damage up to 1942 was too small to establish, and amounted to a reduction in 1942 of 0.5 per cent of German war production altogether. In attacks on military industrial production the loss to the Germans was 1.8 per cent. Only in 1943, when the American daylight raids with specific economic targets began, did the losses begin to have real military significance, but by that time the northern Atlantic was becoming too dangerous for the U-boats. The figures quoted are from those produced by the British Bombing Survey Unit, whose full data have never been published, unlike the American report. This suggests that the losses through bombing in 1942 were 0.25 per cent, and only rose to 3.8 per cent for the second half of 1943.

# CONCLUSION  15

The campaign in the Atlantic lasted for the entire period of the Second World War, and many thousands of men of both sides lost their lives to either enemy action or the 'cruel sea.' Activity in this enormous arena was unceasing, and the hunt for targets unrelenting by all the navies engaged.

The Germans started the campaign with 57 U-boats, a number that was to rise to over 400; the Allied navies began with a few escorts and virtually no aircraft, ending the campaign with escort-ship and air-patrol numbers that were more than sufficient for the job. Mistakes were made by both sides, but the fundamental errors were made by the Germans: all the Allies had to do was persevere and, when necessary, adapt.

In 1939 the German U-boat arm could not close the Atlantic to merchant shipping convoys, and even in 1943 when U-boat numbers were approaching the magic total of 400, they could not find the convoys with sufficient frequency to be in a position to deny traffic routes between the United States and the United Kingdom. Further, Dönitz was hampered in his campaign in the Atlantic by Hitler's insistence on diverting U-boats elsewhere and to Göring's unwillingness to provide adequate and reliable air reconnaissance forces over the Atlantic sea lanes.

Göring's unwillingness to provide adequate aircraft and maintenance to reconnoitre the Atlantic sea lanes was yet another example of the failings of the German command system. Göring, like Hitler, saw no glory in the endless, often fruitless, survey of the sea; so the Fw 200 *Kondor* (or any other long range reconnaissance aircraft) never appeared in sufficient numbers to affect the outcome of the campaign. It is fortuitous that the same did not occur on the Allied side, despite RAF obstinacy and lack of strategic foresight.

It is therefore reasonable to suggest that the real fault laid with the German High Command, from Hitler downwards. Hitler had little knowledge of the sea, and less, apparently, of the importance of the Atlantic Ocean in terms of grand strategy. Raeder was, above all, a surface fleet man. Dönitz was, it seems, promoted above his true ability, that of a senior commander but not a fleet commander.

Unknown to the Germans was the additional fact that Ultra was compromised. The communication system used by Dönitz to contact his commanders at sea was being deciphered at Bletchley Park (with some intermissions) and, although this was never decisive, it was a significant factor in the war against the U-boats.

Most important of all, air cover for the convoys did increase, and the advent of escort carriers finally sealed the fate of the U-boats. Aircraft were the most feared enemy, for they were able to attack quickly, before the U-boats could complete their dives. Counter-measures were implemented, but they were never effective enough to ensure safety for the U-boats, and radar was capable of spotting even a Schnorchel head, denying this expedient any true value.

Radar was perhaps the single most important development in the war against the U-boats. British scientists had invented the means of obtaining a signal return from objects only centimetres in dimension, and this secret was shared freely with the US Government. The appearance of centimetric radar and the Plan Position Indicator meant that the U-boats were no longer free to operate with impunity on the surface at night, which meant that their operations were severely restricted.

Another major improvement in Sonar (Asdic) – the ability not only to find U-boats under the surface but to establish how deep they were – was a further nail in their coffins. This meant that attacking escort vessels could determine the U-boats' underwater position with greater accuracy and allow settings on depth-charges to be more effective. The advent of the forward-throwing 'Hedgehog' (projectiles from which only exploded on contact) added even more to the U-boats' difficulties.

This was a campaign of both raw courage and stamina and of technology. Both sides had men of great bravery, but courage alone was not enough, and the U-boats lost the campaign in May 1943 to superior technology and sheer weight of numbers. The attempts to bring the U-boat war back to the convoy routes was a failure because by that time the economic situation Germany faced would not allow it, and, despite the real innovation of the Type XXI U-boat, it was yet again a case of 'too little, too late'.

# APPENDICES

## THE PREPARATION AND TRAINING OF
## U-BOAT CREWS, 1925–1945

### The Inter-War Years

Despite the provisions of the Treaty of Versailles, which denied Germany construction and use of submarines, the German Naval Command fully intended to remain *au courant* with all matters relating to the subject. In this regard, it was planned that Germany should construct and test U-boats in other countries. From 1922 the opportunity was provided by the setting up of *N. V. Ingenieurskantoor voor Scheepsbouw* (IVS). This firm, capitalised by three German yards, had its head office in the Hague.

In 1925 Naval Ministry funds were put into IVS and an order was obtained from Turkey for two U-boats; there was also the prospect of building elements of a new boat programme for Spain. Korvettenkapitän Canaris ordered the establishment of a submarine office under the nomenclature *Au (Ausbildung – Training)*. In charge was Admiral Spindler. He outlined his field of activity in his first action report of 12 November 1926, which coincided with Canaris's recommendation. A significant part of the report related to the factors affecting the choice of U-Boat type to be supplied to fill the future German naval requirement: one main factor was the teaching materials available for the needs of crew training.

Spindler also needed a combined team of active-service seamen and engineer branch officers to take part in testing the boats for the Turkish Navy. Naval Command considered that on political grounds only retired personnel should be involved, together with highly experienced civilian staff. The connection with the Turkish Navy resulted in two of the officers, who were in the transit crew, being asked by the Turkish Navy to set up a U-boat training school for their own crews.

In Germany Spindler was actively establishing a training programme, and in conjunction with the Navy Arms Superintendent he managed to start a series of theoretical lectures on the U-boat for senior ensigns. These took place from 1927 onwards, during the participants' torpedo courses at the Torpedo and Radio School in Flensburg-Mürwik. The training equipment used was film taken during the First World War on *U35* and *U139*. From 18 to 21 May 1927, 24 ensigns of the recruitment year 1924 received three 3-hour lectures on U-boat subjects.

On the engineering side, Spindler planned a training programme for future U-boat engineers from 1927 onwards. The theme of these courses had already been discussed, questions having been posed as to how the knowledge of the use of the U-Boats in the First World War could be preserved and developed. Also, how were the majority of technical personnel to be provided, and what training equipment was available, and what needed to be supplied.

As far as sea-training was concerned it could be arranged for a select cadre of future U-boat officers to be aboard future projects of TVS. These problems were discussed in a paper issued by the U-Boat Office on 17 October 1927:

> In order to circumvent the Treaty of Versailles and to develop the U-boat Arm to stay *au courant* with the subject, and to enable a limited amount of training to take place, which is not as yet feasible though every effort must be made to rectify this situation ... our Spanish contacts now enable us, by the immediate expenditure of RM 1.5 million and a total of RM 3–4 million over three to four years, to come closer to our aim, i.e. to have our constructors and yard men fully conversant with all that is newest and best in the field of building submarines, and at the same time to train military personnel (seamen' and engineers' branches) in matters relating to submarines.

Various circumstances (e.g., the delay in the start of building in Spain and the subsequent shuffle of personnel following the Lohmann incident) retarded progress during the years 1928 to 1929. The training programme was however initiated by the course for 60 ensigns of the class of 1925 which was given at the Marine Artillery School at Kiel in the early part of 1929. On the debit side was the cancellation of the planned course at Kiel Naval Academy for Engineers. Schottky, who lectured on the course in early 1929, took over the U-Boat Office from Spindler in 1929, and he made efforts to implement simulator training on the UZ Boats and on the Roeder-designed 'F' and 'T' devices (early simulators). The UZ boats were for seamanship and torpedo-firing training. The idea was not, however, adopted by the Naval Ministry, and was not practicable for other reasons as well. However, Schottky and a mixed group of serving officers, retired officers, civilian engineers and officials, managed to gain practical experience during the testing of the two Finnish boats *Vetehinen* and *Vesihiisi* in the summer of 1930.

In 1931, despite certain difficulties, the Spanish boat *E1* was also finished. Due to the close connections between TVS and the Navy Ministry and the further fact that the boat was built with German money, the Navy had a great deal of interest in the tests that were to be made, for it was also to be tested as the prototype for the future submarine element of the German Navy (UA and the two Type IA boats were the result). A notable fact was the close co-operation that existed between the serving naval officers and the builders. Control of the actual building was in the hands of Schottky and Hey (both ex-naval architects and engineer officials), who had under them an experienced team and the support of the naval yard at Wilhelmshaven. The head of the testing team was Kapitänleutnant A. D. Bräutigam, who for some years had been in charge of submarine building in Japan, the boats there being constructed from original German plans. The Chief Engineer was Papenberg, and Rösing was also included, who had been on the team for the Finnish boats. Other officers who had taken Schottky's course also took part, together with a number of men from the Eckernförde torpedo testing station, as well as some naval architecture students. A further addition, as an observer, was the technical chief of the submarine construction department, then existing under the code-name 'Igewit'.

Before submarine training could be set in motion, preparations had to be made at three different levels:

1. Instruction for ensigns in submarine subjects by special lectures:
Class of 1926 – a 3-day course in January 1930:
Kiel Naval Artillery School
Class of 1927 – a five-day 20-hour course in April 1930
Class of 1928 – a course in the summer of 1930
Class of 1929 – a course from 16 – 21 February 1931 at the Naval School, Mürwik
(This last course was cancelled by the C-in-C Navy because of problems over exact dates for the course)

2. Staff Officer courses in submarine subjects down to First Lieutenant level – given from 1930 by Schottky, from 1932 by Schürer and Fürbringer

3. Training of a small number of active-service seamen and engineer branch officers on the TVS boats abroad. It was also decided to send three young officers to join Fürbringer at the Turkish school

Furthermore, following Schottky's instigation, a much greater amount of time was spent on submarine subjects at the Naval School at Mürwik and the Naval Academy at Kiel.

Nevertheless there was still no final date fixed for the start of the submarine programme. This was changed in 1932 following establishment of the building plan for 16 U-boats for the Navy by 1938. This meant

that training was to be more formalised and personnel should gain more experience by taking part in voyages abroad and by occasional lectures. Fürbringer was felt to be suitably experienced to set this up and under the command of Kolbe he gave a six-day course in May 1932 to 49 ensigns at the TNS on the subject of submarines. It was further planned for 1932, under the control of Fürbringer, to train two seamen and one engineers branch officer yearly on an intensive course. The course was to last twelve weeks, with 207 lecture hours, and 1–2 hours daily on the T simulator.

The building of CV707 allowed a much larger number of course members following her completion on 1 April 1933, and on 15 June 32 it was ordered that eight junior officers were to take part, being those adjudged suitable at the autumn promotions date in 1932. To cope with these increased numbers a second instructor was brought in, together with seven other personnel who were particularly qualified in the subject.

The first regular course for future commanders started on 3 January 1933. After three months' training in theory and tactics there was further special training in the working of the gyro-compass, underwater sound-location and escape apparatus.

CV707 began her tests at the end of May 1933 with Fürbringer as Captain and Papenberg as Chief Engineer. Apart from the ten course members, two more reserve officers were present. Following a heart attack suffered by Papenberg, Bräutigam took over command.

The first two fully German U-boats were planned to start building in the autumn of 1933, and the then Reichswehrminister, von Blomberg, ordered the establishment of a submarine school in Kiel-Wik, work on which was to begin on 1 October 1933. Kapitänleutnant Slevogt was named as Commanding Officer, with as Senior Lecturers Fürbringer and Hülsmann, and Rösing and Freiwald as lecturers.

The first class at this school comprised eight officers, and 70–80 NCOs and seamen, all of whom assembled at Kiel in the summer of 1933. The official description of the school was Unterseebootsabwehrschule/UAS ('School of Anti-submarine Warfare') and it came under the organisation of, and technically was incorporated within, the Inspectorate of Torpedoes. As the planned submarine building did not take place, because of the changing political situation, the school ran just one class until 30 September 1934.

Theoretical training included instruction in U-Boat construction from the point of view of seamen and engineers, instruction in maintaining stability, weight distribution and trim maintenance above and below water, in both peacetime and war conditions. Also included was the use of escape apparatus. Seamen received basic training in the firing of torpedoes, and officers and senior ratings in the use of the periscope. Simultaneously, engineering personnel were instructed on the diesel and electric propulsion units. Training equipment included an electrically operated steering machine, as well as an electric periscope and a gyro-compass installation.

Practical training was carried out with the aid of simulators: minesweepers equipped with a periscope stub housed in a covered deck compartment, with an engine installation comprising half the drive of a Type II, and submarine steering equipment. Training took place aboard these minesweepers and aboard CV707 in Finland from 28 May to 4 August 1935. To take part in the latter, seven officers and six NCOs were sent to Finland in the guise of tourists and students. Of the training staff, Braütigam, Papenberg and Freiwald were mainly involved in this venture.

As from 1 October 1934 a further class was formed at UAS in view of the impending construction of six small boats starting in January 1935. The submarine arm then expanded until, in the middle of 1935, it stood at fifteen seamen and nine engineering branch officers, 190 NCOs and men. On 1 December 1934 it was decided to expand the school with a further 580 men by 1 October 1935. This would provide the crews of fourteen large and two small boats from UAS by the middle of 1936.

Following the launch of the first of the U-boats, Braütigam and Hülsmann were transferred from UAS to the newly created Development Board for submarines, which later became the *Ubootsabnah-mekonmmando/UAK* (Submarine Acceptance Authority). Papenberg had already been transferred to have control of U-Boat building. The first U-boat to come into service went to UAS as a training boat in the late summer of 1935.

On 6 June 1935, all matters relating to U-Boats were, with the exception of training, put under the command of the (then) Kapitän zur See Dönitz. U-Boat Flotilla Weddigen was set up in Kiel on 27 September 1935 with *U7–U12* (leaving *U1–U6* for training.) Practical training patrols of from four to twenty days were made in these boats, although no torpedo firings were made at this time. Torpedo firing training was undertaken at Flotilla, where battle-training and tactical instruction were carried out.

As the production rate of larger boats increased, so did the demand for trained crews. Kiel-Wik did not have sufficient training or accommodation facilities to cope with these large numbers, and so a UAS was established at Neustadt (Holstein) in May 1937. The Chief Instructor there was Kapitän zur See Scheer. In 1938 the training boats were established within their own Flotilla, and in 1939 a special school of anti-submarine warfare was set up outside the UAS, which eventually came under the command of the BdU.

### The effect of war

With the outbreak of war in September 1939, the training boats were pressed into active service on patrol duties in the Baltic and North Seas. Half of these were returned to the schools at the end of the Polish campaign, only to be recalled to the front during the Norwegian campaign in 1940. However, all training boats returned to their original duties from July 1940 onwards.

War caused a change in the training programme, for it was no longer practicable to indulge in training at Flotilla level; such training was now reduced to a 'practical' for prospective U-Boat commanders under the eye of the most experienced captains. At the same time training capacity required for the expanded U-boat war programme had to be greatly increased. Thus on 16 November 1939 training was laid down for the following numbers of crews yearly:

1940–54
1941–250
1942–350 (and similarly per year thereafter)

To allow for this UAS 2 was set up at Gotenhafen on 1 July 1940, and UAS 3 in Pillau on 1 July 1941. The Neustadt school was placed under the direct command of the BdU and within the organisation of the BdU service establishment, under direct command of Kapitän zur See von Friedeburg.

Dönitz took the important decision to place U-boat training under the responsibility of the BdU, seeing this as the only way of providing a speedy and easy supply of trained men for the front. The counter-proposal was that all matters relating to training should be placed under the command of the Commanding Admiral, Baltic. These conflicting opinions led to a serious dispute between the BdU and Admiral Raeder. The principle remained, however, of training in specific skills at different training schools with subsequent crew training on board.

Battle-training was provided by extra gunnery and other training schools and 1st Training Flotilla was set up in November 1939, followed by 2nd Training Flotilla in April 1940, both being based in Danzig. A tactical training school was also set up in Götenhafen from January 1940. All three schools were under the command of the BdU.

Commander training was done individually at Flotillas, and despite the anomalous nature of this training, due to the high standards achieved in peacetime, the method was vindicated by results.

When U-boat production rate was stepped up in 1941, another gunnery school was established at Pillau and, to intensify the battle-training schedule in technical matters, a technical training group for combat boats was established at Hela.

In 1940 the entire U-boat training establishment was transferred in April from Neustadt to Pillau, because of danger from air attack, minelaying operations in the training area of the Lübeck Bight, and lack of space at Neustadt. There the school became 1st ULD. The 2nd ULD, set up in July 1940, was based at Götenhafen, but could not come into operation until November 1940 because of building problems. The attached Flotillas were respectively the 21st and 22nd Uflotillas.

For crews already trained at the ULDI, the 1st UAA was set up at Plön in February 1940; this acted as a holding camp for fully trained crews awaiting posting to a boat. Training continued, and there was the addition of military training. Small groups of these men went to the yards on building courses, and others went for short courses at relevant manufacturers.

A delay in building boats, and the resulting back-log of trained crews, caused 2nd UAA to be set up to cope with the personnel overflow from 1st UAA. This was established at Neustadt, with responsibility for the men coming from 2nd ULD. The rising numbers of trained crewmen available, coupled with increasing losses, led to further intensification of building from the beginning of 1943.

In the organisation structure there were two establishments between the BdU, ULD and UAA; these were the HKU, which had overall control of ULD and UAA, and FdU-AusB, commanding certain training flotillas. As boats became available with fully trained crews, they were passed on to FdU-AusB as part of the Home Fleet under FdU-Ost.

HKU was established at Kiel on 15 January 1943. It was responsible for all seamanship and mechanical training undertaken in the ULD and UAA. Increasing numbers led to a further division in the autumn of 1943 when all technical NCOs and men were moved to 3rd ULD.

To train the additional NCOs required for the Type XXI boat, 4th ULD was set up at Memel in February 1944. There, in a short course of three months, men were trained after their time at 3rd ULD. The main part of the course was technical. A motorised training aid for 4th ULD never came into service, and following the fall in the number of commissioned boats 4th ULD became superfluous and was disbanded in November 1944.

Sea time was originally allocated to the men on the basis of ten days for fifteen of the crew aboard school boats, but this was discontinued when 3rd ULD was set up and the new intakes of officers and cadets arrived. Nevertheless the number of training boats grew considerably. The eight-week officer and NCOs' course had one week's theory and one week's practical in rotation, and included 17–18 days sea time. Ratings received dry training in boats in harbour. General seamanship was taught in surface vessels attached to the training flotillas.

All ranks received training in general matters relating to U-boats. Initially training was in the Type II boats, then from mid-1943 the Type VIIC came into use. (From the end of 1944 a short course in the Type XXI was given, but was discontinued because of lack of available detail.) Training in the use of escape apparatus was standard, with equipment available for practising the operation of the valves and in equalising pressures. Each trainee also received first aid training.

The main emphasis of officers' training lay in the important matter of submerged manoeuvre. First principles were taught on the submerged steering trainer at ULD, followed by further training on the school boats. The aim of the training was to ensure complete control in simple manoeuvres, steering a straight course under water, minor adjustments of depth, changes of trim at various points of a course, steering the boat under known conditions and in difficulties, overcoming trim and weight distribution problems and completing successfully a diving manoeuvre of modest proportions. Senior NCOs also had a short basic course in submerged manoeuvring, while seamen-grade NCOs were trained in the use of the hydroplanes. Of equal importance with general boat knowledge was motor and engine training for technical crew members. Training material included complete engines and motors, cut-away models and training diagrams, including charts and diagrams for diagnosing and repairing faults.

Seamen-grade officers and NCOs had only a short machinery course of a few hours. They did however receive detailed training in U-boat tactics and torpedo firing. In addition, there was training in ship recognition, simple navigation, and for officers and senior watchmen training in meteorology and astronomical navigation. Military training for crews included basic infantry training, seamanship and signalling.

When 33d ULD was set up at Neustadt, 2nd UAA had to move from there to Zeren near Bremen, and the task division of the UAAs was changed, 1st UAA now taking all trained seamen from both ULDs (including radio and torpedo men), while 2nd UAA took all technical crewmen. A six-weeks' course for U-boat cooks was set up elsewhere.

April 1943 saw 3rd UAA set up in Schleswig as a holding unit for crews of surface vessels under BdU command. There was also a testing company. The 3rd UAA had no direct connection with the U-boat war, having a purely military function. In mid-1944 it was transferred to Pillau.

During the basic training of U-boat commanders under HKU, FdU had command of the remainder of the crews, preparing them for battle, especially in matters of battle-craft and torpedo firing. As a consequence of the direct contact between FdU and 2SKl, all battle experiences could be immediately incorporated into the training.

Once a newly commissioned U-boat had been put under the command of one of the U-boat admirals, and had a commander and crew, they went to FdU-Ost until undertaking battle training with FdU-AusB. Here the crew was divided into a number of classes for training, which was completed in three months. The training was flexible enough to allow more or less time to a subject according to results.

FdU-AusB also organised training for new commanders, giving them time with their more experienced counterparts who had already commanded a boat at war. Losses from 1943 onwards, however, eventually rendered this part of the course ineffective. The trainee commanders, shortly before taking over a boat, were trained at 3rd ULD in Neustadt in the F-Equipment; this was a simulator for submerged command, having a U-boat type tower with periscope, wheel, gyro-compass and torpedo computer. The trainee saw a battle picture through the periscope and gave details to the computer. Firing the dummy torpedo control stopped everything and mistakes could be analysed. Following this came practical torpedo firing with the special training flotillas in Danzig and Memel.

Seamen branch commanding officers (Reserve Officers, etc.) were trained by FdU, not ULD. There followed a ten-day course of practical work in watch-keeping aboard barges of 19th Uflotilla at Pillau, accompanied by their crews. The 24th Uflotilla at Memel was set up as a sound-locating training school for NCOs and men.

At the end of 1944 a special school was set up at Hela to train officers in underwater sound-location (SU-Gerät 'Nibelung'). This was 18th Uflotilla, but it did not go into operation because of the then war situation.

From mid-1944 onwards a special team was organised and controlled by FdU-AusB to examine the new Types XXI and XXIII in order to optimise future training on these boats. This Test Group for U-boats also looked into and tried out the new fighting methods that these boats allowed. Specially created groups (Sultan and Pascha) tested new location methods, first submerged, then on the surface.

Early in the autumn of 1944 Russian advances cut back on the training programme. The gunnery flotillas moved from Libau and Memel to Gotenhafen. After the fall of the Weichsel Front, the Danzig Bight was denied to the Kriegsmarine. The gunnery schools moved from there to Travemünde and Warnemünde in January 1945. Agru-Front moved to Bornholm at the beginning of March, during which move it surrendered control of tactical Uflotillas. Also, at the beginning of 1945, 1st and 2nd ULD moved west to Hamburg-Finkenwerder and Wilhelmshaven, where they were ordered to surrender soon after setting up. The 3rd UAA at Pillau was ordered into the fighting there.

## ORGANISATION OF THE U-BOAT ARM

### Commander, U-boat Training flotillas
**[Führer der Unterseebootsausbildungsflottillen (F.d.U.Ausb.)]**
**(Gotenhafen)**

This command was established in March 1943. The bases were at Pillau, Kiel, Gotenhafen, Danzig, Eckern-förde, Memel, Libau, Travemünde, Warnemünde and Hela. The flotillas were set up to provide individual training with U-boats specifically attached for the purpose (which remained under the tactical control of Commander U-boats (East).

### Commander, U-boat Training
Kapt.z.S. Schültze (Viktor) May 43–May 45
**Chief of Staff and Chief testing officer, new U-boats**
K.Kapt. Schulz (Wilhelm) Oct 43–Apr 45
**Liaison Officer (Engineering)**
K.Kapt.(Ing.) Looschen Mar 43–Mar 45
K.Kapt.(Ing.) Dipl.-Ing. Gottwald Mar–May 45
**Liaison Officer (Admin)**
K.Kapt.(V) Zander (Walter) – May 45
**Legal Adviser**
MKrGerRat Sieber Mar–Oct 43
MObStRichter Sonanini Oct 43–May 45

### 18th U-boat Flotilla
Established at Hela shortly before the end of the war, it was a radio training flotilla commanded by K.Kapt Franzius Jan–May 45.
U-boats attached: UI161 (ex-Ital S8) Jan–Feb 45; UI162 (ex- intended S10 for Ital Navy) Jan–Feb 45; UA (ex-Turkish Batiray) Nov 44–May 45; UD4 (ex-Dutch O26) Jan–Mar 45.

### 19th U-boat Flotilla
Base: Pillau, from Feb 45 Kiel.
Established Oct 43.

U-boat commander's pre-training school, watch-keeping and harbour duties.
**Commander:**
K.Kapt. Metzler Oct 43–May 45
U-boats attached: U56 July 44–Apr 45; U57 July 44–Apr 45; U58 July 44–Apr 45; U59 July 44–Apr 45.

### 20th U-boat Flotilla
Base: Pillau.
Established Jun 43, disbanded Feb 45.
Pre-tactical training.
**Commander:**
K.Kapt. Mengersen Jun 43–Feb 45

### 23rd U-boat Flotilla
Base: Danzig.
Established Aug 43, disbanded Mar 45.
Captain's torpedo and gunnery training
**Commander:**
K.Kapt. von Bülow (Otto) Aug 43–Mar 45

### 24th U-boat Flotilla
Base originally Danzig, then Trondheim, then Memel. At end of the war transferred to Gotenhafen and finally Eckernförde.
First established in Nov 39, became 1st U-boat Training Flotilla from Apr 40. In July 40 became 24th U-boat Flotilla. Disbanded Mar 45. Training for captains in torpedo and gunnery firing, later under-water sound-location training.
**Commander:**
K.Kapt. Weingaertner Nov 39–July 42
Kapt.z.S. Peters (Rudolf) July 42–Jan 43
F.Kapt. Metten Apr 43–Mar 45
K.Kapt. Jasper (Karl) (in reserve) Apr–July 44

### 25th U-boat Flotilla
(Established Apr 40 as 2nd U-boat Training Flotilla,

renamed July 40) Headquarters Danzig Jun–Sept 41, then to Trondheim, Memel for a short time, and then Libau. At the end of 1944 moved to Gotenhafen, and to Travemünde in 1945.
Gunnery Training.
**Commander:**
K.Kapt. Hashagen (Ernst) Apr 40–Dec 41
K.Kapt. Jasper (Karl) Dec 41–Aug 43
F.Kapt. Neitzel (in reserve) Aug–Dec 43
K.Kapt. Gysae Dec 43–Apr 45
K.Kapt. Schulz (Wilhelm) Apr 45–End

### 2th U-boat Flotilla
Headquarters Pillau, until 1945 when moved to Warnemünde. Established in Apr 41 for gunnery training.
**Commander:**
K.Kapt. von Stockhausen (Hans-Gerrit) Apr 41–Jan 43
K.Kapt. Metten Feb–Apr 43
F.Kapt. Bruemmer-Patzig Apr 43–Mar 45
K.Kapt. Bauer (Ernst) Mar 45–End
U-boats attached: U37 May 41–Mar 42; U46 Apr 41–Mar 42; U48 July 41– Mar 42; U52 Jun 41Mar 42; U80 May 41–Mar 42; U101 Feb–Mar 42; U351 Jun 41–Mar 42

### 27th U-boat Flotilla
Headquarters Gotenhafen.
Established Jan 40 for tactical U-boat training. Renamed July 40.
Disbanded Mar 45. The Italian U-boat training programme was under the command of this flotilla from 1941.
Tactical training, and training of Italian U-boat crews.
Boat attached: UD4 Jan 43–Nov 44
**Commander:**
K.Kapt. Sobe Jan 40–Dec 41
F.Kapt. Hartmann (Werner) Dec 41–Oct 42
K.Kapt. Topp (Erich) Oct 42–July 44
Kptlt. Bauer (Ernst) July 44–Mar 45

### Technical and Training Department, U-boats
(Agru Front) .
Established Sept 41. HQ until Mar 45 Hela, then Bornholm and Eckernförde.
**Commander:**
K.Kapt.(Ing.) Dipl.Ing. Mueller (Hans) Sept 41–May 44
Kapt.z.S.(Ing.) Dipl.Ing. Heintz May 44–End
**U-boat testing department**
K.Kapt. Schulz (Wilhelm)
F.Kapt. Topp (Erich) (Typ XXI) Aug 44–Jan 45
K.Kapt. Emmermann (Typ XXIII) Aug 44–Mar 45

### Training groups and units
### The U-boat School and the U-boat Defence School
On 11 Sept 39 The U-boat Defence School at Neustadt was renamed as the U-boat School, with a subordinate branch named the U-boat Defence School. At the time, and until 1940, this training depot was under the command of the Torpedo Inspection Branch of the Navy, and did not come into the sphere of command of the Commander, U-boats until 1940. In May 1940 the school moved to Pillau and renamed 1st U-boat School. A further renaming took place in Jun 1940, when the school became the 1st U-boat Training Division.

The U-boat Defence School left Neustadt in Nov 1939 and teaching began in Gotenhafen. In July 43 the school moved to Bergen in Norway and remained there until the end of the war. For administration the school came under local area command, although actual command remained with the Torpedo Inspection Branch.

### U-boat School Neustadt
**Commander:**
Kapt.z.s. Scheer (Werner) Apr 38–Sept 39
F.Kapt. Ibbeken Sept 39–(Nov 41)
Chief of Staff
Kptlt.(Ing.) Welsch Mar 39–(Aug 41)

### 1st Department
Established Feb–Mar 40

**Commander:**
K.Kapt. Büchel Mar 40–(Jun 43)

### 2nd Department
Established Feb–Mar 40

**Commander:**
K.Kapt.(Ing.) Zerpka Feb 40–(Jun 43)

### U-boat School Training Flotilla
**Commander:**
Kpfllt. Beduenn Nov 37–Mar 40
K.Kapt. Büchel Mar 40–(Jun 43)
Boats: U1 Jun 35–Apr 40; U2 July 35–Jun 40; U3 Jan 35–Jun 40; U4, U5 Aug 35–Jun 40; U6 Sept 35–Jun 40; U7 July 35–Jun 40; U8 Aug 35–Dec 39; U10, U11 Sept 35–Jun 40; U25 Apr 36–Sept 39; U36 Dec 36–Sept 39

### U-boat Defence School (UAS)
**Commander:**
Kapt.z.S. Dr. Schmidt (Eberhard) Sept 39–Oct 42
F.Kapt. Waller Oct 42–Jan 43
Kapt.z.S. von Selchow Jan 43–End

### Chief of Staff and Chief Training Officer
F.Kapt. Rickert Sept 39–Aug 41
F.Kapt. Waller Aug 41–Dec 43
K.Kapt. Dr. Ing. Peters (Heinz) Jan 44–End
Boats: U8 Jan–Apr 40; U17 May 40–Mar 43; U298 July 44–May 45; U1102 Sept 44–May 45.

### High Command, U-boat training (HKU)
This command was established on 15 Jan 43 in the Deputy Commander, U-boats' department. The HQ was initially in Kiel, then moved to Plön, and in Apr

1945 was moved to Neustadt (Holstein). The U-boat Training Divisions and the U-boat Training Battalions were subordinated to the command. Previously the Training Divisions had been under the command of the Commander U-boats (Organisation) Department, and the latter under the Deputy Commander, U-boats.

### Commander-in-Chief
Kapt.z.S. Schmidt (Albrecht) Jan 43–End

### Chief of Staff
K.Kapt. (Ing.) Miller Jan–May 43
K.Kapt. (Ing.) Schmidt (Heinrich) Jun–Sept 43
K.Kapt. (Ing) Wahl (Rudolf) Nov 43–July 44
K.Kapt. (Ing.) Bahn July 44–End

### Legal Officer
MObStRichter Dr. Meinert Mar 43–Oct 44
MObStRichter Dr. Breinig Oct 44–End

### 1st U-boat Training Division
The U-boat Training School (Neustadt) was put under the command of the Commander U-boats (Organisation) Branch in 1940, and in May of that year was renamed and moved to Pillau as 1st U-boat School. The HQ remained in Holstein. On 13 June 40 it was renamed 1st U-boat Training Division. It moved to Hamburg in 1944, and was disbanded in Feb–Mar 1945.

### Commander:
F.Kapt. Ibbeken Sept 39–Nov 41
Kapt.z.S. Schmidt (Albrecht) Dec 41–Jan 43
Kapt.z.S. Poske Jan 43–Feb 45
K.Kapt. Heyse (Ulrich) Feb–Mar 45

### Chief of Staff
Kptlt.(Ing.) Welsch Sept 39–Aug 41
Kptlt.(Ing.) Bahn Aug–Dec 41
K.Kapt.(Ing.) Schmidt (Heinrich) Dec 41–Nov 42
(no further appointments made)

### 1st Detachment
Commander:
K.Kapt. Buechel Mar 40–Jun 43
K.Kapt. Schuhart Jun 43–Jan 44
K.Kapt. Heyse (Ulrich) Jan 44–Mar 45

### 2nd Detachment
Commander:
K.Kapt.(Ing.) Zerpka Feb 40–Jun 43
K.Kapt.(Ing.) Miller Jun–Nov 43
K.Kapt. Michel Nov 43–Feb 45

### 21st U-boat Flotilla
The U-boat training flotilla was originally commanded by the U-boat School, and on 1 July 40 was renamed 21st U-boat Flotilla. Disbanded Mar 45.
Commander:
Kptlt. Beduhn Nov 37–Mar 40

K.Kapt. Buechel Mar 40–Jun 43
K.Kapt. Schuhart Jun 43–Sept 44
Kptlt. Collmann (Herwig) Sept 44–Mar 45

### 2nd U-boat Training Division
The formation of the 2nd U-boat Training Division was ordered in Jun 40. Teaching began in Nov 40 at Gotenhafen, where the Division was disbanded in Jan–Feb 45.

### Commander:
F.Kapt. Hartmann (Wemer) Nov 40–Nov 41
F.Kapt. Hashagen (Ernst) Dec 41–Nov 43
K.Kapt. Ambrosius (Wilhelm) Oct 43–Feb 44
Kapt.z.S. Neitzel Jan 44–Jan 45

### Chief of Staff
K.Kapt.(Ing.) Looschen Nov 40 –Dec 41
K.Kapt.(Ing.) Bahn Dec 41–Jan 43
(no further appointment was made)

Boat (paid off): U103 Jan.44–Apr 45

### 1st Detachment
Commander:
K.Kapt. Ambrosius (Wilhelm) Oct 40–Feb 44
K.Kapt. Bleichrodt Feb–July 44
K.Kapt. Mueller-Edzards July–Nov 44
K.Kapt. MuellerArnecke Dec 44–Jan 45
K.Kapt. Zahn Jan–Mar 45

### 2nd Detachment
Commander:
K.Kapt.(Ing.) Schmidt (Heinrich) Dec 40–Dec 41
K.Kapt.(Ing.) Looschen Dec 41–Feb 43
K.Kapt.(Ing.) Bahn Jan–Oct 43
K.Kapt. Bahn Jan–Dec 44
K.Kapt.(Ing.) Rohweder Dec 44–Feb 45

### 3rd U-boat Training Division
HQ Neustadt. Established Sep–Oct 43

### Commander:
F.Kapt.(Ing.) Schmidt (Heinrich) Sept 43–End

### Chief of Staff
K.Kapt.(Ing.) Frhr. vo. Engelhardt-Bergshof Oct 43–Feb 44
Kptlt.(Ing.) Subklew Feb 44–End
Boats (all paid off): U48, U52 Oct 43–May 45; U738 Mar 44 until broken up

### 1st Detachment
Commander:
K.Kapt.(Ing.) Bahn Oct 43–Feb 44
K.Kapt.(Ing.) Schulze (Paul) Feb 44–End

### 2nd Detachment
Commander:
K.Kapt.(Ing.) Miller Nov 43–Jan 44

K.Kapt.(Ing.) Frhr. von. Engelhardt-Bergshof Feb 44–Feb 45
Kptlt.(Ing.) Subklew Feb 45–End

### 4th U-boat Training Division
HQ Memel. Established Feb 44 and partially operational in Latvia. Disbanded Nov 44.

### Commander:
K.Kapt.(Ing.) Miller Feb–Nov 44
Boat (paid off): *U29* Apr–Aug 44 (used as target)

### 1st U-boat Training Battalion
HQ Plön. Established as U-boat Training Battalion in Feb 40, and as 1st U-boat Training battalion from Apr 40.

### Commander:
F.Kapt. Rose (Hans) Feb–May 40
F.Kapt. Schmidt (Albrecht) Jun 40–Nov 41
Kapt.z.S. Zechlin Nov 41–Apr 43
F.Kapt. Schuenemann July 43–Feb 45
F.Kapt. Pauckstadt Feb 45–End

### 2nd U-boat Training Battalion
HQ Neustad, then transferred to Zeven/Hanover. Established April 1941.

### Commander:
F.Kapt. Kastenbauer Apr–Nov 41
F.Kapt. Schuenemann Nov 41–July 43
Kapt.z.S.(Ing.) Zerpka July 43–Mar 45
K.Kapt. Michel Mar 45– End

### 3rd U-boat Training Battalion
HQ Pillau, until moved Jun 44 Schleswig June 44

Established April 43

### Commander:
F.Kapt.(Ing.) Hohnwald Apr 43–End

### The scheme of training, 1943 onwards
Crews were under the command of HKU (Kiel) for their initial training, which dealt with seamanship. They were then transferred to the U-boat Training Divisions (and the two Training Flotillas, 21st and 22nd) where they received more basic training. They were then sent to the U-boat Training Battalions.

Crews and officers were then transferred to join their U-boats and came under the command of Commander, East (Danzig). There they were first trained at FlaK School VII at Schweinemünde in anti-aircraft weapons and gunnery (becoming increasingly important as a skill). They then moved to 19th Uflotilla at Pillau for harbour training and seamanship.

The next stop was the Training Group Front at Hela, where they began technical training for operating the boat as a fighting machine. The COs' torpedo course followed at 20th Uflotilla (Pillau) where they worked on pre-tactical torpedo training, followed by torpedo attack training at 25th or 26th Uflotillas (either at Libau or Pillau).

On to 27th Uflotilla at Gotenhafen for operational tactical training, and the whole crew and boat then went for a final shake-down to one of the front training Flotillas (4th, 5th, 8th, 31st or 32nd, based in Stettin, Kiel, Danzig, Wilhelmshaven, Hamburg, Wesermünde or Königsberg).

They were then transferred to the operational command under which they were to work (Commands West, North Sea/Arctic, etc.) and went, via replacement groups, to their operational flotilla.

## U-BOAT FLOTILLAS AND COMMAND ORGANISATIONS

| Flotilla Number | Command | Role |
|---|---|---|
| 1st | FdU West | Operational, Atlantic |
| 2nd | FdU West | Operational, Atlantic |
| 3rd | FdU West | Operational, Atlantic |
| 4th | FdU Ost Ausb | Training: crew training, mainly Type IX |
| 5th | FdU Ost Ausb | Training: Type VII crew training |
| 6th | FdU West | Training initially, then operational |
| 7th | FdU West | Operational, Atlantic |
| 8th | FdU Ost Ausb | Training: seamanship and operational |
| 9th | FdU West | Operational, Atlantic |
| 10th | FdU West | Operational, Atlantic |
| 11th | FdU Nor/West | Operational, Atlantic and Arctic |
| 12th | FdU West | Operational, Atlantic |
| 13th | FdU Nor/Arctic | Operational, Arctic |
| 14th | FdU Arctic | Operational, Arctic |
| 18th | FdU Ausb | Training: crew operational |
| 19th | FdU Ausb | Training: COs preparation, lookout and harbour training |
| 20th | FdU Ausb | Training: pre-tactical |
| 21st | HKU | Training: Flotilla to 1 U-boats training division |
| 22nd | HKU | Training: Flotilla to 2 U-boats training division |

| 23rd | FdU Italy | Operational, Mediterranean. Later became FdU Ausb |
| | | Training: COs torpedo and gunnery |
| 24th | FdU Ausb | Training: COs gunnery, later Sonar |
| 25th | FdU Ausb | Training: crew gunnery, theory |
| 26th | FdU Ausb | Training: crew gunnery, practical |
| 27th | FdU Ausb | Training: tactical |
| 29th | FdU Italy | Operational, Mediterranean |
| 30th | FdU Black Sea | Operational, Black Sea (Type II boats only), 31 |
| 31st | FdU Ost | Training: crew |
| 32nd | FdU Ost | Training: crew |
| 33rd | FdU West | Operational, Atlantic and Pacific |

| Commands | Location | Dates and notes |
| --- | --- | --- |
| BdU and BdU Ops | Sengwarden near Wilhelmshaven | Nov 1939 - Sep 1940 |
| | Paris, Blvd Suchet | Sep 1940 - Nov 1940 |
| | Kerneval, near Lorient | Nov 1940 - Mar 1942 |
| | Paris, Ave Maréchal Maunoury | Mar 1942 - Mar 1943 |
| | Berlin-Charlottenburg | Mar 1943 - Dec 1943 |
| | Bernau, Staff HQ | Dec 1943 - Feb 1945 |
| | Sengwarden | Feb 1945 - Apr 1945 |
| | Plön | Apr 1945 |
| | Flensburg-Mürwik | May 1945 |

| Operational | Location | Commanding: |
| --- | --- | --- |
| FdU West | Angers, France | 1,2,3,6,7,9, 10 and 12 Uflotillas |
| FdU Norway | Narvik, Norway | 11 and 13 Uflotillas |
| FdU Centre | Kiel | Various Schnorkel boats, May-August, 1944 |
| FdU Italy/Med | Rome then Toulon | 23 and 29 Uflotillas |
| Black Sea | Constanza | 30 Uflotilla |
| Baltic | Commander, Cruisers | 22 Uflotilla June-August 1941 |
| France | Lorient Fortress | remnants 2 Uflotilla (no boats) |
| France | St Nazaire | non-operational boats, 6 Uflotilla |
| FdU West | Bergen From Aug 44. | 11,33 and (non-operational) 15 Uflotilla |
| FdU Arctic | Narvik | 13 and 14 Uflotillas |
| Baltic | Admiral, Baltic | various Type VII boats,June 1944-March 1945 |
| East Asia | Malaya, Java, Japan | various Type IX boats |

| Training | | |
| --- | --- | --- |
| HKU | Kiel | 1-4 ULD., I-3UA. (Jan,1943 on) |
| FdU Ost | Baltic ports | 4, 5, 8, 31 and 32 Uflotillas |
| FdU Ausb | Gotenhafen | 18, 19, 20, 23, 24, 25, 26 and 27 Uflotillas. *AgruErnt. Erprobungsgruppe Uboote.* |

| Others | | |
| --- | --- | --- |
| UAK | Kiel | U-boats acceptance from the yards |
| Medicine | Carnac | |
| First Aid | Malente | |
| U-boats research | | October 1943 on. |

## OPERATIONAL STRENGTH ATLANTIC FLOTILLAS

These tables show the strengths of the U-boats in the Atlantic operating from French bases after the fall of France. Other boats were also operational, but these figures give a very good general picture of the number of U-boats actively engaged in the Battle of the Atlantic.

**1939**

| Flotilla | Jan | Feb | Mar | Apr | May | June | July | Aug | Sep | Oct | Nov | Dec |
| --- | --- | --- | --- | --- | --- | --- | --- | --- | --- | --- | --- | --- |
| Weddigen | | | | | | | | | 7 | 7 | 7 | 7 |
| Saltzweldel | | | | | | | | | 11 | 11 | 10 | 10 |

| Fotilla No | Jan | Feb | Mar | Apr | May | June | July | Aug | Sep | Oct | Nov | Dec |
|---|---|---|---|---|---|---|---|---|---|---|---|---|
| Lohs | | | | | | | | | 7 | 3 | 2 | 2 |
| Emsmann | | | | | | | | | 6 | 6 | 6 | 6 |
| Hundius | | | | | | | | | 7 | 5 | 5 | 5 |
| Wegener | | | | | | | | | 10 | 9 | 11 | 12 |
| Total | | | | | | | | | 48 | 41 | 41 | 42 |

**1940**

| Flotilla No | Jan | Feb | Mar | Apr | May | June | July | Aug | Sep | Oct | Nov | Dec |
|---|---|---|---|---|---|---|---|---|---|---|---|---|
| 1 | 16 | 15 | 14 | 13 | 11 | 10 | 11 | 13 | 13 | 12 | 12 | 2 |
| 2 | 15 | 14 | 15 | 14 | 15 | 15 | 15 | 15 | 16 | 17 | 14 | 15 |
| 7 | 11 | 9 | 10 | 10 | 11 | 10 | 11 | 12 | 15 | 17 | 19 | 24 |
| Total | 42 | 38 | 39 | 37 | 37 | 35 | 37 | 40 | 44 | 46 | 45 | 41 |

**1941**

| Flotilla No | Jan | Feb | Mar | Apr | May | June | July | Aug | Sep | Oct | Nov | Dec |
|---|---|---|---|---|---|---|---|---|---|---|---|---|
| 1 | 3 | 11 | 19 | 27 | 26 | 24 | 23 | 22 | 24 | 21 | 20 | 14 |
| 2 | 17 | 18 | 19 | 19 | 20 | 21 | 23 | 25 | 24 | 24 | 24 | 24 |
| 3 | | 1 | 1 | 8 | 23 | 26 | 26 | 25 | 23 | 22 | 21 | 16 |
| 6 | | | | | | | | 6 | 12 | 20 | 21 | 23 |
| 7 | 26 | 26 | 20 | 19 | 18 | 22 | 24 | 24 | 25 | 24 | 23 | 19 |
| Total | 46 | 56 | 59 | 73 | 87 | 93 | 96 | 102 | 108 | 111 | 109 | 94 |

**1942**

| Flotilla No | Jan | Feb | Mar | Apr | May | June | July | Aug | Sep | Oct | Nov | Dec |
|---|---|---|---|---|---|---|---|---|---|---|---|---|
| 1 | 16 | 17 | 17 | 17 | 16 | 16 | 16 | 16 | 19 | 15 | 16 | 19 |
| 2 | 24 | 26 | 27 | 27 | 28 | 29 | 26 | 26 | 24 | 28 | 28 | 28 |
| 3 | 16 | 15 | 19 | 18 | 17 | 15 | 16 | 16 | 20 | 24 | 22 | 21 |
| 6 | 23 | 25 | 21 | 21 | 22 | 11 | 10 | 12 | 14 | 16 | 17 | 17 |
| 7 | 19 | 18 | 21 | 19 | 21 | 19 | 17 | 15 | 20 | 24 | 22 | 22 |
| 9 | | | | 1 | 4 | 5 | 6 | 13 | 19 | 19 | 19 | 17 |
| 10 | | 4 | 4 | 7 | 8 | 10 | 17 | 23 | 31 | 22 | 21 | 23 |
| 12 | | | | | | | | | | 1 | 9 | 11 |
| Total | 98 | 105 | 109 | 119 | 116 | 105 | 108 | 121 | 147 | 149 | 154 | 158 |

**1943**

| Flotilla No | Jan | Feb | Mar | Apr | May | June | July | Aug | Sep | Oct | Nov | Dec |
|---|---|---|---|---|---|---|---|---|---|---|---|---|
| 1 | 21 | 21 | 23 | 22 | 21 | 20 | 19 | 21 | 20 | 14 | 14 | 18 |
| 2 | 27 | 26 | 25 | 25 | 22 | 22 | 19 | 18 | 17 | 16 | 16 | 17 |
| 3 | 23 | 23 | 22 | 20 | 20 | 22 | 21 | 21 | 19 | 19 | 20 | 16 |
| 6 | 19 | 19 | 24 | 25 | 24 | 25 | 22 | 22 | 21 | 21 | 17 | 19 |
| 7 | 23 | 24 | 24 | 23 | 21 | 22 | 19 | 20 | 18 | 20 | 21 | 22 |
| 9 | 18 | 21 | 25 | 25 | 20 | 21 | 17 | 17 | 17 | 14 | 17 | 15 |
| 10 | 25 | 27 | 26 | 24 | 22 | 23 | 16 | 14 | 13 | 13 | 14 | 14 |
| 11 | 12 | 13 | 15 | 18 | 18 | 16 | 13 | 12 | 11 | 14 | 11 | 12 |
| Total | 168 | 174 | 184 | 182 | 168 | 171 | 146 | 145 | 136 | 131 | 130 | 133 |

(1943 Figures do not include 11th or 33rd UFlotillas as their boats were not solely operational in the Atlantic.)

**1944**

| Flotilla No | Jan | Feb | Mar | Apr | May | June | July | Aug | Sep | Oct | Nov | Dec |
|---|---|---|---|---|---|---|---|---|---|---|---|---|
| 1 | 16 | 14 | 13 | 14 | 11 | 12 | 7 | 8 | 3 | | | |
| 2 | 17 | 17 | 16 | 15 | 15 | 14 | 12 | 11 | 4 | | | |
| 3 | 13 | 11 | 13 | 15 | 13 | 11 | 7 | 11 | 6 | | | |
| 6 | 16 | 12 | 15 | 16 | 15 | 15 | 10 | 5 | 4 | | | |
| 7 | 21 | 17 | 15 | 11 | 12 | 13 | 9 | 10 | 6 | 1 | | |
| 9 | 16 | 14 | 13 | 15 | 11 | 14 | 11 | 14 | 8 | | | |
| 10 | 16 | 17 | 17 | 17 | 15 | 16 | 17 | 16 | 6 | 1 | | |
| 11 | 15 | 14 | 10 | 13 | 15 | 14 | 14 | 12 | 11 | | | |
| Total | 130 | 116 | 112 | 116 | 107 | 109 | 87 | 87 | 48 | 2 | | |

(Operations in the Atlantic were carried on increasingly by 11th UFlotilla with 33rd UFlotilla, but operations after the D-Day landings waned to insignificance.)

## THE U-BOAT BUILDING PROGRAMME

U-boats commissioned into the Navy, analysed by Year, Yard and Type. The list does not include experimental boats (such as Type VXVII) nor the mini-boats (such as Biber, Molch etc).

| Type | Yard | 1935 | 1936 | 1937 | 1938 | 1939 | 1940 | 1941 | 1942 | 1943 | 1944 | 1945 |
|---|---|---|---|---|---|---|---|---|---|---|---|---|
| IA | Deschimag | 2 | | | | | | | | | | |
| IIA | Deutsche Werke | 6 | | | | | | | | | | |
| IIB | Deutsche Werke | 3 | | | | | | | | | | |
| | Germaniawerft | 7 | 7 | | | | | | | | | |
| | Flender-werft, Lübeck | | | | | 2 | | | | | | |
| IIC | Deutsche Werke | | | 2 | 5 | 1 | | | | | | |
| IID | Deutsche Werke | | | | | 14 | 2 | | | | | |
| VII | Germaniawerft | | | 4 | | | | | | | | |
| | Deschimag | 5 | 1 | | | | | | | | | |
| VIIB | Germaniawerft | | | | 4 | 7 | 4 | | | | | |
| | Flender-werft, Lübeck | | | | | | | | 5 | | | |
| | Bremer-Vulkan | | | | | 4 | | | | | | |
| VIIC | Deutsche Werke | | | | | 6 | 5 | 13 | 3 | | | |
| | Germaniawerft | | | | | 9 | 10 | 16 | 14 | 9 | | |
| | Flender-werft, Lübeck | | | | | | 3 | 10 | 10 | | | |
| | B&V and Schichau | | | | | 3 | 57 | 69 | 63 | 13 | | |
| | Danzigerwerft | | | | | | 8 | 12 | 12 | | | |
| | Bremer Vulcan | | | | | | 17 | 21 | 14 | | | |
| | Howaldt. Kiel | | | | | | 10 | 8 | 9 | 4 | | |
| | Howaldt, Hamburg | | | | | | 6 | 5 | 9 | 7 | | |
| | Flensburger | | | | | | 5 | 6 | 8 | 1 | | |
| | Neptun, Rostock | | | | | | | | 5 | 3 | | |
| | Stettiner-Oderwerke | | | | | | | | 1 | 1 | | |
| | Nordseewerke, Emden | | | | | | 5 | 6 | 10 | 5 | | |
| VIC/41 | Germaniawerft | | | | | | | | | 3 | | |
| | Flender-werke, Lübeck | | | | | | | | 4 | 8 | | |
| | Blohm & Voss | | | | | | | | 10 | 17 | 1 | |
| | Schichau | | | | | | | | | | 2 | |
| | Danziger Werft | | | | | | | | 5 | 5 | | |
| | Bremer-Vulkan | | | | | | | | 9 | 9 | | |
| | Flensburger | | | | | | | | | 7 | 1 | |
| | Neptun | | | | | | | | | | 2 | |
| | Nordseewerke, Emden | | | | | | | | | 2 | | |
| VIID | Germaniawerft | | | | | | 4 | 2 | | | | |
| | Germaniawerft | | | | | | | | 4 | | | |
| IX | Deschimag | | | 3 | 5 | | | | | | | |
| IXB | Deschimag | | . | | 1 | 13 | | | | | | |
| XC | Deschimag | | | | | 24 | | | | | | |
| | Deutsche Werke | | | | | 12. | 12 | | | | | |
| | Seebeck | | | | | | 4 | 2 | | | | |
| IXC/40 | Deschimag | | | | | | 11 | 17 | 8 | | | |
| | Seebeck | | | | | | | 3 | 5 | 2 | | |
| | Deutsche Werke | | | | | | 11 | 23 | 7 | | | |
| IXD2 | Deschimag | | | | | | 12 | 12 | 6 | | | |
| IXD/42 | Deschimag | | | | | | | | | 1 | | |
| XB | Germaniawerft | | | | | | 3 | 2 | 2 | 1 | | |
| XIV | DW Kiel | | | | | | | 2 | 5 | 3 | | |
| XXI | Deschimag | | | | | | | | | 17 | 23 | |
| | Blohm & Voss | | | | | | | | | 28 | 21 | |
| | Schichau | | | | | | | | | | 19 | 11 |
| XXIII | Germaniawerft | | | | | | | | | 2 | 11 | |
| | Deutsche Werft | | | | | | | | | 29 | 20 | |

## TYPE TOTALS BY YEAR AND SUM TOTALS

| Type | 1935 | 1936 | 1937 | 1938 | 1939 | 1940 | 1941 | 1942 | 1943 | 1944 | 1945 |
|---|---|---|---|---|---|---|---|---|---|---|---|
| IA | | 2 | | | | | | | | | |
| Type total: 2 | | | | | | | | | | | |
| IIA | 6 | | | | | | | | | | |
| IIB | 8 | 10 | | | | 2 | | | | | |
| IIC | | | | 2 | 5 | 1 | | | | | |
| IID | | | | | | 14 | 2 | | | | |
| Type total: 50 | | | | | | | | | | | |
| VII | | 9 | 1 | | | | | | | | |
| VIIB | | | | 4 | 7 | 8 | 5 | | | | |
| VIIC | | | | | | 12 | 141 | 176 | 216 | 110 | 2 |
| VIID | | | | | | | 4 | 2 | 4 | | |
| Type Total: 667 | | | | | | | | | | | |
| IX | | | | 3 | 5 | | | | | | |
| IXB | | | | | 1 | 13 | | | | | |
| IXC | | | | | | | 40 | 14 | | | |
| IXC/40 | | | | | | | | 25 | 45 | 17 | |
| IXD2 | | | | | | | | 12 | 12 | 6 | |
| IXD/42 | | | | | | | | | | | 1 |
| Type Total: 124 | | | | | | | | | | | |
| XB | | | | | | | 3 | 2 | 2 | 1 | |
| Type Total: 8 | | | | | | | | | | | |
| XIV | | | | | | | | 2 | 5 | 3 | |
| Type Total: 10 | | | | | | | | | | | |
| XXI | | | | | | | | | | 64 | 55 |
| Type Total: 119 | | | | | | | | | | | |
| XXIII | | | | | | | | | | 31 | 31 |
| Type Total: 62 | | | | | | | | | | | |
| Annual Totals | 14 | 21 | 1 | 9 | 18 | 50 | 197 | 236 | 282 | 229 | 89 |
| Grand Total 1,146 | | | | | | | | | | | |

## U-BOATS COMMISSIONED AND LOST – MONTHLY

**1939**
Boats in commission at 1.9.1939
(in order of commission):
(1935) U1, 2, 7, 3, 4, 5, 8, 9, 6,
10, 11. 12,13, 17
(1936) U14, 18, 19, 20, 15, 25,
26, 16, 33, 21, 22, 27, 23, 28, 34,
24, 30, 29, 35, 31, 36
(1937) U32
(1938) U45, 51, 37, 38, 56, 46,
57, 47, 39
(1939 to August) U58, 59, 40, 52,
48, 41, 53, 60, 42, 61, 49, 43
Strength: 57

**September**
Commissioned: U54, UA
Lost: U27, 39
Strength: 57

**October**
Commissioned:
Lost: U 12,16,40,42,45
Strength: 52

**November**
Commissioned: U55, 44
Lost: U35
Strength: 53

**December**
Commissioned: U50, 62, 64.
Lost: U36
Strength: 55

**1940**
**January**
Commissioned: U63
Lost: U15, 55
Strength: 54

**February**
Commissioned: U65
Lost:U33, 41, 53, 54, 63
Strength: 50

**March**
Commissioned: U70, 122
Lost: U21®, 22, 31®, 44
Strength: 48

**April**

**Commissioned: U69, 102, 120**
Lost: U1, 49, 50, 64
Strength: 47

**May**
Commissioned: U71, 121,123
Lost: U13
Strength: 49

**June**
Commissioned: U124, 137, 138
Lost: U102, 122
Strength: 50

**July**
Commissioned: U93, 103, 139
Lost: U26
Strength: 52

**August**
Commissioned: U94, 95, 104,
140, 141
Lost: U25, 51
Strength: 55

**September**

Commissioned: U73, 96, 97, 105, 106, 142, 143
Lost: U57
Strength: 61

## October
Commissioned: U74, 98, 107, 108, 144, 145, 146
Lost: U32
Strength: 67

## November
Commissioned: U99, 100, 110, 149, 150, 551
Lost: U31,104
Strength: 71

## December
Commissioned: U75,76, 101, 109, 111, 147, 148, 552, 553
Lost:
Strength: 80

## 1941
### January
Commissioned: U66, 67, 72, 77, 150, 152, 201, 554, 555, 751
Lost:
Strength: 88

## February
Commissioned: U68, 78, 83, 203, 556, 557, 558, 559, 651
Lost:
Strength: 96

## March
Commissioned: U79, 125, 126, 202, 204, 331, 371, 560, 561, 562, 563
Lost: U47, 70, 99, 100, 551
Strength: 102

## April
Commissioned: U80, 81, 84, 127, 372, 401, 431, 432, 501, 564, 565, 566, 567, 652
Lost: U65,76
Strength: 114

## May
Commissioned: U82, 128, 129, 132, 205, 206, 373,402, 433, 451, 452, 502, 568, 569, 570, 571, 572, 653, 752
Lost: U110
Strength: 132

## June
Commissioned: U85, 130, 207,

332, 351, 374, 403, 434, 453, 573, 574, 575, 576, 753
Lost: U138, 147, 556, 651
Strength: 142

## July
Commissioned: U86, 116, 131, 133, 134, 153, 161, 208, 375, 454, 503, 504, 577, 578, 579, 580, 581, 654,701
Lost:
Strength: 159

## August
Commissioned: U87, 135, 136, 154, 155, 213, 333, 352, 376, 404, 435, 455, 505, 582, 583, 584, 585, 655,754
Lost: U144, 401, 452, 570
Strength: 174

## September
Commissioned: U156, 157, 158, 162, 251, 405, 436, 456, 506, 586, 587, 588, 589, 656, 702
Lost: U207, 501
Strength: 187

## October
Commissioned: U88, 117, 159, 160, 163, 171, 209, 252, 253, 334, 355, 377, 378, 406, 437, 507, 508, 590, 591, 592, 593, 594, 657, 703
Lost: U111, 204
Strength: 209

## November
Commissioned: U89, 164, 172, 173, 174, 214, 215, 254, 255, 379, 408, 438, 457, 459, 509, 510, 595, 596, 597, 598, 658, 704, 755
Lost: U95, 206, 433, 560, 580, 583
Strength: 226

## December
Commissioned: U90, 118, 175, 176, 216, 256, 335, 356, 380, 407, 439, 458, 460, 511, 512, 599, 600, 601, 602, 659, 705, 756
Lost: U75, 79, 127, 131, 208, 434, 451, 557, 567, 574

Strength: 238

## 1942
### January
Commissioned: U91, 217, 218, 257, 409, 440, 461, 513, 514, 603, 604, 605, 606, 607 660

Lost: U93, 374, 577
Strength: 250

## February
Commissioned: U165, 178, 210, 258, 259, 336, 381, 410, 441, 515, 608, 609, 610, 611, 661, 757
Lost: U82, 581
Strength: 264

## March
Commissioned: U92, 166, 177, 179, 211, 260, 261, 353, 411, 442, 462, 516, 517, 612, 613, 614, 615, 706
Lost: U133, 503, 585, 587, 655, 656
Strength: 276

## April
Commissioned: U119, 183, 212, 262, 354, 382, 412, 443, 463, 464, 518, 616, 617, 618, 619, 620, 662
Lost: U85, 252, 702
Strength: 290

## May
Commissioned: U180, 181, 184, 221, 222, 263, 264, 301, 337, 444, 445, 465, 519, 520, 621, 622, 623, 624, 63, 758
Lost: U74, 352, 568, 573
Strength: 306

## June
Commissioned: U182, 185, 223, 224, 265, 266, 302, 338, 357, 383, 413, 446, 466, 521, 522, 523, 625, 626, 627, 628, 664
Lost: U157, 158, 652
Strength: 324

## July
Commissioned: U167, 186, 187, 225, 267, 268, 303, 384, 414, 447, 467, 524, 525, 629, 630, 631, 632, 633, 665, 707, 708
Lost: U90, 136, 153, 213, 215, 502, 576, 588, 701, 751, 754
Strength: 334

## August
Commissioned: U188, 189, 226, 227, 269, 304, 339, 358, 385, 415,448, 449, 468,-526, 634, 635, 636, 637, 666, 709
Lost: U94, 166, 210, 335, 372, 379, 464, 578, 654
Strength: 345

**September**
Commissioned: U168, 190, 195,
196, 228, 270, 271, 305, 417, 450,
527, 528, 529, 638, 639, 640, 641,
710, 711
Lost: U88, 162, 165, 222, 253,
261, 446, 457, 589, 705, 756
Strength: 353

**October**
Commissioned: U191, 197, 229,
230, 272, 273, 306, 340, 359, 386,
418, 469, 530, 531, 642, 643, 644,
645, 646, 667, 731,732,760
Lost: U116, 171, 179, 216, 353,
412, 512, 520, 559, 582, 597, 599,
619, 627, 658, 661
Strength: 360

**November**
Commissioned: U169, 192, 198,
199, 231, 232, 274, 275, 307, 341,
360, 387, 416, 419, 532, 533, 647,
648, 649, 650, 668, 712, 733, UF2
Lost: U98, 132, 173, 184, 259,
272, 331, 408, 411, 517, 595, 605,
660
Strength: 371

**December**
Commissioned: U193, 200, 219,
235, 276, 277, 308, 361, 388, 420,
487, 534, 535, 669, 713, 734, 735,
761, 951, 952, 953, 954, 955
Lost: U254, 356, 357, 611, 626
Strength: 389

**1943**
**January**
Commissioned: U170, 194, 236,
237, 278, 309, 342, 421, 470, 536,
537, 670, 736, 737, 762, 847, 956,
957, 958, 959, 960
Lost: U164, 224, 301, 337, 507, 553
Strength: 404

**February**
Commissioned: U238, 279, 280,
281, 310, 343, 362, 389, 422, 488,
538, 539, 714, 738, 763, 841, 848,
961, 962, 963, 964,965
Lost: U69, 187, 201, 205, 225,
265, 268, 442, 443, 519, 44 , 522,
529, 562, 606, 609, 620, 623, 624,
649
Strength: 407

**March**
Commissioned: U220, 239, 282,
283, 311, 344, 363, 390, 423, 489,

490, 540, 541, 542, 543, 671, 718,
739, 740, 763, 801, 842, 843, 849,
966, 967, 968, 969, 970
Lost: U5, 77, 83, 87, 130, 156,
163, 169, 384, 416®, 432, 444,
469, 524, 633, 665
Strength: 420

**April**
Commissioned: U240, 284, 312,
391, 424, 425, 542, 543, 544, 545,
672, 716, 741, 844, 850, 971, 972,
973, 974, 975
Lost: U124, 167, 174, 175, 189,
191, 203, 227, 376, 526, 602, 632,
635, 644, 710
Strength: 425

**May**
Commissioned: U285, 313, 345,
364, 392, 426, 471, 472, 546, 547,
548, 673, 717, 742, 743, 764, 845,
846, 851, 852, 921, 976, 977, 978,
979, 980, 1060, 1089
Lost: U89, 109, 125, 128, 176,
182, 186, 192,209, 235®, 258,
266, 273, 303, 304, 332, 381, 414,
436, 438, 439, 440, 447, 456, 463,
465, 467, 528, 531, 563, 569, 630,
638, 640, 646, 657, 659, 663, 752,
753, 755,954
Strength: 411

**June**
Commissioned: U286, 288, 314,
346, 365, 427, 428, 473, 546, 547,
548, 674, 718, 744, 745, 765, 802,
852,853, 981, 982, 983, 984, 985,
1062
Lost: U97, 105, 118, 119, 194,
200, 202, 217, 308, 334, 388, 417,
418, 449, 521, 564, 594
Strength 419

**July**
Commissioned: U41, 289, 290,
315, 347, 366, 393, 429, 475, 476,
549, 550, 675, 719, 746, 747, 748,
766, 854, 859, 986, 987, 988, 989,
990, 991
Lost: U43, 67, 126, 135, 159, 160,
199, 232, 359, 375, 404, 409, 435,
459, 461, 462, 487, 504, 506, 509,
513, 514, 527, 535, 558, 561, 590,
591, 598, 607, 613, 614, 622, 628,
662, 759, 951
Strength: 408

**August**
Commissioned: U242, 291, 292,

316, 348, 367, 394, 430, 477, 676,
749, 750, 855, 856, 860, 922, 992,
993, 1061, 1161, 1221
Lost: U34, 84, 106, 117, 134, 185,
197, 383, 403, 454, 458,468, 489,
523, 525, 572, 604, 615, 634, 639,
647, 64, 670, 706, 847
Strength: 404

**September**
Commissioned: U233, 287, 293,
349, 478, 677, 720, 767, 803, 857,
858, 861, 903, 904, 994, 995, 997,
1162, 1191, 1192, 1222
Lost: U34, 161, 221, 229, 338,
341, 346, 617, 669, 760, 983
Strength: 414

**October**
Commissioned: U243, 244, 247,
294, 295, 317, 350, 369, 396, 479,
480, 678, 768, 821, 862, 865, 923,
998, 999, 1163, 1164, 1193, 1194,
1223, 1224,UIT21,UIT22
Lost: U220,274, 279, 282, 306,
336, 378, 389, 402, 419, 420, 422,
431, 460, 470, 533, 540, 566, 584,
610, 631, 643, 732, 841, 844, 964
Strength: 415

**November**
Commissioned: U248, 249, 296,
297, 318, 370, 397, 481, 679, 721,
771, 792t, 794t, 863, 866, 924,
1000, 1001, 1002, 1101,
1165,1195, 1196, 1225, 1226
Lost: U86, 211, 226, 280, 340,
405, 508, 536, 538, 542, 600, 648,
707, 718, 768, 842, 848, 849, 966
Strength: 421

**December**
Commissioned: U245, 250, 298,
299, 300, 319, 320, 398, 482, 483,
680, 722, 772, 804, 864, 867, 868,
925, 1003, 1004, 1005, 1166,
1167, 1197, 1198, 1199, 1227,
1228
Lost: U73, 172, 284, 345®, 391,
593, 645, 850
Strength: 441

**1944**
**January**
Commissioned: U246, 321, 368,
399, 484, 773, 869, 871, 1006,
1007, 1052, 1103, 1168, 1200,
1201, 1202, 1229, 1230, 1271,
1272
Lost: U81, 231, 263, 271, 305,

314, 364, 377, 426, 544, 571, 592, 641, 751, 972, UIT 19
Strength: 445

## February
Commissioned: U322, 485, 681, 774, 805, 870, 872, 926, 1008, 1009, 1010, 1053, 1102, 1169, 1203, 1204, 1231, 1273, 1301
Lost: U7, 91, 177, 238, 257, 264, 283, 386, 406, 424, 545, 601, 666, 713, 734, 738, 761, 762, 854, UIT 23
Strength: 444

## March
Commissioned: 1J234, 323, 400, 486, 775, 873, 877, 905, 1013, 1014, 1015, 1051, 1054, 1104, 1170, 1171, 1205, 1206, 1207, 1232, 1233, 1274, 1275
Lost: U28, 223, 343, 358, 366, 380, 392, 410, 450, 472, 575, 603, 625, 653, 709, 744, 801, 845, 851, 961, 973, 976, 1013, 1059, UIT 22
Strength: 442

## April
Commssioned: U324, 682, 776, 793t, 795t, 806, 874, 875, 878, 879, 901, 1016, 1017, 1018, 1055, 1056, 1172, 1208, 1209, 1210, 1234, 1276, 1303
Lost: U2, 68, 108®, 193, 288, 302, 311, 342, 355, 360, 421, 448, 455, 488, 515, 550, 803, 856, 962, 974986, UIT 4®, UIT 5
Strength: 442

## May
Commissioned: U325, 683, 777, 825, 826, 827, 876, 880, 881, 907, 1019, 1020, 1021, 1057, 1131, 1235, 1277, 1278, 1302
Lost: U66, 240, 241, 277, 289, 292, 371, 453, 473, 476, 549, 616,674, 675, 731, 765, 846, 852, 959, 960, 990, 1015, 1234
Strength: 438

## June
Commissioned: U326, 828, 927, 1022, 1023, 1024, 1058, 1105, 1132, 2501, 2321
Lost: U123, 269, 317, 373, 423, 441, 477, 478, 490, 505, 629, 715, 719, 740, 767, 821, 860, 955, 970, 971, 980, 987, 988, 998, 1191, 1225
Strength: 423

## July
Commissioned: U327, 778, 822, 906, 928, 1063, 1064, 1106, 1279, 2322, 2323, 2324, 2502, 3001, 3501
Lost: U129, 154, 212, 214, 233, 239, 243, 250, 319, 333, 347, 361, 390, 415, 543, 586, 642, 672, 678, 742, 872, 1164, 1166, 1222, 2323
Strength: 413

## August
Commissioned: U779, 889, 1107, 1109, 2325, 2326, 2327, 2328, 2503, 2504, 2506, 3002, 3003, 3004, 3502
Lost: U3, 4, 6, 9, 18, 24, 107, 178, 180, 188, 198, 230, 270, 344, 354, 385, 413, 445, 466, 471, 608, 618, 621, 667, 671, 736, 741, 766, 952, 967, 969, 981, 984, 996y 1000, 1166, 1196, 1229, UIT 21
Strength: 389

## September
Commissioned: U328, 929, 1065, 11 10, 1304, 1305, 2329, 2330, 2331, 2334, 2335, 2336, 2507, 2508, 2509, 2510, 2511, 3005, 3503, 3504
Lost: U19, 20, 23, 247, 362, 394, 407, 484, 565, 576, 596,703, 743, 855, 859, 863, 865, 867, 871, 921, 925, 1062, 3509, UIT 1, UIT 15, UIT 16, UIT 20
Strength: 382

## October
Commissioned: U329, 2337, 2338, 2340, 2341, 2512, 2513, 2515, 2516, 2517, 3006, 3007, 3008, 3505, 3507
Lost: U92, 116, 168, 228, 437, 673, 777, 957, 993, 1006, 1060, 1226, 2331
Strength: 384

## November
Commissioned: U1108, 1307, 2332, 2339, 2342, 2343, 2344, 2345, 2346, 2505, 2518, 2519, 2520, 2521, 2522, 3009, 3010, 3013, 3508, 3509, 3510, 3511, 3512
Lost: U80, 196, 322, 537, 771, 1200
Strength: 401

## December
Commissioned: U930, 1306, 2333, 2347, 2348, 2349, 2350, 2351, 2514, 2523, 2525, 2526, 2527, 2528, 2530, 3011, 3012, 3014, 3015, 3019, 3020, 3506, 3513, 3514, 3515, 3516, 3517, 3518
Lost: U297, 365, 387, 400, 416, 479, 547, 735, 737, 772, 877,906,908,1209,2342,2532@
Strength: 413

## 1945
### January
Commissioned: U1308, 2352, 2353, 2354, 2355, 2356, 2357, 2358, 2359, 2360, 2524, 2531, 2533, 2534, 2535, 2536, 3016, 3017, 3018, 3021, 3022, 3023, 3024, 3025, 3026, 3027, 3028, 3519, 3520, 3521, 3522, 3523, 3524, 3525, 4701, 4702, 4703
Lost: U248, 382, 482, 650, 679, 763, 1020, 1051, 1172, 1199, 2523, 3520
Strength: 438

## February
Commissioned: U1406, 2361, 2362, 2363, 2364, 2538, 2539, 2540, 3029, 3030, 3031, 3032, 3033, 3036, 3528, 4705, 4706,4707
Lost: U300, 309, 327, 425, 480, 676, 745, 864, 869, 923, 927, 989, 1014, 1018, 1053, 1208, 1273, 1278, 1279, 2344, 3007
Strength: 435

## March
Commissioned: U883, 1407, 2365, 2366, 2367, 2369, 2537, 2541, 2542, 2543, 2544, 2545, 2548, 3034, 3035, 3037, 3038, 3039, 3040, 3041, 3044, 3526, 3527, 3529, 3530, 4704, 4709, 4711
Lost: U72, 96, 246, 260, 275, 296, 329, 348, 350, 367, 399, 429, 430, 681, 682, 683, 714, 722, 758, 866, 870, 905, 965, 1003, 1021, 1106, 1161, 1302, 2340, 2515, 2530, 3508, 3519
Strength: 430

## April
Commissioned: U2368,370, 2371, 2546, 2551, 2552, 4712
Lost: U56, 78, 103, 183, 235, 237, 242, 251, 285, 286, 307, 321, 325, 326, 396, 486, 518, 546, 548, 636, 677, 747, 749, 774, 804, 843, 857, 878, 879, 880,

982,1001,1017,1024,1055,1063,10
65,1107, 1131, 1169, 1195, 1206,
1221, 1223, 1227, 1235, 1274,
1276, 2509, 2514, 2516, 2537,
2542, 3003, 3036, 3512
Strength: 381

**May**
Commissioned: U4710
Lost: 382 U-boats.

End of hostilities.
1. All boats were either destroyed
by enemy action, or
2. scuttled by their crews or
others, or
3. sunk later in Operation 'Deadlight', or
4. taken as prizes by the victors, or
5. surrendered, and later
destroyed.

Boats taken by the victors may
have been subsequently scrapped,
although three were returned to
Germany, and now stand as
museum artifacts or memorials to
the dead.
Note: ® signifies that the boat was
raised, repaired and returned to
duty; t denotes Walter experimental boats.

## U-BOATS – CAUSE OF LOSS BY MONTH

**Allied Figures**

| 1939 | Sep | Oct | Nov | Dec |
|---|---|---|---|---|
| ESCORTS | I | I | I | |
| Sea | | | | |
| Carrier Sea | | | | |
| Carrier Air | | | | |
| Land Air | | | | |
| Sea/Land Air | | | | |
| Sea/Carrier Air | | | | |
| PATROLS | | | | |
| Sea | I | I | | |
| S/m ptl | | | | I |
| Carrier Sea | | | | |
| Carrier Air | | | | |
| Land Air | | | | |
| Sea/Land Air | | | | |
| Sea/Carrier Air | | | | |
| AIR SUPPORT | | | | |
| BAY AIR PTL | | | | |
| BOMBING | | | | |
| SCRAP, SCUTTLE, P/O | | | | |
| MINE | | 3 | | |
| ACCIDENT | | | | |
| UNKNOWN | | | | |
| | | | | |
| TOTAL LOST | 2 | 5 | I | I |

| 1940 | Jan | Feb | Mar | Apr | May | June | July | Aug | Sep | Oct | Nov | Dec |
|---|---|---|---|---|---|---|---|---|---|---|---|---|
| ESCORTS | | | | | | | | | | | | |
| Sea | | 2 | I | 2 | I | | | | | I | 2 | |
| Carrier Sea | | | | | | | | | | | | |
| Carrier Air | | | | | | | | | | | | |
| Land Air | | | | I | | | | | | | | |
| Sea/Land Air | | | | | | | | | | | | |
| Sea/Carrier Air | | | | | | | | | | | | |
| PATROLS | | | | | | | | | | | | |
| Sea | | 2 | | I | | | | | | | | |
| S/mptl | | | | | | | | I | | | | |
| Carrier Sea | | | | | | | | | | | | |
| Carrier Air | | | | | | | | | | | | |
| Land Air | | | | | | | | | | | | |
| Sea/Land Air | | | | | | | | | | | | |
| Sea/Carrier Air | | | | | | | | | | | | |
| AIR SUPPORT | | | | | | | | | | | | |
| BAY AIR PTL | | | | | | | | | | | | |
| BOMBING | | | I | | | | | | | | | |
| SCRAP, SCUTTLE, P/O | | | | | | | | | | | | |

## 1940

| 1940 | Jan | Feb | Mar | Apr | May | June | July | Aug | Sep | Oct | Nov | Dec |
|---|---|---|---|---|---|---|---|---|---|---|---|---|
| MINE | | | I | | | | | I | | | | |
| ACCIDENT | | | | | | | | | | | | |
| UNKNOWN | | | | | | | | | | | | |
| TOTAL LOST | 2 | 4 | 3 | 5 | I | 0 | 2 | 3 | 0 | I | 2 | 0 |

## 1941

| 1941 | Jan | Feb | Mar | Apr | May | June | July | Aug | Sep | Oct | Nov | Dec |
|---|---|---|---|---|---|---|---|---|---|---|---|---|
| ESCORTS Sea | | 5 | 2 | I | 3 | | | I | 2 | I | 5 | |
| Carrier Sea | | | | | | | | | | | | |
| Carrier Air | | | | | | | | | | | | |
| Land Air | | | | | | | | | | | | |
| Sea/Land Air | | | | | | I | | | | | | |
| Sea/Carrier Air | | | | | | | | | | | | |
| PATROLS | | | | | | | | | | | | |
| Sea | | | | | | I | | | | I | 2 | I |
| S/rn pd | | | | | | | | | | | | |
| Carrier Sea | | | | | | | | | | | | |
| Carrier Air | | | | | | | | | | | | |
| Land Air Sea/Land Air | | | | | | | | | | | | |
| Sea/Carrier Air | | | | | | | | | | | | |
| AIR SUPPORT | | | | | | I | | | | | | |
| BAY AIRPTL | | | | | 2 | I | I | I | | | | |
| BOMBING | | | | | | | | | | | | |
| SCRAP, SCUTTLE, P/O | | | | | | | | | | | | |
| MINE | | | I | | | | | | | | | |
| ACCIDENT | | | | | | I | I | | I | | | |
| UNKNOWN | | | | I | | | | | I | | | |
| TOTAL LOST | 0 | 5 | 2 | I | 4 | I | 3 | 2 | 2 | 5 | 10 | |

## 1942

| 1942 | Jan | Feb | Mar | Apr | May | June | July | Aug | Sep | Oct | Nov | Dec |
|---|---|---|---|---|---|---|---|---|---|---|---|---|
| ESCORTS | | | | | | | | | | | | |
| Sea | I | 2 | 3 | I | I | | 5 | 2 | 4 | 2 | 5 | 3 |
| Carrier Sea | | | | | | | | | | | | |
| Carrier Air | | | | | | | | | | I | | |
| Land Air | | 2 | | | | I | | 2 | I | 7 | 2 | 2 |
| Sea/Land Air | | | | | | I | I | | | | | |
| Sea/Carrier Air | | | | | | | | I | | | | |
| PATROLS | | | | | | | | | | | | |
| Sea | | | | | I | I | I | I | | | I | |
| S/rnptl | | I | | | | | | | I | | | |
| Carrier Sea | | | | | | | | | | | | |
| Carrier Air | | | | | | | | | | | | |
| Land Air | | I | | | | I | I | 2 | I | I | 2 | 4 |
| Sea/Land Air | | | | | I | | | I | | I | | |
| Sea/Carrier Air | | | | | | | | | | | | |
| AIR SUPPORT | | | | | | | | | | | | |
| BAY AIRPTL | | | | | | | 2 | I | I | I | | |
| BOMBING, SCRAP, SCUTTLE, P/O | | | | | | | | | | | | |
| MINE | | | | | I | | | | | 2 | I | |
| ACCIDENT | | | | | | | | I | I | | I | |
| UNKNOWN | | | | I | | | | | | I | | |
| TOTAL LOST | 3 | 2 | 6 | 3 | 4 | 3 | 11 | 10 | 11 | 16 | 13 | 5 |

## 1943

| 1943 | Jan | Feb | Mar | Apr | May | June | July | Aug | Sep | Oct | Nov | Dec |
|---|---|---|---|---|---|---|---|---|---|---|---|---|
| ESCORTS | | | | | | | | | | | | |
| Sea | I | 7 | 4 | 4 | 12 | 3 | 3 | 3 | I | 4 | 5 | 3 |
| Carrier Sea | | | | | | | | | | | | |
| Carrier Air | | | | I | 2 | 6 | 6 | | 5 | I | 2 | |
| Land Air | 3 | 6 | I | 4 | 9 | I | 7 | I | I | 8 | 3 | |
| Sea/Land Air | 2 | | | 4 | | | I | | I | | | |

## 1943

| | Jan | Feb | Mar | Apr | May | June | July | Aug | Sep | Oct | Nov | Dec |
|---|---|---|---|---|---|---|---|---|---|---|---|---|
| Sea/Carrier Air | | | I | I | | | | | | | | |
| PATROLS: | | | | | | | | | | | | |
| Sea | | | I | | | | 2 | 4 | | | I | 2 |
| S/mptl | | I | | | I | I | I | | I | | I | |
| Carrier Sea | | | | | | | | | | | | |
| Carrier Air | | | | | | | | | | | | |
| Land Air | | | | 6 | 2 | 3 | I | 4 | 4 | I | 2 | 2 |
| Sea/Land Air | | | | | | I | | I | | | | |
| Sea/Carrier Air | | | | | | | | | | | | |
| AIR SUPPORT | | | I | | | 3 | | | I | 3 | I | |
| BAY AIR PTL | | 2 | I | I | 6 | 2 | 12 | 5 | 2 | | 2 | I |
| NTransit Area Ptl | | | | | | I | | I | | | | |
| Gib Air Ptl | | | | | | | I | | | | | |
| Gib Air/Sea Ptl | | | | | | | | | | | | |
| BOMBING | | | | | | | I | | | | | I |
| SCRAP ,SCUTTLE, P/O | | | | | | | | | | | | |
| MINE | | | | | I | | | | | | | |
| ACCIDENT | I | I | I | | 2 | | | 2 | 2 | | 2 | |
| UNKNOWN | I | | I | I | I | | | I | | | | |
| TOTAL LOST | 7 | 19 | 15 | 15 | 41 | 17 | 37 | 25 | 9 | 26 | 19 | 8 |

## 1944

| | Jan | Feb | Mar | Apr | May | June | July | Aug | Sep | Oct | Nov | Dec |
|---|---|---|---|---|---|---|---|---|---|---|---|---|
| ESCORTS | | | | | | | | | | | | |
| Sea | 4 | 10 | 7 | 5 | 4 | I | 3 | 2 | 2 | | | 3 |
| Carrier Sea | | | | I | | | | | | | | |
| Carrier Air | I | I | 3 | 2 | 3 | | | I | I | | | I |
| Land Air | | I | I | | | | | | | | | |
| Sea/Land Air | | | | | I | | | | | | | |
| Sea/Carrier Air | | | I | 2 | I | | | I | I | | | |
| PATROLS | | | | | | | | | | | | |
| Sea | | I | | 2 | I | | 3 | 3 | 6 | 3 | I | I |
| S/mptl | | | I | | I | | I | | | I | I | 2 |
| Carrier Sea | | | | 2 | | | 2 | | | | | |
| Carrier Air | | | I | | | I | I | I | | | | |
| Land Air | | | I | I | | I | 7 | | 3 | I | I | |
| Sea/Land Air | | I | | | I | 3 | I | 3 | | | | |
| Sea/Carrier Air | | 2 | 3 | | I | 2 | | | | | | |
| AIR SUPPORT | 2 | 2 | | I | | | | | I | | | I |
| BAY AIR PTL | 2 | | I | I | | | 2 | | | | | |
| N Transit Area Ptl | | | | | 6 | 8 | 4 | | 2 | | I | |
| Gib Air Ptl | | | | | I | | | | | | | |
| Gib Air/Sea Ptl | | I | I | | I | | | | | | | |
| BOMBING | I | 2 | 2 | 2 | | | 5 | 5 | 2 | 5 | | 3 |
| SCRAP, SCUTTLE, P/O | | | | | | | 11 | 3 | | | | |
| MINE | | I | I | | I | | | I | 3 | I | I | I |
| ACCIDENT | | 2 | 2 | I | I | | I | | | 3 | I | 3 |
| UNKNOWN | 2 | | I | 2 | | | | | 3 | I | I | I |
| TOTAL LOST | 15 | 20 | 25 | 21 | 22 | 26 | 23 | 36 | 21 | '13 | 7 | 14 |

## 1945

| | Jan | Feb | Mar | Apr | May |
|---|---|---|---|---|---|
| ESCORTS | | | | | |
| Sea | 3 | 6 | 3 | 9 | |
| Carrier Sea | | | | | |
| Carrier Air | | | | | |
| Land Air | | | | | |
| Sea/Land Air | | | | I | |
| Sea/Carrier Air | | | | | |
| PATROLS | | | | | |
| Sea | 2 | 5 | 7 | 9 | 2 |

| 1945 | Jan | Feb | Mar | Apr | May |
|---|---|---|---|---|---|
| S/rnptl | | I | | 2 | |
| Carrier Sea | | | | | |
| Carrier Air | | | | | |
| Land Air | | I | 3 | 3 | |
| Sea/Land Air | | | | | |
| Sea/Carrier Air | | | | | |
| AIR SUPPORT | | I | | | |
| BAY AIR PTL | | | | | |
| NTransit Area Ptl | | | 2 | 2 | I |
| Gib Air Ptl | | | | | |
| Gib Air/Sea PTL | | | | | |
| BOMBING | 4 | I | 14 | 18 | |
| Air Strike TAF | | | | 4 | 23 |
| Air Strike Carrier | | | | | I |
| SCRAP, SCUTTLE, P/O | I | | I | | |
| MINE | | I | 3 | 4 | I |
| ACCIDENT | I | 2 | | 2 | |
| UNKNOWN | 3 | I | | 2 | I |
| TOTAL LOST | 14 | 22 | 33 | 54 | 28 |

U-boats surrendered at the end of the war are not included.

**Key to Table below**

A  Strength at start of month
B  Commissioned
C  Lost
D  Strength at end of month

## OVERALL STRENGTH OF THE U-BOATS ARM 1939–1945

Initial strength 1.1.39: 45

| 1939 | Jan | Feb | Mar | Apr | May | June | July | Aug | Sep | Oct | Nov | Dec |
|---|---|---|---|---|---|---|---|---|---|---|---|---|
| A | 45 | 46 | 48 | 49 | 51 | 51 | 52 | 54 | 57 | 57 | 52 | 53 |
| B | I | 2 | I | 2 | - | I | 2 | 3 | 2 | - | 2 | 3 |
| C | | | | | | | | | 2 | 5 | I | I |
| D | 46 | 48 | 49 | 51 | 51 | 52 | 54 | 57 | 57 | 52 | 53 | 55 |

| 1940 | Jan | Feb | Mar | Apr | May | June | July | Aug | Sep | Oct | Nov | Dec |
|---|---|---|---|---|---|---|---|---|---|---|---|---|
| A | 55 | 54 | 50 | 48 | 47 | 49 | 50 | 52 | 55 | 61 | 67 | 71 |
| B | I | I | 2 | 3 | 3 | 3 | 3 | 5 | 7 | 7 | 6 | 9 |
| C | 2 | 5 | 4 | 4 | I | 2 | I | 2 | I | I | 2 | - |
| D | 54 | 50 | 48 | 47 | 49 | 50 | 52 | 55 | 61 | 67 | 71 | 80 |

| 1941 | Jan | Feb | Mar | Apr | May | June | July | Aug | Sep | Oct | Nov | Dec |
|---|---|---|---|---|---|---|---|---|---|---|---|---|
| A | 80 | 88 | 96 | 102 | 114 | 132 | 142 | 159 | 174 | 187 | 209 | 226 |
| B | 10 | 9 | II | 14 | 19 | 14 | 19 | 19 | 15 | 24 | 23 | 22 |
| C | 2 | I | 5 | 2 | I | 4 | 2 | 4 | 2 | 2 | 6 | 10 |
| D | 88 | 96 | 102 | 114 | 132 | 142 | 159 | 174 | 187 | 209 | 226 | 238 |

| 1942 | Jan | Feb | Mar | Apr | May | June | July | Aug | Sep | Oct | Nov | Dec |
|---|---|---|---|---|---|---|---|---|---|---|---|---|
| A | 238 | 250 | 264 | 276 | 290 | 306 | 324 | 334 | 345 | 353 | 360 | 371 |
| B | 15 | 16 | 18 | 17 | 20 | 21 | 21 | 20 | 19 | 23 | 24 | 23 |
| C | 3 | 2 | 6 | 3 | 4 | 3 | II | 9 | II | 16 | 13 | 5 |
| D | 250 | 264 | 276 | 290 | 306 | 324 | 334 | 345 | 353 | 360 | 371 | 389 |

| 1943 | Jan | Feb | Mar | Apr | May | June | July | Aug | Sep | Oct | Nov | Dec |
|---|---|---|---|---|---|---|---|---|---|---|---|---|
| A | 389 | 404 | 407 | 420 | 425 | 411 | 419 | 408 | 404 | 414 | 415 | 421 |
| B | 21 | 22 | 29 | 20 | 28 | 25 | 26 | 21 | 21 | 27 | 25 | 28 |
| C | 6 | 19 | 16 | 15 | 42 | 17 | 37 | 25 | II | 26 | 19 | 8 |
| D | 404 | 407 | 420 | 425 | 411 | 419 | 408 | 404 | 414 | 415 | 421 | 441 |

| 1944 | Jan | Feb | Mar | Apr | May | June | July | Aug | Sep | Oct | Nov | Dec |
|---|---|---|---|---|---|---|---|---|---|---|---|---|
| A | 441 | 445 | 444 | 442 | 442 | 438 | 423 | 413 | 389 | 382 | 384 | 401 |
| B | 20 | 19 | 23 | 23 | 19 | II | 15 | 15 | 20 | 15 | 23 | 28 |
| C | 16 | 20 | 25 | 23 | 23 | 26 | 25 | 39 | 27 | 13 | 6 | 16 |
| D | 445 | 444 | 442 | 442 | 438 | 423 | 413 | 389 | 382 | 384 | 401 | 413 |

| 1945 | Jan | Feb | Mar | Apr | May | June | July | Aug | Sep | Oct | Nov | Dec |
|------|-----|-----|-----|-----|-----|------|------|-----|-----|-----|-----|-----|
| A | 413 | 438 | 435 | 430 | 381 | | | | | | | |
| B | 37 | 18 | 28 | 7 | 1 | | | | | | | |
| C | 12 | 21 | 33 | 56 | 382 | | | | | | | |
| D | 438 | 435 | 430 | 381 | 0 | | | | | | | |

Note: the totals include 4 Walter Type XVII boats, and all boats raised after accidents, sinkings etc. which were recommissioned.

| Summary | 1935–8 | 1939 | 1940 | 1941 | 1942 | 1943 | 1944 | 1945 | GrandTotal |
|---------|--------|------|------|------|------|------|------|------|------------|
| Commissioned | 45 | 19 | 50 | 199 | 237 | 293 | 231 | 91 | 1165 |
| Total Lost | 9 | 25 | 41 | 86 | 241 | 259 | 504 | | 1165 |

## U-BOATS SINKING ANALYSIS – TONS SUNK PER U-BOATS SUNK

| Year | Month | All Sinkings GRT | U-boats sinkings GRT | U-boats sinkings % of all sinkings | U-boats sunk | Tonnage per U-boats lost |
|------|-------|------------------|----------------------|-----------------------------------|--------------|--------------------------|
| 1939 | Sep | 194,845 | 153,879 | 79 | 2 | 76,940 |
| | Oct | 196,355 | 134,807 | 69 | 5 | 26,961 |
| | Nov | 174,269 | 51,589 | 29.6 | 1 | 51,589 |
| | Dec | 189,923 | 80,881 | 42.6 | 1 | 80,881 |
| | Totals | 755,392 | 421,156 | 55.8 | 9 | 46,795 |
| 1940 | Jan | 214,506 | 111,263 | 51.9 | 2 | 55,631 |
| | Feb | 226,920 | 169,566 | 63.6 | 5 | 33,913 |
| | Mar | 107,009 | 62,781 | 58.7 | 4 | 15,695 |
| | Apr | 158,218 | 32,467 | 20.5 | 4 | 8,117 |
| | May | 288,461 | 55,580 | 19.3 | 1 | 55,580 |
| | Jun | 585,496 | 284,113 | 48.5 | 2 | 142,056 |
| | Jul | 386,913 | 195,825 | 50.6 | 1 | 195,825 |
| | Aug | 397,229 | 267,618 | 67.4 | 2 | 133,809 |
| | Sep | 448,621 | 295,335 | 65.8 | 1 | 295,335 |
| | Oct | 442,985 | 352,407 | 79.6 | 1 | 352,407 |
| | Nov | 385,715 | 146,613 | 38 | 2 | 73,307 |
| | Dec | 349,568 | 212,590 | 60.8 | 0 | 00 |
| Totals | | 991,641 | 2,186,158 | 54.8 | 25 | 87,446 |
| 1941 | Jan | 320,240 | 126,782 | 42.2 | 2 | 63,391 |
| | Feb | 403,393 | 196,783 | 48.8 | 1 | 196,783 |
| | Mar | 529,706 | 243,020 | 45.9 | 5 | 48,604 |
| | Apr | 687,901 | 249,375 | 36.3 | 2 | 124,688 |
| | May | 511,042 | 325,492 | 63.7 | 1 | 325,492 |
| | Jun | 432,025 | 310,143 | 71.8 | 4 | 77,536 |
| | Jul | 120975 | 94,209 | 77.9 | 2 | 47,104 |
| | Aug | 130,699 | 80,310 | 61.4 | 4 | 20,077 |
| | Sep | 285,942 | 202,820 | 70.9 | 2 | 101,410 |
| | Oct | 218,289 | 156,664 | 71.7 | 2 | 128,332 |
| | Nov | 104,640 | 62,196 | 59.4 | 6 | 10,366 |
| | Dec | 583,706 | 124,070 | 21.3 | 10 | 12,407 |
| Totals | | 4,328,558 | 2,171,754 | 50.2 | 41 | 52,970 |
| 1942 | Jan | 419,907 | 327,357 | 78 | 3 | 109,119 |
| | Feb | 679,632 | 476,451 | 70.1 | 2 | 238,225 |
| | Mar | 693,389 | 627,377 | 90.5 | 6 | 104,563 |
| | Apr | 344,680 | 327,943 | 95.1 | 3 | 109,314 |
| | May | 299,428 | 264,852 | 88.5 | 4 | 66,213 |
| | Jun | 123,825 | 95,753 | 77.3 | 3 | 31,918 |
| | Jul | 365,398 | 252,145 | 69 | 11 | 22,922 |
| | Aug | 119,801 | 86,579 | 72.3 | 9 | 9,620 |

| Year | Month | All Sinkings GRT | U-boats sinkings GRT | U-boats sinkings % of all sinkings | U-boats sunk | Tonnage per U-boats lost |
|------|-------|------------------|----------------------|-----------------------------------|--------------|--------------------------|
| | Sep | 156,419 | 118,841 | 76 | 11 | 10,804 |
| | Oct | 139,861 | 97,407 | 69.6 | 16 | 6,087 |
| | Nov | 144,391 | 66,585 | 46 | 13 | 5,122 |
| | Dec | 348,902 | 330,816 | 94.8 | 5 | 66,163 |
| Totals | | 7,790,697 | 6,266,215 | 80.4 | 86 | 72,863 |
| | | | | | | |
| 1943 | Jan | 261,359 | 203,128 | 77.7 | 6 | 33,855 |
| | Feb | 403,062 | 359,328 | 89.1 | 19 | 18,912 |
| | Mar | 693,389 | 627,377 | 90.5 | 16 | 39,211 |
| | Apr | 344,680 | 327,943 | 95 | 15 | 21,863 |
| | May | 299,428 | 264,852 | 88.5 | 42 | 6,306 |
| | Jun | 123,825 | 95,753 | 77.3 | 17 | 5,633 |
| | Jul | 365,398 | 252,145 | 69 | 37 | 6,185 |
| | Aug | 119,801 | 86,579 | 72.3 | 25 | 3,363 |
| | Sep | 156,419 | 118,841 | 76 | 11 | 10,804 |
| | Oct | 139,861 | 97,407 | 69.6 | 26 | 3,746 |
| | Nov | 144,391 | 66,585 | 46.1 | 19 | 3,504 |
| | Dec | 168,524 | 86,967 | 51.6 | 8 | 10,871 |
| Totals | | 3,220,137 | 2,532,905 | 78.7 | 241 | 10,510 |
| | | | | | | |
| 1944 | Jan | 130,635 | 92,278 | 70.6 | 16 | 5,767 |
| | Feb | 116,855 | 92,923 | 79.5 | 20 | 4,646 |
| | Mar | 157,960 | 142,944 | 90.5 | 25 | 5,718 |
| | Apr | 82,372 | 62,149 | 75.5 | 23 | 2,702 |
| | May | 27,297 | 24,424 | 89.5 | 23 | 1,062 |
| | Jun | 104,084 | 57,875 | 55.6 | 26 | 2,226 |
| | Jul | 78,756 | 63,351 | 80.4 | 25 | 2,534 |
| | Aug | 118,304 | 98,729 | 83.5 | 39 | 2,532 |
| | Sep | 44,805 | 43,368 | 96.8 | 27 | 1,606 |
| | Oct | 11,668 | 7,176 | 61.5 | 13 | 552 |
| | Nov | 37980 | 29,592 | 77.9 | 6 | 4,882 |
| | Dec | 134,913 | 58,518 | 43.4 | 16 | 3,657 |
| Totals | | 1,045,629 | 773,327 | 74 | 259 | 2,986 |
| | | | | | | |
| 1945 | Jan | 82,897 | 56,988 | 68.8 | 12 | 4,749 |
| | Feb | 95,316 | 65,233 | 68.4 | 21 | 3,106 |
| | Mar | 111,204 | 65,077 | 58.6 | 33 | 1,922 |
| | Apr | 104,512 | 72,957 | 69.8 | 56 | 1,303 |
| | May | 17,198 | 10,022 | 58.3 | 37 | 271 |
| | Totals | 411,227 | 270,277 | 65.7 | 159 | 1,700 |

**Overall Totals**

| | Total shipping sunk – GRT | Number of ships sunk | Total sunk by U boats – GRT | Number of ships sunk by U-boats |
|------|---------------------------|----------------------|------------------------------|----------------------------------|
| 1939 | 755,392 | 222 | 421,156 | 114 |
| 1940 | 3,991,641 | 1,059 | 2,186,158 | 471 |
| 1941 | 4,328,558 | 1,299 | 2,171,754 | 432 |
| 1942 | 7,790,697 | 1,664 | 6,266,215 | 1,160 |
| 1943 | 3,220,137 | 597 | 2,532,05 | 463 |
| 1944 | 1,045,629 | 205 | 773,327 | 132 |
| 1945 | 411,227 | 97 | 270,277 | 65 |
| Totals | 21,543,281 | 5,143 | 14,621,792 | 2,837 |

The German Navy adopted a system of lettered and numbered position indicators for security and simplicity. This chart shows how the world was divided into lettered squares, within which were numbered sub-sections.

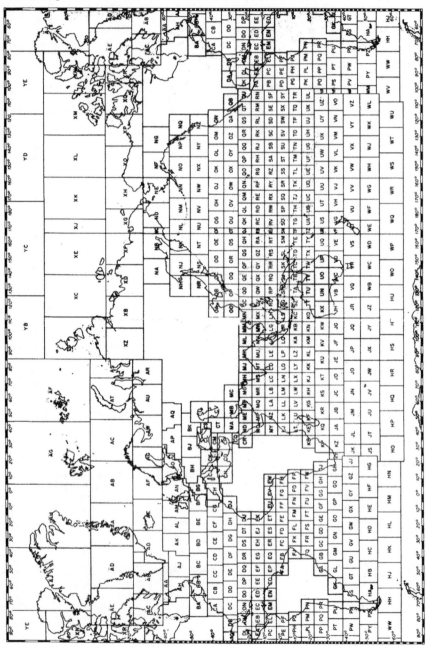

# German Navy quadrant system of position reporting – Atlantic Chart

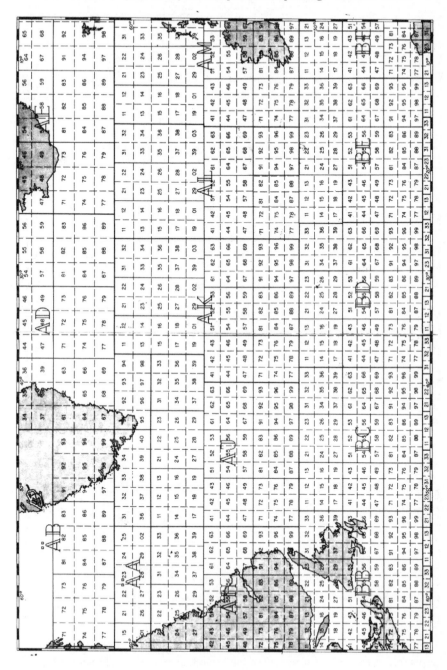

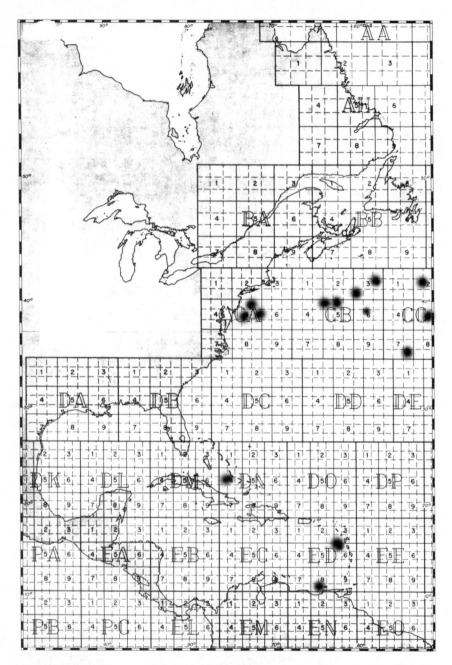

U-boats in the Western Atlantic 14 March 1942, showing the positions of U-boats approaching the eastern seaboard of the United States in the first phase of Operation *Paukenschlag*.

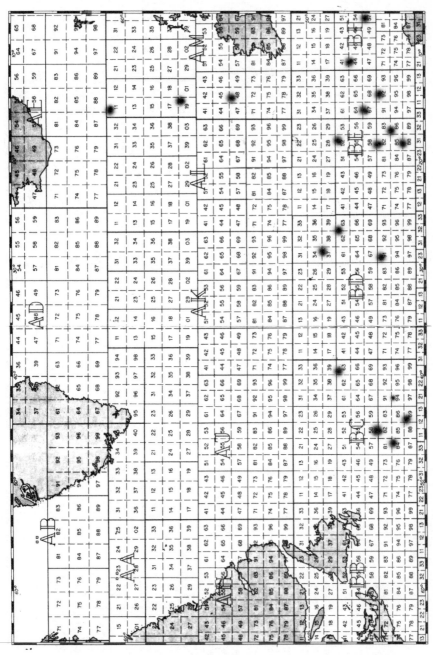

The U-boats' presence off the eastern seaboard of the United states began to increase as 1942 went on. Here a number of boats are plotted in their positions on 14 March 1942. They are en route to their operational areas.

The position of U-boats in the North Atlantic in May 1943, showing Groups Star and Specht and other U-boat positions. Note how many U-boats are plotted and compare this with the plot for June 1943.

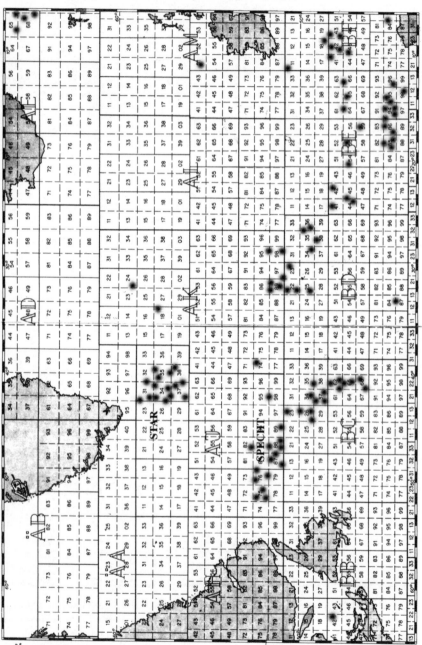

The positions of U-boats in the North Atlantic in June 1943. Compare this plot with that for May 1943 – the withdrawal of the U-boats is clear to see.

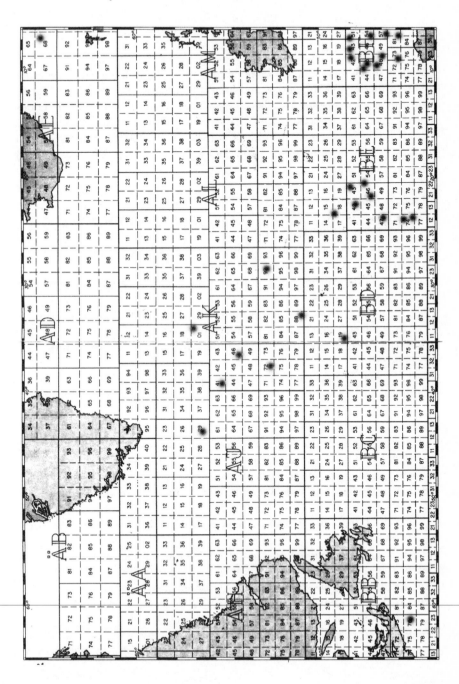

# BIBLIOGRAPHY

Readers should note that this bibliography gives details of the most significant titles in the field of submarine and anti-submarine warfare in World War II, but it is not exhaustive. Details of other titles are to be found in the books cited. The most important single source used was the *Kriegstagebuch des Befehlshabers der U-Boote*, the official War Diary of U-boat Command, which was sent twice-monthly from U-boat HQ to SKL in Berlin. Up to early 1943 this was also Dönitz's personal war diary.

Beesly, P. *Very Special Intelligence*, William Kimber, 1977

British Board of Trade. *Shipping Movement at United Kingdom Ports (1938–1945)*, HMSO, London, 1946

Busch, Rainer, and Röll, Hans-Joachim. *Der U-Boot-Krieg 1939–1945 – die deutschen U-Boot-Kommandanten*, Hamburg, 1996

Dinechin, G de. 'Technique de Sous-Marin pendant la dernière Guerre' in *Revue Maritime*, 1949

*Documents on German Foreign Policy 1918–1945* (Series D, 1937–1945), US Government Printing Office, various dates post-1948.

Dönitz, Karl. *Zehn Jahre und zwanzig Tage* (Ten Years and Twenty Days), Bonn, 1958

Fock, H. *Marinekleinkampfmittel*, Munich, 1968

'Führer Conferences on Naval Affairs' in *Brassey's Naval Annual*, William Clowes & Sons, 1948

Gabler, U. *Unterseebootsbau*, Darmstadt, 1964

Gröner, E. *Die deutschen Kriegsschiffe 1815–1945*, Munich, 1966–8

— Jung, D. and Maass, M. *Die Schiffe der deutschen Kriegsmarine und Luftwaffe 1939–45 und ihr Verbleib*, Munich, 1972

Hessler, Fregkpt. *The U-boat War in the Atlantic 1939–45*, MOD (Navy), HMSO, 1989

Hinsley, F. H. (ed.). *British Intelligence in the Second World War* (Vols I to III), HMSO, 1979–

HM Government. *British Vessels lost at Sea 1939–45*, HMSO, 1947

Jeschke, H. *U-Boottaktik 1900–1945*, Freiburg, 1972

Kruska, E. and Rössler, E. *Walter-U-Boote*, Munich, 1969

Kurzak, K. H. 'German U-Boat Construction' in *US Naval Institute Proceedings*, 4/1955

Lenton, H. T. *German submarines*, (2 vols), London, 1965

Lohmann, W. and Hildebrand, H. H. *Die deutsche Kriegsmarine 1939–1945*,

Bad Nauheim, 1956–64

Milward, Alan S. *The German Economy at War*, Athlone Press, University of London, 1965

MM.5-5.12: US Navy: 'Intelligence Reports on the War in the Atlantic 1942–1945'

Morison, S. E. *The Battle of the Atlantic*, Oxford University Press, London, 1948

—*The Alantic Battle Won*, Boston, USA, 1949. (This and the preceding title form part of Morison's *History of United States Naval Operations in World War II*.)

Operations Evaluation Group, US Chief of Naval Operations. *Antisubmarine Warfare in World War II*, Washington DC., 1946

Public Record Office (now The National Archives), Kew, England:

CAB 87/60: 'Memoranda on Economic Problems and Anglo-American Cooperation, 1942–1946

ADM 1/11133: 'Operation "Primrose": U-Boat Attacks on Convoy OB.318, May, 1941' (includes details of the capture of *U-110*)

ADM 1/18537: 'Operation "Deadlight": Disposal of German U-Boats'

AR series (various): Reports from Convoys

ADM 223/88: 'Admiralty use of Special Intelligence in Naval Operations'

M DEFE 3/705-744: 'Ultra U-Boat Warfare 1942–1945'

Rawlings, J. D. R. *Coastal, Support and Special Squadrons of the RAF and their aircraft*, London, 1992

Reuter, F. *Die Entwicklung und der Einsatz des RADAR-Verfahrens in Deutschland bis zum Ende des Zweiten Weltkrieges*, Opladen, 1971

Rohwer, J. *U-Boote*, Gerhard Stalling Verlag

— *Die U-Boot-Erfolge der Achsenmachte 1939–1945*, Munich, 1969

— *U-Boottyp XXI*, Munich, 1967

— 'Entwicklung des U-Boottyps VIIC' in *Marine Rundschau*, 11/12, 1970

— 'Die Bauvorbereitung für den Walter-U-Boottyp XXVI 1944/45' in *Marine Rundschau 9/1972*

— *The Critical Convoy Battles of March 1943*, London, 1977

— 'Der Einfluss der Allierten Funkaufklärung auf den Verlauf des Zweiten Weltkrieges' in *Viertelsjahrhefte für Zeitgeschichte*, 3/1979

— and Hummelchen, G. *Chronology of the War at Sea*, Parts I and II, Ian Allen, 1974–6

Roskill, Capt. S. W. *The War at Sea*, HMSO, 1954 –

Rössler, E. *The U-Boat: The Evolution and Technical History of German Submarines*, Arms & Armour Press, London, 1981

— 'Die deutsche U-Bootausbildung und ihre Vorbereitung 1925–1945' in *Marine Rundschau 3/1972*

— *U-Boottyp XXI*, Munich, 1976

— *U-Boottyp XXIII*, Munich 1976

— 'Entwicklung des U-Boottyps VIIC' in *Marine Rundschau*, 11 and 12, 1972

— *Die Torpedos der deutschen U-Boote*, Herford, 1984

—*Geschichte des deutschen U-Bootbaus*, Munich, 1975

— 'V-80: The first Walter submarine' in *Aviation & Marine International*, 14/1974

Schade, H. A. 'German Wartime Technical Developments', 1946

Starks, J. F. 'German U-Boat design and production' in *Inst. of Naval Architects*, 5/1948

Techel, H. *Der Bau von Unterseebooten auf der Germaniawerft*, Berlin, 1922

— *Die Entwicklung des Unterseebootes bis zum Beginn des Jetztzeit*, VDI-Zeitung, 5/1938

*The Times* (London) for various dates but particularly 1936 onwards

United States Government:

*United States Strategic Bombing Report*, particularly 'Submarine Industry Report' and 'Submarine Assembly Shelter at Farce', Washington, DC, 1945–8

War Diaries: *Kriegstagebuch der Kriegsmarine, Kriegstegebuch der Seekriegsleitung* and *Kriegstagebuch des Befehlshabers der U-Boote* on microfilm, Operational Archives, US Naval History Division, Washington, DC

Westwood, D. *The Type VII U-Boat*, Conway, London, 2004

— 'The Type II U-boat' in *Warship*, London, 2/1984

White, J. F. *U-Boat Tankers*, Shrewsbury, 1998

Witthöft, H. J. *Lexikon zur deutschen Marinegeschichte*, (2 vols), Herford, 1977

# INDEX